Praise for

MANY LIVES OF
MICHAEL BLOOMBERG

"It is long overdue that a serious biographer appraises this very important and interesting man, as a political leader and administrator, too real for what the major parties today are willing to offer us. Eleanor Randolph, an authoritative, insightful, and lively biographer, introduces a man who, in a different political climate, might be headed for the White House."

—Gay Talese, author of *The Kingdom and the Power*

"This masterful work not only paints a riveting portrait of a fascinating man; it is an absolutely first-rate study of leadership in business, politics, and philanthropy."

—Doris Kearns Goodwin, Pulitzer Prize winner
and author of *Leadership*

"Billionaire, New York city mayor, publisher—Michael Bloomberg has managed to be a towering figure in business, politics, and journalism. How he navigated these often conflicting roles—with amazing success, even if the presidency eluded him—is a riveting tale, brought to vivid life by veteran journalist and Bloomberg observer Eleanor Randolph."

—James B. Stewart, Pulitzer Prize winner
and author of *Tangled Webs*

"Only three mayors merit being enshrined in a mayoral Hall of Fame—Fiorello La Guardia, Ed Koch, and Michael Bloomberg. But none had a broader impact outside the city. Eleanor Randolph's vivid biography of Bloomberg traces the impact of his Bloomberg terminals on the stock market, his much copied innovative management, the spread of his smoke-free restaurants, his early environmental and parks innovations, his fierce championing of education reform, his once lonely assault on the NRA, the deployment of his fortune to help elect a Democratic Congress in 2018, and his generous and targeted worldwide philanthropy. Bloomberg is no saint, as Randolph makes clear. His vanity can be Trumpian. But nothing about Michael Bloomberg is fake. The former mayor and his associates opened the vault to Eleanor Randolph, and readers of this anecdote-rich book are in for a treat."

—Ken Auletta, bestselling author
and writer, *The New Yorker*

"A vivid, timely study of Bloomberg's brand of plutocracy."

—*Publishers Weekly*

"*The Many Lives of Michael Bloomberg* is a smart and engaging book about one of the most important men in our time. Anyone interested in how to become a billionaire, how to run a major metropolis, and how to make the world a better place will want to read it."

—Chris McNickle, urban historian, treasurer,
American Historical Association and author of
Bloomberg: A Billionaire's Ambition

THE MANY LIVES OF

MICHAEL

BLOOMBERG

ELEANOR RANDOLPH

SIMON & SCHUSTER PAPERBACKS

NEW YORK   LONDON   TORONTO   SYDNEY   NEW DELHI

Simon & Schuster Paperbacks
An Imprint of Simon & Schuster, Inc.
1230 Avenue of the Americas
New York, NY 10020

First Simon & Schuster trade paperback edition March 2021

SIMON & SCHUSTER PAPERBACKS and colophon are
registered trademarks of Simon & Schuster, Inc.

For information about special discounts for bulk purchases,
please contact Simon & Schuster Special Sales at
1-866-506-1949 or business@simonandschuster.com.

The Simon & Schuster Speakers Bureau can bring authors to your live event. For
more information or to book an event contact the Simon & Schuster Speakers
Bureau at 1-866-248-3049 or visit our website at www.simonspeakers.com.

Interior design by Ruth Lee-Mui

Manufactured in the United States of America

1 3 5 7 9 10 8 6 4 2

Library of Congress Cataloging-in-Publication Data has been applied for.

ISBN 978-1-4767-7220-2
ISBN 978-1-4767-7221-9 (pbk)
ISBN 978-1-4767-7222-6 (ebook)

For Peter and Victoria

CONTENTS

THE MANY LIVES OF

MICHAEL

BLOOMBERG

INTRODUCTION

THE MANY LIVES OF MICHAEL BLOOMBERG

"I don't have anything in common with people who stand on escalators. I always walk up them—why waste time? You have eternity to rest when you die."
—*Michael Bloomberg, 2014*[1]

When billionaire Michael Bloomberg announced that he was running for mayor of New York in June 2001, the city's pundits scoffed. "Kinda goofy," said one.[2] Another predicted, "There is no turn of events at all, no leap of logic whatsoever, that could make Michael Bloomberg New York's next mayor . . ."[3] Sure, he could overwhelm the city's airwaves and mailboxes with expensive commercials, they noted, and voters could be reminded that he was a generous donor to city charities big and small. But this was a vanity project, the experts decided, another rich man's expensive hobby.

Yet, these doubters were soon confounded by two important realities. First, they had underestimated how a driven Michael Bloomberg would use his energy and his money to achieve his latest goal. They had misjudged him as a tin-eared and boring novice, and they had missed the complex and relentlessly ambitious salesman underneath. When Bloomberg emerged as the billionaire candidate that year, he was not sitting on a yacht somewhere, offering his latest political whims by long distance. He was out there shaking hands and freely granting interviews, studying polls, and giving some of the worst political speeches New Yorkers had heard in years. No matter. He was out there, learning how to be a big-city politician, starting at the top.

Then came the morning of September 11 when New York endured the deadliest attack on American soil since Pearl Harbor. Nearly three thousand people died, a whole swath of Lower Manhattan was destroyed, and the nation's largest city faced the possibility of economic and spiritual decline. Voters began looking for someone who could put the city back together. Bloomberg's campaign literature sold him as "a leader, not a politician," a man who tried to fix problems, not simply complain about them.

When he won, some suggested it was not just his billions, it was a dark form of luck. But, as E. B. White so famously noted, "No one should come to New York to live unless he is willing to be lucky," and Bloomberg was indeed a lucky man. He had started his business at the right time and had run for mayor at the right moment. (An aide once insisted that he led such a charmed life that when he bet on a horse with the longest odds, he ended up stuffing his pocket with winnings he didn't need.) Still, Bloomberg was prepared to work extra hard, to use any turn of events to his advantage. He would not only become one of New York City's most inventive and productive mayors, but he would also become a modern American phenomenon, using his money and his clout in an attempt to improve the lives of millions of people and to preserve the planet where they live.

By 2020, Michael Rubens Bloomberg had come a long way from his modest, working-class roots in Massachusetts. If most people have one career per lifetime, this man had already managed three. He had created a computer product that upended the old guard on Wall Street and made him one of the richest men in the world. Then he had served as mayor of New York City for twelve busy years. After that, he had taken his billions to become one of the world's most inventive philanthropists, pledging to give away his fortune, or most of it, before he died.

As the 2020 presidential election loomed, Mike Bloomberg was clearly eyeing a fourth mission, this time to challenge a president he viewed as a con man and a threat to America. If he could not be the first Jewish president—especially after a costly and brief campaign one writer labeled "a billion-dollar flop"—he would be a political sugar daddy and guru for the often disoriented and underfunded Democratic Party. He would not be idle—that, he promised.

This book is an attempt to chronicle the many lives of a man who chafes at an empty hour on his calendar. He can sit rock-hard-still and listen with a searing intensity when people come to him with proposals for his business or his politics or his philanthropy. (The Bloomberg fidget is never a good sign for anyone asking for his approval.) But mostly this perpetually ambitious man moves and adapts with incredible energy from one pursuit to another to another. He does not rest very long on his successes or brood about past failures. And when something goes haywire or simply ends (like his time at city hall), his first question is often a simple one: What's plan B?

Bloomberg started his adult life on Wall Street. With an engineering degree from Johns Hopkins and extra glister from Harvard Business School, he first learned about the raw, greedy world of stocks, bonds, and big money at Salomon Brothers, a top brokerage in his day. In the late 1960s and 1970s, Bloomberg could fit into the raucous screw-you culture, but he was also different. Unlike many of his elders, the young Bloomberg foresaw the day when computers would eliminate the mountains of paper required to do business. He began to propose a computer system for Wall Street, and the old boys laughed at him. They demoted him to the computer floor and then fired him in 1981 with a generous payout of $10 million.

Bloomberg and three young Salomon techies quickly started a new business. Those beginnings are now the stuff of Bloomberg lore, and he will often say those were the happiest times as a boss—when he knew everybody who worked for him and could hand out paychecks one by one. Bloomberg's computer gizmo began working for bond traders before the Internet had taken hold, and as computers became the gateway and the impetus for a far more complex financial world, his business and his wealth grew astronomically. Career one would provide the funds for his other ventures over the next four decades.

Then came politics. In the late 1990s, after fifteen years as an inventive businessman, Bloomberg told friends he was ready for something new. One associate thought he wanted to become the U.S. ambassador to the United Kingdom. Others saw him eyeing what most people thought was impossible; he wanted to manage the biggest city in America.

In many ways, what made Bloomberg different from his billionaire class was that decision to emerge from his wealth-protected cocoon to face press and public as mayor of New York City. After twelve years and at least $650 million of his own money (nearly half of it spent on his campaigns), the Bloomberg era can now be seen as a testing ground for how a modern businessman could manage a very complicated city. It will undoubtedly attract years of study by academics and urban experts about what worked and what didn't during his busy time as mayor. He would fail in important ways, often involving the city's poor. Too many black and Hispanic youths were stopped and frisked in the name of gun control. Homeless rates soared and public housing suffered. But he improved much of the city, especially the health of its people and the effectiveness of its government. Overall, his time as mayor was a remarkable success.

The third Michael Bloomberg has been a giver, a philanthropist, fighting what he called public health issues that included battles against tobacco, guns, obesity, traffic deaths, and above all the man-made climate changes disrupting the entire planet. He had learned from his time in the city to trust in the power of good mayors. He had seen their problems up close, and he gave millions to cities, arguing that mayors could often solve problems better than distant bureaucrats or politicians. In 2018, he was the second most generous billionaire in America (after the richest man in the world, Jeff Bezos), and by 2019 Bloomberg's staff had calculated that he had given away almost $10 billion so far at age seventy-seven. That left another $45 billion or more to go.

The fourth Bloomberg was the manager who kept hoping he could manage the entire country. In 2019, alarmed at how President Donald Trump was dismantling so many of the protections Americans had enjoyed and damaging the world's environment, Bloomberg began marching through the stations of America's presidential primaries—Iowa, New Hampshire, Florida. But, just as he had done three times before, Bloomberg at first decided he couldn't prevail in the long trek to the White House. Instead, he would spend his time and especially his money on the main goal for 2020—ousting President Donald Trump.

Once again, Bloomberg had a new challenge. If he could not survive as the candidate, he could be the very rich, very savvy techno-mensch that the Democratic Party needed. And he would support those candidates who agreed with his policies, as he had done with some success in the midterms in 2018. He would spend $500 million to fight climate changes and coal-fired power plants. And after that? He once said, with a smile, of course, that he planned to live to 125 (his mother died at 102, and he has the best medical care and advice money can buy). If so, that certainly leaves time for still another version of Michael Bloomberg.

More than a few of Bloomberg's admirers warned that it made no sense to look for a deep, psychological road map to this intense character. He had a stable childhood, tough and loving parents. He was an Eagle Scout. He survived at Johns Hopkins, Harvard. He married a British beauty and kept her as a friend after they divorced. He doted on his two daughters and, as of this writing, his two grandchildren. He was extremely proud to be Jewish, but not overly religious. He was not a philosopher, not an intellectual. (He once claimed his favorite book was a John le Carré novel and his favorite movie was Mel Brooks's *Blazing Saddles*.) Instead, he was a brainy engineer who has always wanted to improve things and make them run better, from a squeaky door to notoriously messy things like city government. He was a doer, "Mr. Fixit," some of his colleagues liked to call him. But he also wanted things done and fixed quickly, as quickly as humanly possible. Asked about how he saw his role in all these careers, he said, "I'm not an investor. I'm not an analyst. I'm not a consultant. I'm not a teacher. I'm not a writer. I am an executive. I make decisions. Some good. Some bad, but that's what I do."[4]

As he became a more public figure, the younger version, the Wall Street, smart-ass Bloomberg, remained mostly tucked under the standard businessman's blue serge regalia. From outside, he was distant, flat, stoic, grumpy to the press and, of course, stilted at the microphone. His face, often set in an inscrutable grin, seemed halfway between the Grinch and the flirt. It could be his distant look or his mischievous look. One colleague called it his "twinkle," a semi-smile that seemed to hint at some risky pleasure.

He was a masterful salesman who packed a variety of Michael Bloombergs into his bantam five-eight frame. He could fraternize in the morning with the muscular "Sandhogs" digging a water tunnel under New York City's streets, and by evening he could be at a gala, blowing air-kisses at the frosty Anna Wintour, editor of *Vogue*. He could be funny and privately raunchy with a full repertoire of old Catskill jokes that were sometimes edgy and sometimes slipped over that edge.

His comments about women, leftovers from his feral Wall Street days, would get him into trouble, even as he denied making them. The response from Bloomberg and his people was that women thrived at his company and that he had been surrounded by strong women all his life, starting with his powerful mother and in later years, his top adviser and confidante, Patti Harris.

Like a lot of men of his era, he showed signs of discomfort that old behaviors were being judged by strict new standards. At one point, he said he had canceled plans to run for president in 2020 because he would not "change all my views and go on what CNN called an apology tour." He added, "Joe Biden went out and apologized for being male, over 50, white."[5]

Michael "Call me Mike" Bloomberg enjoyed a full plate of contradictions. One example: he wanted all his employees to sit around him, to be available and nearby, to be within earshot. Privacy was a luxury in that office-free world, but for Bloomberg, at least, the bull pen always had its escape hatch. Although he pestered his staff by phone or email on evenings and weekends, those private hours were supposed to be completely off the record. While he was mayor, a *Times* reporter nosed around his well-guarded compound in Bermuda. Bloomberg was furious. His aides let it be known that he was a public figure only when he chose to be public. The press, of course, begged to differ.

That same man who craved his privacy also relished the spotlight. Dan Doctoroff, who was a deputy mayor and then the head of Bloomberg's company, described the mayor as being "incredibly anxious" about losing the limelight and the microphone once he left office. Doctoroff said he scoffed at the very idea and told Bloomberg, "You're going to be at the center of whatever you want to be for the rest of your life!"[6]

There was also something of a cowboy inside that expensive suit. Against all sorts of advice from friends and aides, he took on one of the toughest hombres in politics—the National Rifle Association. His anti-gun campaign would help break the NRA's chokehold on politicians who were often terrified to even mention gun control in the face of rising gun deaths in America. It was a campaign that began when he was mayor and grew more intense after he left office.

But if that was a little too theoretical, Bloomberg had also been known to confront the bad guys, face-to-face. When two hackers from Kazakhstan found a way into the Bloomberg LP computers, learning details about Bloomberg's own passwords and credit card accounts, Bloomberg began working with the FBI. Soon he agreed to meet the intruders in a London hotel as part of an "exchange" of money for information about the attack. As he walked out of the room that day, agents walked in. They arrested the two, who were soon extradited to the U.S., and one was convicted; the other deported.[7] Asked years later why he wasn't afraid of being alone in a hotel room with two people from the wild reaches of

Kazakhstan, men intent on robbing him or worse, Bloomberg shrugged and said, with his all-purpose grin, "I don't do fear well."[8]

Almost everybody who talked about working closely with Bloomberg mentioned his view of loyalty. If you were loyal to him, he would be loyal to you, they said, almost as a mantra. And anyone who resigned from his company to work elsewhere was never to be hired again. There could be no going-away parties for someone who had committed his version of corporate treason.

Loyalty would also make a dent in his reputation, however, especially when his police commissioner, Ray Kelly, oversaw a department that stopped, frisked, and too often humiliated hundreds of thousands of blacks and Hispanics in the search for illegal guns. Even after the Kelly version was ruled unconstitutional, Bloomberg would continue to support his police commissioner's efforts for years—as his attempt to stop shootings, to stop young blacks and Hispanics in higher-crime areas from killing one another.

For all his concern about fighting big problems, Bloomberg could also tackle the less serious ones with much the same fervor. One spring, he and Governor Andrew Cuomo competed in what was supposed to be a promotional white-water rafting contest in the Adirondacks. The two teams battled through the rapids in upstate New York, and afterward, the timekeeper announced the governor's team beat the mayor's team by eighteen seconds. Cuomo said Bloomberg complained repeatedly that he felt robbed, especially since the timekeeper worked for the governor. Weeks later, one member of Bloomberg's white-water squad asked him to sign a photo showing the mayor and his paddlers madly churning through the rapids. Bloomberg grinned, took the photo, and wrote: "18 seconds, my ass."[9]

The flat, conventional view of Mike Bloomberg was always missing more than a few more dimensions. He was a natural manager who could give employees plenty of freedom, money, and support but could fire an aide caught playing computer solitaire during working hours. For almost any project, he could gather a group of terrified aides who knew he would ask the hardest questions or redraw their graph or demand better data and a clearer version of whatever they were trying to say. He could be stubborn and cold, refusing to give up some personal pleasure like a golf game when he was needed at a city event. But he also could be generous and thoughtful, calling widows of city workers killed while he was mayor as he left office. He was notoriously impatient, a good thing in government. And he was extraordinarily self-disciplined—adding extra work hours to his schedule or reverting to his "lettuce" diet when his weight hit an uncomfortable number.

He was not easy, but after some disagreement that might normally create an enemy, he could laugh and tell a stupid joke, and all was forgiven if never quite forgotten. Bloomberg could be very thoughtful, but he was not soft. "He's not a warm man, but he's a good man," one former aide said. Instead, he projected a kind of confidence and optimism that could be irritating but also infectious. When it was suggested that he must have a very good shrink, Bloomberg dismissed the very idea. "The only therapist I have," he said, "is the one I see in the mirror when I'm shaving." [10]

This book is a journalist's work, a portrait drawn in part from more than two decades of observing this powerful and complex man. It is not an authorized biography, even though Bloomberg, his staff, and his friends were often very helpful.

During his time as mayor, I was a member of the *New York Times* editorial board and participated in the *Times* editorials on Bloomberg's city. I wrote about many of the events I have described in this book, and I came to know the participants who worked for him and against him. After he left office, I covered him in his new role as a very public private figure. I have also trusted the coverage of Bloomberg by some of the best journalists in the business, and their work for the *Times* has often framed my own recollections. Above all, I found that Michael Bloomberg could not be confined by his public image, and those omissions helped make this work possible.

BORN TO RUN, EVERYTHING

"I thought of myself as the hero patriot, sticking it to old
George III—a maverick role I still try to emulate."[1]

Even today, the working-class community of Medford outside Boston looks like the perfect set for a 1950s sitcom. Ozzie and Harriet could have lived right down the road. Soft hills, modest homes, public schools where everybody knew your grandparents. For the Bloombergs in 1945, it must have seemed like the ideal nest for an ordinary little family.

When Charlotte and William H. Bloomberg chose the small house at 6 Ronaele Road, they were much like millions of young couples who wanted a normal, sedate life. The ugly memories of the Depression and war and especially the Holocaust were still agonizingly raw, and most families craved something quiet and comforting. The Bloombergs selected an Irish and Italian neighborhood where they undoubtedly hoped that Jews might be just another religious group, another ethnic strain in the all-American mix.

It was not that easy, not at first. Charlotte had carefully chosen the house—which was affordable and near William's job as bookkeeper at a dairy in Somerville—only to be told that it was off-limits. The realtors would not sell to Jews. Others might have looked elsewhere. Not Charlotte Rubens Bloomberg. She convinced the family's Irish lawyer, George McLaughlin, to buy the house.[2] He then quickly resold it to the Bloombergs—a transaction that Bloomberg used years later as an example of the insidious ways discrimination works. But as the Medford tale was told and retold in the Bloomberg family, it offered another lesson about how to succeed in a tough world. If you're blocked in this direction, go in that direction. Get over it. Go around. Find another way. Mike Bloomberg learned that lesson extremely well. Throughout his life, a failure meant it was time to try plan B in business, politics, and his personal life.

Young Mike's parents offered what every child needs—one parent who sees only the perfect offspring and the other parent who does all the hard work of managing and coaching a smart child into adulthood. Bloomberg's father was the soft one. His mother was the rock, the disciplinarian, the religious beacon who kept a Kosher house, the guide who eventually had to keep repeating one phrase to her son as he grew more and more successful. "Don't let it go to your head," she would say, tucking her pride beneath that motherly warning.[3] Their story, the story of Bloomberg's parents and grandparents, is the fundamental story of America, the reason so many distressed people leave whatever homes they had and start from scratch in a new country.

Mike Bloomberg, who would later champion the cause of immigration in the face of growing anti-immigrant pressures in his America, explained his background this way: "Three of my grandparents, and six of my great-grandparents were immigrants. All placed education and reverence for the United States at the core of our family values . . . and they made my story possible."[4]

Bloomberg's father, William Henry Bloomberg, was born in 1906, near Boston and grew up in the relative safety of Massachusetts. He was the son of Lithuanian immigrants, and his father, Elick Bloomberg, taught

Hebrew in an immigrant neighborhood near Boston. When Elick filed his intention to become an American citizen in 1898, he declared that he was "renouncing allegiance to foreign sovereigns, especially and particularly to Nicholas II Czar of Russia."[5] Russia's czars and their orthodox Christians had in many ways fed the vicious anti-Semitism that would result in repeated pogroms against Jews living in their empire. America meant the freedom to criticize the czar, on an official document no less.

Bloomberg's father worked most of his adult life as an accountant, earning just enough to support his family. (His son estimated his dad's salary at $6,000.) If there is one memory of Mike's father that made its most durable mark, William Bloomberg took some of those scarce dollars and donated them every year to the NAACP. When asked why, he said simply that "discrimination against one group is really discrimination against all groups."[6]

Mike Bloomberg's mother, Charlotte "Lottie" Rubens, was born into a more comfortable family in New Jersey in 1909. She was the child of strong parents, especially her mother, Ettie, who pushed her four children to take every advantage of America's free education system. Ettie's husband, Max Rubens, was born in what is now Belarus, and when his family fled to England, they struggled to survive in the hard, industrial port of Liverpool. The Bloomberg family would later describe that period as being "as bleak as a Dickens story."[7] When Max finally came to America, he flourished in the wholesale grocery business, carrying around his samples in a gladstone bag and making enough money to buy five brick houses in a German neighborhood of Jersey City. If there is a peddler's DNA, Mike Bloomberg inherited it from his grandfather Max.

Max was suddenly hospitalized in May of 1922 with a lung disorder and died nearly a month later,[8] leaving Ettie to take command of her four children, including Lottie, who was barely a teenager.[9] With the help of her strong mother, Charlotte Pearl "Lottie" Rubens weathered her father's early death and became an unusually independent woman for her day. Her high school graduation photo nearly three years later shows a very determined-looking young woman, and besides being "as bright as a sunbeam," as the 1925 yearbook for Dickinson High School announced, she was a member of the fencing club.[10] (At the time, fencing for women was extremely popular because New Jersey native Adeline Gehrig became a national champion and was chosen to represent America in the 1924 Olympics as a member of the first-ever women's foil event.)[11]

After graduating from high school, Lottie worked in New York City while she also earned a bachelor's degree from New York University's School of Commerce, Accounts and Finance. There were 430 men in the class and 21 women.[12] Obviously, it would have been tough for a girl in her late teens fighting her way in a man's world: night and day, no whining, no excuses. Just set the goal and go for it. It was that personal manifesto of hard work and no complaints that she would pass on to her son.

Lottie soon became an assistant auditor at a dairy company in New York City where she grew to admire another employee, William Bloomberg. Charlotte and William were married in 1934, and soon moved to Boston—first to the neighborhood of Allston, then to the town of Brookline, and finally outside the city to Medford, where she would stay in the same house for the next sixty-six years.[13]

Nearly eight years after Charlotte and William's wedding, Michael Rubens Bloomberg was born at 3:40 p.m. on Valentine's Day 1942 at St. Elizabeth's Hospital in Boston. The baby's parents were on the older side by the day's standards. His father was thirty-six, and his mother, thirty-three.[14] They moved quickly to make the family complete with a second child, Marjorie Rubens Bloomberg, born two years later.

Mike Bloomberg began early testing the standards and limits of Medford's small, confining world. His public version of these early years would concentrate on the science museum in Boston, the Boy Scouts, and evening dinners with his parents, when his mother always used the good silver and every member of the family told about their day.

Friends and associates described a far more complicated youngster. Sure, he could be patriotic and good to his mother, they remembered. Yes, he quickly learned how to be funny, if you were swift enough to get the joke. But he was also a rascal, a smarty-britches who didn't, or couldn't, restrain an urge to show off his brainpower. And underneath all that combustible energy, there was always the ambition—to do something big, to be a force somewhere.[15]

On occasion, even Bloomberg himself would admit that, as a boy, he was a classic handful.

"I had discipline problems. I threw erasers. I dipped pigtails into inkwells—I was totally bored."[16]

William Bloomberg especially loved to indulge his son's mischief and his untapped curiosity. On Saturdays, he would take young Mike for a bacon and egg, greasy spoon, non-Kosher breakfast and then to the science museum in Boston. "It changed my life," Bloomberg said years later. Starting at age ten, the boy who was so bored with the rote learning in Medford during the week would be allowed to hold snakes, porcupines, and an owl named Snowy on Saturdays in Boston.[17] He would learn a few of the basic laws of physics and peek into other corners of the mysterious scientific world.

One day the instructor asked his listeners to give "the age of a redwood tree," pointing to the rings on a stump nearby. Members of the class carefully counted and recounted the rings, and yet with each answer, the teacher kept saying no, wrong. Bloomberg loves to recall what happened next. As he put it, "I don't know what possessed me, but I said it was not a redwood, it was a giant sequoia." Right, the professor said, to Bloomberg's great pride. Even decades later, when he would tell this story, Bloomberg always looked immensely pleased with himself for getting the right answer. But he also gave the museum credit for helping him realize that he needed to "listen, question, test [and] think."[18]

In a very similar way, Bloomberg would talk about his strongest memory of television, which was just becoming a household item in the 1950s. For either financial or educational reasons, probably both, the Bloombergs were among the last in the neighborhood to add TV. What shows did he watch? Bloomberg recalled that one of his favorites was John Cameron Swayze's *Camel News Caravan*.[19]

The Swayze news show—fifteen minutes, five times a week—barely covered the days' headlines from 1949 to 1956.[20] What Bloomberg remembered best were the commercials for Camel cigarettes, which featured a large picture of the company's elegant mascot. Bloomberg, with his head full of Saturday's visits to the science museum, said that he quickly realized that the camel in the commercial was not a camel. It was a dromedary with one hump instead of two. Young Bloomberg could not let such a travesty go unnoticed, so he wrote Mr. Swayze to alert him to the error, thus forcing some feckless aide to write the kid back and explain that, yes, he was right, but the company insisted that the dromedary looked better on the screen (and the package) than the double-humped camel. The dromedary on Camel cigarettes never became a real camel, but much like the sequoia versus redwood story, Bloomberg loved to show how he could be right.

He could also admit, at least occasionally, when he was wrong. Bloomberg often told a family story about how politics entered his world. The Bloombergs were solidly Democratic back then, and he recalled how the family went to see Harry Truman giving a speech from the back of a train as part of a whistle-stop campaign tour in 1948. Years later, a family photo surfaced of the event that Bloomberg had described. The problem—it wasn't Truman giving that speech to the Massachusetts crowd. It was Adlai Stevenson—probably in 1952, he said a few years later to correct the record.

If the museum piqued his scientific interest, the Boy Scouts became an obsession. Going to the scouts' summer camp became such a powerful goal that young Bloomberg sold Christmas tree wreaths around Medford in order to pay his own way. He studiously collected the small embroidered patches that scouts wear like medals on their official uniforms, but one badge was particularly hard to get.

"In the sixth grade I went to Mrs. Kelly—this old battle-ax who I'm sure has since gone on to meet her maker—and I had to get her to sign a paper that I was a good student, for my Boy Scout merit badge. And I remember she looked at me and started laughing.

"We made a deal: that if I stayed out of the principal's office for a month, she'd sign it."

Bloomberg was disciplined enough to behave, at least for a month, since he not only got that merit badge, he also went on to become one of the youngest Eagle Scouts in the country.[21]

If the scouts taught him how to tie knots and make a fire, they also gave him a taste for food that would never touch his mother's table. Food in Bloomberg's youth was often little more than fuel for the day, the Betty Crocker basics that fed most of America in the postwar era. He once wrote in a birthday card to Kitty Carlisle, a noted singer, actress, and advocate for the arts, that his mother's advice for longevity was to "never eat anything that tastes good."[22]

What tasted good to young Mike was junk food. He liked Chinese takeout, and he especially adored the basics served at Boy Scout camp: hot dogs, beans, macaroni and cheese, and particularly the grape-flavored punch called "bug juice."[23] He would later dine at the best gourmet restaurants and enjoy four-star chefs doing their best to impress him. But his tastes still tended toward very thin pizza and Cheez-its and overcooked bacon (burnt, actually), sometimes with peanut butter. When his guests came to dine at one of his many homes, they could easily find an entrée of old-fashioned basics like meat loaf or roast beef.

Bloomberg's parents, who wanted their children to fit in easily in America, also wanted them to keep a solid connection to their Jewish heritage. Religion and his Jewish history were part of his upbringing, of course, but Bloomberg's parents were not overly strict. Although his mother cooked proper Kosher food, she sometimes had a side dish for her son's Chinese favorites. They sent him to Hebrew school, strict enough to keep him in line but not strict enough for his religious grandfather Elick.[24] And Saturdays were as much for science in Boston as religion in Medford.

As a candidate for mayor years later, he startled some members of New York's Jewish community by suggesting that he saw nothing wrong with public school children saying the Lord's Prayer the way he did when he was growing up in Massachusetts.

"Nobody was uncomfortable," Bloomberg snapped at a reporter who had asked him to elaborate. "Only people today would ask a question like that. That is the difference. You want today to find fault in everything that is good and wonderful about America."[25]

His Jewish classmates in Medford were not surprised by the Lord's Prayer comment. Several of them said they could not remember witnessing anti-Semitism firsthand. One former classmate said that maybe it was there, certainly the Bloomberg's roundabout way of buying a house was early evidence, but as young people "we didn't feel it."[26]

Bloomberg's mother, Lottie, tried to describe her rambunctious son as an ordinary boy who, for example, liked to scare his sister with his collection of snakes. ("Have you seen my snake?" his sister remembered with a shudder.)[27] Even years later, he would explain to a reporter how you could trap a snake in the woods near his home by setting up a kind of cave with a piece of cardboard or metal and then catch them when they went inside to sleep.[28] He also attempted to impress his school friends with his skills as a ham radio operator and later his expertise with a slide rule. But, more important, he wanted to take control of everything around him. As his mother explained, "He wanted to be the boss of whatever we were working on. He wanted to run everything."[29]

What his mother once described as young Mike's unusual self-assurance, others in Medford saw as arrogance. He ran with a crowd of older boys, which did not endear him with his own age group, but he managed the bigger friends because he was supremely self-confident. He always wanted to be the one chosen to give a speech. As his mother put it, "It never seemed to bother him to get out in front of an audience and talk."[30]

That love of being noticed did not translate into a passion for being at the top of his class. He barely passed French (his later attempts to learn Spanish made it clear that he could remember words and the grammar, but not the music). At one point he made an A in one math class and a D in another. His version was that he did the answers in his head, and one teacher thought he cheated.[31]

Another school would have noticed that this kid was deeply frustrated, and young Mike rocked along with half an ear tuned to school and the other half focused elsewhere. His favorite book was *Johnny Tremain*,[32] the Esther Forbes novel about the poor boy who becomes a runner and spy for Paul Revere. According to his count, he read it "at least 50 times" or, later he said 100 times.[33]

"I thought of myself as the hero patriot, sticking it to old George III—a maverick role I still try to emulate," he recalled, not missing a chance for a little self-promotion. "I developed a sense of history and its legacy, and remain annoyed at how little people seem to learn from the past: how we fight the same battles over and over; how we can't remember what misguided, shortsighted policies led to depression, war, oppression and division. As citizens, we continually let elected officials pander for votes with easy, flawed solutions to complex problems. As voters, we repeatedly forget the lessons of others who didn't hold their chosen officials accountable."[34]

His time in public school offered different lessons—mainly how education could fail those who wanted more than rote learning. For years, some of the town regulars in Medford mumbled angrily about the way the billionaire Mike Bloomberg would describe his time at Medford High. The building housing Medford's high school in that era was a grim-looking place, dark and institutional. The lessons were keyed to the average learner, and Bloomberg admitted that he was "totally bored until my senior year."[35] That was when he took two honors courses—one in history and the other in literature. If Mike is barely recalled by most of his Medford classmates, his colleagues in the honors classes remember him well, especially because of one telling incident.

"Those of us who did well followed the teachers, did everything they said," said Dorothy Rubin Schepps, a classmate in the honors programs. "Michael riled the teachers."[36]

Schepps and others remembered that Miss Kathleen Sharkey, who ran the literature honors class with an iron will, required a senior thesis. When the students turned in their first drafts, they waited anxiously for a verdict from the teacher famous for terrorizing even the toughest teenagers in her class.

The prim and straitlaced Miss Sharkey could be seen coming down the rows handing back papers and saying, "Good job, Miss Rubin, good job, Miss Davis." Then she got to Mike Bloomberg. She stopped, frowned, and threw his draft onto his desk. "I'm not even going to read this," she announced to a stunned class. Young Bloomberg was shaken by the encounter, his mother later told friends. He had planned to be provocative, not publicly humiliated.

Bloomberg's paper for Miss Sharkey described a widespread conspiracy theory in the 1950s that President Roosevelt knew the Japanese were about to bomb Pearl Harbor. FDR also knew war was inevitable and that it could help pull the country into World War II and out of the Depression. The theory was circulated for years by Roosevelt's enemies, even though historians of the era have repeatedly argued that the president was caught off guard by the Japanese attack. Miss Sharkey was a fan of the mighty Roosevelt, and she would not hear of such calumny. Or even debate it.

"Miss Sharkey, she was so tough. I broke my hand before midterm exam and she made me write left-handed," said the Reverend Richard Black, a retired Methodist minister. That blowup over Roosevelt had to happen to Bloomberg, Black said. "You get two edgy people in a room and you get edges." [37]

Bloomberg does not remember being humiliated by Miss Sharkey's furious rejection of his work. He simply recalls his plan B. He passed the rejected paper over to the honors history class, where the teacher used it to create a full and exhilarating discussion of Roosevelt and the war. Other students in that class believe that he turned young Bloomberg around on Roosevelt in a way that Miss Sharkey could not.

Officially, in the Medford High yearbooks, Bloomberg barely rates a mention. He was president of the slide rule club and a member of the debating society. The yearbook staff winnowed each student's whole personality into one adjective. Mike's was "argumentative," a simple description that many of his friends, colleagues, and competitors over the years would endorse as well.

Marjorie Stone Glau, one of his classmates, said, "All these girls who thought he was the biggest nerd, we missed our chance. Nobody had any interest in him." Too smart, too self-confident, too snarky—he wasn't a first choice for prom night. When they were seniors in high school, Dorothy Rubin Schepps remembered that Mike kept asking her out. The first time, she couldn't go. Her maternal grandfather had died, so they set another date. Then, on that day, Dorothy's paternal grandfather died, and she called again to reschedule.

Was he hurt? Disappointed?

"No, no," she laughed. Instead, he quickly recovered.

"So, okay," he said, "how many grandparents do you have left?"[38]

2

THE WAY UP

"Most of us were just college kids living in the
moment, Mike was living in the future."
—*A friend from college days*[1]

"I was the kind of student who made the
top half of the class possible."[2]
—*A favorite line when speaking to student groups*

Mike Bloomberg's ticket to Johns Hopkins came like a lot of his rewards, as he would say, through old-fashioned hard work. What he did not say was that it also took a certain amount of old-fashioned good luck.

He got into the respected Baltimore university in part because during high school he had a part-time job working—hard, of course—for a small electronics company in Cambridge. The company's "technical genius," as Bloomberg described the MIT graduate and engineer who was his boss, contacted people she knew at the Applied Physics Laboratory at Hopkins and recommended Mike.[3] His grades were middling, but his test scores were far better. Bloomberg says he doesn't remember exactly why he went there, at one point suggesting that maybe it was the best school he got into.[4] Johns Hopkins took a chance on a bright, unchallenged teenager, and years later, after Bloomberg had given his first $1 billion to the school, he usually got a good laugh when he suggested the elders erect three statues on campus—one for Johns Hopkins, one for Mike Bloomberg, and a third for the admissions director who okayed his application.

When Bloomberg arrived in Baltimore in 1960, he had never seen the campus except in brochures. His college interview had been in Boston because "nobody had the money to go down and visit schools." [5] So Bloomberg took the train and, at Baltimore's Penn Station, he shared a cab, a luxury for a youth who would have to work his way through college.

As the car pulled into the school, eighteen-year-old Mike Bloomberg fell in love.

"I'd never seen anything so beautiful in my life. The sun was shining. The flowers were out. In those days, people spent a lot of money on the grounds, and then over the years that went away and now I suppose it's back," he said in 1999. [6] "The campus looks a lot better," he said. "It became a real pig sty [a few years later] . . . but those days, it was beautiful . . . It was everything that Norman Rockwell would have painted in a picture of an American campus." [7]

The undergraduate school was all male (a few nurses, but coeds did not arrive until 1970), and it was like a cloistered academy that nurtured science and engineering for a small, roisterous band of young men. There were rules, of course, to keep these randy boys in line. Sports was there to help let off steam. Suits and ties were the uniform of the day. Fraternities thrived, and girls were often imported usually from nearby Goucher College for parties or events. It was an uncomplicated existence, largely isolated from the growing upheaval over civil rights and Vietnam at other campuses, or even from the urban decay affecting Baltimore.

While Bloomberg and his classmates studied or partied or worked in the college labs, Baltimore was becoming a desolate place as whites deserted the city for the suburbs. Racial turmoil would soon erupt into full-blown riots with the assassination of Martin Luther King in 1968, [8] but while Bloomberg was at Hopkins, the problems for African Americans festered outside the school gates. Inside it was about getting grades good enough to go to graduate school or med school, and about partying as many hours as possible in between.

Bloomberg planned to study physics. That didn't last a week.

"After three days of German, I decided I was never going to learn German, and it was mandatory. And in those days, remember 1960, it wasn't that long after the period when everybody came from Germany in physics. Everything was written in German.

"So, I became an engineering student."[9]

And, as it turned out, most of the time he was not even a particularly good engineering student. "I was a C student," he always admitted freely. "I've always been a C student." Years later, he would often say that "I was one of those students who made the top half of the class possible."[10] That usually drew a delayed laugh, depending on how long it took for people to catch on, but it was not just a joke, at least in his first years at Hopkins.

If most young Americans were starting to enjoy the roaring, marching, dope-smoking 1960s, the Johns Hopkins of Bloomberg's day still sat comfortably in the 1950s. Bloomberg liked to depict his early college years as a local version of John Belushi's *Animal House*—toga parties, drunks, the whole disgusting frat boy bit. His friends from that era challenge that view, at least for Bloomberg. They describe a guy who could pretend to be just another drunken lout but who really wanted to stay sober, or at least sober enough to run things.

John Galotto, who became a physician and one of Bloomberg's closest friends over the years, recalled fraternity rush week, when somebody suggested he go check out this Bloomberg kid. Unlike most eighteen-year-olds, the boy from Medford had a dorm room that was spotless and organized, Galotto recalled. There were notes lined up on the wall. There was a chart his mother made for him, coded to show which shirt went with which jacket, tie, and trousers.[11]

Galotto was impressed with the young man from Medford, and he proudly helped him become the first Jewish member of the Phi Kappa Psi fraternity. As revolutionary as that was, it didn't seem to make much difference to his new brothers. And before long, young Bloomberg moved into the fraternity house and took command—cleaning up the kind of disorder only a few dozen college boys could create. Bloomberg found a local woman who could cook. He hired someone who would clean, and then he divided the expenses among his fraternity brothers.

"He was very fussy about cleaning up. He used to get furious at us," Galotto recalled with a laugh. "Every so often you would see him bustle around with garbage bags and cleaning up and cursing us and making everything look shipshape."

Mostly, it was in good fun, but once, when a frat brother left too many beer cans and dirty athletic gear around the frat house living room, Bloomberg raged at him about being a slob. The boy bellowed back, at one point calling him a "spindly-legged little Jew." Bloomberg dashed up the stairs in a fury, grabbed his ice skates, and pinned the frat boy to the ground with his skates at the offender's neck. "I went up there and got him and calmed him down," Galotto said. The slur was indeed disgusting, but Galotto told him, "'I just made sure you didn't ruin your life over whether someone was cleaning up enough.' He laughed. Finally." [12]

As he emerged as a campus leader, Bloomberg soon would have to clean up more than his own fraternity house. Midway through his senior year, the *Baltimore Sun* reported that a sanitation officer gave two fraternities at Johns Hopkins a deadline of thirty days to clean up "their backyards of rat infestation and accumulated trash and debris." [13] It was a perfect mission for Bloomberg, who by then was president of the Interfraternity Council. He got the two negligent fraternities to clean up and pushed to create an entire system for keeping fraternity row from being a public health hazard.

Bloomberg later told the judge that his council had instituted new rules. There would be a weekly inspection of each of the fourteen fraternity houses by the vice president of the council. And each fraternity had to appoint someone responsible for upkeep during the summer. Also, Bloomberg promised that they would enforce the cleanliness code with fines of up to $200 and would even prohibit functions (i.e., girls and beer kegs) and outlaw the pledging of new members. Serious business, and if Bloomberg's brethren were irritated, the judge was impressed.

"I'm delighted and pleased, not only about the physical work, but because a line of thinking and a method of action has been adopted to ensure, to a great extent, that the action over the past several weeks will be sustained," Baltimore City judge Robert Hammerman concluded.[14]

Four months later, Bloomberg was again in the local news after police were called early one morning to the Phi Sigma Delta house. Neighbors accused the fraternity of "holding some bacchanalian affairs," and they were threatening to sue. The fraternity didn't help. The brothers had responded to a police visit by building a makeshift fort on the front lawn. Enough, Bloomberg's council decreed. They fined the Phi Sigma Deltas $200 and imposed two weeks social probation. As Bloomberg explained to the *Baltimore Sun* reporter, "This means that neither parties nor visits from girls will be allowed during this time." And the money would go to charity, he decided.

Pictures of Bloomberg in his senior yearbook show a very serious, even stern young man. The yearbook writers described his "omnipresent smirk"—more a half smile, an expression that Bloomberg would use to his advantage over the years because it gave away nothing about what was really happening inside. But the serious Bloomberg had a less forbidding side; he designed the college logo—a stylized bright blue jay. Years later, he would appear to dress up like a blue jay as part of an elaborate video holiday card from Johns Hopkins. "The things I do for this university," he would say as he stripped off a huge birdlike shoe for the cameras.

A boy like Michael Bloomberg could not easily afford Johns Hopkins—tuition was $1,600 a year, a lot of money to him and his family. Scholarships didn't exist for C students (and especially those with an occasional D). So Mike got loans from his family and worked and worked and worked.

His main job was managing the faculty club parking lot at night. He earned $35 a week plus dinner. His task was to keep students out of the parking lot reserved for professors. "I would sit there on a chair, some-times under the street light so I could read," as he explained years later.[15] "Holding an umbrella and my slide rule, which was hard to do with one hand, working on physics problems. And they'd drive down the driveway, and they'd see me, and they'd back out. Most times, you didn't even have to get up."

After work, he went inside the faculty club, where the woman running the place provided a meager peanut butter and jelly sandwich. Bloom-berg quickly found a way around such a paltry offering. He went to the club's kitchen and charmed the three women cooks. "You'd walk in, and there were these three big, fat cooks. I think they were sisters, but they all looked alike, enormous women. They loved me and gave me sirloin steaks and slices of roast beef."[16]

Through the undergraduate years, Dr. Galotto recalled, one image of Bloomberg at Hopkins seemed to say it all. "He always acted like he wasn't doing anything, like he wasn't studying, that he was out late par-tying," Galotto said.[17] Colleagues remembered how one night around 2:00 a.m., Mike's friends saw him carrying something large with great effort as he was crossing the campus. As he got closer, they saw it was a gigantic stack of the big, wide printouts that came from the copiers of the day. "He was doing all this stuff sub-rosa so we wouldn't think he was a nerd," one associate recalled.

In an era when many students across America were marching on Washington or protesting in the streets, Bloomberg steered clear of those who wanted to upend the establishment. He gave a small contribution to the NAACP, a poor student's tribute to his father. But he did not march. The only protest involved the dress code at the dining hall. Bloomberg's group, almost certainly led by Bloomberg, followed the dress code all too precisely. They came to dinner shirtless. But they were dutifully wearing coats and ties.[18]

Bloomberg's real talent, his friends and fellow students soon real-ized, was his ability to get along with anybody, to make even disagreeable people agree. He used those skills to become president of his fraternity, head of the Interfraternity Council, a squabbling group of egos, and then president of the senior class. Or, as Bloomberg boasted years later, "an all-around big man on campus." [19]

Learning how to get consensus would certainly serve him well in business and politics. He was a natural negotiator who could easily figure out how to soften the opponent's resolve, and humor was always a part of the repertoire. He could make people laugh—making jokes about others but also himself, about being so short that he agreed to dress up like a leprechaun to tend the bar at a campus Saint Patrick's Day party.

For a college student, Bloomberg had a lot of poise. He would occasionally joke that he would be America's first Jewish president. "How can you talk that way to the first Jewish president? Or, you're going to challenge the word of the first Jewish president?" Mary Kay Shartle, wife of Dr. Galotto and also a longtime friend from college days, remembered. It was always good for a laugh, but later, it became clear that it wasn't just part of Bloomberg's routine. "Most of us were just college kids living in the moment, Mike was living in the future," she said. "I'm not sure even he knew exactly what future." [20]

Bloomberg, the fake frat boy, changed on April 28, 1963. His father, the softer parent, the one who thought young Mike could do little wrong, died suddenly of heart failure at age fifty-seven. To friends, Bloomberg said only that he had to go away for a few days to Boston. When he returned, he showed no sign of the personal torment he would only talk about later and about how he overcame it, how he got back to work. But colleagues at Hopkins suddenly saw a different Mike Bloomberg. Serious. Busy. Maniacally pursuing the serious business of college, grades, leadership, no more nonsense.

He had been known in Medford as a guy who kept his distance with rough jokes and smart-ass commentary. That toughness hardened after his father died. He would soon start telling people not to dwell on tragedy, not to mourn. "Get over it" was like an automatic reaction when there was something awful to get over. That later distance from an openly emotional response, even to national tragedies, was true even at Johns Hopkins. When President Kennedy was assassinated in Bloomberg's senior year, many students were so devastated that they took to the streets or went to Washington to watch the cortege. Bloomberg saw it differently.

"I remember in November I had planned a big fraternity dance in the gym, and we had spent all our budget hiring James Brown and the Flames to play, and then Kennedy got shot and we canceled the dance and couldn't get our deposit back. Never got the deposit back," he said nearly three decades later.

If that memory seemed shockingly beside the point, Bloomberg, the unsentimental pragmatist, saw Kennedy's death as a blip in the real history of his time. "It was like [the death of] Princess Diana, in that everybody thought the world had changed, and the papers were full of it, but a week later people go back to their own work, their own lives, and there was nothing changed, no matter what anybody says."[21]

One of his teachers at Johns Hopkins, Willis Gore, recalled the youth's transformation after a spring semester when Bloomberg got his usual C in Electrical Circuit Analysis. Suddenly, in the next semester he got the sixth-highest grade in class.[22] Bloomberg sometimes explained that the shift into a higher gear came when he decided that, after college, he needed to go to graduate school. This was what Hopkins students did. They became doctors, lawyers, scientists, engineers; they were professionals.

There was another reason for this new intensity, of course. He was now the head of the Bloomberg family. His mother was strong, and she would go to work to help out; his sister would do her part, but he would be the man in charge. It would be another reason to head for the top. And for Mike Bloomberg of Medford, Massachusetts, that meant Harvard.

Years later, he said that although he got a degree in engineering, he knew he wasn't ever going to be a great engineer.[23] Being president of his class and head of the fraternity council and essentially running the fraternity world at Hopkins had given young Bloomberg a taste of management. Harvard was mecca for managers, at least in business. It would teach the finer points of running almost any enterprise. Also, it was just down the road from his mother in Medford.

"Somehow or other, I got into Harvard Business School. Nobody can figure that out, with this grade C average I got in. It was a clerical error, I'm sure," he said to laughter during a speech to the business school years later. "But it turned out okay for the Business School as well." (He would go on to give them millions for a library named after his father, a chair dedicated to philanthropy, and a $32 million grant for the business school to create a Cities Leadership Initiative to help mayors with their management skills.)[24]

When Bloomberg gave the commencement address at Harvard in 2014, a columnist for the *Boston Herald* looked back at Bloomberg's grades in high school and college and wrote a column with the phrase "File Under: Not Wicked Smaht." "If he were a college senior today, Bloomberg would be headed straight to the New England Tractor Trailer Training School, but things were a lot less competitive back then," sniffed Gayle Fee about the ex-mayor's middling grade averages in high school and college.[25]

Perhaps a "smahter" point would be that if Harvard Business School is not on the lookout for a Mike Bloomberg, maybe it's time to rethink the admissions policies. The places that helped young Mike Bloomberg learn about the world—the Boston science museum, Johns Hopkins, and Harvard University—all fared extremely well after their ex-student became one of the richest men on the planet.

In almost any of Bloomberg's versions of his life, Harvard gets a brief, almost dismissive mention. It was like punching a ticket on his way to the moneyed class. While the student world convulsed with protests and LSD and assaults on the establishment, Bloomberg had his head down. Did he sample the free sex? Of course, he told friends and later even some of his employees. Did he do drugs? Marijuana, a bit.[26]

But overall, Bloomberg's years at Harvard were "well spent," as he said later, learning the basics of business. Harvard's methods were brutal.

"There's nothing as educational as the instantaneous feedback of a hundred classmates shouting you down when you're caught unprepared or can't justify a position," he wrote.[27] Anybody who worked for Bloomberg was wise to have that quote pop up when they turned on the computer in the morning. Bloomberg, as mayor, as businessman, as philanthropist, could be merciless when somebody came to him unprepared. City officials quaked when the mayor began to squint at their chart or printout of the latest data. The questions would be direct, and they seemed always to aim at the weakest point on the page. That was perfect Bloomberg, perfect Harvard.

Decades later, Bloomberg remembered a day when he had not read the daily assignment, a case study about a business problem. When the professor asked who wanted to talk about the details of the reading, Bloomberg figured that if he raised his hand, this particular professor would not call on him.

The professor called on him.

Bloomberg quickly moved into high gear: "I'm so thrilled that you called on me," he remembered saying. "I want to thank you so much. It really is a great honor and a great experience to be here with all these smart people and have so many great professors like you, and I thought this particular case was so important you might want to ask others around the room to first lay it out and I would come and pull it all together and give it all the import that it really needs."

Around the room, fellow students were rolling their eyes. Some were chuckling out loud. "It was so obvious that I hadn't read the case. I had no idea what we were talking about," he said years later.

So the professor gave him and the class the day off and told them to come back the next day with the right analysis.

"I had a moral issue that night, no, a risk-management issue. There was no reason if this guy was smart that he was going to call on me the next day, because he would have known I had read the case. So did I have the balls to not read the case?"

He read the case.

It was about the Masland carpet company, which had warehouses and showrooms around the country. Young Mike told the class that he would recommend that the company close the warehouses and just have showrooms and ship from one place.

"This was before FedEx and DHL," Bloomberg recalled. And when he laid out his plans, "they laughed at me, literally laughed at me." The professor told him it wasn't very practical, not smart, Mr. Bloomberg.

Some time later, the professor came into the class with a newspaper tucked under his arm. "I guess we owe Mr. Bloomberg an apology," he said. Masland had decided to consolidate its warehouses and keep its showrooms. Bloomberg, who clearly loves these stories that show him besting the established wisdom, was so thrilled he was still telling the story a half century later. Even so, he always added at the end, the professor only gave him a passing grade, nothing special.[28]

If Harvard's technique provided him a "superior" but not "outstanding" education, as he described those years, it gave him the first brush with big names. He later laughed about his misspent awe as a student, but throughout his business and political years he also would court and clearly enjoy being around the rich and famous. "Embarrassingly, I remember being more impressed by whom I was matriculating with than by their abilities. As a kid from working-class Medford, never before had I met people as close to the limelight," he wrote years later. Just as quickly, however, he dismissed these heirs to the bold names of the day. "Did I think they'd rise to the top just because their dads did? (Generally they didn't.)" Few of their companies would even survive by the end of the century, he added.

"The bullshitters faded away," he said.[29]

When Harvard asked him to give that commencement address, the *Harvard Crimson* chastised those on campus who wanted to stop Bloomberg from speaking. Bloomberg had just left city hall, and some students objected to his police commissioner's overuse of stop-and-frisk policies in black and Hispanic communities. The *Crimson* editors rallied. "Michael Bloomberg is not a dull choice, and that reality is part of what makes him somebody worth listening to," they wrote. "It would be far more troubling if the University chose someone who would deliver a milquetoast speech, devoid of both substance and controversy."[30]

Bloomberg did not disappoint the *Crimson* editors or most of those in the audience. The New York *Daily News* headline about the speech read "Mike in Harvard Rant at Ivy Liberals." He compared the intolerance of some in New York City who objected when a Muslim group wanted to build a community center near the World Trade Center site to those at American universities "where the forces of repression appear to be stronger now than they have been since the 1950s."

He called out college campuses, "including here at Harvard," for a requirement that scholars were funded only if their work conforms to a particular, often liberal or progressive, view. "There's a word for that idea," he said. "Censorship. And it is just a modern-day form of McCarthyism."

He was talking about how students had protested speeches from former secretary of state Condoleezza Rice and also from his police commissioner, Ray Kelly.

"Today, on many college campuses, it is liberals trying to repress conservative ideas, even as conservative faculty members are at risk of becoming an endangered species. And perhaps nowhere is that more true than here in the Ivy League." And, later, "A university cannot be great if its faculty is politically homogenous."

The dignitaries in their multicolored regalia began to shift on the platform behind him, their demeanor ranging from uncomfortable to angry. Perhaps if Bloomberg had been a Rockefeller or a Kennedy or one of those rock-ribbed families that felt Harvard was right up there with the best clubs and the cushiest seats in heaven, he might not have chastised those who ran the place. Not openly, at least. But Mike Bloomberg hated to miss a chance to make a stir and an important point.[31]

During Bloomberg's own Harvard days, of course, the campus was full of rage and debate, especially about the Vietnam War. Again, he did not participate. Bloomberg faced the draft when he graduated in 1966, and he has said he wanted to be an army officer, perhaps in an engineering arm of the military. He was rejected, he insisted later, because he had flat feet. Flat feet always seemed like a privileged-class ailment to keep the select few from marching to war with the less fortunate. And years later, when writer Joyce Purnick questioned how such a minor problem could get such a major exemption during the Vietnam era, Bloomberg angrily took off his shoes and socks and displayed how his arches had failed to arch.[32] Those feet earned him a 1-Y medical deferment in 1966, which meant he would only go to war in a national emergency. (It was the same deferment that President Donald Trump received in 1968 for "bone spurs.")

Over the years he learned to convert his relief about missing the military into humor about his physical deficiency. He said that he and the draft board had a pact—if he didn't call them, they wouldn't call him. Instead of Vietnam, the youth with a new MBA moved swiftly to New York City, where he could begin to enjoy the money scrums of Wall Street.

3

THE SALOMON
BROTHERHOOD

"Hey, Harvard. Get me coffee."

When Bloomberg graduated from Harvard Business School in 1966, there was no army of ambitious young people rushing to earn the easy gold on Wall Street. The few who strayed into the financial world in those days favored the dignified white-shoe firms or started working for Daddy. Selling stocks and bonds like a peddler was grubby, beneath their old-moneyed class.

In contrast, young Bloomberg had already established that he loved selling. The Christmas wreaths in Medford were a first taste. As a Harvard student, he had worked in a small real estate firm, outselling the regulars, as he told it, because he always arrived early and answered the phones to grab new clients before the rest of the staff had poured their first cup of coffee.[1]

One of Bloomberg's Harvard pals suggested that the indefatigable young Mike should try Goldman Sachs or a small family-controlled bond trading firm called Salomon Brothers & Hutzler. Both firms jumped at the chance to bring in a young Ivy grad who was just as eager to learn the selling and trading side of the business.

At Goldman, Bloomberg was interviewed by Gustave Levy, a big-name arbitrageur and philanthropist, one of the lions of Wall Street in his day. Goldman offered him $14,000 a year, a good salary even for a Harvard graduate. At Salomon, Bloomberg met three people including John Gutfreund, the number two man in the firm. He would become known as the "king of Wall Street" in the 1980s before he was forced to leave in disgrace over a treasury bond scandal.[2] Most important, during his tour of Salomon, Bloomberg started talking to a man named Billy, who was "just some easy to talk to, nice person."[3] That "nice person" turned out to be William R. Salomon, managing partner of his family's firm.

Nearly fifty years later, Bloomberg would speak at Billy Salomon's funeral. The address that went out to the media was solid and respectful, but at the end of his eulogy, Bloomberg's voice softened as he talked about how Billy was "more than a mentor, almost like a second father to me . . . And maybe somewheres [sic], my father is now saying to Billy, thank you for all you did for my son," he said, his voice breaking up. "And I say it, too. Thank you, Billy, I couldn'ta done it without you."[4]

What makes that moment so unusual for Michael Bloomberg was that he had spent most of his life carefully hiding that soft side. He could blow up. He could joke. He could be tough and mean and crude. He could be generous and loyal. But soft? Michael Bloomberg didn't really do soft, at least not publicly.

When the young Bloomberg took the job at Salomon, Billy was one of the reasons, and he settled for less—$9,000, plus a $2,500 loan. Even with the Harvard stamp of approval, he started in the business like everybody else at Salomon—in the vault. "We slaved in our underwear, in an un-air-conditioned bank vault, with an occasional six pack of beer to make it more bearable," he recalled. "Every afternoon, we counted out billions of dollars of actual bond and stock certificates to be messengered to banks as collateral for overnight loans."[5] In the mornings, when the stack of documents came back, Bloomberg and his comrades in "the Cage," as they called it, made sure they were counted in the firm's inventory.

After a few months sweating at the firm's lowest level, Bloomberg became a clerk, "putting little paper slips in alphabetical order, all day long." It was so humiliating that Bloomberg said the reason he didn't quit was that he was "too embarrassed" to say what he was actually doing at Salomon. He told his Harvard friends, many of whom had offices by then, private offices with windows and carpets, that he was "studying methods and procedures to simplify the work flow." [6] Within a year, he was a real clerk at the utilities desk on Salomon's trading floor, where he stamped and recorded trades. It was a move up. Barely.

As Bloomberg watched the Salomon methods in his agonizingly slow rise up the company ladder, he witnessed an operation that would soon be as antiquated as the rotary telephone.

Sales only felt real in those days if they were on paper, and those valuable certificates had to be walked across the street to the bank for the night. After the markets closed, a small army of couriers, older men, often ex-cops smoking cigars and looking like nobody to mess with, carted the evidence of the day's trades from brokers to the banks. In 1968, Bloomberg and his colleagues encountered the "Paperwork Crisis," a crucial moment on Wall Street, when the sheer volume of paper overwhelmed the markets. At that point, about 12 million shares changed hands every day (compared to about 900 million a day by 2015), and the back offices (and the boys in the bank vaults) were swamped. The stock exchange eased the crisis by restricting trading to four days a week with some firms closing early to catch up and some going out of business because of the confusion in the back office. [7]

Meanwhile, Mike Bloomberg had been trying to escape that daily paper storm and was growing tired of waiting for his chance to be a real-live broker. He seethed about being the butt of anti-Harvard antics by the golden boy traders. "Hey, Harvard, get me coffee." [8] Enough with the fraternal hazing, enough with the petty, monotonous shuffling of paper and running errands. One day, Bloomberg simply cracked. His job was to sharpen pencils and place them carefully on traders' desks—six number 2 pencils on one and six number 3 pencils on another. Instead, that day he furiously broke the lead tips off the ends of the prescribed pencils, and one trader who saw the pencil carnage on his desk started screaming that Bloomberg should be fired. To Bloomberg's relief, he was soon moved out of that trader's line of vision—to the equities desk, where, as it turned out, he belonged.[9]

Robert Quinn, a colleague from the same era, recalled Salomon's utilitarian offices at 60 Wall Street where Bloomberg would have suffered his initiation rites. "There was a team of seven or eight calculators—mostly mature women—who [recorded] the trades," he said. "They were handwritten on pieces of paper, carbon copies, then sent down in a little basket between floors on a rope." There were runners, mostly young women who ran to help when a trader yelled "Wire" so that a trade could be registered and handed to a cluster of telegraphers. And the women who had calculators "punched a lot of buttons, they were very adept at it. They had to calculate the interest on the bonds and the value and they were very important to the process," Quinn recalled. "And they were lovely ladies."[10]

There were spittoons in those early days, and the smell of sweat and cigars could be overpowering as the trading day reached its daily climax. The noise level in "The Room" was deafening, and there was no real noise buffer, and each day, the decibel level rose as traders vied for who could yell the loudest. "Visitors to the balcony over The Room were often astonished by the zoolike roar that rose from the floor when, for example, the Federal Reserve came into the market at 11:30 in the morning."[11]

If Salomon's pit was a big, open ear-splittingly noisy warehouse, Bloomberg and his colleagues fed on it. And even as the computers slowly made that open room less like an open bazaar, it would be a floor plan that Bloomberg would adopt for his businesses and city hall.

As Salomon Brothers (often, "Solly") grew to become one of the most powerful financial houses on Wall Street, the language of the trading floor would still raise eyebrows at a truck stop. "Fuck you" was a way of saying hello, as one veteran of the Salomon floor explained. Or as another alumnus put it, "The word 'fuck' at Salomon Brothers was a way to take a breath."[12] Everybody was a target—too tall? Too short? And women had to be tougher than any of them. One Salomon alumnus recalled that often he would see an older woman reduced to tears by some young, foul-mouthed trader engrossed in the risky trade of the day.[13] But it was ad-dictive, a kind of "greed-speed," a money-rich high that infected almost everyone who worked on the trading floors in those days.

Quinn, who spent twenty-six years at Salomon and was there dur-ing Bloomberg's time, described the room as "an adult kindergarten and, frankly, it was wonderful. The language was not appropriate for adult men," he acknowledged, "but we were all in the pit together yelling and fussing. It was spontaneous and fast, like an intellectually athletic expe-rience. You had to be quick-witted and think on your feet and express yourself very quickly."[14]

Bloomberg would thrive in that thunder dome, at least for a while. He fed on the electricity, the daily scrum for trades. He also learned quickly that the "easy to talk to, nice" Billy Salomon, or WRS as his staff called him, was not always that easy to talk to or nice. Billy could be gentlemanly, but he also ran a tough school for fast-talking, street-smart ruffians. Still, he would insist that they refuse to exchange expensive gifts with clients—no booze, no tickets, no Thanksgiving turkeys. WRS could listen to dissent, but he was the head man, not the head negotiator. Even for Bloomberg, who believed he was a favorite, Salomon could be tough. One day Billy asked him to go buy a birthday card, and when Bloomberg came back with it, after some careful shopping around, Salomon threw it at him and said, "Not this shit."[15]

Morris Offit, who was Salomon's sales director in Bloomberg's day and later went on to found a bank and an investment house, once de-scribed Billy as "the most underrated Wall Street leader" of his day. "Billy had little compassion, and he did little stroking . . . He had what I used to call the Pit Theory of personnel management—put all these guys into a pit and whoever walks out is the survivor."[16] It would be a rough model for Bloomberg's own system as he later ran a business, a city, and a high-powered philanthropy.

Yet for all the noise and the raw locker-room talk in those days, Billy Salomon demanded a kind of financial propriety that would soon become passé. He would require that traders give up part of their profits to the needy. And Henry Kaufman, once the chief economist at Salomon Brothers, best known as "Dr. Doom" for predicting troubles in the markets, remembered Salomon's code in detail. One day Billy told a trader he had made too much from a deal and had to give some of the profit back.[17] Give the profit back? How quaint, traders would scoff in later years, but Billy Salomon believed that you had to be fair to the customers, not simply suck out every dime on every deal. And when one of the biggest trading stars in the firm cheated on his expense account, Salomon fired him. No appeal, no questions. He was just gone.[18]

Billy Salomon's system worked well in the time that Bloomberg was there. The firm grew from a modest bond house to a legendary investment center on Wall Street. Bloomberg rode that growth into the good times, and he quickly got a reputation as a particularly ballsy salesman who told everybody, including the boss, how to run things.

Bloomberg worked with Jay Perry, an occasionally unhinged block trader (once described as "frenetic and untrustworthy but not vicious")[19] who honed Bloomberg's skills as a salesman to the point the duo "could sell anything to anybody."[20] Bloomberg apparently enjoyed the full Perry madness, and soon he had ridden that high-risk tension executing big trades and earning his chops as an up-and-coming Salomon superstar. It did not hurt that he came in early and often stayed late enough to get a ride home with Gutfreund.

Still, Bloomberg's trajectory was not a straight line upward. In August 1972, when he expected to be named partner, he was not on the list. Everyone else at his level got the nod, not Mike Bloomberg. With tears of fury, Bloomberg recalled muttering, "I'll kill 'em." And "I'll shoot myself."[21] Instead, he went for a run to relieve the tension and arrived back at work the next morning, full of his usual brash confidence and enthusiasm. In December that year, without explanation, he was finally made partner.

Bloomberg's years at Salomon were a little like a raucous childhood he didn't have, the sybaritic frat world that he barely tasted. Wall Street was turning into the famous go-go Gomorrah of Hollywood fame, and even though Salomon was a small firm, it was growing and becoming a part of the fast, mean, ugly, risky, obscene, and seductive world. Temptations were everywhere. The hot breathing over a risky sale, the successful peddling of a new product, a client who bought the line—it was simply another form of Wall Street sex. At day's end, they needed smokes, expensive cigars, good food, and whiskey. The girls were there, if that was what you wanted. The drugs were there—and they brought more than a few of them down. But the money would be the greatest seduction of all and it was everywhere. Piles of it, literally.

At first Mike Bloomberg had gawked at the silverware laid out at fancy dinners and marveled at the genuine artwork in upscale offices. In 1967, for his first trip to the La Côte Basque, a luxurious restaurant on Manhattan's West Fifty-fifth Street that was once anointed "society's temple" by the *Times*, he couldn't stop admiring the excess.[22] His friend Harvey Eisen described those early days as two lower-middle-class guys who didn't have a nickel, and Bloomberg was living in a studio apartment where he put up a curtain and called it a one bedroom.[23] Soon, however, Bloomberg would learn to use the expense accounts like his colleagues. And he would quickly adopt the argot of Wall Street so that even years later, he could all too easily slip back into the mean crudities that traders came to expect from one another.

Richard Levy, a trader who worked for Bloomberg on the equities desk, recalled the day when his grandfather died and he told Bloomberg that he planned to go to the funeral. That was not convenient, Bloomberg told him. It would be a big trading day, and "Would you mind having them change the funeral?" Bloomberg asked. He later apologized, but his instant reaction was to focus on the sale, not on the humans around him.[24]

It would be another example of how Mike Bloomberg would often blurt out exactly what was on his mind, then apologize later—a habit or tic that would cause him more trouble after he escaped the Wall Street of his day.

As Bloomberg was moving up at Salomon, his boss and champion, Jay Perry, was turning into a strange, tortured creature—at one point emptying all the contents of Bloomberg's desk on the floor.[25] Perry screamed at colleagues and even threatened clients. As he wrestled with an ugly divorce, Perry's tasks fell to young Bloomberg, who was considered meek and stable compared to the combustible Perry.[26] Perry's bitter enemy was another complicated man, Richard Rosenthal, and battles between the two had turned into fisticuffs on the trading room floor.

In 1975, the everyday flare-ups between Perry and Rosenthal became so intense that the managing partners decided to bypass both and give the less erratic Bloomberg control over the block trading in stocks. He was thirty-three and his work ethic was legendary. "It's a game for people who thrive on pressure and excitement," he told the *New York Times*. "I love the business. I live and breathe the business."[27]

Bloomberg's life after hours also changed. He moved from his old dating patterns—would you like to take a beer and pizza and join me on the Staten Island Ferry?—to the fast lane. On weekends, he and his friends would party with incredible energy and efficiency. When they rented a place, Bloomberg was, as always, in charge. "He cooked, he did all the food. He wouldn't let anybody do anything," said Harvey Eisen, a friend from the Salomon days who remained a friend. He even bought groceries—two full carts always empty by Sunday evening. Empty? Eisen was asked. He laughed. "You never heard of the munchies?"[28]

Bloomberg would boast, or maybe admit, that he had "a girlfriend in every city." Maybe, for a while, but one British secretary at Salomon Brothers in London turned out to be special. In December 1976, he married Susan Elizabeth Barbara Meyer, née Brown, a twenty-eight-year-old British divorcée. Friends remember his wife as quiet and strong, the family anchor when daughter Emma was born in 1979 and Georgina in 1983. If the new Mrs. Bloomberg had read that interview about how Bloomberg lived and breathed the business, she would have been prepared for the husband who worked hellish hours, who loved dinners and galas, who was seldom at rest, a man who would later say that he loved devoting "twelve hours to work and twelve hours to fun—every day."[29] It was a joke, yes, but what it really revealed was that Michael Bloomberg had begun to agonize over an empty hour. He was a doer, a constant doer. An evening home with a book, more Mrs. Bloomberg's style, was not Mike Bloomberg's idea of a productive night. Soon, they were beginning to enjoy separate lives, a sliding toward what would be a fairly amicable divorce after seventeen years of marriage. Susan Bloomberg told the London *Daily Mail* years later that she had asked for the divorce because her husband was working night and day, and "I was in a country that wasn't my own and very lonely."[30] Bloomberg often said that he had suffered only two bad days in his life—the day his father died and the day his mother died. One longtime associate added a third heartbreak—when his wife, Susan, left him.[31]

More and more, what Bloomberg loved was being out there, meeting people, connecting, networking. It was all part of building the Bloomberg name and the Bloomberg man. He later wrote that "I'm sure someone, someplace is smart enough to succeed while 'keeping it in perspective' and not working too hard, but I've never met him or her. The more you work, the better you do. It's that simple. I always outworked the other person."[32]

Yet even the Bloomberg work ethic wasn't a simple route to success at Salomon. The late seventies were not good for block traders like him, and Richard Rosenthal, who seemed to have a special need to disparage the boy from Harvard. Rosenthal, who did not have a college degree, told colleagues that Bloomberg was a failure, a waste of the firm's money, a burr in the hide of the august Salomon firm.[33]

Suddenly, in 1979, Rosenthal made his play. He convinced the board to allow him to take over equities, Bloomberg's patch. The news sent Bloomberg into a rage, and he stormed across the room to see the bosses, in particular the one he had cultivated for so long, John Gutfreund, and announced that there was no way he was working for Richard Rosenthal. They knew that. Bloomberg would not be working with Rosenthal or Perry, who had by then been transferred to the edge of the known world—Dallas. No more equities for the Bloomberg irritant. Instead, he was going "upstairs" to run the company computer system and the technical side of things. It was, by anybody's lights, a demotion.

For his bosses at Salomon, however, it was obviously a reasonable solution. Bloomberg had been nagging them for years about updating the paper trail needed to sell stocks and bonds. When he pushed in the early 1970s to set up a system that would provide quick and understandable data to traders (who often had to look through piles of ragged *Wall Street Journal*s to find yesterday's index or price or whatever), the bosses told him he could create such a computerized package—but only on his own time. Bloomberg did exactly that, and he and a few others created something he called the "B-page." The *B* meant "back-up or background," not "Bloomberg," although he admitted he enjoyed having people think it was his creation. Never the shy one, Bloomberg's first message to colleagues on his B-page was the announcement in December 1972 that he had just made partner.[34] If he deserved praise and credit for dragging Salomon out of the paper era, Dick Rosenthal made certain he didn't get it.[35]

Rosenthal also conspired to make Bloomberg's last two years at Salomon miserable. Computers, administration, data—to any self-respecting trader this was girls' stuff. He went from being the quarterback to the water boy overnight. Barely a step up from his early days as clerk. Friends remember him at a lonely desk on an upper floor, away from the action, away from the trading thrum that he so loved. But if the big boys were trying to get him to quit, Mike Bloomberg wasn't leaving. Instead, he turned the full force of his energy and his knowledge—the engineering, the Harvard business expertise, the understanding of Wall Street— toward the computers that were supposed to humiliate him.

In his exile, Bloomberg soon became the master of charts and data and the complex logarithms of modern finance. He kept going to Gutfreund to talk about how other, newer computers would make Salomon run better and faster. But Gutfreund and others were not listening. They mostly sided with Richard Rosenthal, who kept making fun of Bloomberg and his "peckers," belittling the Perry acolyte as a misfit in Salomon's high-powered fraternity.

At the same time, Rosenthal was helping craft the sale of Salomon to the Phibro company. The Philipp brothers, who ran Phibro and traded in nearly one hundred major commodities including oil or silver,[36] offered to buy Salomon Brothers for $550 million. In the official histories of this era, the merger happened because Phibro had cash and Salomon had debts.[37] But there were other more personal reasons that some at Salomon wanted this sale. When he was in charge of the company before retiring in 1978, Billy Salomon had made it hard for his employees to draw out their share of the company's profits unless the money went to a charity.[38] Some, like Rosenthal, were anxious to check out with the full share (and he would leave the company with his payout a year after the sale).[39]

Gutfreund and his colleagues also decided the sale would allow them to shed people, paying them handsomely to leave. On August 1, 1981, Gutfreund and others told Michael Bloomberg he had until the end of the year to find another job. They gave him his share—a payout of $10 million.

Almost any telling of Michael Bloomberg's business career, any imparting of advice from one of the nation's most successful billionaires, begins on that August day when he learned that his beloved Salomon Brothers did not love him in return. His autobiography starts there. Once, in a television interview that lasted seven and a half minutes, he mentioned it five times.[40] He would later thank the man who fired him, John Gutfreund, and often mention in speeches that "it turned out okay," which, coming from a famous billionaire, mayor, and philanthropist, always got a good laugh.

For all the talk about that day he was told to leave, Bloomberg has never really explained in much detail how he felt or what he did to make it happen. He has said, "Was I sad . . . you bet. But, as usual, I was much too macho to show it."[41] Sure, he was a rich man, his father would have told him to put it in the bank, but his first purchase was a new sable coat for his wife—just to show her that he was fine.

Actually the young Mike was "devastated," said Kenneth Lipper, who was at Salomon and who watched Bloomberg through his last rocky years. "He loved Salomon Brothers. He loved the tough-guy swagger, the whole trading atmosphere. It was like having your parents stop the car, open the door, and leave you at the side of the road." [42]

Bloomberg's own explanation is that Richard Rosenthal was out to get him and finally did. Others from that wild era see it slightly differently. "He was one of the good guys, working their butts off," said his friend Eisen. He was fired, Eisen believed, "because he has a big mouth, and he doesn't have a governor on it. So, they sent him to Siberia [running the computer system] . . . Then the worst place turned out to be the best." [43] Bloomberg—who bragged about coming in early and staying late to have time with the boss—kept telling those same bosses how to run the place, never a smart policy for an underling.

In his fifteen years at the company, Bloomberg had learned a great deal about bonds, equities, the full panorama of the increasingly complex financial marketplace. But when he was fired, the young Michael Bloomberg took in other important lessons about how to run a company.

Bloomberg's friends who have been fired (or find themselves in trouble) have said that one of the first condolence calls comes from Mike Bloomberg. He would learn to use the corporate ax (unstintingly if someone cheated or failed to do the job—like the city official who was instantly dismissed after the mayor caught him playing solitaire on his computer). [44] But he would also keep connections with many of those he had ousted—a seat on the board, a grant, a golfing date, a part-time aerie somewhere in the company. Howard Wolfson, who worked for Bloomberg as a deputy mayor in city hall and a political adviser, said that he took Mayor Bloomberg aside one day and complained that one top member of their team was a dud. He wanted the authority to fire that person as soon as possible. Instead, the mayor lowered his voice and explained that firing people is dangerous. It hurts the person who gets fired, of course, and he or she can then go off and bitch about the Bloomberg operation, even to the press. It also hurts the others who stay and fear that their loyalty to him is misplaced. Loyalty deserves loyalty, he said often, and that loyalty pact became early dogma at Bloomberg LP.[45]

The mighty Salomon Brothers made one particularly important mistake when they gave Michael Rubens Bloomberg his golden boot: they also released him, in every sense of the word. Besides the money, Salomon handed Bloomberg, and later three colleagues, the keys—the expertise they needed—to build one of the most successful financial enterprises in the world. Bloomberg would insist that he and his associates had made sure they did not take anything that belonged to Salomon, no papers, no computer data. But what was in their heads was enough. As Gutfreund acknowledged later, "In the eighties, Bloomberg built his business and sold the services he had developed at Salomon back to Salomon. We paid for it twice. I congratulate him." [46]

Bloomberg tried to make certain another Mike Bloomberg couldn't happen to him. People who work in Bloomberg's many enterprises sign a confidentiality agreement before the first paycheck. They vow not to use their wisdom about the Bloomberg operation or even gossip about life in the Bloomberg capsule or badmouth the boss. In 1981, when Salomon Brothers fired Mike Bloomberg, they failed to do that.

Salomon Brothers thought they were shedding a young troublemaker. Instead, as he has said repeatedly over the years, they made it possible for Michael Bloomberg to change Wall Street and become one of the world's most powerful billionaires.

4

THE MAKING OF
A BLOOMBERG

"He pushed me and other people out of our comfort zones into places where he saw opportunity, and he was willing to take the risk."
—*Thomas Secunda, co-founder, Bloomberg Terminal*

Walking through Bloomberg's New York headquarters in 2019 with its sleek starship look, its aquariums filled with exotic fish, its vast beehive humming with any hiccup of news in the world economy, it was hard to imagine the hunt-and-peck beginnings of Mike Bloomberg's terminal.

Newly fired by Salomon Brothers, Mike Bloomberg has always said he worked his normal twelve hours on his final day at Salomon, and then started his own company the next morning.[1] He took $300,000[2] from his $10 million payout and rented two small rooms in a high-rise full of low-rent offices on upper Madison Avenue. He wanted four other Salomon employees to come with him. One decided it was a gamble he couldn't take, but three young geeks signed on for the adventure. Bloomberg took the office with a window and a classic New York view of the back alley.[3] The three other Salomon alumni shared another room, and the makeshift sign on the door said "Innovative Market Systems." The project that would make them all members of the "three comma club," billionaires whose net worth would someday require three commas, all started very slowly.

Their first year, 1982, would not be a particularly good time to start a business. The financial world around them was in retreat. President Ronald Reagan was overseeing what was then the worst recession since the Great Depression, and the lines of people looking for jobs lengthened as the unemployment rate hit nearly 11 percent.[4,5] The Dow hovered around 1,000[6] and the prime interest rates, which had soared to a meteoric 21.5 percent in December 1980, had begun to come down slowly to the still-astronomical mid-teens.[7] As for Bloomberg's new company, there was a far more important benchmark: *Time* magazine's "man" of the year was The Computer.[8]

Computers were not alien to Wall Street. David Leinweber, a computer scientist and historian, likes to begin his story in 1823 when the "eccentric and obnoxious" Charles Babbage invented (but did not build) his "calculating machine."[9] Then came the telegraph and the ticker tape (which Thomas Edison improved by repeatedly dropping it and then fixing what was broken).[10] Then there were the big computer machines—the first one in 1946 "weighed 30,000 pounds and blew a tube every 45 minutes."[11] Bell Labs invented the modem (telephones required). The machines steadily improved and grew smaller each year.[12]

By the time Bloomberg and his colleagues left Salomon Brothers, there were already the cumbersome mainframe IBM computers and Quotrons or Telerates, boxy contraptions that were little more than computerized ticker-tape machines. Personal computers were edging onto desks by then. They were better than the paper logs of the past, but the Bloomberg team knew these machines could not offer the broker an idea of the "what-ifs" (what if the Fed rate changes or what if OPEC raises the price of oil). The financial computers of the day did not compare one product with the rest of the market. They did not help a trader recognize a good deal from a clunker. As they had packed up their family photos at Salomon Brothers, this foursome would begin their adventure years before most people would even hear the word "Internet."[13]

At Innovative Market Systems, the young Salomon refugees began by figuring out what exactly they wanted their machine to do. Bloomberg was the visionary and the banker. Duncan MacMillan would eventually help figure out who would buy their product. Chuck Zegar worked on the software, and Tom Secunda was the whiz kid who helped write the formulas and analytics to make the Bloomberg Terminal unique.[14]

All four brought key advantages to their new venture. They had been traders, and they knew firsthand what the guy on the phone, the broker desperate to make a sale or buy the lot, really needed. Also, they knew more about computers than most of those on Wall Street. How to knit those two advantages into one great package would be no easy business.

Bloomberg's official version of this period generously spreads the credit around to those who took a chance with him. But the real spark behind the Bloomberg machine came from Thomas Secunda, who was twenty-seven years old when Bloomberg, then thirty-nine, recruited him.

"He's like a Steve Wozniak [who co-founded Apple with Steve Jobs]," recalled Morgan Downey, a long-term Bloomberg employee who left to create a lower-cost competitor called Money.net. "Mike was the money; Tom was the coding brains, if you will."[15]

Bloomberg and Secunda met in the 1970s when Secunda was a young bond expert and Bloomberg was one of the hotshot equities traders in the business. When Bloomberg asked Secunda to dinner one day, it was like being tapped for an insiders club, the younger man remembered. Since Mike was quite the dashing Wall Street superstar, they went where stars gathered—the Quilted Giraffe on Madison and Fifty-fifth. It was a restaurant of choice in Manhattan in the 1970s and '80s, and regulars included Jackie Onassis, Woody Allen, Henry Kissinger, and, that evening, Mike and Susan Bloomberg. Bloomberg, the Medford kid, had once marveled at such glamour, the extra forks at the place settings, the masterpiece paintings on loan from the Met. Now it was Tom Secunda's turn to gawk. "My girlfriend got so flustered that she called me Bob most of the time."[16]

In what might have seemed like a fairly routine question that night, Bloomberg asked Secunda what he could do to help him. The youth gave the right answer. He wanted a computer on his desk so that he could get more work done quickly. "In those days, you didn't have a keyboard," Secunda recalled. Instead, traders would take their requests to a central computer room to get data from the big computer. Traders used this time waiting for the big computer as a break from the phones, he said. "People spent most of their time just shooting the shit and hanging out" while they waited, but Secunda wanted to skip that step and the leisure that went with it. So the next day he came in and one of the few available terminals was on his desk, "which made me dramatically more effective and pretty soon everybody had one, and I happened to be one of the most hated guys for a while because I took away your excuse for not working."[17] Mike Bloomberg saw real promise in someone who knew about these confounding new computers, someone like him who wanted to work smarter and faster and who refused to slow down with the four o'clock bell.

Secunda tended to be soft-spoken, a gentler contrast to Bloomberg's sharp edges. Even years later, he would have the look of a sixties folk singer, short beard, easy smile (all of which betrayed an inner toughness, some of his colleagues suggested).

"The thing I'm really proud of is that we changed the way Wall Street works," he said. "The emphasis shifted from who you knew to what you knew. The trend would have happened whether there was a Bloomberg or not. I think we sped it up. We made it affordable. We made it possible."

Before the Bloomberg, you went to a trader and he sold you the bonds he had or thought he could get. It was a little like going to a used-car lot and saying, I want a blue Malibu. And the salesman would say, we only have a nice, red Impala. The Bloomberg let its user get a better idea of what was really under the Impala's hood and whether somebody else at the lot across the street might actually have an affordable blue Malibu.

This was nothing short of a revolutionary system that let the air out of a lot of inflated deals and the egos that went with them.

Other data and information providers, like Reuters, were eyeing the market, and it was obvious to many of the younger, computer-savvy traders that this confetti of a system based on paper was as arcane as the old days when some of the first traders sent offers and prices by stagecoach or semaphore.[18]

"Nobody knew for sure where computers were going, and later where the Internet was going," remembered John Holman, who helped create what would be an unsuccessful Bloomberg competitor with a system called Shark. The Shark was produced by Walsh Greenwood Information Systems, but didn't survive on its own. Like Bloomberg's terminal, Shark arrived before Al Gore's bill to create the "Information Superhighway" in 1991 or the revolution created by the World Wide Web two years later.[19] For those who couldn't understand why anybody would spend so much energy and money on computers, this looked like a risky gamble, a fantasy tethered to that airy thing called the Internet. No paper; no reality.

"Now it seems obvious," Holman said. "Then it was a huge risk."[20]

Risk, of course, had been the drug of choice at Salomon Brothers. The big risk takers were known in the trade as the Big Swinging Dicks, and they acted like high-wire artists, buying and selling sweat-free and without a net. Bloomberg had learned to savor risk, to court it personally and financially. He skied on the double black diamond slopes. He flew airplanes and helicopters, relishing Wall Street's code about the need for adventure. "Happiness for me has always been the thrill of the unknown, trying something that everyone says can't be done, feeling that gnawing pit in my stomach that says, 'Danger ahead.'"[21] Clearly, even with all that hard work and careful planning, this love of risk also came with a surprising allotment of good luck.

By the end of the first year at Innovative Market Systems, Bloomberg's bank account began to dwindle, and friends described a tense and anxious man with little of the bravado from his Salomon days.[22] Help came just in time. Bloomberg had been doing a little consulting for Merrill Lynch & Co., and Edmond Moriarty, who was Merrill's executive vice president for capital markets, offered to give him a hearing about his dream project.

In Bloomberg's telling, one daunting scene made all the difference, and the hero, as is often the case in these renderings, was Bloomberg himself. It was a small Mike from Medford versus a whole squad of well-tailored corporate giants at Merrill Lynch. To a roomful of skeptics, Bloomberg pitched and pitched, making this glorious machine (which did not yet exist) sound like the answer to every bond trader's dream. Some in that group remembered being transfixed by Bloomberg's dazzling spiel but also troubled that Merrill was already working on a similar project with IBM. And the man who had been running software development for Merrill scoffed at the very idea of going outside the company. He told the group that he could do the same thing—internally. It would take six months, he estimated, as long as there were no interruptions.

Six months? Bloomberg huffed. He could get a machine prototype in six months—and, here was the clincher, there would be no charge if Merrill didn't like the thing.[23]

Six months? His colleagues back at the little office gasped. Who even began creating a new computer system in six months? For the next very intense nine months—Merrill allowed extra time for contract negotiations—the four men worked six days a week, dawn to midnight some days. On Sunday, they would often come into the little office "just to talk," Secunda remembered.

"We were all family," he said. "We sort of lived what we were doing, and we were on a mission . . . we really thought we could change the way Wall Street worked."[24]

Bloomberg often remembered those days as the best in his business life. "Never before or since did I have as much fun and as challenging a time," he would say later in his many speeches to young entrepreneurs. "I'm not sure the company wasn't better off then either."[25]

What they created would look like a kid's toy. Named the Market Master by the Bloomberg team, it was basically a cathode-ray tube (think 1950s television set) with everything tucked inside. The innards were based on Intel,[26] the microprocessor company that later became the world's top producer of this computer necessity. Having Intel from the beginning made it easier to switch from their self-made machines to the commercial ones when they became available. One early witness thought their machine looked a little like a contraption cobbled together for a high school science project that had more promise than reality. Others quickly saw the future.

Secunda described how they designed and assembled their own keyboards—focusing on how to simplify their offerings enough for the bond trader who was coping with an increasingly bewildering marketplace. They called their first keyboard in 1983 the Chiclet because the keyboard buttons looked vaguely like the little squares of gum popular at the time. Instead of "Enter" on the keyboard, you pushed "Go." Different markets had different keys—munis, government, mortgages, et cetera. The dreaded QWERTY system of letters that had tortured typists since the 1870s remained, however, even though Bloomberg and his people knew that the world's bullheaded old brokers of the 1980s would not deign to "type." Typing was for women and flunkies, "peckers," as they were known on Wall Street. So Bloomberg and his crowd would argue that this was not typing; this was punching keys. One early ad for the machines even shows a trader aiming only one index finger at the keyboard—to punch, not peck, at the terminal.

Over the years, learning how to use the terminal allowed one to enter a kind of insider's universe—one user compared it to the *Star Trek* language of Klingonese—but once you learned, you were so easily hooked that another extremely satisfied user would compare it to drugs. For traders, it was like a company "selling heroin."[27]

In early 1983, it became a joke at Merrill that if Bloomberg made the deadline of nine months, he would deliver the first on-time software project in history.[28] When Bloomberg brought the prototype of his machine back to Merrill Lynch, he presented it in the afternoon of the day it was due.[29] But even the outwardly self-assured Bloomberg was not sure if his makeshift machine would work. There had been weeks of computerized nightmares—crashes, failures, bugs of all varieties. There had been plenty of yelling—Bloomberg himself admitted to a lot of it—and hours of despair. At the demonstration to Merrill's executives, Bloomberg focused on promoting the wonders of his creation while desperately waiting for it to actually turn on. Finally, out of the corner of his eye, he saw the little flashing message "Loading software." It meant that his team had dispatched the latest glitch,[30] and the machine worked enough to show promise. A few at Merrill opened a bottle of champagne, but there were doubters who worried about whether IBM would match this one-man dervish of a Mike Bloomberg and his homemade terminal.[31]

Bloomberg had already softened the ground at Merrill's executive suite when he began consulting for the financial behemoth. In his version, he would start out in the early mornings when most workers were still wrestling with their alarm clocks. He would buy several cups of coffee and tea—black or with milk, sugar, stirrers at hand. He would roam the corporate halls of Merrill holding his coffee tray as a way to introduce himself to the bosses. Oh, you don't like coffee, you like tea? I've got tea. You want sugar with that coffee? I've got sugar. Let's talk. (Those were the days before security, he said, and you could walk right in with a smile and the sheepish look of a lackey who was forced to get the boss coffee.)[32]

The Starbucks method apparently worked.

Merrill eventually invested $30 million in the fledgling Market Master, and almost equally important at that point, the company supplied Bloomberg with its own data for pricing bonds. Unlike the stock market, the bond market was built on contacts with different traders who could offer different prices for bonds at different banks or brokerages.[33] Any real information about some bonds could be extremely slippery because the price was affected by all sorts of shifts—in repayment rates or early redemptions or other arcane matters.[34] A trader could use this complexity to make a ton of money at the buyer's expense. The Bloomberg team wanted to eliminate that confusion for any financial pro who need only peer into their machine and ask it whether a particular bond offering was really a good deal. The Bloomberg would not only give out numbers, it would help the trader make sense of it all by answering a trader's questions immediately.

Graphs helped, of course. The machines of the day took far too long to create a graph at the same time the broker was working a sale. So Bloomberg hired an engineering company to make what was a "two-plane board"—a way to have the needed information about a bond and a graph about it at the same time. By later standards, it was the horse-and-buggy stage of computing. But for the day, it was as futuristic as the George Lucas Jedi. The clunky Market Master would give you the numbers and the graph almost at the same time—a delicious new combo for a trader who wanted some context while still negotiating on the phone.

The Bloomberg team would install new machines at night when most offices were empty. City building codes? What codes? "A half dozen of us dragged wires from our computers to the keyboards and screens we were putting in place, stuffing the cables through holes we drilled in other people's furniture—all without permission, violating every fire law and building code and union regulation in the books. It's amazing we did not burn down some office or electrocute ourselves." The reward, of course, was when they turned on the machine and, magically, it worked.[35]

Bloomberg watched over every person and every detail at his new company, and each challenge became a mission, especially for the boss. He came in early, started the coffee, fed the goldfish (he would always have fish tanks, perhaps as a touch of serenity in the midst of chaos, and these were the only fish he could afford in those days). He hired the newcomers, looked them in the eye. He wrote the checks and handed them out to employees. He bought the snacks. Ever the neatnik, he swept the floors and dusted the windowsills. (Even later, as a very rich man, Bloomberg would confess to being outraged when he saw anybody drop a paper towel in the bathroom or a scrap of paper and leave it on the floor. "I want to scream," he said. "Perhaps I'm compulsive, but I stop and pick it up, even at someone else's place."[36])

Bloomberg's fury at some misstep or disappointment often meant a telephone slammed or thrown across the desk. Some employees remembered gauging the length of the telephone wires before approaching the boss with questionable news. "I do tend to break phones all the time," Bloomberg admitted. That was when telephones were still safely tethered to telephone wires.[37] He often resorted to his rough Salomon vocabulary and his favorite dirty jokes to relieve the tension, much of which he had created on his own.

Bloomberg later argued that the secret was not simply these fourteen-hour days, it was picking the right project, producing it on time, building an interactive machine full of data added bit by bit by bit. Producing the Bloomberg box was like learning to read, he would say, you start with one-syllable words. "If you try to read Chaucer in elementary school, you'll never accomplish anything."[38] Later, as he grew older, he would add luck to that equation, but often with a standard caveat. "Work hard enough and you make your own luck," he said.[39]

Bloomberg's timing to focus on bonds for the early Market Master looked brilliant, especially in retrospect. As the economy was beginning to sour, Paul Volcker, the Federal Reserve Board chairman, announced that bond interest rates would float, and as Michael Lewis wrote, "Overnight the bond market was transformed from a backwater into a casino."[40] Bloomberg, with his machine focused on the bond market, was there to rake in the house proceeds.[41]

When Merrill made their early deal with Bloomberg, he promised not to sell the machine outside the company. Soon, however, he got the okay to see if other customers were interested. Bloomberg and Secunda would lead the team going around the country to market their machine with the Merrill Lynch bull logo on it.

To go to conventions where their machine was always "between the Great Bear water jug and the ladies room," as Secunda remembered, the duo flew "in the back of the plane," tourist class. They slept in seedy third-rate hotels like the one in Chicago with a McDonald's in the lobby, a room with a broken sink, and a communal bathroom down the hall.[42]

Bloomberg did the talking; Secunda did the demos. "In the early days, people were either amazed or they just couldn't understand," Secunda recalled. One executive groused, "Why do I need all that? I get a report at the end of the day." Secunda just shook his head at a smart man's ignorance.[43]

Soon, however, word got out about the Bloomberg machine that bond traders quickly grew to love. A Market Master made them smarter, made them money. The financial press also began to discover the bond traders' secret, and *Institutional Investor* lavished early praise on Bloomberg's machine. "Market Master has become one of the most popular additions to the fixed-income manager's crowded desk," the respected magazine gushed. "Market Master can examine one security or an entire market."[44]

One early problem was the name. Market Master sounded like a kitchen appliance. And almost nobody could remember the name of the company. What was it? Innovative, uh, something?

So Michael Bloomberg named the company and the machine after himself. His argument was that somebody else was using the name Market Master and, "anyways," as he always said, people kept calling it "Bloomberg's machine" or the Bloomberg. Like the Dows and the Reuters, the Fords, the Chryslers, and of course his beloved Salomon Brothers, in 1986 Bloomberg stopped any pretense of humility about the increasingly coveted machine. The company became the Bloomberg Limited Partnership and the box became the Bloomberg Terminal.[45]

His old friends were not surprised. One recalled that each time the younger Mike made a phone call—to hire the cook for the fraternity, to rent the summer cottage in the Hamptons—he stressed his name, repeatedly, to make sure the person on the other end could remember it. "That's Mike Bloomberg, B-L-O-O-M-B-E-R-G," he would say, spelling it once or more, just in case.

Thus, the brand was born. Soon, there would also be Bloomberg News, Bloomberg Television, radio (WBBR), *Bloomberg Businessweek*, *Bloomberg Markets*, *Bloomberg Pursuits*, Bloomberg Politics, Bloomberg

Government, Bloomberg Law, Bloomberg Tradebook, Bloomberg Philanthropies, to name a few. His autobiography is titled, what else, *Bloomberg by Bloomberg*. When he ran for mayor in 2001, his financial declaration to city officials would list thirty-nine subsidiaries with such names as Bloomberg Services LLC or Bloomberg Bondtrade LLC or Bloomberg Philippines LLC. His philanthropy would spread his name to universities, hospitals, art galleries, and Boston's science museum where the Bloomberg tag would be added to a room or a branch or some vital operation.

The name became the profit center, the business. But it was also attached to the very proud Mike Bloomberg. Protect the company; protect the name; protect the man. In 2014, his lawyers registered about four hundred web addresses when a new city domain became available. The idea, of course, was to make certain they didn't fall in the wrong hands. They included normal links to Bloomberg and his empire, but they also included MikeIsTooShort.nyc and MikeBloombergisaDweeb.nyc, several versions of Fuckbloomberg.nyc or Bloombergthespoiler.nyc.[46]

The key to the continued success of the Bloomberg—and a way to ward off competitors—was to keep adding data and explanations of data and getting it organized faster for the customer. During the rocky first years, Bloomberg had one of his many fortuitous coffee dates—this time with a man named John Aubert, who owned something called Sinkers (not fishing gear, this was data about bonds being paid off). Aubert was an enthusiastic data nerd, but he was unhappy with his business. After the two talked, Aubert agreed to take over and organize a good part of Bloomberg's data collection. He had one requirement. "I didn't want to live in New York," Aubert recalled years later.[47] Aubert lived outside Princeton, New Jersey, in a little community called Skillman. It is peaceful and quiet, a Grandma Moses landscape come lazily to life. So Bloomberg agreed, as long as it was near an airfield so that he and others could get out easily to the "brain," as it was called, and back to the city.

Aubert's operation was housed in a small building that could have been a rural dentist's office. The staff grew steadily so that by 2017 nearly 1,200 people worked in two new, high-tech buildings that looked like almost any corporate back office or the bookkeeping center for the university.

Workers in this comfortable field office lived by the mantra "Data is the key to the kingdom," and Bloomberg created a cushy world for them with elaborate free luncheons and their own garden, games on the lawn on nice spring days. But when the corporate reports came in over the years, they raced to get them onto the computers so that they could be massaged into charts and added to the historical record for the company and the industry.

Data had been key to Bloomberg's kingdom from the beginning. One especially important cache came early from the New York Federal Reserve in downtown Manhattan. The Fed was the source for the rates of U.S. Treasuries that could affect every company, every CD holder. It was on the list of must-reads every day for stock and bond traders around the world.

But even in the 1980s, the New York Fed still used a system straight out of the 1950s. Late every workday afternoon a Fed worker would give handwritten lists of prices to a runner who would then scurry to midtown, if you could scurry during the city's notorious rush hour. At Rockefeller Center's offices of the Associated Press, a harried typist would hurriedly punch in the details to the AP's many clients. In 1987, Bloomberg convinced the Fed, the Associated Press, and others including the *Wall Street Journal* to scrap this "pony express,"[48] as he called it, that resulted in plenty of mistakes, mostly typographical errors. Instead, Bloomberg offered to take over the task and transmit the numbers immediately (or in about five seconds),[49] and electronically at 5:00 p.m. every day. Bloomberg then got the credit for providing what some felt was the most important piece of financial information published in the

U.S. every day. Bloomberg celebrated, of course: "That, needless to say, made me very happy."[50]

Eventually the data banks at Bloomberg would bulge with information, and the Bloomberg became a kind of Google for business. From the beginning, the big selling point was that you could ask the terminal questions, and "we'd pull data from different sources and combine it to give you an answer," Secunda said.[51] If there were three guys offering a three-year-note, Bloomberg showed them together, an instant comparison, and if you wanted a graph to go with it, sure, Bloomberg would create one for you. And, more important, as Wall Street became more complex and data seemed to come from everywhere, the Bloomberg analysts could usually provide guidance.

Mike Bloomberg was always moving, pushing the company to expand its reach, more customers, more offerings on the terminal. When the fixed income business was a rousing success, Bloomberg decided it was time to expand. He wanted to add equities to the terminal, not just bonds. It was time for the big stock markets, too.

"At one point, Mike says, 'We're gonna take some of your resources away . . . and we're gonna repurpose people to start doing equities, and I want a significant amount of the sales force to go out because it's a hard sell.'"

Secunda remembered the panic it caused in the company. "I'm like, 'Oh, my God, you're going to wreck us because we have such an opportunity here [where we are],'" he said. "But, of course, he was right . . .

"He pushed me and other people out of our comfort zones into places where, you know, he saw opportunity, and he was willing to take the risk."[52]

As the market grew more complex so did the terminal. By 2016, for example, there were about fourteen thousand different functions on the machine, so many that few company insiders, much less customers, had tried to use all of them.[53]

Other additions turned out to be not only helpful to clients, but also vital to the business. The best example was the Bloomberg machine's internal email. It was not simply a closed chat room for traders. It was a club. "Bloomberg Me" was its password, and membership required $12,000 a year (and later $22,000 a year) as the basic rental for the Bloomberg machine.

Pioneered in the early 1990s, the messenger service was fairly basic. "We thought being able to talk to customers was a lot more powerful than a broadcast for everybody," Secunda explained. And since almost everybody with a Bloomberg had email, you stood a better chance of contacting the CEO, not the summer intern. It was "the world's most expensive email," one user said.[54] Expensive and exclusive—for many, that was exactly the point.

On September 22, 1988, Bloomberg's magic machine had been anointed from on high—by the *Wall Street Journal*. On the front page of the *Journal*, two financial reporters, Matthew Winkler and Michael Miller, described the mastermind of this new financial machine as a "breezy, profane" former trader who not only had "a puckish sense of humor and a prodigious temper," but who also had an "audacious plan" to transform the $4 trillion global bond market.

The bond market was "a chaotic bazaar where prices and products vary depending on where you are shopping," they wrote. What if Bloomberg could provide a single quotation system, a central market for bonds, for example? The article was heavy on possibilities, once again portraying the plucky little Bloomberg operation versus the giants like Reuters and even Telerate (the *Journal* company, Dow Jones, owned 56 percent of Telerate at that point).

Miller and Winkler compared Bloomberg's growing system to the sudden breakthrough by American and United Airlines, which had hooked agents on their electronic reservations and ticketing systems. And they advised Merrill that it was time to break their old agreement that barred Bloomberg from selling his machines everywhere, even to Merrill's competitors. Because Merrill owned 30 percent at that point,

Bloomberg's success would only add to their bottom line. Brokers at the excluded Wall Street firms were "hungry" for the Bloomberg machine and were even ready to swap their bond prices for the analysis.[55]

Bloomberg proudly added the page to his office wall. But he was also ready to do more than enjoy a moment's praise, even from the *Journal*.

5

BLOOMBERG MAKES
THE NEWS

"I was so addicted to [the] Bloomberg . . . In a few
seconds, I could learn an incredible amount."
—*Floyd Norris, former* New York Times *columnist*

If timing is everything in the financial world, Michael Bloomberg believed in 1990 that it was the right moment to get into the journalism business. He watched the Berlin Wall come down in 1989 and, as he saw it, "Capitalism had triumphed."[1] At the same time, journalism was in trouble. The big international story—the cold war—had fizzled, and readers were looking elsewhere for news. Two newspaper towns were barely sustaining one newspaper. Lots of journalists needed jobs, and few news organizations knew how to cover the new obsession—with money.

"Readers might not have realized it to start with," Bloomberg said, "but here was a hole. I knew Bloomberg could fill it."[2]

He also knew just the man to do it, that combustible, thirty-three-year-old *Wall Street Journal* reporter named Matthew Winkler, who had been one of the authors of the 1988 article on his wall. Winkler's own story reads like a guidebook for the classic Mike Bloomberg hire. When he decided he needed his own wire service for his terminals, Bloomberg turned to the highest-energy journalist he knew, a man who also understood what his company was doing.

Matthew Winkler had discovered Mike Bloomberg's moneymaking machine[3] when he was in London writing for the *Journal*. A recent graduate of Kenyon College with a degree in history, Winkler was suddenly swept up in a financial journalist's dream job: he was covering the European markets in the 1980s for the *Wall Street Journal* just as Prime Minister Margaret Thatcher ordered a major deregulation of the financial industry in London. The upheaval in the markets was so dramatic that it became known as a Big Bang.[4]

One of Winkler's main sources during that tumultuous time was a bond expert at Merrill Lynch who shared insights that "were always right and always impeccable," as Winkler put it. One day Winkler asked his source, "I know you're brilliant and all, but how do you come up with all this stuff every day when we talk?" The secret, the trader admitted, was that he had "a Bloomberg on his desk," and Winkler rushed over to see this strange new device. He knew about other computers, Quotrons, Telerates, but this "diminutive screen" was obviously very different. The Bloomberg "in its infancy could tell whether one security was cheaper or more expensive than the others. There was no system that could do that at that time," Winkler remembered. What surprised him was that other companies and news organizations had access to some of the same data, the prices, plus information of all sorts going back years, for example. They knew stuff that they weren't really using; it was stacked in a basement somewhere. In contrast, Bloomberg was scraping whatever facts and numbers he could find to give historical context, the relative value of financial products. And to give it quickly.

Back in New York in December 1987, Winkler, by then quite the expert on bonds, and Michael Miller, who covered technology, started comparing notes over lunch at the *Journal* cafeteria. The two journalists quickly recognized what would become the most important story in Winkler's career. They called Mike Bloomberg to ask if he would sit for an interview. It was like asking a struggling actor if he'd like the title role in a new film called *Batman*.

Bloomberg quickly invited the duo to his now-expanded offices in an I. M. Pei building at Park Avenue and Fifty-ninth Street. The man who had so admired the open hub at Salomon Brothers had an old-fashioned office with an old-fashioned wooden door that you could close to seal off his staff, now numbering about 220 at various offices around the country. As soon as Winkler and Miller sat down, Bloomberg began telling them about how he had the best company "in the world" and even the best employees, who would jump out the window for him to serve his happy customers. "Right," Winkler replied. "And the dish ran away with the spoon."

Suddenly Bloomberg stood up and stomped away, furious at these skeptics, these journalists doubting his word. Winkler and Miller weren't certain whether they were supposed to find their way out. But, a few minutes later, Bloomberg came back, this time lugging a large stack of computer printouts, which he dumped in Winkler's lap. "There," Bloomberg said, pointing to the list of his customers. "If you don't believe what I'm saying, call 'em yourself."

The list with names and phone numbers was pay dirt for newspaper reporters, and Winkler and Miller spent the next five months calling dozens of Bloomberg clients to ask how they fared on his machines. The result was the story on September 22, 1988, that was like a coming-out in the financial world for the Bloomberg Terminal.

About a year later, Winkler[5] got a call from Bloomberg, who said he wanted some advice. Winkler guffawed. Advice from a mere reporter? Bloomberg was serious. He wanted to get in the news business. How could it be done? Winkler quickly began to muse about how Bloomberg could marry his data and analysis with up-to-the-minute news. Winkler told him, "You'd actually have something that right now doesn't exist. Nobody has it." Something that doesn't exist, something that nobody else had—Winkler was dangling a tantalizing prospect before a man who was busy creating a machine that nobody else had, that didn't exist elsewhere.

At a Japanese restaurant later that day, Winkler mapped out a more detailed plan for Bloomberg to follow, starting small with five reporters in Tokyo, five in London, and five in New York. (Bloomberg wanted two in each city, Winkler said.) "Good," Bloomberg concluded. "I'm gonna do it. You're gonna do it for me. When can you start?" Winkler said it all happened so fast he didn't even ask about his salary. (Like top Bloomberg hires, he didn't suffer, of course.)

Winkler's colleagues at the *Journal* were flummoxed that he would suddenly dive into such a murky, risky venture. But as many others learned over the years, Mike Bloomberg was like a magus who hypnotized his prey into working long hours on his crusade to change Wall Street and, of course, to help themselves and Bloomberg get very, very rich.

On his first day, February 5, 1990, Winkler arrived at 8:00 a.m., a version of daybreak for journalists, but as he settled in, his new boss walked by. "Hello, Winkler. Nice of you to show up," Bloomberg said as he handed his newest employee a piece of paper. "An outline," Winkler remembered. "It was neat, typical Mike, but it filled the page on both sides. Number one, then a,b,c,d. Two, a,b,c,d. It was like a scientific experiment," he said, one laid out carefully by a man who organized his thoughts and linked the stages of a new project like an engineer. The mission was as simple as it would be difficult: create something that gave a Bloomberg user financial news so that they didn't need to go elsewhere, certainly not to Reuters or Dow Jones or the radio or even the *New York Times*. Bloomberg handed Winkler the daunting and exhilarating task of creating an entire financial news empire. From scratch.[6]

The official birth date for the Bloomberg news operation (then called Bloomberg Business News, or BBN) was June 14, 1990. It was not a painless delivery. As almost anyone who worked for Matt Winkler would explain, it was like a club, and you had to be initiated, you had to be "Winklerized," as they called it. At the smallest provocation, Winkler would yell and grow red in the face, a color that would often contrast with a sedate plaid bow tie that did little to soften his appearance. Bloomberg would yell back, on occasion, but mostly Winkler's bottomless font of anger would land on his besieged workers. If they could stand it, survive it, really, they learned to value the advice from the man who would push and cajole and bellow and give birth to Bloomberg News.

At first, Winkler had his writers rewriting the dailies. His team would beat even Bloomberg to the office by arriving at their desks before 3:00 a.m., when they read and digested the financial news as soon as they could find it—in the *Journal*, the *Times*, the *FT* in London, the *Nikkei Asian Review*, anything else that they could harvest. Then they summarized each important story—fifty to sixty summaries a day, most of them available on the Bloomberg Terminals by 7:30 a.m. These press summaries gave credit, of course, the copyright lawyers saw to that, but as Winkler put it proudly, "When you saw the headline, you thought, oh, Bloomberg News is covering all these things." Winkler soon added the public relations announcements—company A buys company B—a headline with the press release attached. That moved hundreds of other items onto the Bloomberg wire.

Winkler and Bloomberg called this early period their *Wizard of Oz* era, when Bloomberg machine users were simply too busy to look behind the box. (Except, of course, for the people at Dow Jones.) About two months into the *Oz* era, Dow Jones announced that their company would no longer do business with Bloomberg because it was a competitor. But Winkler said the Dow Jones crowd soon learned they had a contract to provide their news to Bloomberg and their reports would stay on the terminals for another ten months. After ten months, he noted that DJ kept quietly renewing their contract as the terminals grew more popular on Wall Street. At the same time, the news offering to the Bloomberg Terminals was growing. "It was beginning to actually look like the fire hose, which Mike delighted in. He loved the idea that people could drink from a fire hose, of all things, from him," Winkler said.[7]

In Washington, D.C., however, there was one barrier that could bring that fire hose down to a disturbing trickle: the powerful committee of journalists who gave out press passes to government agencies. The House/Senate Standing Committee of Correspondents was created in 1879 to separate the press from the lobbyists. Over the years, as newspapers changed into all sorts of news delivery systems, this group maintained a choke hold on who could get into the press pens.

The committee, made up of people who knew Winkler from the *Journal*, refused to give his Bloomberg News reporters credentials to cover the Commerce Department, the Labor Department, all the Washington agencies and departments that affect the financial world. The press passes were the golden tickets of journalism, and without them, Bloomberg News could not cover the breaking economic news that terminal users found so necessary.

"What are you?" the chairman of the committee of correspondents asked, according to Winkler. "Where are you published?" When Winkler fumed that they were published on the Bloomberg Terminal, that they were an "electronic newspaper," he was told that there were no "criteria" for that kind of electronic news.[8]

So Bloomberg and Winkler knew they had to get published. Somewhere. Their solution soon came from Floyd Norris, a respected financial columnist at the *New York Times*. The *Times* writers like Norris wanted a Bloomberg machine, so Bloomberg agreed to give the paper a free terminal if the *Times* would give Bloomberg credit when they published any of Bloomberg's news items. Norris got the editor to agree and once Bloomberg pieces were published in the *Times*, it was like being sanctioned by the news Vatican. The press passes arrived quickly, and as other news organizations asked for the terminals, Bloomberg said, "That's great, put 'em in."

Soon, Bloomberg had his machines tucked into the wire rooms of more than four hundred news organizations[9] across the country, and Winkler's staff was growing. (After five years of free terminal use, Bloomberg began to charge. Most news organizations like the *Times* paid to keep a machine.) Norris said that when *Fortune* magazine later offered him a job, one of his first questions was whether they had a Bloomberg. "I was so addicted to Bloomberg," he said, because as a columnist on deadline, he often needed background information instantly on a company or a financial trend. With the Bloomberg, he said, "in a few seconds, I could learn an incredible amount" about the day's subject.[10]

From a few dozen workers in the beginning, the Bloomberg News operation doubled in size, then doubled again. When the *Times* and the *Washington Post* started firing people during a downtime, the whisper as they went out the door was always "Bloomberg's hiring." It wasn't normal journalism for most reporters, but it was a fat and comfortable paycheck.

As the news operation expanded, Bloomberg increasingly left Winkler alone. He had promised to protect his news operation from corporate types who didn't like his coverage, and when his fellow CEOs called to whine, Bloomberg usually simply transferred the complaint back to Winkler. Bloomberg also did very little to interfere with Winkler's rules and his chain-gang management style.

Winkler enforced what he soon began to call "The Bloomberg Way" for his growing army of journalists. He quickly put out a spiral notebook with his rules of journalism—a 376-page tome handed out to every journalist on day one.[11] Leaked versions of what was really Winkler's *Way* made him most famous for outlawing the word "but," which he argued might confuse traders who didn't have time for nuance and conflicting ideas. When the book went public in 2011, it became clearer that Winkler's advice to his journalists was far broader than a few basic rules. He gave detailed instructions on how to make the news "lucid enough, even to Aunt Agatha."[12] His demand for the Five F's meant every story was supposed to be First, Factual, Fastest (isn't that like "First"?), Final, and keyed to the Future. Adverbs and adjectives were considered too "imprecise." Labels like "moderate" or "activist" were verboten. Although much of *The Bloomberg Way* is a description of good journalism, it reads today like a daunting rule book for a reporter who knew that the man in the bow tie was breathing fire over his shoulder.

There was also forbidden territory. Bloomberg News would not write about Bloomberg, the company or the man. That rule would become more troublesome as Michael Bloomberg became a top news maker, a big name in politics, finance, and philanthropy.

6

LIFE IN THE
BLOOMBERG FISHBOWL

"You either caught on or you left us."
—*Thomas Secunda*[1]

As Bloomberg steadily expanded his private company—225 employees by 1988 to more than 7,000 by 2001,[2] and as he prepared to step aside to run for mayor—he still relied on Salomon's floor model. He insisted on the open plan, a bull pen with a cluster of desks where nobody was out of sight or beyond a shout from the boss. His open floor would never be as noisy as Salomon's, but even as Bloomberg LP expanded to offices around the globe, the culture was there, the back-alley rowdiness so beloved on Wall Street, the sense of mission that made it all seem okay. There would be protests from women about being encouraged to wear short skirts and then being asked to get things from that file drawer near the floor.[3] For years, it was a tolerated misbehavior that Bloomberg and his lawyers would strenuously deny, especially when complaints reached the courts.

The Bloomberg Way could feel very strange to somebody who had worked for, say, the more conventional Chase or Goldman Sachs. "It's almost like a patrician family structure," said one ex-employee.[4] Once, during a Bloomberg television interview with Bloomberg and hedge fund mastermind Ray Dalio, then moderator Stephanie Ruhle noted that some people had described both of their massive corporations as cults. Dalio, who had dismissed such charges before, denied any exotic culture in his company. Bloomberg folded his arms, crossed his legs defensively, and rejected the very idea at Bloomberg LP.[5] "It's very regimented, and it feels kinda like a boot camp. You basically have a drill sergeant—a command goes out, and everyone acts on that command," said another ex-employee. That top commander, of course, was Bloomberg, whose word traveled almost as fast as his data. He liked to be in control of everything, even as the business grew far beyond his natural reach.

"Moving from 'hands-on' to 'hands-off' has been a gradual, and not that pleasant, process for me," Bloomberg admitted as the company grew in the 1990s. "I'm an operating guy as opposed to a strategic person. I like doing things myself, getting my hands dirty," he added. "If we're to grow and not be dependent on yours truly, turn it over I must. But that doesn't mean I'm happy about it."[6]

Employees' office emails showed the time they arrived at work or when they returned after a rare lunch outside the building. Meetings were sometimes held without chairs, with everyone standing—they didn't last as long that way. And if the intense twelve-hour days were too much—even with the comfortable perks and paychecks—there were the elaborate staff parties. In New York City in recent years, Bloomberg has rented a large patch of parkland on Randall's Island to create an elaborate carnival—with a carousel, rides, games, concerts, and food for thousands. In 2011, Geoffrey Croft of NYC Park Advocates estimated the Bloomberg party cost about $9 million, including at least a $750,000 yearly donation beginning in 2009 to the Randall's Island Sports Foundation.[7] Croft and others objected to the exclusive use of a public park by a private corporation, especially one then affiliated with the mayor, but for young Bloomberg employees and their families it was much needed downtime.

By far the most famous of these relief parties was the Seven Deadly

Sins gala in London in 2000. A large warehouse was converted into a pleasure palace for about 1,500 employees. Each section depicted a "sin": lust, gluttony, greed, sloth, wrath, envy, or pride. For a mere million pounds, give or take a few thousand, there were rooms for sushi, sweets, and truffles for the Gluttony section; manicure and massage rooms, live bands, drag queens, and a massive silk-covered bed for the Lust pavilion. Greed was there, of course, with entertainers waving bills and shouting, "Money, ain't it gorgeous?"[8] A party lover and party giver, he made news in Los Angeles when his celebration for Democrats at their 2000 convention was a little more subdued, featuring a bed of oysters topped with a woman in a tasteful mermaid suit.[9]

Bloomberg set the tone, especially in the early years. It was a boisterous place. Work hard. Laugh hard. Be tough or be gone. Bloomberg wanted to welcome every new employee. Some early Bloomberg workers remember their first day, suddenly looking up from the desk to see their new boss. In one moment that became famous for a while, a bright but taciturn hire suddenly found Bloomberg at his side. The terror in the young man's eyes was obvious to those around him, and Bloomberg, who could converse with a stone, found this youth particularly difficult. Finally, he asked where the young man went to school.

"Brown," the youth choked.

"Ah, Brown," Bloomberg chuckled. "That's where I got my first blow job."

The employee froze, desperately searching for a response.

Finally, he said, "In Providence?"

Other employees erupted in laughter, and for a while, when anyone made an off-color remark the response was a question: "In Providence?"[10]

Bloomberg, who became well known for his closed computer system, also became famous for the Bloomberg biosphere. The open-plan office was meant to be self-sustaining. The snacks and coffee or tea became more elaborate over the years, and a light lunch was free at a central location where people did not exactly meet—there never seemed to be time for that. Free lunch, however, could be a little intimidating for anybody who wanted to have lunch at, say, the sushi bar down the street. Bloomberg once said, "If people believe it's really free, you don't understand the business model."[11]

The money was good, even in tough years, and the race to sell terminals or help a struggling trader or break a bit of news was often exhilarating. This was a high-speed workplace, where success was increasingly timed in seconds, and if it ultimately exhausted some workers, others relished the pace, the competition, and the raucous camaraderie. Bloomberg, who often said he loved Sunday nights because he could go to work the next day, continued to arrive shortly after daybreak, as a rule. He would have difficulty understanding people who failed to enjoy hard work as much as he did. He complained about consultants, outsiders, who stopped work at 5:00 p.m. while employees work "till 7:00, 8:00 or 9:00 at night, until the project is done."[12] And unions? Not at his private company. As Secunda would put it, as nicely as possible, "You either caught on or you left us."

Those who left quietly spread the word that if Bloomberg was an exhilarating ride, you had to be ready to cede life for work. Some workers called themselves Stakhanovites, after the Ukrainian miner who became a Soviet hero for supposedly digging out an impossible 227 tons of coal in a single shift. One former news employee, Hal Davis, saw younger employees already wearing wrist bandages because of repetitive stress syndrome. "They're grinding people into the ground," he said.

It was very steady employment, especially in an age when so many jobs seemed temporary. Few people were fired, but a resignation in Bloomberg's world was the company's form of treason. Going-away parties were taboo, and once you left, you were a nonperson. The company was not supposed to hire you back. Ever. Well, maybe, if you left to take care of a sick relative or to get a graduate degree, but even then, it was hard to do. He once explained, "God forbid one of our people [should] go to work for a competitor, then we all heartily and cordially really do hope they fail. In their new job, they have an avowed purpose to hurt their old coworkers. They have become bad people. Period. We have a loyalty to us. Leave and you're them." [13]

Bloomberg explained that although he didn't allow anyone to hire family members at the company, "I'm a big believer that organizations are family, and you can't be perfect and sometimes you make mistakes, but we have to make sure that people understand if they devote themselves to the good of—either it is the city government where I worked or this company, or the foundation or whatever—it is a two-way street. We have to take care of them." [14]

Certainly, one reason some people stayed was the generous annual bonus. Based loosely on the Salomon Brothers system, [15] Bloomberg gave each employee a share of the company's profits for what he called Equity Equivalent Certificates, or EECs. These gifts, called simply "certs," could usually be cashed out a year after they were granted—but you had to be working at Bloomberg to get the check. One detail: when your cert was announced, it was based on the company's performance that year. The actual value might be slightly different.

Bloomberg kept most of his employees, who loved the feverish competition as well as the dependable paycheck, the good health care, the camaraderie, and the chance to move up the corporate chain. Some were not so content, however, and Bloomberg and his company have faced a number of lawsuits, most notably in the 1990s, including those from women who felt they were being belittled in the company's raunchy climate or were demoted when they became pregnant. These women portrayed a work environment that was a throwback to the 1950s, and by the twenty-first century, that hard humor of the Wall Street boys' club wasn't so funny anymore.

Mike Bloomberg would consistently deny that women were being treated differently, and he would feverishly deny the specific charges that these employees made in court.

Perhaps the most famous suit was filed by a sales employee named Sekiko Sakai Garrison. She charged that when she met Bloomberg in the corporate snack bar in 1995 and told him she was pregnant, he sneered, "Kill it." She added that Bloomberg began grumbling about how many women at Bloomberg LP were pregnant and thus not able to work as hard as everyone else.

Garrison said Bloomberg left a private voicemail message on her machine at work. "I didn't say it," he said in her version of the conversation. "I didn't mean it. I didn't say it."[16] He tried to get her to come back to work, she said, and when she turned to lawyers instead, Bloomberg's muscular legal machine went to work.

Garrison's suit stated that Bloomberg and his executives subjected females to repeated sexual comments and unwelcome sexual overtures. Women were encouraged to wear short skirts, high heels, and tight blouses, Garrison charged. She sued, seeking more than $15 million[17] in damages for five counts of harassment and discrimination.[18]

Bloomberg repeatedly denied Garrison's claims, and one of his lawyer's responses to her accusations included a copy of her self-evaluation in 1994. In that document, she rated herself an eight out of a possible nine on "Quality Image." She added, obviously adopting the jargon of her workplace, "With a boob-job, this could be a '9.'" She also wrote that Bloomberg is "the best fucking co [company] in the world." Her salary went from $35,000 in 1989 to $206,070 in 1995.[19]

Depositions in the case accused employees of activities that were both alarming and simply crude. In one affidavit to the New York State Division of Human Rights, Rowland Hunt said he was fired after he complained about a Christmas party when a female employee who had recently given birth was presented with a "pair of rubberized women's breasts that squirted fluid through the nipples. At the party, people were squirting the breasts at one another. I wanted nothing to do with it."[20] There were other times when the jokes weren't so harmless. Garrison, who is Japanese American, accused Bloomberg of calling her a "Jap," and said that she was such an aggressive saleswoman that she had destroyed "centuries of Japanese culture."[21]

Bloomberg's early response to employee complaints about the tone of the workplace was just short of dismissive. Asked in a deposition in 1999 if he had said he would like to "do" this or that woman employee, he said, "It does not have a real life meaning. It is a term that is used in jest, not as a serious term." He added about such commentary, "If it happens very seldom, I see nothing wrong with it. I can't control everybody's conduct and have no right to keep people from having normal conversation."[22]

The Garrison complaint was quietly settled before the 2001 elections with a confidentiality agreement and no admission of liability by Bloomberg and his company. "After a long period of time, I settled because the lawyers believed the suit could drag on for years and disrupt the company's focus,"[23] Bloomberg explained later.

Another complaint had surfaced in those years from Bloomberg employee Mary Ann Olszewski, who accused males at the company from Bloomberg on down of harassing and degrading women. Her case was closed in 2001 after a dispute with her lawyer. Another plaintiff withdrew her suit, and a fourth lawsuit in this period was dismissed.

These cases brought out details about Bloomberg, the person, and Bloomberg, the company, that might have been an inside joke for some, a private humiliation for others. In one important deposition in 1998, Bloomberg said that even though he might tolerate the frat house atmosphere and the after-hours mischief, he kept himself separate from the workers.

"I don't socialize with anybody in the company," he said. "That is my policy, correct."

Q: Have you at any time leered at any employee?
Bloomberg: "No."

Q: Or looked up their dresses.
Bloomberg: "No."

And later,

Q: Have you ever had an intimate relationship at any time with any employee of Bloomberg?

A: "Certainly never." [24]

Bloomberg not only denied everything, he also took a lie detector test and passed, his aides insisted, although they refused to release the results. Instead, Paul K. Minor, the FBI's former chief polygraph examiner who administered the test for him, put out a statement that "all Mr. Bloomberg's responses were truthful." Bloomberg later said his company had investigated all of the cases thoroughly and that these women were basically saying, "If you don't give me what I want, I'm going to make a fuss." [25] He had once put it a little differently. "As far as I am concerned, that is out-and-out extortion, and I think companies caving in to that sort of thing are making a terrible mistake. And we will go and fight all three of these, and I, in my heart of hearts, believe that we have done nothing wrong." [26]

As the company grew, there would be other lawsuits from women and from those of both sexes complaining about the long work hours (and lack of overtime pay).[27] The most important of these was a complaint that reached the Equal Employment Opportunity Commission in 2007. The commission argued that Bloomberg LP had routinely discriminated against pregnant women who took maternity leave, and their action eventually included seventy-eight individuals. Bloomberg was mayor at the time and contended that he knew nothing about these problems. But he was still the owner of the company and forced to testify. A clearly irritated Bloomberg argued that his company valued hardworking employees and did not create a hostile environment for women. "Around the world we treat everybody the same," he testified.[28]

The case went to Chief Judge Loretta Preska of the U.S. District Court in Manhattan, who was an appointee of President George H. W. Bush and was on the short list for supreme court nominees for President George W. Bush. Judge Preska would dismiss charges of discrimination against Bloomberg in a sweeping and pointed sixty-four-page order. The EEOC had argued that the Bloomberg company "has tended to follow Wall Street's model of having few women in top management positions." But the judge said the EEOC had relied on anecdotes, not data, and that "J'accuse" was not enough.

Perhaps more important, she stressed that the law did not mandate a work/life balance. "In a company like Bloomberg, which explicitly makes all-out dedication its expectation, making a decision that preferences family over work comes with consequences."[29] The judge quoted the EEOC's version of Bloomberg's "code of standards" for employees that included the admonition that Bloomberg "is your livelihood and your first obligation." She cited Bloomberg's lawyers, who had produced numbers that showed many of the 78 women complainants (of 603 female employees who were pregnant during the time period of February 1, 2002, and March 31, 2009)[30] were compensated better on average than others who took leave for other reasons like a family emergency. The work may have been relentless, but they made good money—one woman's salary went from $219,534 in 2001 to $304,187 in 2008.[31] The judge quoted Jack Welch, the former head of General Electric, who said, "There is no such thing as work-life balance. There are work-life choices, and you make them, and they have consequences."[32] She concluded that Bloomberg's company did not have "a pattern or practice of discrimination."

Her ruling outraged many women, especially members of the New York chapter of the National Organization for Women. "I don't know if it's too harsh to call the judge ignorant," said Sonia Ossorio, then the group's executive director. "But she certainly has a fundamental misunderstanding of how discrimination plays out for working mothers."[33]

The Preska ruling could not give much comfort in later years to Michael Bloomberg, the very public billionaire. Social views were shifting, and women had launched a new era in the fight against years of abuse and discrimination. Questions about Bloomberg's view of women and the occasional eruptions of his old Wall Street vocabulary would not go away.

7

THE BLOOMBERG
WOMEN

"Don't let it go to your head."
—Frequent advice from Bloomberg's mother

"I've worked for him for 25 years, and women have
always been in senior leadership roles."
—Patti Harris

It might have seemed easy to turn the Mike Bloomberg of Bloomberg LP into a crude, two-dimensional, Wall Street macho man, given
the easy patter about women's cleavage or his proclamations that females
need to wear high heels or dye their hair when the little gray roots started
to show.[1] There was plenty of that which he would deny. And deny. And
deny.

But in the end the undeniably rough talk or old jokes that would
cause him trouble as he became a public figure were overshadowed and
largely forgotten as the media charted the astonishing upward trajectory
of this billionaire politician. And in reality, Bloomberg, who had spent his
life surrounded by powerful women, would owe much of his public success to one woman, Patti Harris, who would eventually become an adviser,
friend, chaperone, guide, nothing short of privy counselor.

Bloomberg hired Patricia Edith Harris in 1994, when she seemed to
be a quiet thirty-eight-year-old who knew a lot about public relations.

Bloomberg had just gotten divorced, and he seemed to be having trouble arranging his schedule and organizing his philanthropy. He had his schedule in a little black book in his pocket, and he was taking all press calls himself. He hired Harris as a kind of quasi–press secretary (there are few titles at Bloomberg LP), but slowly this stealth-like woman took control of more than his daily routine. She would soon advise her boss on every difficult question about politics, arts, culture, philanthropy and, in general, life beyond Wall Street. Perhaps more important, she became the one person who could get Mike Bloomberg to listen when he was being unusually stubborn or apologize when one of his outbursts had given offense. As he moved steadily into the limelight, Harris moved even more steadily into her role as guide and guardian.

Once, during a deposition after a former political consultant stole Bloomberg's campaign funds for his own personal use, Bloomberg was asked about his relationship to Harris.

Q: Now, Ms. Harris, how long have you known her?
A: Seventeen years.

Q: And she's a close friend, is that fair to say?
A: She is a close friend and a business associate and my confidante, yes.

Q: A close confidante?
A: Very close. She runs my foundation and she is the first Deputy Mayor of the City of New York authorized to act on my behalf when I am out of town.[2]

Harris has told colleagues about an incident that happened shortly after she was hired. Bloomberg sent her to a board meeting to represent him as a big donor, and the males on the board began referring to her as "Mike's girl." When she came back to report on the meeting, she added that she was now known at that board as "Mike's girl." "Outrageous," Bloomberg fumed. "That's not cool." So for the next board meeting, he came along with Harris, and every time one of the elders asked Bloomberg a question, he bounced it to Harris. Finally, they got the message that she was Bloomberg's representative, not his girl.[3] And very quickly, word got around that Patti Harris was the go-to person in much of Bloomberg's world.

By most accounts, Harris had pitch-perfect instincts, especially about everything outside Bloomberg's business empire. She nudged him into the art scene, helping him collect and support the arts as an individual and as a donor. She directed his philanthropy, guiding the way a mogul like Bloomberg could move upward in the social strata of New York and even London. When he was mayor, she would promote public art and even helped him take on such dramatic projects as *The Gates*, the 7,503 tangerine-colored panels by Christo that billowed throughout Central Park, brightening the winter of 2005. And she would be the first woman to hold the top job as first deputy in any New York City administration. "Run it by Patti" was often the first task for anybody who had a new idea or a problem in city hall.[4]

A native Manhattanite, Harris went to Ethical Culture Fieldston, a progressive private school in the Bronx, then graduated in 1977 from Franklin & Marshall College in Lancaster, Pennsylvania, with a degree in government. (Bloomberg later surprised her by matching donations up to $1 million for a building at her college that is now called the Patricia E. Harris Center for Business, Government & Public Policy.)

Harris always seemed to be around for any big Bloomberg moment. Watching her, you saw a kind of calm, as if she had some magical power that kept everything under control. Dressed immaculately for the cultured world, she seemed to make everyone around her look rumpled and slightly frantic.

Former police commissioner Ray Kelly, a very tough ex-marine, had been impressed watching Harris negotiate with the U.S. Secret Service in 2002. Shortly before the first anniversary of the 9/11 attacks, a team of U.S. Secret Service agents met with her to describe their demands before President George W. Bush would attend the ceremony. They wanted everyone to walk through metal detectors. Harris would explain, quietly and repeatedly, that family members still grieving would not be asked to go through the detectors or face searches by agents. This was New York City, and those were the mayor's rules. The Secret Service eventually retreated.

"She is not a yeller," Kelly said later. "She gives you the sense that this is what she wants and she is going to get it with a smile and she is going to get it collegially, but she is going to get it done."[5]

Married to Mark D. Lebow, a New York lawyer, they raised three children, and despite her duties that seemed to increase every year, Harris made certain she could wrangle time to scuba dive at the best reefs around the world. It was no accident that shortly after she took over Bloomberg Philanthropies, saving the oceans became a growing concern. When she was not around, the mischievous old Mike could slip back into his old ways. Dirty jokes, the chuckles with the boys about how he would "do" that particular woman "in a minute." Soon that one was shortened to just "in a minute." Her appearance could quiet even the ribald references to the eel in the main office aquarium.

Harris avoided interviews and maintained a tight smile through virtually all public appearances. Aides explained that she always seemed to be "in charge of everything," and Bloomberg looked to her to get things done and to keep him out of trouble. Bloomberg once put it this way: "She has the ability—not just with me, but with everybody—to tell you when you don't have any clothes on, but in a way that you say she's right, and you don't want to strike out at her."[6]

Harris knew her boss well and knew details of the criticism and the lawsuits by women at the company. When asked about it, she responded that "I've worked for him for 25 years, and women have always been in senior leadership roles. I've seem countless women grow professionally, earn more opportunities, and get promoted as they also raised families.

"Not long after I started Mike told me: Make sure you make time for your kids. He meant it," she continued. The company benefits were "extremely family-friendly," and even though "there are going to be complaints," she added, "anyone who works hard and performs well is going to be rewarded, regardless of gender or race or sexual orientation or anything else."[7]

Bloomberg had learned early in life about the powers of a strong woman. His dominant mother certainly offered plenty of evidence that even if he enjoyed the sexism of the fraternity or Salomon Brothers or Wall Street, he should recognize that women could have a full set of brains and often a lot more wisdom. His wife, Susan, who left after she grew tired of his high-energy and increasingly public lifestyle, would remain friendly and even work in his campaigns.[8] And his two daughters inherited the Bloomberg family mettle.

In many ways, Emma and Georgina Bloomberg were like separate versions of the man himself, as one Bloomberg friend noted. Emma, born in 1979, was the brainy Bloomberg, the one who graduated magna cum laude from Princeton[9] and then earned two master's degrees from Harvard in business administration and public administration. She helped with some of her father's most important issues in city hall—like the establishment of the city's 311 information line. She also worked hard to organize the Republican Party convention in 2004 (a success for Republicans, a horror show for protestors who were arrested by the hundreds). Emma would go on to help fight poverty with the Robin Hood Foundation and her own political nonprofit called Murmuration (named for a flock of starlings), but, in this case, designed to help the nation's children. She has said she likes golf,[10] which must please her golf-obsessed father. And occasionally she could be seen in the society news pages, like when she and her husband, Chris Frissora, "combined their names into a portmanteau," as the *Times* wrote in 2015.[11] Their daughter, Zelda, would have the last name Frissberg, as in half Frissora and half Bloomberg.

Georgina, nearly four years younger than Emma,[12] inherited her father's sporting and social genes. A superb equestrian and a regular on the glamorous side of the philanthropy circuit, she often shared the limelight on her father's arm, later alone as she grew more famous herself.

Georgina had a shelf full of awards for her horsemanship, besting other riders in Florida, New York, Spain, Canada, and France. She also co-wrote a series of popular books about girls and horses for the teen set. But Bloomberg's elfin daughter also inherited her father's grit. She won third place in the Hampton Classic in 2013 when she was pregnant with her son, Jasper. And she suffered mightily in other ways. George, as friends call her, broke her collarbone three times, fractured an ankle, broke her back twice, and suffered one concussion when the saddle slipped and she fell in 2010. After that tumble, she went to the nearest bar with friends. But when even a drink did not stop the pain, she finally made it to the emergency room, where doctors found another break in her back. Soon, she agreed to have surgery to straighten a crooked spine (spondylolisthesis). Surgery in 2011 kept her off the horses for months, but by the summer of 2012, she had won her first post-surgery jumping event in Massachusetts. This was one tough woman.[13]

Bloomberg has made his daughters and their families comfortable. He has given money to their causes and even learned not to flinch as George and her horse took the high jumps. But there was one particularly special gift that only the mayor of New York City could give his two daughters. In 2007, the Sandhogs, the union workers who dig tunnels deep under the city, offered to let the mayor name the massive Herrenknecht drills that would grind through underground Manhattan to extend the number 7 subway line. Bloomberg named the giant machines Emma and Georgina.[14] For Mike Bloomberg, the trained engineer, that was love.

With help from friends, Bloomberg managed to hide any hurt about his failed marriage, and soon, he could be seen with some of New York society's most glamorous women. He mostly liked women his age, a bit unusual for the Wall Street crowd, but that still could include Broadway or movie stars like Ann Reinking and Marisa Berenson. He escorted friends like Barbara Walters and Annette de la Renta to the city's most luxurious galas. He told the London *Guardian* in 1996, "I am a single, straight billionaire in Manhattan. What do you think? It's like a wet dream."[15]

By the time he was hinting that he might run for mayor, the *New York Post* had labeled him the anti-bimbo billionaire, and Bloomberg's explanation for his maturing tastes in companions was that he had tried the Wall Street world of girls, girls, girls and decided older women were a better option. "I find women my age more interesting, I guess. Maybe it's just that I have less in common with younger women. It's also safer. Somehow or other, the wives of your friends find it much more reassuring." [16]

Indeed, he always seemed to be keeping his options open. He scoffed at the idea of getting married again, and even enjoyed teasing anyone who was getting married about the hazards of legalizing a relationship. He professed to like the freedom of knowing he could stray when he wanted.

Despite his very vocal anti-marriage stance, Bloomberg would spend most of his mayoralty and post-city years with Diana Taylor. Taylor, a financial executive, was beautiful, scary slim, gracious, intelligent, and dressed like someone straight out of Anna Wintour's wardrobe room at *Vogue*. A graduate of Dartmouth with an MBA and a degree in public health from Columbia, she was widely viewed in New York's social circles as "a catch for any man, no matter how powerful," as one of Taylor's social peers put it. [17]

Yet too often Bloomberg seemed to treat her like a politically appropriate appendage, as far as some of his friends, especially female friends, were concerned. They talked of painful dinners with Bloomberg using Diana as a foil for his heavy-duty humor. Mostly, in public, he gave her an easier time, and she was a perfect substitute first lady for his time as mayor—always there, smiling at even the most tedious public event. [18]

Once, shortly after he left city hall, Bloomberg was asked why he had returned to the top job running Bloomberg LP. "Well, the alternative is for me to stay home every day and talk to Diana about feelings," he told a Bloomberg television audience that laughed nervously. "If that doesn't get you back to work, I don't know what would." [19] A joke, but ouch.

Any such militantly unmarried male over thirty-five in New York City could raise a few questions and some latent hopes from the gay community, and Bloomberg, even when he was nominally a Republican, supported gay marriage and civil rights. But simply watching him work a crowd might have helped dispel such notions. Once, after accepting an award at a gala for the Citizens Union public interest group in 2013, Mike Bloomberg spotted a tall blond woman in a small huddle of people. The mayor maneuvered himself so that as he passed by the makeshift receiving line, he could give her a hug, a kiss on each cheek. Then he moved a little to shake hands with a few admirers. Then he came back to the blonde. Another hug, two more kisses. He even seemed to be angling for a third round when the blonde suddenly moved on. Out of reach.

Bloomberg worked throughout an era when women evolved from docile or fake-docile homebodies into corporate tycoons, from timid secretaries and lowly assistants to vocal activists for women's rights. Like many men in his generation, Bloomberg would eventually seem bewildered by the so-called Me Too movement, the army of women who complained about mistreatment and abuse in the earlier times. He would update the company's rules to protect female employees and make sure they were given premier benefits. But the real test would come when he stepped out of his private company, his private world, to become a public figure. He would soon hire, and depend on, a group of powerful women to help run his campaign and his city.

8

RUNNING ON MONEY

"He doesn't get bought. He's the one doing the buying."
—*Former New York assemblyman Richard Brodsky*

"Why the hell would you want to do that?"
—*Richard Ravitch on hearing Bloomberg wanted to run for mayor*

Michael Bloomberg told his colleagues that if he ever tried politics, he would not be a legislator, not even a senator. He was a natural boss, and he had to be in charge. But he also wrote that, overall, his "impatience with government kept me away from politics. All elected officials should stop worrying."[1]

As it turned out, candidates for mayor of New York did need to worry. When his publisher, John Wiley & Sons, was packaging his autobiography, *Bloomberg by Bloomberg*, in 1997, the man himself had already begun to make his moves on the city.

At fancy New York dinners, especially at charity events where his money had turned him into a social and philanthropic superstar, Bloomberg began hinting that he was interested in politics. It was often a question, an invitation to hear encouragement from the moneyed class. "Do you think I should run for mayor after Rudy steps down?" he would ask, trying to make it seem that he had not already decided on the answer.

New York's elite swooned at the very idea of a man with experience as a real manager running their city, but the political professionals, the veterans of the city's mean political wars waged precinct by precinct, saw little more than a rich man's diversion. Some wondered aloud whether this was simply one more way of advertising the Bloomberg brand.[2] Others saw it as a foolish gamble that could only damage his reputation as a successful businessman, an excess of vanity for a man whose considerable assets would, at best, provide a healthy living for campaign consultants.

Richard Ravitch, a respected city elder who revived New York's decrepit subway system in the late 1970s, was shocked when Bloomberg broached the subject. Over a private lunch, the gruff Ravitch, who could make a comment on the weather sound like a stormy edict from Mount Sinai, questioned the very idea. "Why the hell would you want to do that?" Ravitch remembered saying. An unsuccessful candidate for mayor in 1989, Ravitch reminded the very private Bloomberg, who ran a very private company, that candidates have no privacy. Their every peccadillo lands on the front page of a tabloid. The media eats politicians, he warned. They will know the family secrets, he predicted. But Bloomberg didn't seem to care, Ravitch recalled. "Or perhaps he didn't think it would happen to him."[3]

Bloomberg's friends also wondered how a man who had wallowed in the money pits of Wall Street could suddenly turn politically respectable. Their pal, who insisted on being called Mike even by underlings at his company, was well known for blurting out whatever crudity or politically suspect idea that came to mind. He was smart and more ethical than most of his peers, but his tough wit straight from the trading floor was too often, well, misunderstood. To the uninitiated, it could simply sound mean, and his jokes could offend—especially women. The claims of inappropriate sexual remarks and harassment of women in his company would begin to seep out as he became more serious about running for office.

But Bloomberg was very serious. Sometime in the late 1990s, he had decided that nearly twenty years building Bloomberg LP was enough. He had conquered Wall Street. He had become a business media baron. He had made his billions. Now it was time to succeed at something different, he told friends.

"I thought twenty years at the company, it's time for somebody else to do things," he said years later. "A new guy can always do it better."[4] (He smiled when he said that in 2018, recognizing he was still running the company he started more than thirty-five years earlier.) At some point, after all that mentioning the idea to friends and asking for advice, Bloomberg's name appeared on everybody's list of possible candidates to run for mayor. His sister teased him, he remembered; making the point that the newspapers had said he was only good enough to be mentioned as mayor, not as a candidate for president.

Bloomberg laughed it off. Being mayor of New York City was "a better job than even the president's," he remembered telling her. "It's the ultimate political job. You don't have a Congress to deal with."

Also, the city needed his kind of help, he said. "You've got a budget bigger than the GDP of half the countries in the world. You've got more embassies here than any other city in the whole world because of the UN." Plus, the man who liked to run things and fix things wanted his city to work. "And I was tired of people saying, 'Oh. You can't do things.'"[5]

Moreover, Bloomberg knew his strengths. And his weaknesses. "I'm not an investor. I'm not an analyst. I'm not a consultant. I'm not a teacher. I'm not a writer. I am an executive. I make decisions . . . in government, the president, the governor, and the mayor are executive jobs." As for details, Bloomberg wanted to hire good people who would bring him the best choices. "We ask [candidates] about policy. But you have other people that do policy. And you don't know what policy you're going to need down the road. So to ask you when you're running what your policy is . . ." He shrugged. "The problems of today aren't going to be the same problems by the time you get down the road."[6]

Michael Bloomberg, the executive, the decider, the manager, started working toward his new goal with the customary precision and pragmatism of his other expertise, as the engineer. Campaigns are messy, as a rule, and he wanted to begin methodically, even if things couldn't stay that way for long. First, as always, he hired the best (and often most expensive) people in the campaign business. Patti Harris had already convinced Bloomberg to hire Kevin Sheekey, a handsome, fast-talking political whiz who could spin the dullest detail into a good story. A veteran of then senator Daniel Patrick Moynihan's Washington staff, Sheekey dazzled almost anybody in his headlights. There was always some question about how many frills he added as he unfurled his latest tableau. But Patti Harris obviously recognized a political force, and Mike Bloomberg spotted a fellow salesman.

Sheekey, who had been advising the company on the ways of Washington since 1997, was one of the first political people Bloomberg asked about whether he should run for mayor. Never admit you're *not* running, Sheekey counseled. With a direct line to some of New York's best political reporters, Sheekey kept sowing hints that Bloomberg would run to succeed Giuliani. He knew Bloomberg enjoyed the attention, but, like Harris, he also began to worry that this descent into politics was not going to be neat and easy.

By January 2001, Sheekey and Harris were working hard to talk their boss out of running when Bloomberg invited them to dinner.

As they sat down, Bloomberg ordered wine, and when it came, he raised his glass. "Okay, if we're going to do this thing. Let's toast on it," he said. Sheekey and Harris were stunned, but as Bloomberg explained later with a grin, "We decided to take a vote, and one vote carried it."[7]

Soon, Bloomberg had hired political strategists like Frank Luntz, who had helped Republicans, and Doug Schoen, who had helped guide President Bill Clinton through his reelection in 1996, and the seasoned pros at Squier Knapp Dunn, known for creating the advertising for Democratic campaigns going back to Hubert Humphrey's presidential run in 1968.[8] Harris had already been making certain Bloomberg met the key people in the city, including those who knew its politics. She also helped Bloomberg hire not only the political bigwigs, but also the intellectual experts on urban matters like Mitchell Moss of New York University, Ester Fuchs of Columbia, and civil rights activist Alan Gartner, a professor at Queens College of New York.

But, the prize consultant, David Garth, the guru of political gurus who had helped elect mayors and governors, seemed out of reach. Garth had added his magic to the winning campaigns of three mayors—John Lindsay in the raucous 1960s and early '70s; scrappy, "How'm doin'?" Ed Koch, who brought the city through the eighties; and the current mayor, Rudolph Giuliani. Garth's television ads were legendary. When Koch was running against incumbent mayor Abe Beame in 1977, the Beame campaign was pleading with voters to let him finish the job. "Finish the job," Koch sniffed in Garth's powerful ad. "Hasn't he done enough?"[9]

Garth had sent word he was not ready to take on a losing campaign, even for a winning paycheck. Harris and Sheekey, however, were not ready to give up. They arranged a clandestine meeting at Garth's chosen spot—the Café des Artistes, an elegant cave-like restaurant with nymphs painted on the walls and some of the city's most powerful people maneuvering at the tables. Garth was a tough, plainspoken character, part ogre, part wizard. After Harris and Sheekey convinced him to meet Bloomberg, Garth came away with a rough assessment of the candidate: "This guy was in love with himself. He's a prick, all right? But he also has empathy for people—blacks and Jews, you know? And I never liked the people around him, except for Kevin, who knows politics and Patti, who has excellent instincts,"[10] Garth said later. He signed on anyway. It would be an interesting campaign, he told Sheekey, and the money turned out to be better than good.

Away from the public eye, at least at first, Bloomberg also shifted more of his philanthropy beyond the city's cultural centers, adding an astonishing seventy-nine organizations, many of them smaller charities and nonprofits in the five boroughs. They included the Doe Fund to help the homeless and the Staten Island Children's Museum, the Children's Health Fund to help pay for a "doctor's office on wheels" for poor children.[11] They were worthy causes, of course, but they would also help introduce Bloomberg across the city to make the super-rich new candidate look as generous as he certainly was.

Not everyone saw charity, of course. Among the most vocal was former New York assemblyman Richard Brodsky, a Democrat from the city's suburb of Westchester, who viewed the Bloomberg contributions as a form of political largesse. "He doesn't get bought," a political hazard for poorer candidates, Brodsky said dismissively. "He's the one doing the buying."[12]

As the money for the campaign spread into the millions, the city's political insiders scoffed. They saw the pollsters and the admen, the analysts and the advisers, and even some of the charities, "taking him for a ride."[13]

But Bloomberg was looking at the odds a little like the money managers he knew from Wall Street. What he and his advisers saw was a political assumption that a Democrat would win after Rudy Giuliani's eight years of arch Republican rule. Every Democratic leader with an ounce of ambition seemed to be eyeing the mayor's job. The Democratic public advocate Mark Green clearly thought he was next in line. The city comptroller, Alan Hevesi, another Democrat, was making his play for the top job. The Democratic city council speaker, Peter Vallone, was running, so was the Bronx borough president, Fernando Ferrer, who hoped to be the first Hispanic mayor. On the Republican side, Herman Badillo, a former Democratic congressman and star in the Puerto Rican community, was making his sixth run for mayor, this time trying out the GOP line. At age seventy-two, and after losing the race for mayor five times, Badillo was little more than a placeholder for the Republicans, who had almost no hope of holding on to city hall. To Bloomberg, a Democrat, that meant he was in the wrong party.

So in 2000, Michael R. Bloomberg quietly switched his registration from Democratic to Republican.[14]

For every successful candidate, there has to be a good answer to this basic question: Why you are running? It cannot be simply ambition, although a good supply of determination is necessary to sustain the hard work of campaigning. It cannot simply be a love of attention, although it has certainly helped the likes of Donald Trump. In Bloomberg's case, there was another reason. He believed he could run the city better than anybody else. So Bloomberg and his team slowly compiled an encyclopedic wish list of things he wanted to do as mayor. He wanted to keep the city safer, of course, but also healthier. He wanted full control of city schools, a goal other mayors had failed to get. He wanted to improve the business atmosphere, create a central place for information (which became 311), develop more and better housing, help the unfortunate, make the mayor's office nonpartisan, and generally make the city hum nicely like one of his famous machines.

His list of promises compiled later by one political staffer, Bradley Tusk, included an astonishing 349 items. (By 2004, Tusk would claim that 211 were achieved, 113 launched, and 25 were reconsidered.[15] Tusk estimated that in his first term Bloomberg had launched or completed 94 percent of his campaign goals.) Some were far out of his reach like election reform and renovation of the dungeon-like commuter terminal at Penn Station or imposing congestion pricing on city drivers—all of which were controlled by a notoriously inept state government in Albany. Some plans were canceled, like requiring public school students to wear uniforms. (They were costly, and other cities had found few benefits from the one-look-fits-all school dress, the mayor decided.)[16] One item on the list—to move the city hall press room from city hall to Staten Island—may have been a joke. Even so, it managed to irritate two groups Bloomberg needed—the press and the conservative voters on Staten Island.

Overall, however, it was a useful political package for that era, especially since Bloomberg could afford to spend $92.60 per vote on ads, promotions, and advisers to sell his competent, entrepreneurial image.[17]

As he turned from the finance world that counted dollars to the business of counting votes, Bloomberg started shedding bits and pieces of the high-end existence he had worked so hard to acquire. Shortly before he announced, Bloomberg resigned from several mostly white private clubs that could offend a diverse city. Wall Street regulars collected clubs like personal tokens, and in this way, Bloomberg had followed his pack. He quit the Harmonie Club in Manhattan and the Century Country Club in Purchase, New York—two exclusive enclaves established more than one hundred years earlier by Jews who had been excluded from most other clubs in the city.

At the same time, he quietly turned in his resignation to two all-male societies. One was the Brook Club, a clannish operation founded, according to legend, by men who were ousted from another club after they tried to poach an egg on a member's bald head.[18] Bloomberg also resigned from the militantly all-male Racquet and Tennis Club in Manhattan, a club known for refusing to allow even tennis star Evelyn David to practice on their courts in 1987.[19] Denying her time in their pool, which was rumored to feature males routinely paddling around in the nude, might have made sense. But their tennis courts?

Still, he was not left without a club or golf course or other high-end sanctuary. He remained a member of the Bond Club, the Century Association, the Council on Foreign Relations, the Harvard Club, the New York Yacht Club, the Kappa Beta Phi fraternity, the Golf Club of Purchase, New York, a favorite of Wall Street types,[20] the Caves Valley Golf Club, a course for serious golfers near Washington, D.C., and, in Bermuda, his weekend getaway of choice, the Coral Beach & Tennis Club, and the Mid Ocean Club.[21] He sold his half of a billionaire's requisite yacht, an admission of excess that Bill Cunningham, a top campaign adviser, insisted was not a big deal. "It's not an aircraft carrier. It's not a submarine," he said. "It's just a boat."[22]

Bloomberg's problems with women at his company hovered as a potential hazard, but news accounts of the harassment charges by female employees and the vehement denials by Bloomberg came early—even before he had announced. Did his campaign leak the news in order to inoculate the candidate? The answer is almost certainly yes, as author Chris McNickle wrote in 2017.[23] That's the standard campaign way to downplay a bit of bad personal history—get it out early.

Ten weeks before Bloomberg announced, the New York *Daily News* had trumpeted the women's accusations, the lawsuits, the accusations of things Bloomberg allegedly said (like "Kill it" to a pregnant worker), and the vehement denials by Bloomberg.[24] Political regulars chuckled privately as a nonpolitician tried to air out his past before he went public. An aide to Peter Vallone, said that the ruckus in the tabloids "reinforces the fact that Bloomberg is not a serious threat, and his candidacy isn't quite ready for prime time."[25]

Far from being disheartened, Bloomberg's advisers saw the muted response and believed they had won a pass. If reporters brought it up later, the campaign could point out that Bloomberg had already denied it and passed a lie detector test. The cases were settled, and it would be old news.[26]

Undaunted, or more characteristically even encouraged by the naysayers, Bloomberg finally declared his candidacy on June 5, 2001. His speech announcing his run for city hall was three and a half pages long and used the pronoun "I" 117 times, as columnist Gail Collins noted in the *Times*.[27] No matter. The actual announcement, the real introduction to city voters, was on television, the beginnings of a televised blitz that would be part of a campaign that would eventually cost Bloomberg a stunning $74 million.

As Bloomberg began his first run for public office, surveys for the Quinnipiac University Poll showed him more than thirty points down, just one step over invisible.[28] Most Republicans didn't think he had a chance, but Bloomberg, who once estimated that he would not spend more than $30 million to get elected, was now ready to fork over whatever it took to get the nomination. As one writer put it, the GOP "welcomed Bloomberg with open pockets."[29]

Soon, even then governor George Pataki ditched Badillo and endorsed Bloomberg. At their first joint press conference, Pataki was standing next to the freshly initiated Republican when a reporter asked the billionaire candidate if he was really, truly a Republican, given that he seemed to be awfully liberal. "I AM a liberal," Bloomberg answered as

Pataki flinched. And after several more questions like those about his liberal views on guns, abortion, and gay rights, Bloomberg grinned and made himself perfectly clear: "I'm a liberal. I'm a liberal. I'm a liberal. I'm a LIBERAL," he said. Pataki remembered working hard to keep a smile on his face. This was not on the talking points memo, but, as the governor would soon learn, it was standard "I am what I am" Bloomberg.[30]

The business community rallied, of course. But others did not fall in line so easily. Betsy Gotbaum, a high-energy force around the city, had been a parks commissioner under Mayor Dinkins and president of the New-York Historical Society, saving it from a dusty bankruptcy and the loss of a splendid building on Central Park West. Bloomberg supported the society and had become a social friend.

So Bloomberg assumed Gotbaum was on board. Not so fast, she explained. A lifelong Democrat whose husband, Victor, had been a prominent labor leader, she was running for the job of public advocate, the city's ombudsman. Endorsing a Republican or criticizing Bloomberg's opponent would be political treason in her world, even for a friend. Bloomberg, however, saw her political attachment as a form of desertion.

When they both won, Gotbaum expected an easy relationship with the mayor, not like the daily spats between former public advocate Mark Green and ex-mayor Rudy Giuliani. That wasn't going to happen, she was shocked to learn. She had been disloyal, she was told, and he would have no trouble cutting her budget and getting city voters to drastically limit the public advocate's position, in other words, her job. It was a very public war. But when her husband died nearly a year and a half after the mayor left office, Gotbaum said that the first outsider to call and offer his sympathy was Mike Bloomberg.[31]

If Bloomberg had plenty of money to run for office, a successful candidate also needs something even Mike Bloomberg could not buy—pure, old-fashioned luck. In 2001, this political newbie enjoyed three unexpected advantages, the most important being the disaster on September 11 that alarmed the city and rattled its voters.

But there were also other circumstances that favored this political novice. First, nobody thought he could win, including himself. A few months before he announced, Bloomberg told Israel's prime minister, Ariel Sharon: "Am I running? Probably. Will I win? Not a chance."[32] So he made a lot of his mistakes (and gave a lot of really terrible speeches) early, while nobody was really looking. The press and the political diggers from the opposition mostly gave him a pass—until it was too late.

"If you go back to when he first announced that he was running, people were cracking jokes. He was just kind of goofy," recalled Joe DePlasco, who ran the campaign of his main opponent, Democrat Mark Green.

"I remember [a *Times* reporter] calling after the election and saying, you know, he was sorry that they did not give Bloomberg a bigger and deeper look," he said. "All that stuff you would have investigated—the background, the expenditures on political stuff, business decisions, personality flaws, whatever, that didn't take place," he groused. "They didn't have the immediate scrutiny that you would have normally in an election."[33]

The second bit of good fortune for Bloomberg was that his Democratic opponent was Mark Green. Green, who had been a steady and sometimes strident voice for reform as the city's public advocate, was an arrogant and abrasive man. He had a talent for offending people, even if they agreed with every single word he said. Green managed to divide the Democrats, offend key unions, alienate blacks and Hispanics, and generally drive a sure win by the Democrats that year into a humiliating loss.

Still, the most fateful event for that election and for America in the years ahead was the terrorist attack on the World Trade Center towers on September 11, 2001. With what would become 2,763[34] city deaths and the catastrophic destruction of the massive Twin Towers, even tough New Yorkers were shaken. Suddenly, enough city residents would yearn for stability, and Mike Bloomberg's wooden but dependable candidacy fit the needs of that moment. Bloomberg looked like a successful manager, a qualified chairman at city hall, a steady hand that could control the budget, supervise the city's 300,000 workers, and generally reign as a paternal figure who could take care of the city's eight million residents.

Some voters went to the polls four times that fall. The city primary on September 11 was quickly canceled. There were even people who said the election saved their lives because they stood in the polling place waiting to vote before going to work at or near the World Trade Center. Most New Yorkers could tell you exactly what they did that day, how they watched the destruction on TV or, in real time, who they called, where they were. Bloomberg was in his campaign office, eye on the television, phone at his ear. Voting for mayor was not a priority that day, even for him.

A new primary was set for September 25, and Bloomberg easily bested his Republican opponent with 72.3 percent of the vote, even though Badillo had tried, and failed, to make an issue of Bloomberg's money and the lawsuits from women in his company. Most people, including most of the media, were watching the Democrats, where Green was forced into a runoff with Fernando Ferrer because neither candidate won 40 percent of the vote. Green, who eventually clawed his way to a win against Ferrer, was so confident he could beat Bloomberg that he had already begun offering jobs in his future administration. He repeatedly scoffed at the idea of Bloomberg as mayor, at one point calling Bloomberg's plan to add schools on Governors Island off the Manhattan shoreline "the naivete of a novice." "I don't think he knows the city, and I don't think he understands government," Green sneered. "When he's been to all the neighborhoods like I have, perhaps he'll be slightly more insightful and credible." [35]

Although his opponents and the press had mostly failed to notice, Bloomberg had been going to all those neighborhoods. He had been steadily meeting people in every borough and finding, to his relief, that all sorts of New Yorkers felt comfortable with his stiff but genuine salesmanship. When he worked to make people like him, they liked him. He was indeed odd, even for a billionaire. He droned through his speeches, like a schoolkid reading a book report, and he had this strange way of speaking—part Massachusetts, part Bloomberg. The word "anyway" always turned into "anyways." But, hey, he wasn't fake, New Yorkers figured.

While Bloomberg was shaking hands and promising a better city, his campaign staff was working just as hard trying to introduce this very rich white man to a very diverse city. Jonathan Capehart, who had been a Bloomberg reporter before he began working to help Bloomberg connect with the African American community, tried to get his subject to loosen up, especially when he visited the city's powerful black churches. Capehart explained to the candidate that religion in a black church is physical. The organ thumps and the choir soars and people clap and stomp their feet and sing and sway to worship joyously with their whole bodies.

Bloomberg would just stand there, once in the same church as Green, who tried to rock along with the congregation. Capehart remembered asking him, "Mike, you know, it's church. You can't clap? You can't move? He said, 'Hey, listen, I could try to pander and pretend like I know what to do and that this is part of my tradition or I've been around this all my life, but I haven't. And it's not part of my tradition so I'm not going to pretend to be someone I'm not.'"

Capehart added, "I thought, you know what, good for him. There's nothing more terrible than to see a politician, and particularly a white politician, trying to get down in a black church when they've never done it before."[36]

To reporters covering his campaign, this stiff candidate seemed odd for a man who had a reputation straight out of the high energy and low morality of Wall Street. To some, it became clear that he was trying hard, sometimes painfully hard, to stop from blurting out what he might have said on the Salomon Brothers trading floor. Still, he could occasionally go off script and offer a few glimpses of the inner Bloomberg.

In a key economic address at a breakfast given by *Crain's* business magazine in October 2001, he began advising executives from the city's top corporations to avoid hiring people from the suburbs. They are not "the best and the brightest," he explained. "This is a self-selection process. People who want to go there [Connecticut or Westchester, for example] aren't the people that you want to have in your company."[37] It might have hurt him with his richer suburban friends, but it sounded right to New Yorkers. Whether he understood that it might be helping him with the voters, it wasn't planned, wasn't in the text. It was just what he wanted to say at the moment.

During one early interview, Bloomberg was asked what had become a standard question for politicians—had he ever smoked marijuana? Bloomberg said, "You bet I did. And I enjoyed it." A national pro-marijuana campaign later used the quote as part of an ad that showed a very bleary-eyed Bloomberg with the line: "At last, an Honest Politician." (Bloomberg would later admit that although he regretted the remark, it "was the truth." And he would later oppose decriminalization of the drug, especially in his city.)[38]

At another point early in 2001, he was talking about how students could apply for jobs. He said that too often students from the city's public schools "don't know how to present themselves. They have personal hygiene problems. These are the things that drive employers crazy."[39]

As Bloomberg's poll numbers went up, the state Democratic chair, Judith Hope, put out a list of Bloomberg's "offensive remarks" and "blunders." They included items from the Bloomberg birthday book of quotes compiled in part by a former Bloomberg employee, Elisabeth DeMarse, for Bloomberg's fiftieth birthday. After DeMarse admitted she had released the book and some of the quotes were printed in *New York* magazine in September,[40] she got a call from a Bloomberg lawyer suggesting, as she put it, that "they were going to take all my money" because she had broken her confidentiality agreement with the company.

"I didn't worry," DeMarse laughed years later. "At that point, I didn't have any money."[41]

As Bloomberg made headway in private polls, the Democrats pulled out those old jokes and tried to make them sound like campaign statements by the Republican candidate. Their list included:

"I make it a rule never to go to Queens, and since that eliminates both airports, I don't travel very much."

"The three biggest lies are: The check's in the mail. I'll respect you in the morning, and I'm glad that I'm Jewish."

Hope wrote that "New Yorkers deserve to know about the offensive things their Republican candidate for Mayor has said about women, the borough of Queens and being Jewish."

There was, of course, no suggestion by the opposition that these might have been jokes, even terribly old ones. Bloomberg labeled them old "Borscht belt" standbys.[42]

Not funny, the joyless Green campaign argued. Green tried desperately to add these quotes as an antidote to the television ads and expensive flyers stuffed in mailboxes of potential voters. These Bloomberg ads showed a strong-looking guy who described himself as "a self-made man from a working-class family." Television commercials hammered the idea of a competent businessman who had an impish grin and who exuded the kind of confidence of a man who was in control of the world around him. Many voters could see through Green's umbrage and once again registered Bloomberg's "blunders" as a little crude authenticity not unknown in the big city.

The real issue, Green and other Democrats said, was his money. How could people tolerate a rich man buying his way into office? the Green campaign asked. Bloomberg and his campaign turned the question on its head, arguing that it was so much better for him to pay his own bills than to take money from some leftover Tammany Hall wannabe who would ask for favors if he won. (He would later help the city pass a law limiting contributions to candidates from companies that do business with the city. That law would eventually impose a $25,000 fine for taking donations from those on the "doing business database".)[43]

In the end, the *New York Times* editorials, which had supported the Republican Giuliani in 1997, backed the Democratic candidate Green and argued that Bloomberg's money was indeed the main issue in the campaign.[44] New York City had a model system of public financing for political campaigns that parceled out matching funds to candidates who participated, followed the rules, and ran legitimate races. The system encouraged competition, and it was supposed to provide a hedge against rich candidates like Bloomberg. The problem was that even New York City's campaign budget could not offer much protection from nearly $74 million. Bloomberg, of course, did not participate in the system.

As the campaign took off, Stu Loeser, Mark Green's prime researcher, put together a package he called the "Bloomberg White Paper," designed to reveal the underreported flaws of their billionaire opponent. The Loeser team criticized the Bloomberg company's treatment of workers who made his keyboards in Mexico and accused him of running his company like "an electronic sweatshop"[45] with hours rivaling the Salvadorean sweatshops that, incidentally, made his campaign T-shirts. (Bloomberg canceled the T-shirt contract shortly after he was asked about the treatment of those workers.) The candidate had indulged in what the Green investigators called "abusive/boorish behavior" about women, and the man who made his money in the world of computers had said repeatedly that classrooms should not have computers for the youngest students. (He wanted children to focus on books and the blackboard and the teacher, not on individual machines—an idea which drew jeers from the Green camp.)

DePlasco and Loeser tried to peddle the details not mentioned in Bloomberg's smooth television ads, but Bloomberg's flaws barely made the news. And in the end Loeser didn't find enough to sour on his target. In 2005 he joined the Bloomberg political team, and in 2006 he became Bloomberg's press secretary in city hall.[46]

The 2001 campaign reached its peak in mid-October, even though most New Yorkers were focused elsewhere after 9/11. Each day seemed to bring the painful sound of bagpipes keening "Amazing Grace" in memory of another firefighter or police officer lost at the World Trade Center. The media was full of alarming new warnings about anonymous letters containing powder—some of it lethal anthrax, some of it talcum powder sent more to harass than to harm. A journalist in Florida died after opening a letter seeded with anthrax spores. Two assistants to NBC anchor Tom Brokaw grew violently ill after dealing with his mail—a "letter that looked as if it were written by a child."[47] Mail rooms around New York City were on alert, watching for strange packages or envelopes, and some mail clerks had to have hazmat suits ready if a suspicious letter appeared. The economy, already showing signs of weakness before 9/11, was slipping dramatically in New York, as tourists canceled Christmas vacations in the newly damaged city. New York was sliding into hard times.[48]

Green's real troubles began during the rough Democratic brawl of a primary season that really started when he had to compete with Ferrer in a runoff. One incident during that runoff probably lost Green the election. A Jewish lawyer in Brooklyn printed and passed out flyers showing a cartoon of Ferrer kissing an enlarged behind of black activist Al Sharpton. The idea was to scare whites into the Green camp,[49] but the flyer infuriated Ferrer and Sharpton as well as their followers in the Hispanic and black communities. Green never really apologized for the flyer. Instead, he denied knowing about it, and, in a debate with Bloomberg that year, said, "How can I apologize for something that we weren't responsible for?"[50]

The Bloomberg people enjoyed contrasting that pettiness to Bloomberg's reaction when a Staten Island Republican printed a brochure featuring Green and former mayor David Dinkins, the city's first black mayor. The brochure was printed and distributed by the Republican Party chairwoman of Staten Island at the time, and it was clearly what politicos call a "dog-whistle" to racists in the borough. The Bloomberg coordinator in Staten Island apparently knew about the printing but did not tell those running the campaign.

When reporters began calling, Bill Cunningham, who often dealt with the media, remembered that Bloomberg was so upset he fired the campaign coordinator on the spot and called the chairwoman, demanding that she withdraw and shred every copy. When Bloomberg arrived at the campaign office a short time later, he was as red-faced and angry as some of his advisers had ever seen him. "He slammed the table when we explained what was going on, just slammed his hands on the table," said Cunningham. Bloomberg then went on the radio that night and told a mostly African American audience what had happened. And he apologized. He called former mayor Dinkins and apologized. And when anybody asked over the next few days, he apologized again and again. That was ten days before the general election, and Bloomberg had been earnestly courting black and Hispanic voters. He needed them to know he had not weaseled out of the responsibility for a mistake that had his campaign's name on it.[51]

In the final days of the campaign, Bloomberg and his team realized that they desperately needed one particular man's help—the mayor he wanted to replace, Rudy Giuliani. After September 11, Giuliani had become a national hero, and he became so buoyed by his newfound fame that he tried to get the legislature to extend his term ninety days to deal with the damage to the city. Both Bloomberg and Green agreed, a mistake for Green because it infuriated many of his old liberal allies. But when the legislature failed to sanction such an undemocratic move even for "America's Mayor," as he was being called at the time, Rudy had to go.

Even so, Giuliani resisted sharing his glory with Bloomberg. Twice, the newly sainted Rudy had failed to appear for the endorsement taping.[52] Finally, on October 27, the outgoing mayor appeared, but when he finally gave Bloomberg his blessing, his commanding voice had died to a near-whisper, and his endorsement had the lifeless feel of a man reading his own warrant.

"I am very, very confident that the city would be in absolutely excellent hands in the hands of Mike Bloomberg," he mumbled. "If he can have half the success with New York City that he has had in business, New York is going to have an even greater future."[53]

With only ten days to go, the Bloomberg squad had Giuliani's endorsement on the air in twenty-four hours. Public polling still showed Green ahead, but Bloomberg was almost even with Green in the candidates' private polling. The Green team became more frantic as they saw their Republican opponent inching up to the finish line.

In the last days of the campaign, Green launched what his campaign saw as their blockbuster: they ran a television commercial charging a sinister-looking Bloomberg with advising a pregnant employee to "kill it." Bloomberg once again denied he'd ever said such a thing, and his aides also began feverishly selling the idea that Green had gotten what one member of the Bloomberg team called "a bad case of the flop sweats."[54]

Green's desperation became even more obvious during a kind of French farce that occurred the night before the election. At the last minute, then Miramax honcho Harvey Weinstein and a few other seasoned Democrats tried to engineer a peace mission between Ferrer and Green in order to get much-needed votes from the black and Hispanic communities. DePlasco, who said "everyone was freelancing at that point,"[55] recalled that Al Sharpton, who saw himself as the key to the black Democratic vote, suddenly seemed to be the arbiter of the whole plan. It was supposed to be a last-minute lovefest with Green, Sharpton, Ferrer, and former president Bill Clinton. What newspaper would be able to resist a front-page photo of that foursome on the next morning, on Election Day?

Clinton drove to the Four Seasons Hotel to meet Weinstein, then still a friend, but as his limousine inched closer to the hotel and the news crews turned their lights toward the former president, his limo suddenly sped away. Some said Clinton was furious about the media attention. That doesn't seem likely. Green said years later that the presence of Sharpton in any group photo was "a deal breaker" for him and that he believed Clinton felt the same way.[56]

"At that point, it looked like Mark Green's campaign was a sandcastle with the tide coming in," Bloomberg's Bill Cunningham recalled gleefully.[57]

The next day Green and his friends were preparing for a celebration, and exit polls were showing him ahead.[58] What Green's supporters failed to notice was that the unions had endorsed him and done little else. No real ground troops. The unions were suddenly busy elsewhere. No calling in the dependable voters, helping them get to the polls. Democrats sat on their hands in the Bronx.[59]

While Green was preparing to celebrate, Mike Bloomberg and his friends were planning an election night party at B. B. King's Blues Club and Grill on West Forty-second Street to savor the evening, even if they could not stomach the night's news. Bloomberg began promising his workers that he would get them good jobs in the private sector—he still had plenty of friends in business, he kept saying. The public polls showed Bloomberg gaining votes, but Green was still ahead. It did not look like a happy night.

The vote count came in slowly, but as the numbers started coming in from Staten Island and Queens, Pataki and Giuliani began smiling and nodding over the results. The excitement in the room grew minute by minute, and at one point, Garth grabbed Kevin Sheekey's arm and said, "Oh, my God, I can't believe we did it. I can't believe we did it." A stunned Sheekey replied, "Whattya mean? You always told us we could do it." Garth answered, "Yeah, yeah, yeah but I lied."[60]

The final election tally would eventually show that Bloomberg had lost in Manhattan, Brooklyn, and the Bronx. But Queens and Staten Island voters, plus those pulling the levers on the Independence Party line, would grant him a narrow win with 744,757 votes compared to 709,268 for Green.[61]

As returns became more obvious that night, Mark Green called Bloomberg to concede. Then he went out to tell his distraught followers shortly after midnight, even before most of the crowd or the media knew he had lost. "Apparently, they're not kidding when they sing, 'It's not easy being Green,'" he told the stunned and silent crowd, most of whom were young enough to get the reference to *Sesame Street*'s beloved Kermit the Frog.[62]

Before the campaign, Bloomberg had said that he would not spend more than $30 million because "At some point, you start to look obscene."[63] But even Bloomberg did not know how far beyond obscene the bill would be. A final tally turned out to be $73,391,461. For 744,757 votes, or $98.54 per ballot.[64] The $16.5 million that the Green campaign said they spent looked paltry by comparison.[65]

The campaign budget looked like one for a presidential race more than a contest for mayor. David Garth earned $1,020,318. Pollsters Penn,

Schoen, and Berland came away with more than $12 million, as did the Baughman Company, which specialized in direct mailing and did a lot of direct mailing for Bloomberg that year. The political team got bonuses ($300,000 for Cunningham and $100,000 each for Harris, Sheekey, and press spokesman Ed Skyler). And the big winners were ad makers Squier Knapp Dunn, the firm led by advertising guru Bill Knapp. Bloomberg paid at least $34 million to the company for ads, which so dominated the airwaves that *Times* columnist Gail Collins once worried that the city had "a hologram running for chief executive."[66] Still, if that was the cost of being mayor, it was cheap at the price for a man then worth $4 billion.[67]

9

FIRST HUNDRED DAYS

"And, Don't Fuck It Up."

—*Mike Bloomberg to many a new hire*[1]

Michael Bloomberg wanted to send a signal that he would be a different kind of mayor, a man of his word. One way to do that, as some on his political team realized, was to make good on a campaign promise to Tony of Bensonhurst. During the campaign, Anthony Santa-Maria, a sixty-two-year-old building security officer, had confronted Bloomberg at a Brooklyn stop to say that he was just like all candidates. Bloomberg, the candidate, would forget about guys like him once he was Bloomberg, the mayor. Not me, Bloomberg had promised. He would be different.

So on day one as mayor-elect and with only minutes of sleep, Bloomberg headed out to that same New Utrecht subway station in Brooklyn where he had met Tony of Bensonhurst. A media crowd had already gathered—media from around the world had been alerted that the strange billionaire mayor was making his first public appearance.

Kevin Sheekey, Bloomberg's political strategist, loves to tell what happened next. Into all the madness, suddenly, along comes Tony. Tony SantaMaria, who lived nearby. "He says, 'Hey, he's here to see me' and some cop says, 'Yea, yea, buddy, he's here to see all of us. Keep moving.'" An aide hears the rising voices and yells, "He's our guy." Tony, who had clearly been alerted to this event, goes up to Mike and hugs him. (Mike winced a little; he was not a natural hugger.) Tony puts an arm around him and tells the cameras, "See this guy. This guy is different." [2]

Sheekey and Bloomberg liked this event so much that the mayor returned to Bensonhurst the morning after every win—in 2005 and again in 2009 for smaller and smaller crowds that nevertheless included Tony SantaMaria.

Bloomberg insisted in other ways that he wanted to break old rules, and he spent his time in those early days in unexpected places for a Republican, even one in name only. After Tony of Bensonhurst, he had a very public post–Election Day breakfast in the Bronx with Democrat Fernando Ferrer, who sat with the mayor-elect at the Court Deli in the Bronx and said, pointedly, "Welcome to 'the Other New York.'" [3] It was a reference to Ferrer's slogan in his failed primary campaign against the Manhattanite Mark Green.

Bloomberg made other rounds that had been off-limits for a Republican. He visited union leaders and liberal Democrats like Randi Weingarten, head of the teachers union, and he recognized Al Sharpton with a well-staged handshake, all moves that separated him from the public seething and snarling Rudy Giuliani, who would reluctantly hand over the office almost two months later. Again and again in those first days, Bloomberg kept sending the message that he would be different.

Officially, Mike Bloomberg, Wall Street billionaire, became Mayor Michael Bloomberg amid the raucous New Year's Eve celebration to end the year 2001 in Times Square. It was a scene to remind New Yorkers that even after the devastation of 9/11, they could still celebrate and hope for a better 2002. In those first cold minutes of January 1, 2002, the usual taut face of Michael Rubens Bloomberg seemed to soften for a moment as the power passed to him from Giuliani. As he waved to the crowd on the street below, couples kissed and tooted their plastic horns, some even celebrating a new mayor.[4]

Bloomberg had already paid his fifteen pennies as his official filing fee to the city clerk, a requirement established by law in 1898 when the city's five boroughs were consolidated. And at his public inauguration later that day, he strolled out of city hall as a massive American flag unfurled with a gentle thump behind him. New York's divine Bette Midler sang "The Star-Spangled Banner." Al Leiter, famed pitcher for the New York Mets, was the emcee. New York's chief judge Judith Kaye, a friend, did the swearing-in ceremony. (He would ask her a few days later if she wanted to be his new schools chancellor. She said she had laughed and refused.)[5] His family was there, including his slight mother, Charlotte "Lottie" Bloomberg, who beamed as she stood in a long fur coat to witness her only son take his first oath of public office.

In a dreary monotone that would become the nasal voice of New York City for the next twelve years, Bloomberg read his first inaugural address. The audience applauded when he thanked people—especially his predecessor—but there were scattered boos when he warned that he would be "asking all parts of my city government to do more with less."

He advised his friends in the corporate suites nearby, "This is no time to leave the Big Apple." He promised New Yorkers that after suffering a temporary loss of confidence that was out of the city's robust character, "We will rebuild, renew and remain the capital of the free world."

It was a dutiful speech, touching all the right bases, thanking all the right people. Elegant? No. Rousing? No. Memorable? Not really. But it suited the cold weather and the dark mood of the city. "We are the toughest, most resilient and most determined people on the planet," he told an audience of those worrying that their city was slipping quickly into a post-9/11 despond, and perhaps even a return to the bleak 1970s.[6]

A few blocks from city hall, workers at the still-smoldering World Trade Center site were carting away what would be nearly two million tons of debris and human remains to Staten Island.[7, 8] The sixteen acres destroyed in the attacks would soon have the look of an untended construction site with the wind stirring dust in slow circles as politicians, business leaders, architects, engineers, and families of the victims endlessly debated what should replace the Twin Towers.

The losses from 9/11 were estimated at $83 billion by the city's prime business organization, the Partnership for New York City.[9] Nearly 430,000 jobs would disappear after 9/11. Nearly 18,000 small businesses were either destroyed or forced to move elsewhere to survive. The financial industry, one of the pillars of New York's economy, reeled, not only from the loss of so many lives in the Twin Towers, but also as the nervous company executives considered plans to relocate outside the city.

The other pillar of the city economy—tourism—also took a hit. Tourists from around the world canceled trips to the broken city. Hotel occupancy suddenly dropped below 40 percent.[10] And the city budget was now $4.76 billion in the hole.

Where to start?

Bloomberg had that long list of promises he had made in the campaign, plus he wanted to make the city simply work better. Advisers repeatedly said that he wanted to fix the government, not abolish it. To do that, he started the way he would always start a major project. He would find the best people who would sacrifice their time and often their lush salaries and even their privacy to work for him—seven days a week. There is no way to dismiss as too obvious this key part of the Bloomberg strategy for running things—from his business to his campaigns to his city hall to his philanthropy. Over and over, Bloomberg would make this point. First, hire the best people who will work for you. Pay them what you can (not much of an option in the city). Tell them to come up with the best ideas, make them accountable, and then promise to protect them even if they try their hardest and fail and the boss gets a call from the *New York Post*.[11]

It did not always work, of course. And those bare bones left out a lot of detail—like the private calls from the mayor at 6:00 a.m. "What WERE you thinking or were you thinking?"[12] He could be surprised when he made demands, and employees would decide something should be done differently. If they made it work, he would say, "I wouldn't have done it that way, but it looks right." And, of course, there were the mistakes—a social friend who couldn't run the schools, a former mayor of Indianapolis who couldn't step into the big time as deputy mayor, a few who stayed too safely inside the box. But mostly, the people who worked for Bloomberg starting in 2002 turned out to be smart, loyal, enthusiastic, and available by phone or email at virtually any hour of the day.

Years later, when Donald Trump had been president for a full eleven months, Bloomberg's main public criticism of him was that he had not hired the best people to do such a massive job. "The bottom line is, this president, as all presidents, needs a team and let them make decisions. You have got to hire people and give them authority to go along with responsibility. And you have got to hire people who are experts in each facet of government, rather than people who just happen to agree with your political point of view," Bloomberg said, in what turned out to be a classic understatement. "And he's not separated out the politics from the knowledge that we need."[13]

As Bloomberg prepared to move into city hall in the winter of 2002, he really had only his political team, and they were better at winning than actually governing. A few had gone off to spend their considerable pay packets, courtesy of the billionaire candidate for mayor. Patti Harris was always there, of course. She would be the first woman to become the city's first deputy mayor and she would stay there, at the top, all twelve years. Ed Skyler, a key campaign adviser, would be a key press strategist, eventually rising to the position of deputy mayor. Sheekey would remain in city hall as an all-purpose adviser, then deputy mayor in the later years, and Bill Cunningham would wrestle with the media as communications director. But the city had more than 300,000 workers and 50 departments. He needed help.

Harris knew just the man, Nathan Leventhal, an expert in transitions from one mayor's team in the city to the next. Leventhal was the former president of Lincoln Center, and he turned out to be a good match for Bloomberg. Brainy, meticulous, and tough, the new transition guru had been chief of staff to former mayor John Lindsay and deputy mayor for operations under former mayor Ed Koch. He had also helped with the transition for former mayor David Dinkins.[14]

A few days after the election, Leventhal and Bloomberg and a few aides sat around Bloomberg's kitchen table in his Upper East Side town house. They were putting together a new team to start at full speed on January 1. At one point, Leventhal asked the new Republican mayor, "And how many Republicans do you need to hire?" Bloomberg answered by pressing his thumb to his index finger to create a meaningful zero.

Mike Bloomberg did not need to hire anybody, he insisted. There were no donors to appease, no supporters who had bargained their endorsement for some city favor. With such freedom, Bloomberg's hires—with a few exceptions—would be the best that he and Leventhal believed they could find at the time.[15] Bloomberg told reporters that he would not ask potential hires about party, even whether someone had worked for his opponents like Mark Green. And there would be no effort at diversity, he added. "I am not looking at race, ethnicity, gender, whatever."[16]

Even outgoing mayor Rudy Giuliani had little pull with his successor. Few of Rudy's team were kept in the city's top jobs. Nicholas Scoppetta, who was in charge of children's services for Giuliani, took over the city's fire department still reeling from devastating losses in 9/11. Iris Weinshall, married to U.S. Senate Minority Leader Charles Schumer, stayed on as transportation commissioner. Taxi Commissioner Matthew W. Daus remained. John Doherty, who had been sanitation commissioner during Giuliani's first term, returned to the job. At the top level, there were also a few others who satisfied Bloomberg's political supporters, but not many. Bloomberg, who often said aloud what others were thinking, told reporters that when he took a look at Giuliani's team, he decided that "not all of his appointments were brilliant."[17]

Bloomberg let it be known that he liked strong personalities. He admired passion, and he enjoyed arguments, or as he saw it, debates. He wanted people who would move fast, far beyond the comfort level of the city's workforce. He expected data—data about the problem, data about the proposal to fix it, data about whether it worked once he'd tried it. And he especially wanted people who could sell their mission to the public, whether it was anti-tobacco or pro-bicycle or rebuilding a whole new region of the city.

Two of the biggest and most immediate challenges were public safety and a shrinking budget.

There were rumors that Bloomberg planned to ask Bernard Kerik to stay on as police commissioner,[18] after a little more than a year on the job for Giuliani. Fortunately for Bloomberg, that didn't happen, and a few years later, Kerik would be imprisoned for tax fraud and lying under oath[19] (thus requiring city officials to chisel his name off the entrance to the Bernard Kerik jail in Lower Manhattan).

Instead, Bloomberg chose Raymond Walter Kelly. Highly educated, highly capable, an ex-marine and police officer, he had already been police commissioner for two years under former mayor David Dinkins. Hours after he won the election, Bloomberg had called Kelly to offer him the job. He did not waste words. "So, you want to be police commissioner?" Bloomberg asked impatiently. Even though the $150,000-a-year salary was a pay cut for Kelly, who had been in private business, he answered, "It would be an honor." It was like the ex-marine answering with a salute.[20]

The other immediate challenge was an emergency budget. An obvious candidate for the job was Marc Shaw, who had become a master at wrestling with big government budgets in New York—the city's, state's, even the troubled Metropolitan Transportation Authority's that ran the buses and subways. Soon after the election, Leventhal introduced Shaw to Bloomberg. The mayor-elect sat quietly as the chronically disheveled budget maestro talked about the possibilities and hazards of city budgets—especially the one with a big hole in it that the mayor would be forced to announce only forty-five days after he took office. After about twenty minutes of attentive listening, Bloomberg picked up a pen and, in his tiny, left-handed script, wrote, "Hire this guy" on Shaw's file. "It was my dream job," Shaw said later of his position as first deputy mayor for operations. "I was also the one who worked for Mike Bloomberg, the mayor who happened to be a billionaire. Others were working for Mike Bloomberg, the billionaire who happened to be mayor."[21]

There would be plenty of other star players. For development, Bloomberg would choose Daniel L. Doctoroff, a forty-three-year-old, high-energy financier who had been pushing for New York to win the Olympics in 2012. Even with strong support from Bloomberg, however, Doctoroff did not get everything he wanted as deputy mayor for economic development and rebuilding. Mainly, he had decided to hire Alex Garvin, a respected urban expert at Yale, as the city's planning commissioner. Not so fast, the newly elected mayor told Doctoroff.

To help plan how the city would grow, Patti Harris had brought in Amanda Burden, a well-known socialite and urban planner. She and the domineering Doctoroff would not be an easy team. There were shouting matches, usually out of the mayor's earshot.

Then there were the people who the overconfident Mark Green had already offered jobs even before the election. Most of those commissioners-in-waiting kept waiting. One exception was Dr. Tom Frieden, a talented public health physician who had been in India fighting tuberculosis for the World Health Organization. When Green had called to offer the job of health commissioner, Dr. Frieden had wisely suggested they wait until after the vote.[22]

Frieden would become another superstar in the early Bloomberg years. When Bloomberg first met Frieden, in what was supposed to be a job interview, the two had what one official called an instant "mind meld."[23] Both supersmart, they talked rocket-fast. And Bloomberg cared deeply about Frieden's work as a public health physician and advocate.

It would take a while for Bloomberg to find someone ready to overhaul the Department of Education. After the state legislature granted him full control, Bloomberg looked for someone with the strength of a four-star general to manage 1.1 million students, 75,000 teachers, and

1,600 schools. Joel Klein, who had been the lead prosecutor in the anti-trust case against Microsoft, had almost no education credentials. But he was tough—tough enough to take on an education system that had become a bureaucratic quagmire.

Adrian Benepe, who became Bloomberg's parks commissioner, was the scion of a park-loving family (his father helped turn the festering drug den at Union Square Park into an urban market and playground). Benepe would focus on using private funds to help develop public spaces, and he would oversee the restoration of Central Park and the addition of more than seven hundred acres of new parkland including the High Bridge and Brooklyn Bridge Park.[24]

Peter Madonia, who became Bloomberg's chief of staff, had worked for Mayor Ed Koch as deputy commissioner for the fire department, among other jobs, until his family needed him to help with the Madonia Brothers Bakery in the Bronx. When Patti Harris, a friend from the Koch days, called, Madonia agreed to have lunch with Bloomberg, who seemed to be asking for advice about a potential run for mayor. Asking for advice, however, was a standard Bloomberg ploy. Yes, he wanted advice, but he also wanted to judge whether this person could work for him as his chief of staff, his doorkeeper and one of the toughest jobs in the city. Madonia did a lot of the unpopular stuff, like cutting the budget for the mayor's office by 20 percent and culling twenty-five cars from the mayor's fleet.[25] He sorted through the daily blast of unresolved questions that reached the mayor's office because they could not be solved down the line. And his job was to solve those issues before they reached the mayor, or worse, the press.

Madonia, a rough-hewn character with a good bit of the Bronx under his belt, knew how to deal with problems big and irritatingly small. The captain at a firehouse was trying to get porn off the computer—the problem bounced to Madonia. War games were necessary for the city as part of emergency preparedness—over to you, Peter.[26]

Dennis Walcott, who had been head of the Urban League in New York, took the post of deputy mayor for education and stayed with

Bloomberg all twelve years. Michael A. Cardozo, a top-flight lawyer, would become corporate counsel known for fighting long and hard before settling any complaint big or small.[27] Verna Eggleston, who had worked in children's services for Mayors Koch and Dinkins and had helped advise Bloomberg in his campaign, would be commissioner for the Human Resources Administration.

To deal with the business community, Bloomberg and Doctoroff worked to bolster confidence by hiring from the business world. Among the first was Andrew Alper, who had been chief operating officer of investment banking at Goldman Sachs. Alper would encourage investment through the city's Economic Development Corporation and would help guide the city into better times.[28]

At every level, Bloomberg aimed at the top of the list, and this high-powered crew was Bloomberg's step one. When the press or public asked what the mayor was doing in his first hundred days, the answer was that he was hiring the best team he could find. Yes, but what is he actually doing? they would ask. The answer would come again—the mayor was hiring the best team he could find. In virtually every case, the new hires told the same story. With the final handshake, Bloomberg would welcome the new team member. Then he would say, usually in a whisper, "Don't fuck it up."[29]

10

A BILLIONAIRE'S
CITY HALL

"Happiness can never buy money."
—*A favorite Bloomberg joke*

Michael Bloomberg would always be the first billionaire mayor of New York City. His campaign ads stressed that he came from a working-class family—no family money, no trusts to help start out—but by 2001 Bloomberg himself could not pretend to be a regular nine-to-five kind of guy. Sure, he rode the subways—the express trains on Manhattan's East Side that regulars claimed suddenly looked a lot cleaner during his time as mayor. Like many self-made moguls, he enjoyed being recognized for his net worth, and the rich man kept slipping out of his prepared texts. He admitted repeatedly that he liked wealthy people and wanted more of them in his city. "I am what I am," he would say—his Popeye defense, his staff called it when somebody thought he was showing off about his money. Or he would sometimes joke, sort of, that "happiness can never buy money."[1] Such comments would get him in trouble when he couldn't resist reminding people that he wasn't just another politician; he was Michael Bloomberg, one of the richest men in the world.

The transition to public official number one in New York City was never going to be easy for a man cosseted in the private citadels of the rich and immune from meddling stockholders at his very private company. He was constantly annoyed at a press corps nosily trying to find out where he was on weekends. The *New York Post*, at one point, ran a front page with his face on a mock milk carton.[2] And when it was obvious that he was playing golf in Bermuda, the *Post* began calling him "Bermuda Bloomy." The mayor was said to be "furious" when journalists including those at the *New York Times* revealed details of his lavish weekends with fifteen hours of golf, dinners with friends, and his planes ever ready to whisk him back from his Bermuda mansion to the city in a little more than two hours.[3]

The billionaire also wanted to keep a lot of his personal and company details private, to reveal only what was absolutely necessary to city officials and the media. Bloomberg's first public report of his finances had come during the 2001 campaign, and the *Times* complained, in what was certainly a *Times*ian understatement, that the billionaire candidate was "frugal with the details."[4] The document, which the candidate's aides called a "reconstructed tax return," said that Bloomberg had paid 39.56 percent of his income in taxes, which amounted to payments of more than $500,000. How much more? Not telling.

There were a few bare details.[5] Bloomberg had established trusts for his sister, Marjorie Tiven, and a former girlfriend, Mary Jane Salk, and there was a loan to his ex-wife, Susan Brown Bloomberg. There was a list of boards that counted him as a member (the Metropolitan Museum of Art, the Jewish Museum, Lincoln Center, the Old Vic, the Big Apple Circus, Johns Hopkins, and fourteen others).

He had invested $10 million[6] in a film called *Focus*, based on an Arthur Miller story about a nebbish of a man who, in 1944, begins to learn about anti-Semitism firsthand when his new glasses seem to make him look Jewish. Released in 2001, *Focus* struck too many reviewers as preachy and heavy-handed, and it made almost no money, even with Bloomberg's help and Miller's name.

Journalists, who had to take notes and were not allowed to copy the documents, complained that Bloomberg's first release of financial details was so limited that there were only four precise figures in his thick, official-looking folders. Those were about his philanthropy, which went from $26,592,284 in 1997 to $33,693,286 in 1998 to $46,969,972 in 1999 and then more than doubling to $100,451,454 in 2000 shortly before he actually announced he wanted to be mayor.[7]

As he prepared to take office, he listed five homes, each worth more (a lot more) than the city's highest category of $500,000 and up. There were two estates in Westchester, outside the city (Armonk and North Salem); a sprawling penthouse apartment in Vail, Colorado; his beaux arts mansion in New York City, where he would live instead of staying in the mayor's home, Gracie Mansion; and a massive "cottage" in Bermuda.[8] (By the time he left office, he would own twelve homes, including in London, Westchester County, Southampton, Long Island, Wellington, Florida, Bermuda and, of course, his ever-expanding town house in one of the deluxe neighborhoods of New York City.)

Once he was in office, the city had rules designed to make certain there were no conflicts of interest. There were rules about what he could own and rules about whether he could pay bonuses to his favorite employees. And even though he had technically resigned from his positions at Bloomberg LP, there were new rules about how much he could get involved with his company. To negotiate these complicated matters, Bloomberg encountered New York City's admittedly timid Conflicts of Interest Board, which had never dealt with a politician whose financial network was as large and diverse as Mike Bloomberg's. It took a full eight months before the board and the new mayor could finally come to terms over what he could own and how involved he could be in his company.[9]

As Bloomberg was giving the shreds of information to the conflicts board in 2002, *Forbes* ranked his wealth at a hefty $4.8 billion from his successful data/news/research business. It was a good reason why he took only $1 a year as salary from the city's taxpayers.

The city's conflicts of interest agreement opened the door ever so slightly into Bloomberg's shuttered world. Bloomberg had to sell or donate to charity his vast stock and hedge fund portfolio within ninety days—eighty stocks worth more than $500,000 each and ten more worth over $250,000 each. A group of money managers would invest his money and report to Bloomberg generally about how well they were doing.

Bloomberg could keep his large portfolio of tax-exempt government bonds—fifty-nine of them at this point, each worth more than $500,000 (the largest category of an asset that the city had). Many of these bonds helped fund such local projects as the city's subway system, the City University of New York, the water finance authority, and other public necessities. The conflicts board decided that they did not want to discourage anybody from owning government bonds, so he was advised not to sell the bonds and even, if necessary, buy more.[10]

The report revealed that there were Bloomberg Terminals at "virtually every major banking and investment firm" in the city, but the board saw no real conflict there. How could a mayor operate, especially after 9/11, if he could not talk to the business community?

The company was a different story. One important issue for the city and the conflicts board was how this billionaire mayor could continue to own his multibillion-dollar corporate empire. Bloomberg owned 84.55 percent of Bloomberg Inc., which in turn owned 80 percent of Bloomberg LP. Bloomberg's company owned thirty-four subsidiaries, at least thirty of which used the name Bloomberg in their titles. Other employees from the early days like Thomas Secunda or Duncan MacMillan or Charles Zegar mostly owned a few bits of the company, although it was enough to make them very rich in later years. Merrill Lynch still owned 20 percent of the Bloomberg bonanza (until Bloomberg bought that share back for an estimated $4.5 billion during the recession of 2008).[11] The mayor vowed to recuse himself from any city matter that involved his old friends at Merrill Lynch.

Bloomberg agreed to resign from all top positions in his company, but he argued that as a major stockholder, he needed a little leeway. The board granted him access to Bloomberg LP in four cases: (1) the possible sale of Bloomberg LP or a significant part of the company; (2) the sale or purchase of "a significant asset"; (3) a major financial commitment, such as a major borrowing; (4) any major change in the company's employee compensation policy or structure.[12] It was not exactly a blind trust, but it was the best the ethics board could do.

Meanwhile, Peter Grauer, an investment banker who got to know Bloomberg when their daughters rode horses together, took over Bloomberg's company along with Alexius Fenwick, Thomas Secunda, and Matthew Winkler.

Still, Mayor Bloomberg could not make himself scarce at his old company. Employees recalled seeing him stroll through their offices, not often, but often enough. He would hover over a model of his London offices (a "significant asset" under the ethics agreement, he could argue). It was being built while he was still at city hall, and Mike Bloomberg, the engineer, would take part in virtually every major decision.

The new mayor had a Bloomberg system on his desk, and he used the four-carat Bloomberg email to check in with his old friends in the industry and his trusted allies at the company like Secunda.[13]

The man in charge, Peter Grauer, said he felt free enough to modernize the business, but for one series of changes, he decided he needed Bloomberg's okay. One day Grauer took his proposals to Bloomberg at city hall, and the mayor barely looked up. "You do it," he told Grauer. "It's your job." Grauer said that the mayor's "involvement in what we did over those 12 years was *de minimus*."[14]

That did not mean that Mayor Bloomberg would avoid actions that could affect his company's bottom line. As he was trying desperately to keep corporations from leaving town after the attacks on the World Trade Center, he canceled a $14 million tax benefit for his own company's lavish new building on Lexington Avenue. There was no way the mayor's headquarters would be leaving town, he told colleagues. Bloomberg waived rental fees for terminals being used by the city comptroller and others, and he promised he would not use the city as part of his company's advertising. His promotions could list the Vatican and much of Wall Street, the London financial district, or virtually everybody concerned with finance in Washington, but not the City of New York.

One item caught the eye of Wayne Barrett, the fearsome investigative reporter at the *Village Voice*. Because the mayor of New York had some control over the city's cable matters, Bloomberg had promised not to get involved in any negotiations for Bloomberg Television, which was then in the upper reaches of the dial at channel 104. However, shortly after he hired his former deputy mayor Dan Doctoroff to run his company in 2008, the Yankees channel moved elsewhere and Bloomberg News magically shifted to the far more advantageous channel 30. It was like switching from the top shelf at the grocery store to the average customer's eye level.

Barrett was outraged. He wrote about how in other cities, Bloomberg TV languished in the "hinterlands," as he put it: channel 224 in Los Angeles, 252 in San Diego, 246 in Boston. The Bloomberg people insisted it was not about favoritism for the mayor or trickery of any kind; it was simply a question of paying more for a lower slot in the listings.[15]

There were other more trivial adjustments. The conflicts board also noted that Bloomberg's 1997 book, *Bloomberg by Bloomberg*, enjoyed a sudden spurt in sales in 2001. (More than forty thousand were sold by the time he left office.)[16] Some copies were undoubtedly bought by the mayor himself, who routinely gave the book to visiting dignitaries, sometimes in their own language after it was translated into Chinese, German, Portuguese, Japanese, Korean, French, and Spanish.[17] The city's Conflicts of Interest Board decided that it was okay for the book's biographical data to note that he was mayor, but the publisher should not use his city position "to market or promote the book."[18]

Bloomberg, who had rigid anti-nepotism rules for his company, nevertheless got the conflicts board to okay the hiring of his daughter, Emma Bloomberg, another employee earning $1 a year. (He added his sister at the same rate to help the city's relations with the United Nations.) The ethics board decided it was okay because "Although [Emma] will receive an advantage [by working in city hall for the mayor], it will not come at the expense of the City. Rather, she will be conferring on the City the benefit of uncompensated services that you have judged her qualified to render based on her work in your election campaign."[19]

The board made plenty of other exceptions for Bloomberg while he was mayor. He could give extra pay to members of his staff like his executive assistants. He argued that he wanted to reward them for their extra time helping him out with his "private logistical and family matters." The conflicts board chair at the time, Steven B. Rosenfeld, cautioned that the extra pay could not be for any work done as part of the city job, only the extras. The letters from the conflicts board did not list dollar figures, but Bloomberg said he would pay for an additional twenty to thirty hours a week "over and above" the regular city workweek. That meant a sixty to seventy hour workweek or ten-hour days and goodbye weekends.[20]

In the end, the conflicts board saw so few conflicts for Bloomberg that Barrett wrote in the *Village Voice*, "If the board was viewed as toothless before Bloomberg's terms, its advisory opinions [for this mayor] have raised questions about the health of its gums as well."[21]

If Bloomberg got off lightly in his dealings with the city's Conflicts of Interest Board, he held firm to his own ethos about how his money should be spent and how rich people contributed to the city. He had tapped into his own fortune, spending more than $650 million during his time as mayor, and he defended the wealthy during a time when city reformers and, later, protestors would demand more taxes on the city's rich. "We want rich from around this country to move here. We love the rich people," he said at one point, thus earning the title Mayor Moneybags. But he was firm about his views on sharing the wealth. "People say, 'Oh, well, you know if the income were redistributed throughout the system more fairly.' I don't know what fair means. You can argue that if you make more money, you deserve more money."[22]

Plus, he argued, these rich people "buy things and create jobs for waiters, limo drivers and the like."

By 2003, Bloomberg, the businessman, had begun to explain more openly how he saw the future of his city. In a speech for business and civic leaders, Bloomberg made it clear he was counting on New York City to lure the best and the most energetic people, no matter how expensive it was to live and do business there. "If New York City is a business, it isn't Wal-Mart," he said. "It isn't trying to be the lowest-priced product in the market. It's the high-end product, maybe even a luxury product. New York offers tremendous value, but only for those companies able to capitalize on it."[23]

So Bloomberg's New York really was a fur coat and Rolls-Royce kind of town, and Bloomberg wanted the world to crave it the way he once did. He wanted his city to provide something that would be called "magnetic infrastructure,"[24] an alluring collection of place and people that would bring in some of the smartest and most sought after talents in the world, a buzzing hyperkinetic society that shared various amounts of space on 302 square miles of highly congested land.

This was the view of Bloomberg, the businessman, the old-style Republican side of a man who believed that the path to a better society came when individuals got a good education, found a job, and worked like a demon to get ahead. There was also a Democratic Bloomberg in there, of course, who believed in civil rights and gay rights and women's rights, and public health, which he soon argued would include gun control and climate control. But he was a rich man who believed in the power of capitalism to improve people's lives and who intended to use his own wealth to do his part.

In the twelve years he was mayor, Bloomberg could certainly afford any luxuries denied most public officials because, as the economy recovered, so did his business as run by his appointed managers. They would expand the business and add considerably to its bottom line. In 2000, the company was worth $2.3 billion. By 2014, when Bloomberg returned, his company was worth $9 billion.[25] As the company expanded, so did Bloomberg's own bottom line. Worth about $4 billion when he took office, he had amassed a comfortable $33 billion by the time he was leaving city hall. Put another way, *Forbes* magazine, which assessed big money, ranked Mike Bloomberg as the eighty-second richest man in the world when he became mayor.[26] In the spring of 2013, a few months before he left office, he had become the thirteenth richest man on earth.[27]

II

A LABORATORY FOR URBAN REFORM

"When you need to talk to me, come by my desk and when
I'm off the phone, we'll talk. When I need to talk to you, I'll
come by your desk and when you're off the phone, we'll talk."
—*Bloomberg to Deputy Mayor Robert Steel*

There are a lot of moving people and parts in New York, all running at the unnatural speed of the nation's largest city. As Pete Hamill, one of the great chroniclers of New York, liked to say, New Yorkers always act like they're double-parked.

In 2002, when Mike Bloomberg arrived at city hall, there were nearly 300,000 employees at 50 major departments serving just over eight million people. New Yorkers spoke an estimated 800 languages,[1] mostly English, often in dialects not yet flattened by cable television. There were about 3.6 million workers of all varieties[2] and 420,000 welfare recipients and 1.1 million public school students—all living on a little more than 300 square miles in five separate counties. Residents produced more than 11,000 tons of trash every day[3] that the city had to pick up and send elsewhere, and they enjoyed nearly 30,000 acres of parkland that almost always needed tending.

There is more, always. New York City is the center of world finance,

American media and publishing, a cluster of exceptional museums, prime theaters, sports stadiums, major hospitals, famous universities. Movies are being made on many a photogenic corner and hot new fashion trends migrate from the streets in SoHo or Brooklyn to the runways in the city or even Paris. There is food of any variety in 27,000 restaurants,[4] plus cafés, bodegas, and food carts. There are technology start-ups and big-time developers and small-time landlords; there are bus drivers, subway drivers, limo drivers, truck drivers, taxi drivers, and ordinary citizen drivers. There are gyms and undertakers, plumbers and realtors, lawyers and construction workers, to scratch only the surface. And all of them need some kind of license or approval or assistance or comfort or service from their city government.

For a man who hated downtime, this was the perfect job.

On the very first day that Mayor Bloomberg's newly formed, fix-it squad of administrators arrived at city hall, they were ushered into what had been the old Board of Estimate chamber. Instead of the rows of benches once used for meetings, the big room had been overtaken by a sea of fifty desks and converted into the Bloomberg Bull Pen. For anyone who had been in the building earlier, it was a shock. For those who once enjoyed the sanctity and prestige that came with an office, it was an insult. This was Wall Street's roisterous workplace imposed on city government. There were fish tanks, a Bloomberg signature addition since the beginning of his company, but if they were supposed to relieve tension, they were a waste of the city's water supply.

Nobody was a big deal except the guy in the middle. And that guy, Mike Bloomberg, clearly loved it. He sat in the center like a king surrounded by his courtiers. Bloomberg believed such openness encouraged creativity and productivity and a lot less intrigue. He once said of the system at his company, "It may seem like chaos, but every single thing that goes on here is carefully planned. Like an explosion."[5]

"The room was a player. You needed to understand the room—that was part of his management style," said Ester Fuchs, a professor of international and public affairs at Columbia University and a key adviser for Bloomberg in his early years as mayor. You could watch who talked to him, she said. You could see his reaction, frown, smile, or what Fuchs liked to call his "twinkle"—that look that said, yes, this is something that nobody else would dare to try but him.[6]

Robert Steel, a former banking business executive who joined as deputy mayor in Bloomberg's last term, asked the mayor how often he liked to meet. Once a week—the weekly staff meetings? Every morning? Bloomberg answered, "When you need to talk to me, come by my desk and when I'm off the phone, we'll talk. When I need to talk to you, I'll come by your desk and when you're off the phone, we'll talk."[7] Bloomberg had long ago declared a personal war on process—meetings were supposed to be rare and short. He disliked paperwork, extra forms were a scandal. And friends spread the word that he could once be seen at his company dramatically ripping a proposed form into shreds. Just get it done. Go for the results, not the impediments along the way.[8]

At city hall, it wasn't quite that simple, of course. There were city rules about process, and meetings that were required. Peter Madonia, Bloomberg's chief of staff, remembered a time when he needed to discuss a very sensitive union matter and asked to go into one of the few remaining offices. Bloomberg said he preferred to go to a table on a platform above the bull pen where everyone could see them chatting. Bloomberg told him, "You hide in plain sight. You go into an office, everybody wants to know what you're doing."[9]

Bloomberg thrived in the clatter of his open workroom. Not everyone else did. Marc Shaw, the mayor's chief budget strategist, hated being deprived of a closed private space. An office. He would slide into the nearest conference room or move out into the park in front of city hall to smoke a cheap cigar and talk on his cell phone. Patti Harris, Bloomberg's most important deputy mayor, would repeatedly try to coax him back inside, but Bloomberg didn't want to tamper with the budget wizard. Shaw got a pass.[10]

Some of those in the room learned other ways to manipulate the system. Near the platform where Bloomberg met with important people like Madonia in the open, there was also a bull pen coffee machine. And Bloomberg had decreed that everybody—even the mayor himself—had to fetch their own drinks. When Bloomberg would take some official to the platform, a crafty aide with good hearing might use that opportunity to spend a little extra time getting a cup of coffee.

Timing was a major part of Bloomberg's equation, and nearly every major project had a real deadline. How real was it? Bloomberg always wanted results sooner, and he shortened virtually every time frame. Perhaps more important, when he announced a plan to the media, he wanted to add the date it would open or start or become real. He often pushed those inside city hall by handing the estimated deadline outside to the *Daily News*.[11] (By his second term, Bloomberg had installed a highly visible countdown clock, which had to be adjusted when he engineered a third term beginning in 2010.)

Unlike most politicians, Bloomberg relished open disagreements—even if they rose to full-throated shouts. Bill Cunningham, who joined the Bloomberg campaign as a political adviser and became the mayor's first communications director, often said that he was hired because he was not afraid to argue with the man. Once, after the mayor "tore my hide off," as Cunningham put it, the underling fought back, and as the two sparred openly, the bull pen grew quiet. The room waited. Would Cunningham be fired? Demoted? Hardly. Only a few minutes later, Bloomberg and Cunningham were getting cups of coffee at the end of the room and sharing a few laughs. A dirty joke, Cunningham remembered.[12] The swing from angry to okay in a few short minutes was a reminder that Bloomberg didn't encourage prissy debates. He wanted the few disagreements to ignite, explode, and then dissipate quickly—inside the bull pen, of course.

Bloomberg pushed his hires to be inventive, to think about new ways of solving the same old problems. If X didn't work, make a case to try Y. Or Z, even. For the big projects, he wanted to see the data about what was needed before he would approve the proposal to fix it. And in many cases, he wanted data to show whether it worked. Or didn't. His enthusiasm for new ideas meant city workers came up with plenty of suggestions big and small, serious and even provocative. In one case, officials trying to come up with new ways to remind pedestrians to look both ways before crossing the street suggested a sign at busy street corners that read "Wearing Clean Underwear?" Alas, that one never went public.

"Nobody tried more different things, brought more new policy, created more opportunities," said Joel Klein, who was Bloomberg's first schools chancellor. In his view, Mike Bloomberg wanted to make New York City "the laboratory for urban reform." [13]

While Bloomberg's new army wrestled with the giant centipede of city government that touched and sometimes meddled in virtually every aspect of urban life, Bloomberg would soon become a major cheerleader for his city and the power of cities in general. At his inaugural address in 2001, he had beseeched corporate leaders to stay in the city, especially after the 9/11 attacks. To stress that point, he would soon declare that "the golden age of the suburb is over." [14] He would even mock those living in the pricey suburbs as workers who did not have the guts and energy to thrive in the big, fast city.

"Even before he was sworn in as mayor, Mike called the CEOs of major companies pledging he would do everything in his power to keep the city safe," recalled Kathryn Wylde, [15] the president of the Partnership for New York City, New York's premier business group. She expressed the relief of many business leaders in the city when Bloomberg was elected. It was an important message from the businessman mayor, and they made major corporate decisions based on those phone calls. They might never have believed that from a mere politician, but they trusted Bloomberg to have their interests in mind whenever he made city decisions.

Besides all the promises and the showy meetings with any public official or superstar who came through city hall, Bloomberg had a more urgent duty—a necessity before any reforms could even take place. His first city budget was due forty-five days after he took office, and it would draw complaints from all quarters.

The attack on 9/11 had already eroded New York's economic fortunes,[16] and a global recession soon added to the city's woes. Mayor Giuliani had left Bloomberg with one of the worst deficits in years; the new mayor would scramble to fill a $4.76 billion hole in what would be a $41.4 billion budget.[17]

His first budget was what he called a "spread-your-pain, no-sacred-cow kind of a solution to our problem."[18] Nearly every department had to cope with a yearly PEG—the dreaded acronym that meant cutting each budget by finding a "program to eliminate the gap." That first year, the cuts ran to 7.5 percent citywide with some departments facing setbacks as steep as 26 percent. Bloomberg cut social services, even police and education budgets. But it turned out there would be one sacred cow, as a clever *Times* headline writer noted, and that was the mouse—computers would get extra, even in a downtime. Bloomberg carved out $25 million a year for two years to create his planned 311 information and complaint system. To some, it looked like the mayor who loved numbers had deserted millions of human subjects in favor of a fancy new tech experiment.[19]

Bloomberg stunned sports fans and especially Giuliani, who saw new sports stadiums as a key to his legacy, when he canceled plans for the city to help build new stadiums for the Yankees and the Mets. He labeled the massive packages of tax write-offs and city support as "corporate welfare." (In later, fatter years, he would relent and give city support to help build these two stadiums, plus another one in Brooklyn.) More pointedly for some of his old friends on Wall Street, he canceled Giuliani's elaborate package of enticements offered to help build an expansion of the historic stock exchange in Lower Manhattan.[20]

Bloomberg also rolled back recycling, saving $40 million[21] and stunning the city's environmentalists. It would be a harsh opening shot for a man who would later become one of the world's most intense advocates for a greener world. He raised taxes on cigarettes from eight cents to $1.50 a pack, then the highest tax in the nation. A pack of cigarettes that cost about $7.50 in Bloomberg's first year in office ran to about $13 when he left. The tax not only added revenue so badly needed by the city, it helped bring down smoking rates considerably, an administrative twofer. Sales dropped immediately from 29.2 million packs in July 2001 to 15.6 million packs in July 2002.[22, 23]

Finally, he resorted to breaking one of his key campaign promises— he borrowed $1.5 billion to pay operating expenses. That tactic is often explained as a government's version of taking out a mortgage to pay for groceries, and it was one of the key reasons that New York City went into financial decline in the mid-1970s. Bloomberg assured the rating agencies that the city was not going to mortgage its future, and, as promised, his future budgets would essentially pay the money back and patch this hole in his operating accounts.

Most surprising to the public, especially to Republicans who had backed Bloomberg, was his 18.5 percent increase in property taxes starting in 2003—the highest one-time increase in the city's history.[24] Desperate to balance his budget, Bloomberg had already convinced Albany to allow the city to add temporary surcharges on the sales tax and the personal income tax. The clothing tax exemption, beloved by most city residents, was also canceled by the state, thus infuriating almost everybody who bought shoes and items of clothing worth under $100. But the property tax was the only one that the city could essentially levy on its own, and that tax for homeowners clearly had Bloomberg's name on it.

New Yorkers, of course, thrive on complaints and especially seem to enjoy the sport of mocking their mayor. Mike Bloomberg was an easy target. A rich stiff who wanted to take away their cigarettes and raise their taxes? Bloomberg often recalled parades, especially in Staten Island, when there were "a lot of one-finger waves."

A New York Times poll in 2003 registered those complaints—with 74 percent of those polled unhappy about the property tax increase. Another poll in 2003 found that 61 percent of New Yorkers would reject an invitation from the mayor to have Thanksgiving dinner.[25] Overall, midway through his first term, Bloomberg had an approval rating of 24 percent. It was the lowest rating in the twenty-five years that the *Times* had been assessing the popularity of New York City mayors.[26]

12

THE "NANNY" MAYOR

"Just before you die, remember you got three extra years."
—*Bloomberg, on a healthier New York City*[1]

Michael Bloomberg loved doing business over dinner. It was not idle time, those hours taken off to savor food and drink. And the talk was not usually about the food (even at his posh dinners, he served meat loaf or roast beef, barely one step up from the cafeteria specialties of his youth). Meals were a time to devour whatever was happening outside his cloistered world, to seek out experts in his big three interests—business, politics, and philanthropy.

He met and interviewed countless future employees at a favorite Italian eatery in Manhattan. And after he left city hall, Bloomberg's homes, especially the elegant limestone town house in Manhattan, would become a kind of modern-day salon, post-university seminars where a rotating cast of ten people or so would sit around a large table and debate his chosen subject of the evening.

Still, he would be a guest for one of the most important dinners in his long career—one of many events in the late 1980s for rich trustees at his alma mater, Johns Hopkins. By chance that night, Bloomberg and his then wife, Susan, met Dr. Al Sommer, dean of the university's School of Hygiene and Public Health, or simply "hygiene," the students' dismissive label for the place where doctors promoted such necessities as working toilets. "It was the poor cousin of the university," Dr. Sommer recalled. "By definition, people who go into public health have no money. They weren't particularly valued alumni. There were none—zero—on the board of trustees." [2]

So when Bloomberg, the richest alumnus of all, suggested, in a light and sociable way, that if Dr. Sommer and his wife ever got to New York, they should all have dinner, Dr. Sommer managed to hold out for two weeks.

Over a meal at a small Manhattan restaurant Sommer made his pitch. "Public health is about preventing disease, and if you prevent a disease, nothing happens," he remembered saying. "Nobody's grateful they're not getting smallpox. They're grateful if the doctor saves them from a heart attack, and they walk out of the hospital cheating death, at least for the moment." [3]

Bloomberg listened intently. He quickly got that public health isn't about that stent in a heart that gives someone extra time (including, later, even him). It's about millions of people *not* getting heart trouble in the first place. The salesman was sold, and he came up with a slogan to market public health, a way to make it sexier than something called hygiene. Imagine saving lives—millions at a time, Bloomberg began telling associates and friends. "When I heard it, I quickly copyrighted it, and it became our official motto," Dr. Sommer said. [4]

The Hopkins school soon began to advertise that its mission was "Protecting health, saving lives—millions at a time." And after Bloomberg gave $350 million (a mere down payment on his later contributions), the name of the school changed in 2001 to the Johns Hopkins Bloomberg School of Public Health. [5]

Bloomberg had indeed helped Dr. Sommer. But even more important, Dr. Sommer had given Mike Bloomberg a cause that would guide him through the next decades. As a politician and philanthropist, Bloomberg would soon launch his own public health campaigns against smoking, obesity, guns, drug addiction, coal-fired power plants, dirty water, accidental drowning, traffic deaths and, above all, climate change.

Others in his class of billionaires were helping the world's poor, trying to cure people of basic diseases or eradicate illiteracy. Bill Gates was spending billions to fight AIDS and to win the "mosquito wars" against malaria and to help out poor schools both in America and in developing countries. Warren Buffett was giving more than $3 billion a year to the Gates Foundation to draw down his considerable net worth before he died. Other billionaires were choosing their causes, some of them attached to favorite politicians. But Bloomberg soon recognized that as mayor of New York City he could save even more lives—millions at a time—by changing the way an entire city of eight million–plus people lived. No health issue would be too small or too politically risky—from a ban on smoking in bars and restaurants to a warning about a circumcision rite. He would later say, "My obligation is to protect the citizens . . . The job is not to have high ratings."[6]

Shortly after Bloomberg was first elected, his top advisers began hearing about Dr. Thomas Frieden, an infectious disease specialist who was then traveling around India to fight tuberculosis for the World Health Organization. A graduate of Oberlin College (in philosophy and pre-med),[7] Frieden received a medical degree and a masters in public health from Columbia University. After a fellowship in infectious diseases at Yale, he became assistant commissioner of health in New York City, where he helped curb a sudden increase in drug-resistant tuberculosis.[8] By the time he had joined WHO, Frieden was an international expert on lung diseases, tuberculosis, of course, but also how smokers invited cancer and emphysema. He had already decided that his next big job would be to curb tobacco use in India, in America, maybe even in New York City.

Dr. Sommer, who was by then helping Bloomberg find a commissioner, emailed the forty-one-year-old doctor in India and suggested he should come to New York City to meet the new mayor. As Dr. Frieden sat down for his first encounter with Bloomberg, the mayor-elect suddenly launched into a lecture on the dangers of tobacco.

"I walk in and sit down and for the first ten minutes Mike talks about tobacco," Frieden recalled.[9] "He talks about how it's like three airliners crashing every day. A terrible problem. Don't know what we can do about it . . . In a sense I felt he was making a commitment to me to do tobacco, but *he* didn't need convincing." Bloomberg, ever the pitchman, was sealing the deal to have Dr. Tom Frieden as his first health commissioner.

Once in office, Frieden moved quickly to curb tobacco use. "For the last five years, my enemy has been mycobacterium tuberculosis," he said early on. "Now, it's tobacco executives." One of his first meetings with the mayor was about making New York a smoke-free city. When Bloomberg's political team heard the proposal, they were stunned. Ed Skyler, the top press officer, was horrified. Budget guru Marc Shaw saw trouble, as did Dan Doctoroff, deputy mayor for development.

Peter Madonia, Bloomberg's chief of staff and a plainspoken man, said that as the mayor cut the city budget, laid off workers, and raised property taxes, he worried that "now you're going to tell people you can't smoke in a bar. Like, who the fuck needs this now?"[10]

But the political team eventually had the data the mayor and Frieden needed. Despite polling that showed nearly 40 percent of New Yorkers thought you should be able to have a cigarette with your drink, Bloomberg's private polls revealed that 85 percent of those surveyed felt it was unfair to impose that deadly smoke on the bartender with asthma or the waitress just working to feed her family.[11] An internal report from Frieden's office on the prospects for a ban had an elegant couple featured on the cover. The young man was saying, "Mind if I smoke?" with the young woman answering, "Care if I die?"[12]

Frieden recalled taking his proposal to the mayor in the open office plan—with the Bloomberg team all sitting around their boss and listening warily.

"I did my spiel and he said, 'Are you certain that this is going to save lives?' And I said, 'Yes,' and he said, 'Then do it,'" Dr. Frieden recalled, and then he hesitated. He wanted to make certain the mayor was ready for battle.

"It's gonna be really rough. They're gonna go after you, and it's gonna be ugly," he told Bloomberg.

"And he interrupts me. 'Do you know the first rule of sales?'" Frieden shook his head, no. "'Once you make the sale, leave. It happens all the time. A new salesman comes into the company, and he makes a sale. He's so excited about it he starts talking to the customer and pretty soon the customer's having second thoughts and they lose the sale.'"

Frieden hurriedly backed out of the bullpen and returned to work, his first big pitch to the city's top salesman a success. In fact, when he talked almost twelve years later about the city's fight against tobacco, Frieden seemed to bounce in his chair. An energetic man on any occasion, simply recalling this particular battle fired up the old weaponry as he raced through his memories of a favorite campaign. It was easy to see why Bloomberg admired him. He could sell health the way Bloomberg sold terminals.

"It wouldn't have happened without him," Frieden said of the mayor, who backed him steadily through the political turmoil the proposed ban created in 2002. Like Dr. Frieden, Bloomberg seemed to enjoy defending his smoking ban even when it was unpopular. A smoker until his early thirties, the mayor often explained how he quit—he simply imagined his worst enemy outliving him.[13] Who? He wouldn't say.

The main opposition came from bar and restaurant owners and their friends in city government. "Giff Miller [then City Council Speaker Gifford Miller] was a pain in the butt [pun apparently intended]," Frieden remembered. "He wouldn't let it pass, wouldn't bring [the bill] to the floor."

Miller demanded separate smoking rooms for restaurants or bars, so with the mayor's okay, Frieden and others engineered the bill to allow separate smoking rooms, so separate they would be similar to the isolation rooms used for people with infectious diseases like Ebola. The rooms would have to be state-of-the-art, negative air pressure, exhaust fifteen feet away from any window or door, and they would probably cost around half a million dollars each. Oh, and that whole system? It would be approved for only three years.[14] The law passed the city council in late 2002 and went into effect on March 30, 2003. (The state would follow four months later.[15]) Smokers were furious. Some called it Stalinesque. What about the city's smoke-filled history? The Camel billboard that puffed white smoke in Times Square?[16]

A few worried politicians came to Bloomberg asking for exemptions from the law. They proposed "smoke-easies"—places where like-minded people could smoke themselves into the hospital. Frieden scoffed, "We don't allow asbestos-easies. We don't allow benzene easies."[17] To the chagrin of some of his political aides, Bloomberg sided with Frieden.

At parades, especially on conservative Staten Island, Bloomberg recalled that people booed and threw cigarette butts at him as he passed. Mostly, he said he loved the attention, but at one contentious city council hearing, Bloomberg had eventually snapped at a crowd of rough-looking tavern keepers clearly gathered by the tobacco lobby.[18]

"Does your desire to smoke anywhere, at any time, trump the right of others to breathe clean air in the workplace?" he seethed. "The need to breathe clean air is more important than the license to pollute it."[19]

At the Old Town Bar in Manhattan, a favorite hangout of Bloomberg's political team, one of the owners, Gerard Meagher, groused to his customers from city hall about the smoking ban—yet another intrusion into his business, and by a Republican, no less.

The bar is often used as a movie set since little has changed since it opened in 1892. The original "tin" ceiling of embossed steel was painted a light blue in the 1950s, but by 2002 it had become a thick, dull brown, a vivid reminder of what undoubtedly happened to the lungs of regular patrons and workers. More important for the business, the bar was often as full after the smoking ban as before, and Meagher said that it helped profits and turnover at the tables because diners didn't linger too long after they ate.[20]

Ten years after the ban, Mayor Bloomberg came back to the Old Town in 2013 to celebrate how exiling smokers to the sidewalks had been good for business in his city. He boasted that six thousand bars and restaurants opened after the anti-smoking law went into effect. And many, like the Old Town, had prospered.[21]

A smoking ban was only one of Frieden's controversial plans to improve the health of New Yorkers. Soon, the commissioner outlawed trans fat, those industrially engineered fats used in margarine and other 1950s-style foodstuffs that turned out to be more dangerous than lard to human arteries.[22] Bloomberg supported the ban, which affected most restaurants, and he agreed with Frieden that it was time for restaurants to post calorie counts. He even sanctioned Frieden's promotion of condom use, the "Get Some" campaign that was announced on Valentine's Day 2007, Bloomberg's sixty-fifth[23] birthday. (The city eventually gave out three million a month[24] to reduce pregnancy and sexually transmitted diseases.)[25] When he announced the new condoms, the commissioner apparently couldn't restrain himself. "We are now unveiling, unfurling, unrolling, if you will," the city's new prophylactics, he said. In his office, Frieden kept a bowl of the official NYC Condoms (fashionably black, of course).

Bloomberg's conservative supporters feared promoting condoms meant promoting, well, you know, free sex. He heard from some in the same group again when his administration required more sex education in schools, allowed school nurses to provide birth control, and gave teenagers access to the morning-after pill (labeled "Plan B" by insiders at city hall). Bloomberg saw the numbers and left his health commissioner alone.

After trans fats, salt became another of Dr. Frieden's prime targets. He wanted salt content in restaurants and processed foods to be lowered by a full 25 percent by 2013.[26] If Bloomberg enjoyed controversy, this one hit home. The mayor loved salt. He put salt on pizza. Extra salt on popcorn. He sprinkled it on chips, and Dr. Frieden swore he once saw him shake a little extra salt on a piece of bacon. This would be an uncomfortable test for the public health mayor. (At the time, reducing salt was beginning to encounter resistance from a few scientists, and one writer in *Scientific American* would soon conclude that "The zealous drive by politicians to limit our salt intake has little basis in science."[27])

When Frieden called together CEOs of some of the biggest food companies for a "salt summit" to talk about lowering the amount of sodium in their foods in 2008, Bloomberg opened the meeting by immediately straying off script. He was supposed to confess that he liked a little extra salt, but too much was not healthy. Instead, Bloomberg began by explaining how much he loved those salty little squares called Cheez-its. He would be happy if he could mash up Cheez-its and sprinkle them on a pizza, he said.[28] The Cheez-it producers (representatives from the Kellogg Company) applauded, even though only a handful of Cheez-its provides more than 10 percent of a day's recommended sodium.

The company executives were polite about Dr. Frieden's request, but in the end, they mostly pretended to help.[29]

After much effort, a group of sixteen big food producers—Starbucks, Mars, Au Bon Pain, Heinz, and others announced they would participate in the effort to cut salt in restaurant and packaged goods by 25 percent by 2015. Bloomberg declared the goal achieved by the time he left office. But by a year later, one report estimated salt content reduction by major companies was "modest" at about 7 percent.[30]

At each point in the mayor's health campaigns, his political protectors tried unsuccessfully to steer him away from the most ambitious and controversial plans of his health commissioners, and they worked in vain to shield him from those who would soon mock him as the Nanny Mayor. Maybe the Frieden health agenda would save lives, yes. But they worried about saving Bloomberg's political future.

Bloomberg dismissed such worries. If you have a high approval rating, you're not doing enough of the hard stuff. Or, as he would sometimes put it, if you're not falling on your skis, you're staying too long on the baby slopes. One day in the bull pen, he was urging his commissioners to think big thoughts, even if his approval rating tanked. "Okay, it's time to be controversial," he said loudly.

Across the room, the deep voice of Ed Skyler rang out, "We're counting on you, Tom," as Frieden and Bloomberg smiled in unison.[31]

In Bloomberg's final years at city hall, Frieden left to be director of the Centers for Disease Control and Prevention in Atlanta and Dr. Thomas Farley took his place. Farley, who had been an epidemic intelligence officer at the CDC and Frieden's second-in-command in the city, worked hard to battle obesity, a worthy mission that nevertheless caused Bloomberg the most national grief about his health campaigns. In what became known as the Big Gulp issue, Farley wanted to limit the sales of soft drinks to sixteen ounces each. As Farley remembered, he told Bloomberg about the idea and said, "This will be controversial." Bloomberg simply laughed and said, "Oh, you figured that out?"[32, 33]

Bloomberg and Farley failed to sell the idea that it was not really a ban on big soda. You could always buy two sixteen-ounce drinks, they said, probably for the same price as one thirty-two-ounce Big Gulp. The idea was that buying two drinks might make people think twice about buying that second vat of liquid sugar. But it quickly became a match of the titans—Mayor Bloomberg versus Coke, Pepsi, their political surrogates, and even the late-night comics.

The jumbo soft drink debate moved into national politics with former Republican vice presidential nominee Sarah Palin drinking what was supposed to be a bucket-size soft drink during a 2013 speech to cheering conservatives. "Oh, Bloomberg's not around," she cooed. "Our Big Gulp's safe."[34]

Mississippi[35] and North Carolina quickly enacted "anti-Bloomberg" laws to ward off limits on food, drink, or diet. North Carolina's law was especially sweeping. It was called the Commonsense Consumption Act,[36] and it prohibited local governments (i.e., cities) from limiting the size of soft drinks for sale. It also made certain that food manufacturers, advertisers, sellers—the whole make-'em-fat industry—could not be sued for someone's obesity and the costly health problems that went along with it.

After Mississippi had passed its version, Bloomberg scoffed, "You gotta love it. In the state with the highest rate of obesity, they pass a law that says you can't do anything about it." At the time, 34.9 percent of adults in Mississippi were overweight or obese, compared to 24.5 percent in New York State.[37]

The soft drink industry's billboards showed people who looked like they could run a marathon while protesting that Bloomberg's bureaucrats might be keeping them from a big 513-calorie[38] drink. They hammered their opposition on the sides of trucks delivering drinks and even on banners attached to airplanes over Coney Island.[39] At one point, executives from Coca-Cola offered an alternative plan that would involve more diet sodas and smaller sizes, but no shift on the big ones. When Bloomberg sat down with the executives and listened to their pitch, it was the only time Dr. Farley could recall seeing the mayor uncomfortable.[40] This was the businessman Bloomberg warring with Bloomberg, the public health advocate.

In New York, the limits on big sodas won in city hall but lost in the courts. The high-priced lawyers from the soft drink industry argued that Bloomberg's Department of Health had exceeded its authority and strayed into lawmaking. The 2014 majority ruling of 4–2 by the New York State Court of Appeals was written by a judge appointed by Republican governor George Pataki, and it was a major loss for the city's health department and Bloomberg's health activists. The dissent written by another Pataki appointee, Judge Susan P. Read, was just as passionate. She wrote, "The majority misapprehends, mischaracterizes and thereby curtails the powers of the New York City Board of Health to address the public health threats of the 21st century."[41] She spoke to a new form of public health that had moved from only fighting diseases like typhoid and TB to battling the way human choices contributed to obesity, heart disease, and cancer.[42]

After the public fuss subsided, Bloomberg would tell people that he had actually won the soda war. All that bad publicity for him was also bad publicity for Coke and Pepsi. The news media might call him the Nanny Mayor, but some analysts on television had also displayed a pile of nine sugar cubes like that found in a seven-ounce cup of soda and a giant pyramid of eighty-seven sugar cubes in a sixty-four-ounce drink of soda (which supposedly was sold to quench the thirst of an entire family). Soon the sales of soda, and even diet soda, were declining steadily and water seemed to be the favorite drink of weight-conscious Americans.[43] And in 2014 Gallup found that more than 60 percent of Americans now said they were avoiding soda in their diets.[44, 45]

In the final Bloomberg years as mayor, Farley worked hard to help the mayor take Frieden's missions to the next level. City parks and beaches became smoke-free, and shortly before he left office, Bloomberg signed a law raising the age for anyone to buy cigarettes from eighteen to twenty-one.[46] Farley introduced letter grades for restaurants, which some restaurateurs groused about as ridiculous. Tomatoes, for example, had to be cold—a terrible idea, salad lovers would protest—and fines were sometimes exorbitant—one private school got a $900 ticket for having fruit flies.[47] Soon most restaurants got A's, however, either by conforming to more rigorous rules against vermin or unwashed vegetables or by appealing to city officials about overzealous ticketing. Bloomberg declared success when salmonella infections in the city dropped 14 percent after the first year of giving out A, B, Cs and listing the unappetizing reasons for those grades publicly on the health department's website.

At one point Farley went too far even for the mayor when he appeared to be angling for curtailing pub hours like in the old days in Britain. That didn't fly. Instead, Farley came up with the "Two Drinks Ago" campaign to fight binge drinking. "Alcohol takes a devastating toll on our health and well being," Farley's statement began. "New Yorkers are surrounded by ads selling alcohol, and the messages are enticing. Beer, wine and liquor may look like passports to sophistication and romance. But even two extra drinks can turn a good time into a disaster . . ."[48]

The anti-drinking ads on the subway showed a man with a big gash on his forehead and a woman slumped dangerously on what looked like subway steps. "Two Drinks Ago you could still get yourself home," the ad warned. The mayor, who enjoyed wine at his Italian restaurant, or the politicos, who relished a few beers at the corner pub, worried that this taking on alcohol was not in their best interest, politically or personally.

Even more controversial was an effort encouraged by both Drs. Frieden and Farley to warn Hasidic families about a medieval circumcision ritual. Bloomberg's health commission began requiring parents to consent before baby boys were circumcised during a ritual called *metzitzah b'peh*. The mohel, the person who performs the rite, uses his mouth to suck blood away from the child's penis after the foreskin is cut away. Bloomberg, the secular Jewish mayor, warned that children had died or gone blind because of this unsanitary procedure.

Members of the huge Hasidic community in Brooklyn were outraged. But Bloomberg again seemed to thrive on the controversy.

"I think it's fair to say that nobody else would take that on. I mean, come on!" he told one journalist. "Who wants to have 10,000 guys in black hats outside your office, screaming?"

Bloomberg added, "But there is a reasonable chance that this is dangerous to kids' health. There have been some kids who we believe die or have brain damage from the practice."[49]

In the Jewish community, many heard only one thing—the ten thousand guys in black hats. "For the mayor to identify an entire religious group by the clothes they proudly wear is the basest of insults," said one Orthodox Jewish official, City Councilman David Greenfield. "It is even more offensive coming from a secular Jewish mayor."[50]

• • •

In his twelve years, Bloomberg easily earned the title as New York's premier public health mayor. The percentage of adults who smoked in the city went down by an astonishing 35 percent while he was mayor.[51] The rates ticked up slightly when women began smoking more—television's *Sex and the City* effect, as health officials like Dr. Frieden called it. Then too many men resumed the habit for the *Mad Men* effect. Still, rates continued to go down in the next few years as smokers were banished to the sidewalks, where they often looked embarrassed that they were unable to resist their dangerous habit even as users moved to electronic cigarettes. Sophisticated and romantic, it was not.

The campaign against Coke and Pepsi may have lost in the courts, but the ads on the subway (which Bloomberg's successor kept on the Health Department website) were intentionally repulsive. One famously showed nauseating blobs of fat pouring out of a soda bottle. People suffering through their daily commute often turned away, but the image was hard to forget.

Bloomberg also worked to make the city's air and water cleaner—his administration began phasing out the dirtiest heating oils (number 4 and 6 grades),[52] and the black smoke from buildings began to thin out, then virtually disappear. Bloomberg, the ex-engineer, got the city to commit $4.7 billion to complete a key part of a new water tunnel that was authorized nearly sixty years earlier to supplement Manhattan's aging underground network. "It's not sexy," the mayor admitted when he turned the ceremonial wheel to open the massive water pipes in 2013. "And nobody says thank you."[53]

Altogether there were more than one hundred health initiatives in the Bloomberg era—from more bike lanes and smoke-free zones and no trans fats and dozens of Green Carts bringing fresh produce to communities where it was hard to find even a fresh apple. *Scientific American* magazine asked whether all the Bloomberg programs made New Yorkers healthier. Their conclusion, "Yes, but it's complicated."[54] For all the good in Bloomberg's legacy, the rates of obesity and diabetes overall got worse during his twelve years in office. Still, that left such a wide array of improvements that even Bloomberg's highly critical successor, Bill de Blasio, was forced to mumble a little praise occasionally for the Bloomberg health agenda.

When the city's life expectancy increased three years, compared to a national average of 1.7 years, Bloomberg boasted, "If you want to live longer and healthier than the average American, then come to New York City."[55] More pointedly, as he promised New Yorkers complaining about his various restrictions on some of their favorite vices, "Just before you die, remember you got three extra years."

13

THE GEEK SQUAD

"This isn't just some stuff. This is the stuff that
makes a difference, day in and day out."
—*Bloomberg, on plans to make New York a digital city, 2011*

One bright October morning in 2005, the city's telephone operators suddenly began receiving bizarre calls to Mayor Bloomberg's 311 citizens' complaint line. Manhattan residents reported that the air outside didn't smell right. Instead of the normal odors of the big city, their neighborhoods smelled sweet, kind of like maple syrup. Veterans of 9/11 worried—weren't there some poison gases that smell like ripened fruit? Could this be some devious terrorist's cover for a deadly cloud? When it happened again a few days later, city officials assured the public that the odor was not dangerous. One sniffer scoffed that this had been a case of crazy Manhattan overreacting to the "Aunt Jemima wing of al Qaeda."[1]

Still, city officials wanted to know where the smell came from, just in case it was a prelude to something more dangerous. The city's experts on dangerous gas plumes (or radioactivity) helped out, as they mapped the locations of the 311 callers. They charted the winds for those days. They cross-checked and analyzed the data. And finally, the city confirmed what many New Yorkers had suspected all along—the smell was coming from New Jersey. The culprit was a "flavor enhancement" used by a "natural flavor" factory to turn a form of fenugreek into mock maple syrup. The odor had wafted innocently over the Hudson River to Manhattan.[2]

Bloomberg loved it. He loved the way his 311 line and the city's data nerds could figure out what was going on. "Given the evidence, I think it's safe to say that the Great Maple Syrup Mystery has finally been solved," he crowed, offering praise for his "smelling sleuths."

In far more important ways than tracking aromas from New Jersey, Mike Bloomberg would use the skills that made him a billionaire to help operate the big city. He wanted to be the data mayor. He wanted New York City to work as well as one of his machines. Outside city hall, this meant encouraging the new technology business to create "Silicon Alley," as DoubleClick, a company later bought by Google, tried to rename the Flatiron area of Manhattan. Soon, a cluster of tech start-ups would set up shop in the old manufacturing section of Brooklyn, and eventually Bloomberg would create a new graduate school, Cornell Tech on Roosevelt Island, to provide technological expertise for commercial, government, or nonprofit sectors in the city. But it was inside city hall where Bloomberg first began to use data to change the culture of his government.

If you came to him with a proposal, he wanted the numbers. He pounced on any weak details. He spotted holes in the worksheets. He redrew graphs—a graph should tell a story, he would say. He wanted new ideas and reforms to start immediately without baking in years of planning. And he wanted long-range, data-rich proposals for keeping the city on top in the future.

For the nation's largest city with its vast retro infrastructure, this was a massive undertaking, and Bloomberg and his army would succeed in important ways and bog down in others. Creating the 311 phone system was a triumph, yet he would struggle with modernizing the 911 telephone system that had become a giant tangle of warring interests among emergency responders, especially police and firefighters. (What other New

York politician would dare even try to make police and firefighters work better together, even for emergencies?) He would inherit and fail for years to recognize a major data scandal involving contractors building a new digital payroll system called CityTime for the entire city workforce. But overall, his aim was to make New York the "top-ranked digital city," and it would take years and billions of taxpayer dollars for Bloomberg and his people to drag much of the city government's technology into the twenty-first century.

When Bloomberg moved into city hall, aides groused that some computers could have been on display in the Smithsonian. Department systems could not talk to one another or get their latest information fast enough to an impatient public. A few experts warned the new mayor about the city's technical gaps. Bruce Bernstein, then president of the New York Software Industry Association, a trade group supporting information technologies, described the nest of networks as "one of the most complex information systems in the world." Also one of the oldest for an advanced city's not-so-advanced government.[3]

Pre-Bloomberg, there had been a few attempts to modernize the technology. The city, like most of the rest of the computerized world, nervously tried to prepare for the year 2000 when computers failed to go berserk as predicted in the Y2K frenzy. But as Bloomberg was dutifully touring agencies early in his first term, he was shocked to find that many in the outer boroughs didn't have email. That was also true, he soon learned, even for some in city hall.[4] And some systems were working so erratically that many of Bloomberg's new hires began using their own laptops to do their jobs. (Bloomberg, of course, had his own terminals set up at his central bull pen desk. And he kept his private email from his perch at Bloomberg LP throughout his twelve years as a public official.)

The Department of Information Technology and Telecommunications, which oversaw much of the city's computer world, barely functioned by Bloomberg standards. Insiders called it DoITT (Do-it), which some Bloomberg staffers quickly renamed "Don't do it." Bloomberg energized a dispirited DoITT; he became the "hammer," as one insider recalled,[5] and DoITT was no longer a sleepy outpost in the vast city bureaucracy. Gino Menchini, who was commissioner for DoITT during Bloomberg's first term, recalled how his agency went from a backwater, scrambling for funds, to a prime mission. "My biggest challenge was not selling technology but keeping up with Mike's expectations," Menchini said. "He represented a game changer in that respect."[6]

Bloomberg had 311 near the top of his to-do list, and he repeatedly promised New Yorkers that they would have two numbers to reach their government—911 for emergencies and 311 for everything else.[7] Idea maven Ester Fuchs of Columbia University remembered early in his first campaign when Bloomberg asked how a New Yorker would call or email or get in touch with their city. How did they know where to complain if the garbage wasn't picked up or the noise level had become unbearable? An aide handed Bloomberg a regular telephone book with a government section that included the city. You had to call one of those numbers and hope you would not be transferred, "ping-ponged" back and forth, or put on hold. Forever. "He was completely horrified," Fuchs recalled.[8]

The city still had at least forty separate call centers, an assortment of hotlines and customer help numbers, not to mention those eleven pages dedicated to the city government in the public phone book. Savvy New Yorkers forked over $20 for a small, green directory that had numbers and often names of every deputy and sub-deputy. The ordinary citizen was stuck waiting on hold.

Bloomberg dove right into this mess. His first budget, which cut funds to virtually every department including police, added funds for the city's technology. In his first State of the City speech in January 2002, he promised what most people thought was impossible—a "citizens' service center" that would allow people to reach the city by calling three digits—311. This was the toll-free number that the federal government had long ago reserved for nonemergency community services, and some cities like Chicago, population nearly 3 million, and Baltimore, with 640,000 people, had already started 311 service. But an easy, efficient way for 8 million New Yorkers to complain was widely considered little more than this amateur politician's fantasy.

Menchini, the city's chief information officer, remembered helping Bloomberg write the section of his budget speech about 311. But when the mayor gave it, he added a zinger. He said it would be up and running in a year. "I knew that was not in the prepared text," Menchini said, remembering how his colleagues started kicking the back of his chair. A year, huh? They laughed. Normally government takes a year to study the problem. At least. But that was a "Mike Bloombergism" and a key ingredient to his success—an extremely tight time frame. That meant everybody had to scramble, extra effort, extra hours. Menchini's DoITT went into hyperdrive, and the 311 system opened successfully in fourteen months.

To achieve a working 311 quickly took an astonishing level of organization—some of it by the mayor's own daughter, Emma Bloomberg. She faced early resistance—"DOT is stalling move," Emma wrote about the Department of Transportation on one committee report in December 2002.[9, 10] Everybody seemed to have a reason for delay—the default position in government that Mike Bloomberg often saw as failure.

Workers answering phones in some offices didn't want to change jobs, especially if their salary and benefits might freeze as a result. Turf battles surfaced, but the mayor of New York City has a lot of power, and Bloomberg had no trouble using it. He wanted this system now, he kept reminding his people. In the first year. No excuses.

As city officials scrambled to find ways to make it work, staff members toyed with marketing strategies, some of them apparently keyed to Bloomberg's peppery sense of humor. Suggestions for slogans included "All help and no attitude." One inside favorite for an operator's opening question to a New Yorker was "So, what's *your* problem?" (Vetoed, of course.)

The staff also looked at sixty different ways to name this new service. They ranged from "Call Liberty" to "EZ-Apple" to "This is NYC." Eventually it became known simply as 311, the city number for "everything but emergencies."[11] One important feature borrowed from other cities like Chicago was that a real human being would answer, even if that meant a slight delay.

Officially, 311 started operating on March 9, 2003. A new way to complain? New Yorkers caught on quickly. They could ask questions or, more frequently, grouse to an actual person paid to listen—about noise or garbage or even how new surveillance cameras were screwing up their television reception. More often, calls would be worth the city's time, like school closings or storm warnings or the one from a veteran from Oklahoma who had worked at Ground Zero and wanted to come back and plant a seedling somewhere in the city.

The mayor himself was one of the first callers, and after he carefully punched 311, an operator asked for his name. "Mike Bloomberg," the mayor replied, prompting the operator to ask how to spell that. "B-L-O-O," the mayor began as his aides burst out laughing. The mayor grinned and declared success. A live operator had answered and made sure his name was spelled right.[12]

A common complaint was noise—almost a thousand calls a day about booming construction sites or blaring music or whining air conditioners. The noise numbers were so strong that Bloomberg decided it was time to have a new law about the growing racket in his city, even a limit on the amount of time your dog could bark—five minutes at night, ten minutes in the day. "Most complaints about noise are not frivolous," Bloomberg said, citing the data from 311. He didn't want to stop construction or close down the local bar, he insisted, he just wanted to "turn down the volume,"[13] even for the Mister Softee ice cream trucks. This brought a new clamor—from parents of toddlers. So Bloomberg compromised. The jingle was allowed to jangle nerves while the truck was rolling through the streets. Once the truck stopped, the music was supposed to stop.[14]

What surprised Bloomberg and many of those computer-savvy aides around him was that there was plenty of raw data buried in the city's many departments. The problem was that too often nobody seemed to know how to use it. This, of course, was Bloomberg territory. He used 311 as an investigative and management tool. At morning meetings, he would carefully examine the weekly 311 reports, including the city's responses. If the garbage teams took too long in Staten Island and residents kept calling, Bloomberg noticed.

"He could see in those numbers whether any agency was performing," said Bill Cunningham, Bloomberg's press spokesman in his earlier days as mayor. "He called 311 himself a lot, even from his car—there are homeless people here, trash still there, and he would get his ticket and then follow up about it."[15]

There were plenty of examples of how Bloomberg demanded data to run his city, but Michael Flowers became one of his rock stars. A former prosecutor in the Manhattan district attorney's office, Flowers was originally hired to analyze why mortgage-backed securities had caused the meltdown during the Great Recession. He outgrew that job swiftly. Soon Bloomberg asked Flowers to become head of the Mayor's Office of Data Analytics, also known as the Mayor's Geek Squad.

Flowers surprised city insiders by going directly to Craigslist to find a group of mostly new college graduates he would soon call "the kids." They were techies, of course, and some had economics degrees. Flowers also looked for a creative side—one was a former music major. Another was a huge fantasy baseball expert.[16] The key prerequisite for the job— never think first about what was impossible. There were plenty of people in government to do that.

Flowers instructed the kids to soak up data and analyze it, but also to listen to the frontline experts and try to be humble about it. The inspectors in the field could smell a problem long before it reached the official complaint stage, and Flowers wanted to balance those gut instincts with hard data.[17]

When the Geek Squad began collecting and cross-pollinating the city's data, some of their work quickly became city legend. The fight against FOG—or, fats, oils, and grease in the sewers—was a constant urban battle. The "fatbergs," as giant globs of fat were sometimes called, caused more than half of the backups in city sewers.[18] So when the city's Department of Environmental Protection couldn't identify culprits pouring grease directly into the drains, they called in the Geeks. Instead of inspectors going door-to-door—or back door–to–back door—in hopes of catching somebody in the act, Flowers and Co. found data from the Business Integrity Commission. The small agency created in 2001 to investigate and control the criminal influences in the garbage and waste-hauling business[19] had been collecting a lot of formerly unnoticed details about which restaurants paid for private trucks to haul away their grease. Then the Flowers crew matched that data of those that didn't pay for the haulers with the city drains most often choked with FOG. They handed inspectors a list of potential dumpers, many of whom were quickly caught and ticketed for clogging the city's sewers.[20]

Bloomberg's Geeks also worked to discover the residential buildings that had been subdivided into firetraps, the "illegal conversions" hidden in homes and apartment buildings around the city. Finding these nests of renters and their unscrupulous landlords was far from easy. The buildings, tax, and housing preservation departments all used different ways to identify the same building. The police used its own mapping system. The fire department often identified a structure by its proximity to the nearest fire "call boxes."

The Flowers team started with a ton of building data—the thousands of registered properties in the city. They added complaints or comments from nineteen other agencies plus crime rates and the number of ambulance visits to specific sites. They followed inspectors around, and when one took a quick glance at a building and said no problems there, the Flowers team members asked why. When the inspector explained that the brickwork was new, he said it was an indication somebody was taking care of the building. Flowers found another knot of data—the agency that gave out permits to do brickwork. That went into the mix. The conclusions of the Geek Squad shocked even the old pros. When inspectors used the lists, they found violations severe enough to vacate a building rose by about 70 percent.[21]

The Flowers model sounded like a game plan taken straight from Bloomberg's desk. "They took massive quantities of data that had been lying around for years, largely unused after it was collected, and harnessed it in a novel way to extract real value,"[22] concluded one team of independent data experts who analyzed Bloomberg's data strategies.

The success of 311 gave Bloomberg confidence to take on a far more difficult task—modernizing and streamlining the emergency call system at 911. Early on, Bloomberg's team analyzed the patchwork and sometimes rickety 911 system that averaged eleven million calls a year and found that it "was the worst example of outdated technology" in the city.[23] It badly needed an update, but city experts warned the mayor that 911 would be far more difficult than 311. Getting the police, firefighters, and emergency workers and their unions to work together was a no-win task for any politician. As one adviser put it during a key meeting with the mayor, the unions would "park dead bodies on your doorstep if they don't like what's happening."[24] To Bloomberg, that sounded less like a warning than a challenge.

Before 911, many people had a list of emergency numbers by the phone—police, fire, ambulance, helpful neighbor. Or they simply dialed 0 and gambled that the operator knew what to do. The three-digit code 911 was established nationwide on January 12, 1968, and New York City soon replaced its seven-digit emergency number for calling the police station with 911. The system in New York for police steadily added new services—the fire department and emergency medical units—but the rivalries between these different branches seemed to grow more intense over the years. The police and firefighters in particular were the Sharks and Jets of emergency services, and they refused to share blame when anything went wrong or to cede control when somebody tried to fix the system. Previous mayors had tinkered with the problem or pretended the system was better than it was.

As a result, Bloomberg inherited a jerry-built 911 system that could barely cope with a real emergency. The police had been using a modified airline reservation created in 1969. The dispatching system was so creaky and unpredictable that it had to be shut down one hour every other week for maintenance. On occasion, dispatchers resorted to paper and pencil.[25]

The test that Bloomberg needed arrived at 4:10 p.m. on August 14, 2003,[26] when the lights across a steaming city began to flicker, then died altogether. Elevators shuddered to a halt. The subway froze and stoplights went dark. It would be the beginning of the Blackout of 2003, the city's worst loss of power since 1977, when widespread looting and arson and crime levels signaled a low point for an already depressed city.

Bloomberg, who had been in Brooklyn, rushed back to city hall, where the backup generators were roaring.[27] He called officials. He called the press. He spoke in what was, by then, a comforting monotone, this time heard only by any New Yorker who had a battery-powered radio: "The first thing that everybody should do is to understand that there is no evidence of any terrorism whatsoever," he said. Police would be at the big intersections, he said. Subway officials were plucking people out of steamy cars underground. He told people their evening events were probably canceled and that they needed to take it easy trying to get home. "With a lot of luck, later on this evening we will look back on this and say, 'Where were you when the lights went out?' But nobody will have gotten hurt."

Bloomberg and his security detail even walked a few yards away from city hall to the Brooklyn Bridge, to hearten those trudging home in the unrelenting heat. "Walk slowly," he said as temperatures hovered in the nineties. "Stay cool." "Walk slowly?" one woman complained. "We're going to get home around 10!"[28]

After most of the lights came back on seventeen hours later, Bloomberg ordered an inquiry, and the first details he saw were alarming. There were no clear emergency protocols for city hall officials. Children were stranded in recreation centers as parents without phones sat in traffic without stoplights. At least one major hospital had no Internet to access emergency data. City pools, which might have provided relief, were closed without electricity to circulate the water. The parks department welcomed residents and tried to keep them safe as they slept on the grass or on benches during the steamy night hours.

Most alarming of all, many callers to 911 sat too long on hold. Police reported that 911 received 132,000 calls that day—86,000 more than normal. The fire department, which normally took about 1,200 calls a day, received 6,646 calls and responded to 3,619 incidents. There were fifty-five serious fires, thirty-four of them caused by people resorting to candles.[29]

Bloomberg ordered a full report on how to improve the city's response. The task fell to Andrew Alper, then president of the city's Economic Development Corporation, and Susan Kupferman, director of the Mayor's Office of Operations. Within three months—a long time in business, a nanosecond in government—they reported that even with no mass trauma and no spike in crime, the 911 system had coped with six times as many serious fires and three times as many medical emergencies. A network of seven different dispatch centers and three dispatch systems "leads to an inefficient on-scene incident command structure." Some callers had to repeat their information three times in order to get the right kind of help.

Mike Bloomberg and his team vowed to fix it, but their plans for 911 were barely noticed by the city's press. Bloomberg announced his proposal on October 28, 2003, when there was a huge spray of cameras, a full house of reporters. They came, however, not to read a twenty-four-page report written by bureaucrats. The draw was the mayor's new Latin Media and Entertainment Commission chair—at the same event, the mayor announced that it was Jenny from the Block, Jennifer Lopez from the Bronx.

Almost nobody asked about 911.

Still, tucked in that document was a plan to iron out the many wrinkles and duplications of a system essentially run by three separate and often competing teams—the police, the firefighters, and the ambulance workers. It would be one of the biggest jobs of the Bloomberg era, and they almost got it done. Almost.

Bloomberg proposed consolidating and integrating all these call-taking services for an estimated cost of $1.3 billion. By 2007, the price tag had risen to $1.5 billion, with additional plans to add a new call center in the Bronx that would cost even more. This would give the city a backup facility if the primary one failed. But as redoing 911 kept getting delayed, the city's problems with 911 did not.

The Christmas blizzard of 2010 became another rough reminder of lapses in the emergency system. But the real problem that weekend was that nobody seemed to be in charge to declare a snow emergency. The mayor's plane was spotted in Bermuda for the holiday.[30] The deputy in charge, Stephen Goldsmith, was away in Washington, D.C., dealing with his own emergency marital problems. With no warning for private cars to stay off the streets, the ambulances and fire trucks could not get through. Streets in the outer boroughs, in other words, not Manhattan, went unplowed for days, and the mayor was forced to apologize. "We did not do as good a job as we wanted to do, or as the city has a right to expect," he said, three days after the blizzard. "We'll figure out what happened this time and try to make it better next time."[31]

Another weather disaster, another report. This one listed failures that sounded all too familiar. The 911 system "became overburdened with calls," and Bloomberg's advisers recommended that the mayor "accelerate" his plans for the new Emergency Communications Transformation Program, or ECTP, to reform 911.[32]

It would take a little over a year before Bloomberg announced "major milestones" for 911 NYC.[33] Consolidation of the services would work eventually, but it would cost $2.36 billion by the time Bloomberg left city hall.[34] There were still a few rough edges, but before he left office, Bloomberg boasted that for the first time in city history, all emergency call takers (police, fire, and medical personnel) were on "the same floor and operating on the same technology." This new organized force could handle fifty thousand calls per hour, forty times more than the average daily rate and nine times more than the peak call volume for 9/11.

Investigators for Bloomberg's successor, Bill de Blasio, spent a year looking into the cost increases for the new 911. Their report in 2015 was overseen by Mark Peters, de Blasio's campaign treasurer who had become head of the city's Department of Investigation. Peters said that after looking at 1.5 million documents and conducting fifty interviews, he found "persistent mismanagement," but "no overt criminal conduct."[35] Bloomberg, who had warned his former city staffers not to respond to his successor's insults, made an exception for the Peters report. Caswell Holloway, Bloomberg's former deputy mayor, issued a point-by-point response, labeling the de Blasio administration's charges as "untrue." The delays were understandable, given the human and technological complexities. And the increase in cost came when Bloomberg decided to add a backup system that certainly made sense after 9/11.[36]

What ultimately mattered was that the Bloomberg team upgraded 911 before they left in 2013.[37] And in the end, if Bloomberg did not perfect 911 in his city, he made it vastly more efficient than he had found it.

If there is one blot on Michael Bloomberg's record as the data mayor, it was his administration's failure to recognize that contractors who were supposed to be creating a new payroll system called CityTime were stealing from the city. What became known as the CityTime scandal was a massive case of an outside data contract gone berserk. New York's most famous prosecutor of the era, U.S. Attorney for the Southern District of New York Preet Bharara, would call it "perhaps the single largest fraud ever perpetuated on the city of New York."[38]

Bloomberg and his team often preferred getting outside contractors to do their work. It was a way of getting around city employees who too often said, "It can't be done that way." Or, "It can't be done that quickly."

Bloomberg's predecessor, Rudolph Giuliani, originally approved the CityTime contract with Science Applications International Corporation, known for their expertise in organizing payroll services for employees of the military and the intelligence agencies. The new system was designed to scan the hands of workers as they clocked in and out. The unions hated it. It was degrading, some argued. One union executive called it "a backdoor form of fingerprinting."[39] More to the point, the installation of

CityTime was supposed to cost about $63 million. The final bill, before the federal investigators and prosecutors got involved, was nearly $700 million.

Why didn't Bloomberg or his data-savvy team notice? Why didn't the city's comptroller, who sanctioned every increase in the costs of this contract, raise the alarm? To be sure, once Bloomberg's Department of Investigation realized the outrage, the city informed federal prosecutors that contractors had been stealing millions of dollars from the city. And when Bharara, then U.S. prosecutor in Manhattan, announced the outcome of the case, he said that Bloomberg's chief investigator, Rose Gill Hearn, had been "our extraordinary partner" in the matter. "Commissioner Hearn deserves enormous amounts of credit for her leadership in uncovering graft and corruption in the city," he said.[40] But that was later, after the graft and corruption had been going on for years.

Bharara managed to get the company to pay back more than $500 million—with most of it returned to the city of New York. Three of the contractors were convicted of bribery and fraud and sentenced to twenty years in prison. The contractor who helped federal investigators got three years probation. Two other perpetrators fled the country and were believed to be hiding in India. At the sentencing of the three main characters, U.S. District Judge George B. Daniels said that the CityTime scam was "the largest city corruption scandal in decades."[41]

In early 2011, sources within the Bloomberg administration had tried to pin the problem on a budget expert who kept assuring them all was okay. Another backup also failed—the city comptroller who was supposed to check on a mayor's contracts. Comptroller William Thompson's supporters would claim that Thompson had expressed concerns privately about CityTime. But during his eight years in the job, Thompson's office conducted 626 audits. Not one uncovered the fraud at CityTime.[42] The new comptroller, John Liu, elected in 2009, made CityTime a major issue.

Bloomberg, who valued his reputation as an honest man, was said to be furious in private. When the scope of the scandal was announced, he said, "We just have zero tolerance, absolutely zero tolerance for any kind of corruption whatsoever. And going forward, we've taken some steps to ensure this doesn't happen again."[43]

To his radio pal, John Gambling, on New York City's radio station WOR, Bloomberg did a better job of shouldering the blame. "You can't look everyplace. If you want to know how big projects have things that slip through the cracks, this is as good an example as you need," he said. But ever the cheerleader, Bloomberg also found some comfort. "We actually did a pretty good job here, in retrospect," he said. "We were lucky ... because with the fines and paybacks, the final price tag was $100 million and cheap at the price. And in the end it turned out because of the recovery [by Bharara] that we saved a lot of money."[44] He would talk about a "few bad apples," the ones that appear no matter who is in charge. "We actually did a pretty good job here, in retrospect," he kept saying as the issue came up again and again.[45]

To his critics, however, CityTime was an important warning about the limits of Michael Bloomberg's management style as adapted to government work. At his company, this system mostly worked. One former company executive described the way he ran Bloomberg LP:

"Mike is very results oriented. What that means is that *how* you get there is much less important than the result. When you work for a person like that you have much more freedom and discretion to make your goal ... and you have autonomy ... Mike gave you the freedom to reach your goal. It was very common for him to review an outcome and say, that's not the way I would have done it, but, hey, you got it done." But he was always watching warily, and "If he felt like the goal wasn't being met, he would parachute in and become a micromanager."[46]

That worked at his company, which had about 7,000 employees when he left for city hall in 2001 to be in charge of 300,000.[47] To do their work the Bloomberg way, his top city officials got more freedom. Obviously. They succeeded in important ways, but there were also times when Mayor Bloomberg needed to be a micromanager—to curb abuses at his police department, which caused so much personal distress in his city, or to save taxpayers money by doing a better job of monitoring the contractors for CityTime.

As he left office in 2013 and the CityTime consultants were being convicted of corruption charges, Bloomberg defended his record as "the cleanest administration in New York City's history."[48] City historians can certainly argue that point, but as one of his critics noted a few years later, "The main thing about the CityTime system is that it actually works."[49]

As mayor, Michael Bloomberg's goal was to make New York "the Nation's Leading Digital City."[50] To do that, he pushed to make it more open, accessible, and responsive. He used the mass of data to improve the way the city worked. His administration sidelined many of the rickety, outdated systems to make room for faster, more modern technology. And by the time he left, virtually every office had email.

The Bloomberg way was to put a lot more of the city online, to make the Geek Squad's data available and understandable for anybody with a phone or a computer. There would be hackathons and app contests—all efforts to figure out the best way to get New Yorkers in touch with their government and better ways to prod that government to respond. By the time Bloomberg left office, you could pay your water bill online and you could even see how much water you were using week by week. It cost the city $89 million to put 835,000 residences online, but you could figure out how much it cost for that relative who stayed a week and took forty-five-minute showers.

Even more important, the city spread its digital footprint to the latest favorite media outlets—at that point, Facebook, Twitter, Foursquare, and Tumblr. The Bloomberg teams wanted plenty of places for people to find news in case of an emergency. If the electricity went out, your city app would still work—at least for a while.

"This isn't just some stuff," Bloomberg said at the time. "This is the stuff that makes a difference, day in and day out." Still, the mayor didn't like all those extras personally. "I'm very old-fashioned," he said to the consternation of some of his younger techies. "I still use email." (That email would become controversial in later years when he failed to put it on the public record.)

Even more important for Bloomberg's world, the city was doing a better job of keeping up with the boom in private technology. When he signed off at city hall, New York City had nearly 7,000 high-tech companies with 100,000 jobs with an average salary of $118,600 compared to $79,500 average for everyone else. Venture capital firms invested $1.3 billion in high-tech in 2013 alone.[51] And the city was ready to provide more talent to these companies with Bloomberg's new graduate school on Roosevelt Island.

As the New York *Daily News* put it at the end of Bloomberg's time in office, "New York is Nerdville-USA."[52]

14

THAT PUBLIC
SCHOOL BUSINESS

"I was hired to make the schools better. Hold me responsible."
—Mike Bloomberg, 2003[1]

Michael Bloomberg ran for mayor of New York City in 2001 promising to fix the largest and most complex public school system in the country. It was hardly a novel pledge for city politicians who had long recognized that the system was a mess—an impenetrable bureaucracy and a management structure so tangled and slow that a frustrated Mayor Giuliani once suggested it "should be blown up." Most city politicians would only complain about the problem for 1,200 schools, 1.1 million students, and 80,000 educators. They could not, or would not, attempt to actually make the public education system work for so many students. Once again, Bloomberg vowed to be different. For him, the city's schools were much like a distressed and mismanaged enterprise that could not serve enough of its students, or customers, as some Bloomberg people liked to call them. For starters, no one was really in charge. Then there were too few good choices for students who were too easily shoved into a failing school in their neighborhoods. It soon became clear that Bloomberg's plan for city schools was nothing short of revolutionary.

A graduate of the public schools in his hometown of Medford, Massachusetts, Bloomberg was not an obvious advocate for public education. Both his daughters went to Spence, an elite academy in Manhattan. The children of most of his rich friends had also opted for expensive private institutions rather than the neighborhood school where your kid might be lucky and get a brilliant teacher, but could also get stuck with one who could dampen a child's curiosity for years to come.

Even so, public schools were at the very top of Bloomberg's list of city services that needed fixing, and Bloomberg knew that to throw out "the toxic stew of dysfunction,"[2] as he once called the system, first he needed control.

The new mayor had inherited a disorderly network of thirty-two elected community school boards overseen by a central board that had strings attached to virtually every local politician. It was an almost-perfect recipe for stagnation, with an average graduation rate of 50.8 percent to prove it. Yet, it had served the political establishment well—if nobody was really in charge, then nobody was ever to blame.

Any major changes—like abolishing disruptive school boards or certainly taking control of the entire system—had to go through Albany, and that had been a problem for mayors who wanted to be in charge, going back to Abe Beame in the 1970s. Bloomberg's predecessor, Rudy Giuliani, had tried, but the state crowd, many of them tucked comfortably in the pocket of the teachers union, refused and refused, just as state Republicans would make it hard years later for Bloomberg's pro-union successor, Bill de Blasio, who was at first granted control over schools for only one stingy year at a time.

Bloomberg's contributions to Republican lawmakers would help in Albany, but for Democrats, he needed support from the teachers. And the teachers needed a new contract. On June 6, 2002, Bloomberg and

Randi Weingarten, the head of the teachers union, announced a two-year contract, with overall raises of 16 to 22 percent and the biggest increase in starting salaries.[3]

A few days later he was in control of the largest public school system in the country.[4] The Albany crowd gave him seven years.[5] That would nearly get him through two terms, and it was a clear signal from New York's political veterans that the city's troubled school system was now Mike Bloomberg's problem.

Merryl Tisch, an education activist who became the powerful chancellor for the New York State Board of Regents (2009–2016), knew Bloomberg socially. She also knew Albany. "They were personally intrigued by him, and I think kind of mesmerized," she said later.[6] (It certainly did not hurt with a Republican governor and Republicans in control of the state senate that he was considered an easy touch for contributions to their many campaigns.)[7, 8]

A key player in Bloomberg's success, Tisch remembered once asking him why he wanted school control so badly. "'Cause they wouldn't give it to Rudy," he replied, making one of his jokes that often edged very close to reality. Then he added, "The only way I can succeed turning around a complicated enterprise is by having the ultimate responsibility."[9]

Bloomberg would exert his power in large and small ways. Once, when a panel of education experts under his control refused to change the way students were promoted from grade to grade, he simply had the dissenters removed and replaced with people who saw things his way.[10] Bloomberg was sending a message about his management style, in case it was needed. When the head man spoke, you listened, and if you disagreed and couldn't convince him of your view, it was time to go.

"This is what mayoral control is all about," Bloomberg said at the time. "In the olden days, we had a board that was answerable to nobody." He went on, "Mayoral control means mayoral control, thank you very much." He added, "They are my representatives, and they are going to vote for things I believe in."

Any questions?[11]

• • •

Once the mayor had control, Bloomberg moved to step two—closing the old Board of Education. For seasoned educators there was a standing joke that involved the unwelcome appearance of a school official who said, "Hello, I'm from Central, and I'm here to help." [12] "Central" was the central Board of Education's office at 110 Livingston Street in Brooklyn, and it was such a dense bureaucratic hive that only an outsider could have dismantled it. One former educator suggested activating the building's fire alarm and then locking the doors to keep everybody out. [13] Shortly after he took office, Bloomberg essentially pushed the alarm button.

The new mayor stunned the education community when he suddenly announced that he planned to move the city's education bureaucracy from Brooklyn to the nineteenth-century Tweed Courthouse behind city hall. The Tweed had been an embarrassment since Boss William Magear Tweed, the old Tammany Hall boss, had it built with bribes and kickbacks and other schemes that cost the city $13 million in 1878—about $178 million in 2002 dollars. [14] Giuliani had helped renovate the building for another $89 million with the idea of using it for the Museum of the City of New York.

A museum? No way, Mike Bloomberg decreed. It would be the headquarters for education, just a short walk from his city hall bull pen. There would be a real, live school in the grandiloquent Tweed fortress, a school that would remind administrators "why they have jobs, what they're supposed to focus on," he insisted. "And if every day they see children getting an education, that will remind them when they go upstairs what their mission is." [15]

Bloomberg would use the move to great advantage. He would pare forty district superintendents down to ten and eliminate nearly 75 percent of the jobs at the Brooklyn headquarters, essentially ordering an army of former teachers back to the classrooms. Many retired instead. [16] The cuts included workers of all levels, from top administrators to ten "window shade repairers." [17]

Step three for Mayor Bloomberg was even more important—finding a new chancellor. The task of finding someone to take over the New York City schools had often been so difficult that, as veterans often put it, "nobody who was smart enough to do the job was dumb enough to take it."[18]

His staff proposed big names in education, Paul Vallas who ran Chicago schools, chancellors in Cleveland and Atlanta, even Donna Shalala, former U.S. secretary of Health and Human Services.[19]

Bloomberg was not looking for an educator, as it turned out. He wanted somebody tough enough to execute his radical reforms. When a friend suggested Joel Klein, Bloomberg liked the idea of a supersmart lawyer who would have to be lured away from a very cushy job as chairman of the American operations of Bertelsmann media group.[20] Klein was a grasshopper-thin man whose nasal Queens accent had survived Columbia, Harvard, and the Justice Department in Washington, D.C. He was known for outsmarting even Bill Gates in a seminal anti-trust case against Microsoft. Bloomberg liked the idea. Anybody who could take on Microsoft could take on the city school system. His record as an educator? *New York* magazine wrote that Klein's "experience in the education field seems to consist chiefly of—well, of having gone to school."[21]

"Jesus Christ wasn't available," as Bloomberg told one interviewer after the stunning appointment of Klein. "And I thought Joel was smart and tough as nails for a job that really required that."[22]

Shortly after the announcement stunned and horrified New York's public school establishment, David Yassky, then a city councilman, ran into Bloomberg at city hall. Yassky told the mayor that he had once worked for Klein and that he was one of the ten smartest people he had ever met. Bloomberg grinned, his classic impish grin, and whispered, "And nobody saw it coming." That jazzed him, Yassky said. "He liked to surprise people and show that something people don't think is going to work, it works."[23]

Bloomberg approached education reform like a businessman. He wanted a market-based system, where customers (i.e., students and their parents) would be able to choose the best schools possible. What he and Klein envisioned was a kind of educational emporium where students, especially high school students, could pick and choose among public schools. Then, with considerable push from his administration, the worst schools—the failing ones—would wither and die like any business that failed to serve its clientele.

To die-hard supporters of public education and the unions, the term "choice" was conservative code for dismantling much of the public system in favor of private, charter, and parochial schools. Bloomberg insisted his idea of choice was different. He wanted students to choose among *public* school options, including well-regulated public charter schools. He insisted that he saw "choice" as a way to enhance the public school system, not destroy it.

Never one to aim low, Bloomberg promised what most people thought was impossible:

"If four years from now reading scores and math scores aren't significantly better," he said in 2001, "Then I will look in the mirror and say that I have been a failure. I've never failed at anything yet, and I don't plan to fail at that." [24]

In his first days as chancellor, Klein learned how the old system had worked. Much of it ran on old-fashioned political clout. One assemblyman quietly suggested to Klein, "Protect this principal's job, and I'll protect you politically." [25] Another politician, a borough president, couldn't get certain children placed in certain schools and fumed at the new chancellor, "Fuck you. Why can't we work together?" [26]

Klein ignored the meddlers and began to carry out the Bloomberg list of priorities. He would close failing schools, add choices, streamline the bureaucracy, give principals more power, try to reward good teachers, and sideline most of the "lemons," the system's term for those who could not do the job but bounced from school to school. Yet, he would not earn much love for these efforts. Nobody likes the disruptor.

Closing the failing schools, the "dropout factories," as they were so often called, would stir the most anger from students, parents, teachers, and even former students. Alumni of these troubled high schools, even the worst ones, rallied to keep the doors open. One particularly raucous example involved Jamaica High School in Queens.

Jamaica had once been a star in the city's public school system. Luminaries like Stephen Jay Gould, Art Buchwald, and former U.S. attorney general John Mitchell were alumni. But, by the time Bloomberg was in charge, Jamaica High's glory days were long gone. The school of four thousand students had a graduation rate far below 50 percent, and it ranked in the bottom 7 percent of the city's high schools. That record did not stem the outrage. One particularly angry alumnus was George Vecsey, an author and sports columnist for the *New York Times*. Vecsey compared Joel Klein to Cambodia's genocidal dictator Pol Pot, arguing that "The city destroyed a piece of history because of its own failure."[27]

Jamaica High's same grand building, a Georgian revival–style structure with columns and a great lawn suitable for a great school, became four specialized high schools: Jamaica Gateway to the Sciences, a math and science academy with about 400 students and a four-year graduation rate of 91 percent by 2016; Queens Collegiate, a college preparatory school with about 650 students and a graduation rate of 77 percent; Hillside Arts and Letters Academy for arts and music, with about 420 students and a graduation rate of 81 percent; and the High School for Community Leadership, with 357 students and a graduation rate of 84 percent.[28]

Closing a school also caused a backlash among the teachers because it gave Bloomberg and Klein an opportunity to cut the staff. The new school principals could hire teachers who fit their new programs—violin teachers for the music academies, computer experts for the data centers, et cetera.

School closings so angered local communities that Bloomberg's successor decided he wanted to spend more than $700 million to improve them instead. That didn't work, as it turned out, and Mayor Bill de Blasio eventually canceled his expensive program to prop up failing schools in 2019.[29]

Meanwhile, the Research Alliance for New York City Schools at New York University was one of the first to begin assessing how closing these big schools by Bloomberg had affected the students. They found "meaningful benefits" for those who went on to the smaller schools. Not surprisingly, those who stayed behind as their school withered and died fared about the same as those at other failing schools still operating in the system.[30]

Bloomberg and his education team would eventually close 164 failing schools and create 654 new ones, including 173 charter schools. "To tie this to Bloomberg and his philosophy about how this is all supposed to work, this is a market process," explained Sean Patrick Corcoran, associate professor of economics and education policy at New York University. "They saw themselves as facilitating this marketplace and making sure people had enough information to make choices."[31]

Still, choice was not a simple concept for the city's teenagers, not like picking Nikes over Adidas. Eighth graders were required to apply to twelve high schools as options, listing their preferences. Those possibilities were advertised in a 626-page directory—online or printed out to be about the same size as their grandparents' old Sears, Roebuck catalog. They had to slog through the school data to pick, say, a high school for contemporary arts and a collegiate academy in the Bronx and then ten others. Then the administration would let them know which school would be theirs.

This array of choices, like those in any bazaar, put a great deal of pressure on the consumer—in this case a student already coping with all the stress of hormones and social media. For many, it worked far better than the old system. For some, who had no parent or guidance counselor or friend to help, the tyranny of choice was more like a crapshoot. It was easier for too many of them to simply stay in the neighborhood and live with a school that offered far less.[32]

Just as Bloomberg was leaving city hall, Corcoran and other NYU researchers issued a critical report[33] showing that, despite the efforts to expand options for all students, "low-achieving students attended schools that were lower performing," and that this was no accident. These students tended to pick those schools as the less challenging ones—i.e., the easier ones—when they made their high school choices.[34]

Michael Bloomberg ardently promoted public charter schools as another option, especially for lower-income kids. Public charters, launched in New York in 1998 by Republican governor George Pataki, were independent, not-for-profit public schools set up to have more freedom to experiment with ways to educate. In New York, the unions had little say over these schools, but unlike in some other states, the charters were closely monitored to make sure they were doing the job.

When Bloomberg arrived there were seventeen charter schools in the city. Unions and other groups worked to disparage the charter movement, arguing that they picked off the better students, disciplined too many kids, got rid of those who couldn't keep up, and drained money from the main public school system. But every year, the charter schools advocates claimed, about 50,000 students[35] languished on their waiting lists after entering, and then losing, in lotteries to go to such schools as Success Academy or the Harlem Children's Zone or KIPP academies, some of the best-performing charter schools in the country. By the time Bloomberg left, the 183 charters served more than 72,000 students—nearly 80 percent of whom qualified as poor enough for the free lunch program.[36]

Public charter schools were supposed to be laboratories, experimental classrooms providing guidance about what worked and, of course, what didn't. One positive assessment of Bloomberg's city charters came from Stanford's Center for Research on Education Outcomes, which concluded in their 2013 report that the city's charter school students performed far better than those in similar public schools. The Stanford analysts were concerned that reading scores for charter schools were sliding in some schools, but overall, it was as if the charter students had an additional month of reading instruction and five months more in math than those in the regular public schools.[37]

These charter students were often poor, mostly Hispanic and African American. But they shared one important advantage. Each student had that parent or grandparent or guardian or friend or adviser—in short, an advocate—who worked hard to get them into those schools. This was clearly a problem for the many kids who didn't have an adult at their side or for those who were homeless and shifted from address to address. And even for those who had all the support, the lotteries to determine who could go to these schools became truly heartbreaking when a student's name was not called.

Not all charters were successful, of course, even when they were encouraged and carefully vetted. Some failed like the charter school anointed to be a showcase in the Tweed Courthouse near city hall. The Ross Global Academy eventually closed in 2011 after the city and state cited its poor performance.[38]

Some critics argued that the charter schools suspended too many students—their way of culling the troublemakers and sending them back as another problem for the regular public schools.[39] Critics also questioned whether charters got rid of those students with emotional or learning problems who had accidentally won their lottery.

Bloomberg didn't waver. The main idea behind these public/private schools was basic to the Bloomberg ethos—competition. They added a few more kiosks to the city's education market. For Bloomberg, "school choice is an important way to hold schools accountable for success because when people vote with their feet you know that it's real, and it's pretty obvious which direction they are going."[40]

If closing failed schools and introducing more choices for students was the basis for Bloomberg's educational reform, dismantling the old power structure would be both basic and disruptive.

At the same time, word got out that Bloomberg's school system would be an exciting place to work. Instead of slogging your way up from the lowest ranks to the top, reform-minded educators were welcomed by Bloomberg and Klein if they were ready to experiment with new ways to make the system work better. David Weiner, who worked as a principal and later as an administrator in charge of a teacher evaluation system, said New York became a haven for energetic and innovative educators.

It was a vibrant, exciting, "kinda sexy" place to work, Weiner said shortly after Bloomberg left office and Weiner moved on to help raise private funds for public schools.[41]

Bloomberg liked to boast that he was keeping the good teachers in city classrooms. Before he arrived, an estimated twelve thousand of eighty thousand teachers either left (often to work for better salaries in the suburbs) or retired every year, and the city had trouble filling those slots with certified teachers. "Today," he boasted in 2008, "we have 50-odd thousand teachers a year from around the country who apply to teach in the New York City schools system, and we have only about 5,000 vacancies."[42] It helped, of course, that Bloomberg had eventually raised starting teachers' salaries by a healthy 43 percent.[43]

Bloomberg and Klein also shifted more power to the principals at the city's growing number of schools. A new Leadership Academy trained up to seventy principals a year in management skills, often over a short summer course. The academy's programs "focused on developing the principal as CEO, placing particular emphasis on the use of data to determine and manage the improvement process."[44] Very, very Bloomberg.

Klein also offered principals a different deal. They could have far more control over their schools, more freedom to hire and to budget for their students, but in return, they would sign five-year contracts, promising to improve student achievements.

It was quite a gamble, and some in the principals' union advised against it. If the school didn't improve, the principal went on the "ladder of consequences,"[45] a form of probation that sounded like a medieval torture device. A first-year failure meant the principal needed a new plan. The second year, the principal could be removed. The third year on the ladder, the school could be closed altogether and the principal might even return to teaching.

Klein boasted the contracts were a success because more than three hundred principals agreed that "If I don't hit the ball, they'll be sending me to the minors." [46] Not all principals were ready for such independence and the risk that went with it, [47] and Bloomberg's successor quickly moved back to a system that had less independence school by school and more control from above.

The move to the Tweed Courthouse and the major trimming of the bureaucracy also helped Bloomberg save money and redirect it into schools. The budget for city schools grew from $11.4 billion to $19.9 billion while he was mayor, plus he invested $27 billion in new schools and other capital improvements. [48] And the billionaire mayor reached into his own pocket on occasion to fill in the gaps. He used his Fund for Public Schools, a nonprofit corporation, to add part-time consultants to the department. He gave money for a makeup date as a second chance for those who did not do well on a first try on the exam for the city's best high schools, and he provided money to help train principals, to name a few ways he used his private wealth and connections to help his public schools.

Of course, the Bloomberg team also depended on data, which would not always work out to the mayor's advantage. An early analysis of a massive school system by McKinsey & Company found lots of paper, few emails, and a system that took months to find out the number of kids who had a school lunch on a specific day. [49] Klein found that solid data was "a shockingly rare commodity," and not simply because of outdated technology. [50] He recalled early in his term innocently asking which teachers were doing well in schools with the most students from low-income families. The reply: "I can't do that. [51] The union doesn't let us do things like that." Klein spent most of the rest of his term pressuring for numbers in a world that viewed data as sterile and unproductive.

Test scores for students became a particular embarrassment for Bloomberg and Klein. At first student scores on state tests soared from 39 percent of students proficient in several grades in English in 2002 to 69 percent in 2009. Math scores were even better—up from 37 percent to a stunning 84 percent. When the state scores came out, Bloomberg declared that this success was "nothing short of amazing."[52] As it turned out, it was very short of amazing.

When the state made the tests harder and less predictable, 42 percent of students in the city were proficient in English and 54 percent in math. Better, but certainly not amazing. And after Bloomberg left office in 2013, data in the city's education department became another unacceptable four-letter word.

The relationship between Mike Bloomberg and the teachers union was promising in the beginning. At first Randi Weingarten, then the forceful and media-savvy head of the United Federation of Teachers, stood shoulder to shoulder with Bloomberg, who promised more money for her members. Bloomberg even joked in 2008 that when he proposed performance-based bonuses, Weingarten's response was "Well, in New York City, we've already got performance pay and that's why the Mayor makes a dollar a year."[53]

Such public cheerfulness lasted while Bloomberg increased teachers' salaries and benefits,[54] which brought in more applicants and slowed the stampede of good teachers to the suburbs. Bloomberg praised the way Weingarten cooperated on the "third-rail" issues, like trying to eliminate the so-called "rubber rooms," where ineffective or troublesome teachers were exiled while the system tried to fire them.

Behind the scenes, it was not so cozy. Weingarten's relationship with Chancellor Klein grew more acidic with every shake-up. She increasingly saw an amateur meddling with, not fixing, the problems at hand. And overall, she concluded that the Mike Bloomberg years were a distraction, a series of lost opportunities and wasted time.

"I like the guy," she said years later about Bloomberg himself. "We still like and respect each other," but, but, but, but. Pushed to come up with something positive about the Bloomberg education era, she paused, then praised the ex-mayor for recognizing that teachers should be considered professionals. They should stand as a solid part of the middle class, which meant more pay. "I worked with many a mayor who would not have recognized that need."[55]

Bloomberg did pay better salaries. But he wanted to pay even more to the best teachers. Merit pay was generally against the union code—their question was who was qualified to pick the "best" teachers? Weingarten's United Federation of Teachers and Bloomberg agreed to a compromise announced in 2007 for about two hundred "highest needs" schools. Instead of determining pay teacher by teacher the way Bloomberg's company would decide employee by employee, a compensation committee at every school (two school leaders and two union representatives) would decide how to parcel out funds.[56]

Well, that didn't work. Teachers weren't motivated by the extra money since the committees almost always decided to share the bonuses with every teacher, good, mediocre, or awful.[57] Bloomberg liked to say they tried some things that worked, and when they didn't, he was not afraid to admit it.[58] This program was a good example, and after $56 million in uninspiring bonuses, he canceled it.[59]

Bloomberg seemed to have a special gift for infuriating teachers. Once, when speaking to students at the Massachusetts Institute of Technology in 2011, he mused about how he would run the ideal school system: "If I had the ability, which nobody does really, to just design the system and say, ex cathedra, this is what we're going to do, you would cut the number of teachers in half, but you would double the compensation of them, and you would weed out all the bad ones and just have good teachers. And double the class size with a better teacher is a good deal for the students."[60]

When Bloomberg got back to the city, teachers were fuming. Understandably. Half of them were bad? Bigger class sizes?

Such comments only added to the simmering anger among teachers, especially those active in the union. Accustomed to hearing praise about how they had sacrificed their lives for the next generation, teachers were increasingly irritated that their worth was being judged more and more by data and by test scores and by a cold, rich mayor.

During Bloomberg's final years running the city, his relationship with the union was a lot closer to open warfare. Randi Weingarten was the kind of tough negotiator who could manage an unruly union crowd but could also survive a social dinner uptown. She wooed the media and had friends at every level in government and finance. But by Bloomberg's third term, she had moved up to become president of the American Federation of Teachers in Washington. Her replacement was Michael Mulgrew, a muscular negotiator who could turn on all the charm of a nightclub bouncer.

A Catholic school graduate who once apprenticed as a carpenter before he became a vocational education teacher, Mulgrew always seemed ready to box rather than negotiate with the well-heeled crowd at Mike Bloomberg's city hall. Or file a lawsuit. Mulgrew's teachers union joined the NAACP to sue the city over what they saw as Klein's destructive methods of closing schools. At one point, the courts required the city to have more public hearings and community input before they shut down the big schools and replaced them with smaller ones (and, of course, sidelined many teachers in the process).[61] The case went back and forth in the courts, but in the end, the Bloomberg team still managed to close 164 schools (and open 654 including 173 charters).[62]

One confrontation in this era was particularly intense. When a local radio station, WNYC, and the *New York Times* submitted a Freedom of Information request to see the test scores of students, identifying the teachers in each case, the union leaders were furious. But Bloomberg's administration handed over the data to the press. At one point, WNYC reported that the Bloomberg people had tipped off the press to request the test scores naming each teacher. Bloomberg himself was unrepentant. "We should have all of the data out there."[63]

After that, Bloomberg's relations with the union went from frosty to glacial. The increasingly bitter conflict provided an easy path for a pro-union Democrat to replace Bloomberg in 2014, to clean out Bloomberg's administration and roll back many of his reforms.

It would be hard to criticize Mike Bloomberg and Joel Klein for trying to shake up and reorganize New York City's Byzantine and lethargic school system. The problem for many was that there was shake-up after shake-up, with too little time to recover.

"Slow down and consolidate," advised education experts from the American Institutes for Research, a nonpartisan social science organization. The rapid pace of change and change and more change made educators worry that no one really knew what was happening. Researchers for the institutes suggested rather gently in 2011 that the mayor and his chancellor should "resist the temptation to continually tinker with the tools, even if they perceive the changes as clear improvements."[64]

Hunter College education expert Joseph Viteritti also wrote about attempts to upend the old bureaucracy. "By the time Klein got to the third reorganization, educators and parents were confused. They wondered if Klein and his team knew what they were doing." He concluded, "The result was chaos."[65]

That view infuriated Bloomberg alumni. "The thing that characterized the Bloomberg era was an openness to try new things on behalf of the students. If they benefitted, it continued. If they didn't, we would try something else. Several stages—later stages—contradicted earlier stages," countered Eric Nadelstern, one of the most dynamic and outspoken leaders in Bloomberg's education department.[66]

Asked about how he and the mayor dealt with such criticisms and even failure, Klein chuckled and remembered how the phone would ring at 6:00 a.m. with a very unhappy mayor on the line. "There were the stupid things like changing the bus routes in the middle of the winter," Klein said, grimacing as he thought about the students left standing in the snow, the blast of phone calls from irate parents. "It's like the old Ed Koch line [borrowed from La Guardia, no doubt]. When I make a mistake, it's a beaut.

"The way you always deal with Mike—and this is so Mike—is that you go to him. He wants to know everything. You tell him this is going to be a painful period. He obviously was not happy with us. He says, 'What were you thinking. Or were you thinking?' That kind of stuff. But then he backs you. He's very good about saying, look this was the right move at the wrong time, or something like that."[67]

And if it doesn't work? You change it, Klein said. "In the past in the field of education, when we have something that's not working we put more resources into it; whereas, in the real world, when something's not working, you usually put in fewer resources." Expand and move money to the programs that are successful, not the ones that are struggling. It was a standard business practice.

One problem for Bloomberg was that his control of schools began to run out in 2009. The crowd of state politicians, who lost clout to Bloomberg and Klein, were ready to take some of it back when Klein and Bloomberg returned to Albany. Klein wanted a four-year extension of control, and the teachers union, whose leaders had begun to see Klein as a mortal enemy, were ready to fight.

Rather than deal with such a political difficulty, New York's state lawmakers did what they often do in such cases—nothing. They simply allowed the law to expire after its seven-year run. Political leaders in the city scrambled to fill a sudden void by reestablishing a makeshift board of education. A furious Bloomberg called several legislators cowards for not voting, and even labeled one "meshugenah," a Yiddish term for someone who's completely bonkers.

One lawmaker shot back that the mayor was "treating us like we're some people on his plantation." Another, Senator Hiram Monserrate, called him "the Bernie Madoff" of education. (That was the same Hiram Monserrate who was thrown out of the State Senate a few months later for beating up his girlfriend.)[68] Finally, the Senate returned to Albany a month after the law had expired and approved the bill to give Bloomberg back his power. The reconstituted Board of Education that met only once for nine minutes evaporated, to the relief of the mayor,[69] who continued to control the schools for the rest of his time in office.

• • •

As criticism of Klein mounted, the mayor and Klein realized that it was time for the chancellor to go. Klein had become a liability, and like any drastic reformer, he had made too many enemies. "Did he stir things up?" Bloomberg said after announcing Klein's departure. "You betcha. That was the job, and the great beneficiaries of that stirring were our children."[70] But aides saw that Bloomberg was also unhappy that Klein couldn't do a better job of touting his success in improving the schools. By late 2010, Bloomberg felt the schools needed a better salesman. Or a saleswoman. His pick, apparently a spur-of-the-moment decision, turned out to be a disaster.

Whatever her credentials as the former head of the *USA Today* newspaper and the longtime president of Hearst Magazines (*Cosmopolitan*, *Esquire*, *Elle*, etc.), Cathie Black was not qualified to run one of the nation's most complicated school systems. Merryl Tisch, the state chancellor, was aghast when she learned about Black, and she forced Bloomberg to install a respected educator, Shael Polakow-Suransky, as a kind of shadow chancellor. Black scrambled for support from her many friends in the media. Email exchanges show a frantic effort to get Ivanka Trump, Suze Orman, Deborah Norville, Nora Ephron, and Gloria Steinem to sign letters of support. She wanted Oprah to provide a good quote to the *Daily News*. In an email to Gayle King, later a CBS morning news anchor and Oprah's best friend, Black sounded frantic. "All of this is coming down to the wire," she bleated. Asking King to help with "a brief, exclusive call with Adam Lisberg of the *Daily News* in which Oprah would offer her support."[71]

Even Oprah couldn't help, as it turned out. Insiders complained that Black wasn't prepared to dig in and learn the details. And some of her meetings with parents made matters worse. During one session in Lower Manhattan, parents were complaining about crowded schools when Black said, "Could we just have some birth control for a while?" Angry parents didn't see the joke.

And during one particularly noisy session as parents protested the closing of a neighborhood school, she provoked a loud "Awww" from the crowd when she pleaded for sympathy. In response, she returned the "Awww" for the television cameras. She looked like a society matron peering down her nose at those poor unfortunates who were not rich enough to send their children to the city's private academies.

Most parents and teachers started counting the days until she left. When she did, 95 days after taking the job, Bloomberg said, "I take full responsibility for the fact that this has not worked out as either of us had hoped or expected." Then he announced that the new chancellor would be Dennis Walcott, a veteran educator who had worked hard as a deputy mayor to promote Bloomberg's education agenda. The next two years would be quiet by comparison.

What had stunned people around the city was how quickly the mayor had chosen Black, how little advice or counsel he had taken from those around him. Was this the hazardous side of relying on those lightning-fast instincts, the Salomon broker who pushed the "Buy" button, who often saw success come in mere seconds? When the gut speaks, you listen. But sometimes, of course, the gut is wrong.

Much later, Bloomberg was meeting guests at his foundation when he suddenly began talking about the Black fiasco. "I want you to know that Cathie Black gave up an awful lot to do that job. Some of those boards . . . they earn $250,000 a year." He paused for a breath, then added, "Once Mort and Rupert turned against her, I knew." That is, once Mort Zuckerman's *Daily News* and Rupert Murdoch's *New York Post* turned against her, she had to go. He sounded irritated, mostly at himself, for this obvious chip in his legacy.[72]

How did he do as CEO of the largest public education system in the country? Even if Bloomberg's successor had picked education officials who spurned all things Bloomberg, he streamlined a sluggish bureaucracy and made improvements for many students. The abysmal four-year graduation rate that had stalled for years at around 50.8 percent as Bloomberg arrived rose to 66 percent by the time he departed, with even higher graduation rates in the new smaller schools.[73]

Independent research had begun to validate the push for these smaller schools. One study from researchers at New York University, Syracuse University, and Arizona State University concluded that "the introduction of small schools improved outcomes for students in all types of schools, large, small, continuously operating and new. Small school reform lifted all boats."[74]

The big "drop-out factories," as the *Times* editorials often called those high schools with three thousand or more students, had graduation rates of 62.2 percent, better but still too low. Students at smaller high schools of about four hundred students had graduation rates of 71.6 percent, or sometimes higher. Most graduated in four years, not five, and many went on to college. For young black men, 42.3 percent went from a small school to college, as opposed to the control group of 31 percent.[75]

Bloomberg had succeeded in adding choice for public school students in New York City.[76] Maybe it was not the full cafeteria the businessman/mayor had envisioned, but there were many more possibilities for many more students. He introduced accountability practices and tried to find better ways to assess teachers' skills in the classroom. He and Klein pared back the stultifying bureaucracy allowing successors to start from a simpler bureaucratic base. (It's always easier to add layers of people than subtract them.) And most important of all, he took control of the entire system, boasting about any progress, but, in a way that was almost unheard of for a politician, also shouldering the blame when things went wrong.

His efforts resulted in educational reforms that were "among the most ambitious of any large urban system in the country," as one important group of education experts found toward the end of his time as mayor.[77] His failures meant that no future mayor or chancellor would try those particular options, and his successes were far more modest than he had hoped. But primarily because he took responsibility for the schools and put his emphasis on the students—or the customers for this massive enterprise—Michael Bloomberg left the nation's largest public school system better off than he found it.[78]

Were there still problems? Plenty. Union leaders had a long list. Bloomberg moved too fast for some communities, and he and Klein stubbornly refused to acknowledge much of the criticism about the upheaval created by his reforms. The reliance on test scores became an embarrassment when tests were made more difficult and scores dropped. Graduation rates went up, but too many students needed extra help in college or at a new job. His choice of Klein and later Cathie Black sent a message that he valued noneducators more than those who had dedicated their lives to the classroom.

One of his strongest critics, Diane Ravitch, saw Bloomberg as a destructive force killing neighborhood schools and giving charter schools an unfair edge, as opposed to the needy students left behind. "Managerialism without experience," she called it.[79] When a new mayor was elected and named an educator as the new chancellor, Ravitch celebrated. "The era of punishing, blaming and shaming professional educators is over . . . This is a great turn of events, not only for New York City but the nation."[80]

Despite any missteps, the mayor would always emphasize that his highest priority was the students. He made that view especially clear one day in 2007 when the teachers union and the newspapers were railing about his latest upheaval. He attacked the teachers union for trying to roll back his reforms. He took aim at the newspapers that criticized him daily. He even compared those naysayers with narrow interests to the National Rifle Association, leaving open the question about whether he was including the teachers union in that group.

Then, when one reporter asked whether he classified everybody as being either "with us or against us," the mayor exploded. Wagging a finger at the journalist to emphasize every word, Bloomberg raised his voice to full volume.[81]

"No! No! No!" he said as a few of his supporters applauded. "You're either with the children or against the children. With 'us' doesn't matter."[82]

15

OFF HOURS

"What's great about golf, it's just about you."
—*Bloomberg, about playing with Tiger Woods, 2018*

By the time he was an international figure about midway through his years as mayor, Mike Bloomberg's image was fixed in the public eye as the businessman-mayor in a suit, often a dark $2,000 suit, white shirt with either a purple tie, as in Mike Bloomberg, the independent, or later, a bright green tie, as in Mike Bloomberg, the environmentalist.

Mostly hidden from public view were the times when the mayor had on helicopter earphones and his hands on the controls of his favorite flying machine. Or the times when he could be seen in garish, golfing outfits—the taxicab-yellow or salmon-pink open-collared shirts, the Bermuda shorts that needed only oxfords with cleats to have him ready for the first tee.

Bloomberg had for years carried his engineer's curiosity into his after hours, often in pursuit of the Wall Street broker's high-risk pastimes. He loved the aeronautic intricacy of the whirlybirds and the interlocking calculations of flight—wind speed, engine speed, drift, fuel consumption.

And he attacked golf the way you would build a bridge—this bit goes this way, this bit goes that way. If it doesn't sound like fun or relaxation to most of us, it was his version of relief.

Bloomberg remembered taking his first flight in a private plane in 1973, and he recalled the details vividly. It was a twin-engine Beech Baron, and he was with Dick Rosenthal and another colleague from Salomon Brothers. It was the same Dick Rosenthal who engineered Bloomberg's firing in 1981 and who died piloting another Beech Baron in 1987.

Bloomberg soon got his pilot's license (he still keeps it in his extremely organized wallet and will proudly show it to anybody who asks). And he flew fixed-wing planes or helicopters whenever he could get to an airfield. Bloomberg moved to piloting helicopters, he said, because they are "a lot more fun." He added, "If you take your hands off the controls [in an airplane], it will tend, for a brief period anyways, to continue to go same speed, same altitude, same direction. A helicopter right away will start going [down]." The copter needs all your senses, hands, feet, eyes, ears. "I like to fly it, so I never use the auto pilot because that's so fun," he explained. It is a rich engineer's perfect gizmo, a place to lose yourself in the complicated calculations of vortex and speed, rotation and lift or yaw (to turn left or right).

Twice in the earlier years, he almost crashed. Once, in the winter of 1976, he was in a rented helicopter, an Enstrom F-28, when smoke suddenly filled the cockpit. In his telling, he calmly turned off the engine and used emergency auto-rotation procedures to land on a tiny island off the coast of Connecticut. It was so tiny, so the story goes, that the tail of the helicopter was in the water when he was rescued by the Coast Guard.[1] Nearly twenty years later, he was taking a nephew on a sightseeing trip above Manhattan when he heard a popping noise and the aircraft suddenly lost power.[2] With aviation crews assembling fire trucks on the ground, Bloomberg managed to guide an aircraft that had become what he called "a very heavy glider" back to a Westchester airfield, where he landed safely, to the great relief of everyone, especially his sister and her young son.[3]

Soon after that, Bloomberg could afford his own executive jet, and he also would start bringing along a copilot, mostly to sit and watch him fly the plane. "If I'm unconscious," he explained with a grin, "that's when they take over."[4] Or, of course, the copilots would get plenty of flying hours when Bloomberg was napping in the cabin—his way of turning a flight to Europe or across country into a useful time to sleep.

On the ground, Bloomberg discovered golf, a game he became more serious about shortly before he ran for mayor in 2001. It was the latest in a long line of athletic pursuits, none of them a lazy diversion, even for a part-time sportsman. Bloomberg took his play seriously. In college, he was an avid ice-skater. The stress of Wall Street often drove him into the streets of New York to run off a bad day. And soon, when he had the money, he spent time in Vail—schussing and snowboarding like a teenager. (One story told in Bloomberg's skiing community was that he apparently shocked his daughter by wearing a baseball hat and fake ponytail [no helmet?] as he rode a snowboard down the teen's favorite mountain).[5]

As mayor, he decided against his daredevil ski trails in Colorado. Wearing a cast to a press conference could raise questions about the health-nut mayor not taking his own advice. But in the spring of 2017, a very tan Bloomberg limped into a book party at his philanthropy headquarters. When told he looked particularly fit, Bloomberg admitted that his latest skiing venture left him with a pulled muscle.[6] The black diamonds? he was asked. Yes, he answered, and shortly after his seventy-fifth birthday.[7]

Golf became Bloomberg's steadiest sport over the years, and it is generally a good game for the comfortably rich—riding around in a cart, having somebody hand you the right club, outdoors but not really inconvenienced. It is also a very good way, its devotees will tell you, to uncover personal quirks about your golfing partners, and, at the same time, for them to learn more about you. Percy Boomer, a famous British golfer and trainer once wrote, "If you wish to hide your character, do not play golf."[8]

Thus, Bloomberg, the golfer, was another version of Bloomberg, the tycoon, and Bloomberg, the politician. He did not take an easy swing at the sport; he tackled it with a passion, sometimes even a fury, that surprised many of his fellow golfers, but not those who knew him well. On weekends, often at his private enclave in Bermuda, Bloomberg would play thirty-six holes of golf—walking eighteen, taking a cart on the next round. It would be a form of speed golf, the famous Bloomberg impatience on display even in his off-hours. One partner called him "intense." Another labeled him a "grinder" who played with grit and determination. Mike Bloomberg did not play golf; he assaulted it.

John Gambling, a radio personality on New York's WABC-AM and later WOR radio, shared Bloomberg's passion for golf, and almost every Friday morning while he was mayor, Bloomberg would chatter on the air with Gambling about issues big and trivial. It was a relaxing time, the end of an overscheduled week with golf on the horizon, and with that ease often came the possibility of an inappropriate slip, a "Bloomberg blurt" as journalists came to know it. Once the pro-immigrant Bloomberg was trying to explain how immigrants keep America going by doing jobs nobody else wants to do. "You and I are beneficiaries of these jobs. You and I play golf. Who takes care of the greens and fairways in your golf course?"[9] he asked, assuring his Saturday spot in the next morning's tabloids. One golf club manager hurriedly assured the *Daily News* that all those working on *his* fairways and greens were not in the country illegally.

Even after that, however, Gambling and Bloomberg continued to mock each other's golfing skills. "He does not rise to the level of good," Gambling laughed after the mayor left office, "but he's a lunatic about it." And he added for emphasis: "I think the reason why he is such a fanatic about golf is because he doesn't excel at it. When he can't do something, it drives him nuts."[10]

Bloomberg often set himself impossible goals whether in business, politics, or his personal life. Once, welcoming a group of leaders from

Latin America to his New York offices, he said that there were two things he wanted to do before he died—"speak Spanish like a native and hit a golf ball like a pro." This got a chuckle from many in the crowd of Latin officials who had just heard the former mayor speaking Spanish like a native Bostonian.

Indeed, the trained engineer at first approached golf as a challenge that simply needed to be solved, like everything, with the right equation, the right step-by-step process that could turn him into New York's Arnold Palmer. Bloomberg hired experts, trainers, and, at one point, Joseph Bruno, then the Republican leader of the New York Senate, recalled giving Bloomberg a trick club designed to improve a golfer's swing. Swing badly, and the club head would nod and droop, an obvious rejection of the effort. Bruno told the *Times* that when Bloomberg tried it, "the thing flipped and flopped, and I could see he was getting pretty upset."

It didn't end there, of course.

A few weeks later, Bloomberg saw Bruno and tried the club again. This time there was no flipping, no flopping. It was a perfect swing, so perfect that Bruno said later that "he must have gone out and bought a dozen of those things and swung them everywhere he went."[11]

Bloomberg explained it this way: "I can tell you every part of my body, where it should be at every part of the swing. You can't do a thousand calculations in a quarter of a second. That's why it's so hard, I think for me, to learn how to hit a golf ball." He smiled, then added, "But I think engineering is a great background."[12]

Bloomberg's golf scores were never Olympian. Early in his effort, he shot 121. At nearly fifty strokes over par, bringing in a duffer's score apparently increased his determination. But the fact that he admitted such a humiliating effort also helped confirm what many of his fellow golfers report after a round with Bloomberg.[13] The man was scrupulous about counting every shot. No gimmies. No cheating allowed. Soon, his handicap index was a respectable 13 or sometimes 15.

Bloomberg loved hanging out with celebrities in the city at galas or a press conference, any media city event that featured Salma Hayek or

Jennifer Lopez or Lady Gaga. But he also loved to play golf with the sport's rock stars, like Tiger Woods, even if their scores were considerably different.

"What's great about golf, it's just you. If you play tennis, Roger Federer on the other side of the net, you will never return a serve. I can play against Tiger Woods, and he has nothing to do with me," he said. "You're playing your game. He's playing his game. As long as you don't slow anybody up, you have a fine time together."

Those fine times apparently included games with Presidents Clinton, Obama, and even Donald Trump, the president whose scoring was the opposite of Bloomberg's meticulous count-every-stroke version. (Former *ESPN* columnist Rick Reilly once said of Trump's golf game that "when it comes to cheating, he's an 11 on a scale of 1 to 10."[14])

During his years as mayor, Bloomberg's enthusiasm for golf only increased, and city officials soon learned that if they wanted to interrupt his golfing plans, it had better be an emergency.[15] He could focus on details about golf that would not seem to matter to such a busy man. For example, he wanted his favorite golf courses to flow from green to green with no interruptions from the outside—like a road cutting between fairways. After visiting the La Tourette Golf Course on Staten Island, for example, Bloomberg became concerned that golfers had to stop for traffic to get from one hole to the next. He wanted a signal, to give priority to golfers, even though traffic engineers resisted. In the end, six months after he left office, the city's transportation department finally agreed to put up a flashing yellow light that turned red when golfers were trying to get across.[16]

Similarly, in 2016, Bloomberg slipped into the Southampton Town Hall on Long Island[17] one day to try to talk officials into closing a road through the Shinnecock Hills Golf Club. The club is near Ballyshear, his sumptuous $20 million, thirty-five-acre estate in the Hamptons. The proposed rerouting of this road infuriated neighbors who enjoyed the scenic shortcut through the golf course, and when word got out, they bristled at Bloomberg's interference. By 2018, the club and the town and Bloomberg had reached a compromise. The road would be closed only when the US Open was being played at Shinnecock, but would reopen after that busy week.[18]

To his golfing partners, Bloomberg did provide an inside glimpse of his character. They reported that he was intense about every swing and meticulous about his scorecard, but he was also funny, full of ribald jokes, making fun of their trips to the sand trap and his own visits to the rough. Mainly, for the restive Bloomberg, this was a rare tonic, a place where he could actually come as close as possible to relaxing before returning to his overloaded schedule at business, philanthropy, or his next round of political activism.

16

BLOOMBERG'S BULLDOG

"New York is the safest big city in the nation."
—*Bloomberg,* Washington Post, *August 18, 2013*

"It's like burning down a house to rid it of mice."[1]
—*U.S. District Court Judge Shira Scheindlin on stop-
and-frisk policies in the Bloomberg era*

When Bloomberg took over as mayor in 2002, crime was one problem he figured he didn't have. Rudy Giuliani, his predecessor, had vigorously attacked crime in the city for eight years, and the murder rate had dropped more than half—from 1,560 a year to 649, not counting 9/11. Giuliani had taken the fear out of daily life for most New Yorkers and visitors from around the world, and Bloomberg's task was to find someone who could keep crime going down and also address the city's heightened threat of terrorism.

The mayor elect picked Raymond Walter Kelly, a tough, thirty-year veteran of the NYPD, an educated man who had experience in Washington and on Wall Street. Plus, he had been police commissioner before, when David Dinkins was mayor.

Ray Kelly had the city in his bones. He grew up dodging cars to play stickball on Manhattan's Upper West Side and learning the hard lessons of both Catholic school and the streets of New York City in the 1950s.[2]

196

He worked his way through Manhattan College (where a student commons building was named after him fifty years after he graduated). In his junior year he joined a police cadet corps—a paid opportunity to learn about the best and the worst of the city's police force.

Five days after he was sworn in as a young city police officer, he took leave to join the marines. He married his teenage sweetheart, and after Vietnam, went back to the city police force. He got a law degree at night from St. John's University (the late governor Mario Cuomo was one of his professors). As he moved up police ranks, he also earned a master's degree in public administration at Harvard, then, after his time as police commissioner from 1992 to 1994, Kelly served under Clinton in the Treasury Department's enforcement arm. Then he was head of global security at Bear Stearns.

Kelly also looked the part of the toughest cop in the nation's biggest city. In public, he barely smiled, offering instead a thin-lipped Cagney grin. He was fit, a muscular barrel of a man whose buzz cut grew shorter with every decade. By the time he took over One Police Plaza for Bloomberg, the police commissioner was so trim in his custom-made suit, with his perfectly tied Charvet tie, his perpetually fresh handkerchief carefully tucked in a breast pocket, that even Bloomberg seemed a tad mussed by comparison. Jaw jutted as if always ready for a fight, Kelly looked so indestructible that the city's headline writers quickly labeled him "Bloomberg's Bulldog."

Over twelve years, Bloomberg and Kelly would enjoy plenty of success keeping the city safe. Crime went down steadily. There were no more terrorist attacks—sixteen failed attempts, some caught by chance but most after considerable effort on the part of the police. And Bloomberg became the anti-gun mayor who would take his mission fighting to control the spread of guns to other states with lax controls and even to the powerful National Rifle Association.

Yet, that very battle against illegal guns left a deep scar on his mayoral legacy—a rise in street stops by police of hundreds of thousands of city youths, mostly black or Hispanic. To his critics, this was another racially charged police tactic, one so outrageous that a federal judge eventually ruled it unconstitutional. Bloomberg would defend his stop-and-frisk record vigorously until late 2019 when he issued a surprise apology shortly before announcing plans to run for president. Even then, for him, frisking young people for guns was, once again, a health matter. It was about saving lives.

When Kelly said yes instantly, to Bloomberg's offer to return to his old job, he promised to work to keep the city safe, to curb crime and terrorism, and to improve relations with communities in high-crime areas, often blacks and Hispanics who had learned to distrust police under Giuliani. He called his mission "the three C's"—Counterterrorism, Crime Fighting, and Community Relations.[3] Bloomberg would celebrate how much Kelly succeeded in keeping crime down and blocking terrorist attacks. The question for the new mayor, the political neophyte, was how well he would stand up to a tough police commissioner if his methods of controlling the city became excessive.

Lowering the already low crime rate would be hard, but Kelly adopted and refined a workable system that his predecessor (and sometime adversary) William Bratton had established. Bratton had streamlined communication between the brass and the cop on the street. Bratton's CompStat system pinpointed higher-crime areas that needed more police officers in order to prevent crime, not merely catch criminals after the fact.[4]

Kelly added security cameras to monitor the streets of the city, and he kept track of the details, bringing those numbers to the one-on-one meetings with the mayor, no aides, no extra ears, no pushback.[5]

The weekly police sheet suited the data-loving Bloomberg. One of Kelly's regular collections ran 263 pages. It included details about quality-of-life arrests (76,000 arrests over the decade from 2001 to 2011), a graffiti database of 11,018 "chronic vandals," and color photos of their "tags," plus more serious concerns like the twenty-seven prisoners who escaped in 2010 and the way Chinese gangs trafficked in drugs like Ecstasy. It seemed that Mike Bloomberg had found his crime-fighting avatar.[6]

Fighting terrorism would be harder. New York City had plenty of alluring targets for anyone trying to kill and terrify Americans. Times Square. The Brooklyn Bridge. The Statue of Liberty. As Bloomberg put it, look in the pocket of any terrorist and you'll find a map of New York City.[7]

From his Washington experience as undersecretary for enforcement at the Treasury Department, where he was responsible for the Secret Service and the Bureau of Alcohol, Tobacco, Firearms, and Explosives, Kelly knew that New Yorkers could not count on Washington to protect them from terrorists. Where were they before 9/11, for example? Local police were not on the feds' need-to-know lists, and the only way to get information from the big investigation networks was to trade with them—tidbit for tidbit. "I worked in Washington, remember?" Kelly would say later.[8] So he decided he would have to protect the city with his own local version of the FBI and the CIA.

Bloomberg relished the idea of creating the city's own intelligence operation—especially when Kelly managed to nab a thirty-five-year veteran of the Central Intelligence Agency, David Cohen. Here was a spy's spy, and he now would be running New York City's secretive intelligence operation. At the press conference announcing the new intelligence squad, reporters trying to get a little biographical information asked Cohen his age. He replied that he was between twenty-eight and seventy.[9] Cohen hired seven hundred police officers who spoke fifty languages and dialects—from Egyptian Arabic and Farsi to Spanish spoken in Mexico and the Caribbean.[10]

During the Bloomberg-Kelly years, terrorists failed at sixteen attempts to attack the city. Part was luck, like the time a T-shirt vendor in Times Square saw smoke coming out of an SUV and called over a cop on horseback. The streets were cleared almost immediately, and the car, which failed to explode, gave investigators clues they needed to find the driver and examine his methods.[11]

Other attempts failed because Kelly and his intelligence squad had prepared for the likes of Iyman Faris, a sleeper al-Qaeda agent. Faris wanted to destroy the Brooklyn Bridge—more than 100,000 vehicles a day; 8,000 people on bikes, skates, and running shoes; lovers posing for historic mementos and people in wheelchairs enjoying the spectacle. Kelly got word about the threat and had police officers crawling over the bridge, "the Godzilla bridge" as some of the al-Qaeda terrorists referred to it in intercepted emails. And when Faris spotted Kelly's forces, he abandoned his mission, emailing his handlers in Pakistan that "The weather is too hot." [12] Faris was caught and eventually sentenced to twenty years in prison. [13]

Kelly's success soon came with its detractors. His "Demographics Unit" was designed to track people who had been to Pakistan or other areas suspected of fomenting terrorism. Officers in plain clothes went to mosques looking for potential terrorists and listening for radical rhetoric—a tactic that drew intense criticism from the Muslim community. Kelly later bristled at the criticism. "We'd get leads," he said, "and we'd follow them there. If they went into a mosque, we'd follow them. If they went into St. Patrick's Cathedral, we'd follow them." [14]

Likewise, when Kelly's surveillance teams began monitoring student websites in the northeast, the president of Yale protested that spying on Muslim students was "antithetical to the values of Yale." Bloomberg scoffed in response. "Of course, we're going to look at anything that's publicly available, in the public domain. We have an obligation to do so, and it is to protect the very things that let Yale survive." [15]

Bloomberg supported Kelly in pursuing terrorists, even into the mosques. But the mayor also made it clear repeatedly that he did not want New Yorkers—or any Americans, for that matter—to single out Muslims for the murderers among them. Other religions had murderers as well.

In one of the most forceful examples of his unswerving support of religious freedoms, Bloomberg defended the building of an Islamic center to offer interfaith meetings near the World Trade Center site. Some of those who lost family members in the attacks were horrified since the attackers had been radical Muslims. The proposal ignited an outcry from conservatives like Newt Gingrich. "Nazis don't have the right to put up a sign next to the Holocaust Museum in Washington," Gingrich huffed.[16] If that comment was not ugly enough, Mark Williams, a Tea Party conservative, called the project a monument "for the worship of the terrorists' monkey god."[17]

Such bigotry infuriated Bloomberg. He quickly spoke out in favor of the developer of the center, Imam Feisal Abdul Rauf, whose goal was to create a place for people of different religions to talk with each other. Plus, Bloomberg, the businessman, believed strongly in the imam's right to build a religious center on his own property.[18]

The mayor's most powerful response to the anti-Muslim crowd came on August 3, 2010,[19] when he gave a speech on Governors Island with an array of city officials and religious leaders around him. With the Statue of Liberty pointedly as background, Bloomberg made a passionate plea for Americans to understand how basic are the nation's freedoms of—and from—religion. He cited the Flushing Remonstrance of 1657, when a group in Queens petitioned the Dutch governor Peter Stuyvesant to allow Quakers to set up a house of worship. Stuyvesant had them arrested. But their effort began the long and crucial trek to religious freedom and property rights in an increasingly diverse New York City. As Bloomberg said of the Islamic center, "The simple fact is this building is private property, and the owners have a right to use the building as a house of worship."

More pointedly, when the city's police and firefighters scrambled into the World Trade Center towers to help people on 9/11, more than four hundred of those first responders died trying to save people. "Not one of them asked, 'What God do you pray to?'" Bloomberg said. "'What beliefs do you hold?'"[20]

As an unseasoned politician, Michael Bloomberg had an unexpectedly rough introduction to the gun control issue. At one campaign stop early in his 2001 campaign, a potential voter asked Bloomberg about the Second Amendment. He paused. "And that one is?" he asked before aides frantically whisked him away for a quick reminder about the constitutional amendment that gives "the right of the people to keep and bear arms."[21]

Then, as mayor, the first time an off-duty police detective was stabbed and died in the hospital, it was a weekend (March 31, 2002) when Bloomberg was out of town. His aides crassly suggested to reporters that he did not go to the hospital or meet the family right away because this was some of the mayor's well-deserved and fiercely protected private time. And, they added, that he had only been out of pocket three of the last thirteen weekends. Ed Skyler, his communications honcho, then compounded the error. "Mayor Bloomberg agrees with the 80 percent of New Yorkers who feel he's entitled to a personal life."[22]

But with each later trip to the hospital, each wrenching call to the family, each visit to people keening over police officers who were shot or a youth shot by police officers, Bloomberg grew steadily more concerned about the deadly abuse of guns in America. He learned that the illegal guns killing his New Yorkers came from states where anybody with the money could buy a deadly weapon. By the time he was reelected to his second term, Bloomberg had declared the lax gun culture "our most urgent challenge," adding that "we will not rest until we secure all of the tools we need to protect New Yorkers from the scourge of illegal guns."[23]

Guns were a health issue, he would argue. Yes, smoking killed people. Fat and sugar killed people. But guns, which were protected by the zealous lobbyists from the National Rifle Association, killed thirty thousand people a year. Nobody bucked the NRA then and got away with it, Bloomberg was told. They proudly killed off political careers like ducks in a carnival shooting gallery. Go against the NRA and somebody would almost always mention Jack Brooks. Brooks, a Texas Democrat, had been an NRA stalwart for forty years until he voted for a crime bill that included an assault weapons ban. The NRA defeated him a few months later. When members of Congress considered gun control measures, somebody would quietly whisper the name of Jack Brooks.

Bloomberg was more than ready to fight this political Goliath that most in Washington were too scared to challenge. And he would increasingly call on mayors in other cities in the next decades to tackle such problems that Washington couldn't manage to solve.

On a fine April day in 2006, Bloomberg gathered fourteen other mayors at Gracie Mansion to support a simple, straightforward message: "Stand up to fight against illegal guns." Inside the historic mayor's home and against a backdrop of American flags, Bloomberg had seemed subdued that morning as he read prepared remarks to begin the conference. Then the mayors moved outside onto the lush front lawn to meet the press and sign their proclamation.

Before the cameras and the microphones, Bloomberg suddenly shifted from dutiful administrator to passionate advocate. He was no longer reading a script; he was a man on a mission. Squinting into the full April sun and a nest of cameras, he reminded reporters that while Washington dawdled, the mayors had to make "that terrible call that a member of your family was killed by guns. And what do you say?" he asked. "That we didn't have the courage to stand up and do something about it?" His face was hard and he shook his head slightly, signaling a barely contained anger as he raised his voice for the cameras. Finally, he offered what sometimes served as his strongest admonition against a public wrong: "Shame on us if we don't do something about it."

A lot of that shame belonged in Washington, of course. Congress was throwing up roadblocks, writing NRA-friendly laws that made it harder to track down illegal guns or even analyze the gun data. "One of these laws goes so far as to say that the only ways that data can be shared in this day and age is on microfiche," Bloomberg fumed. "I don't know if anybody makes a microfiche reader anymore," said the billionaire mayor from the data industry. "That is deliberately designed to keep the police departments of this country from getting the information they need to protect the police officers, to protect the public, to get guns off the streets."[24]

One statistic kept driving the issue home to the mayor: 82 percent of the illegal guns recovered on the streets of New York were sold from outside the state. For the "iron pipeline," as law enforcement experts called it, guns could be easily bought in, say, Georgia or Virginia, and driven up I-95 to be sold at a hefty profit on the streets of New York.

One way to clog the pipeline, the mayor and his legal team figured, was to sue the people who were selling these guns to people who had not passed the background checks. But how to find out where people were buying these guns and bringing them into the state illegally? Bloomberg's anti-gun squad decided to run their own sting operation—so secret that they slipped across state borders without telling state officials or the federal government.

Bloomberg and Kelly dispatched private investigators in teams of two, to see if they could make purchases illegally. One undercover officer asked about the gun, how it worked, what it could be used for. The gun was clearly for that buyer. But his partner was the one who filled out the required forms in order to pass the background check.

In May 2006, Bloomberg filed a federal lawsuit against fifteen "rogue gun dealers" in Georgia, Ohio, Pennsylvania, South Carolina, and Virginia. Over a six-year period—1994 to 2001—more than five hundred guns recovered after crimes in New York City had been traced to these fifteen dealers.[25] Within a few months, six of the fifteen dealers agreed to settle with the city and allow a special monitor to oversee their records and inspect their inventories. Then, in December 2006, the Bloomberg team sued twelve more gun dealers in the same five states.[26] (Some of the dealers countersued, but those cases ended in settlements or losses on appeal.)[27]

There was another side to the story, of course—the dealers who bought those guns and sold them illegally in the city. One such merchant was an aspiring rapper named Matthew Best. If a good rapper raps about the real life around him, Best couldn't help boasting about his sideline business. At one point on Instagram, he bragged about "packing more guns than the Air Force." And he couldn't resist crowing about his illicit loot. He flashed one picture of his own hand clutching a wad of $100 bills. As it turned out, others besides his rap fans were watching.

One of the rapper's collaborators brought guns in from North and South Carolina, packing as many as fourteen at a time in an old zebra-striped suitcase. The middleman transported the cache by "Chinatown bus," for years the cheapest way to travel from the South to New York City. Then, out of his makeshift recording studio, Best sold his contraband guns. Eventually Best and eighteen others were nabbed and the NYPD brought in a total of 254 illegal weapons, many of them courtesy of Best's Instagram account.[28, 29] Bloomberg exulted in what he called the largest gun seizure in city history.

These stings and subsequent arrests and lawsuits infuriated some state officials who had failed to catch the gunrunners. After Bloomberg accused Virginia's then attorney general Robert McDonnell of defending "rogue gun dealers," McDonnell warned the mayor that any more sub-rosa operations in Virginia would be violating a new state law enacted by his legislature precisely to combat Bloomberg's meddling in the local gun business. "It's not the job of the mayor of New York to enforce the criminal laws of Virginia," said McDonnell (who eventually became governor, then was convicted of corruption for taking lavish vacations, a costly Rolex watch, and other goodies from a businessman selling dietary supplements, and finally was given a reprieve by the U.S. Supreme Court).[30]

Lawyers at the federal Bureau of Alcohol, Tobacco, Firearms and Explosives were also miffed at Bloomberg's unorthodox methods. When the city sent its findings to the bureau, the result was not only an investigation of the dealers. Federal officers and a few state officials began to investigate Bloomberg's operatives, who had essentially broken the law to prove it was so easily breakable. The result was little more than a scolding by government lawyers. But the Justice Department offered a stern reminder that there are "potential legal liabilities" when private investigators break the law, even to prove their point publicly.[31]

This was the kind of political fight that would have most elected officials cowering in fear of the backlash from donors, the NRA, and a few rabid gun owners, if not the actual voters. Instead, it energized Michael Bloomberg. He presided at press briefings trumpeting his team's interstate successes like the proud father of a revolution.

Kelly's third promise—to improve the department's relations with local communities, especially blacks and Hispanics—would start off well as he visited churches or mosques to erase the anger over the Giuliani years. He marched in the West Indian Day Parade and the Puerto Rican Day Parade, among others.[32] The police sponsored cricket and soccer leagues. He had a new unit that reported directly to him about issues, especially in rougher areas or in ethic enclaves. And he worked to increase the number of police officers who came from these diverse communities.[33]

That goodwill began to sour, especially in black and Hispanic communities, as Kelly's officers increasingly misused and overused an established police tactic officially called "stop, question, and frisk." In 1968, the Supreme Court ruled in *Terry v. Ohio* that if a police officer sees unusual conduct, which leads that officer to reasonably conclude there may be criminal activity, the person may be stopped. And if the officer has reason to fear the suspect may have a weapon, then the officer is allowed to frisk, or pat down, the suspect. And if that frisk suggests a weapon is present, then a full search is allowed. These Terry Stops, as they were known, were soon adopted widely as a policing tool. But the standard was a "reasonable suspicion" or "specific reasonable inferences," not merely "inarticulate hunches."[34]

The practice was "a basic tool" for police work, according to Giuliani's police commissioner, William Bratton,[35] but it had to be done by the book. Under Kelly, the number of "street stops," as he called them, rose from 97,296 in 2002 to a high of 685,724 in 2011, down to 191,851 as he left in 2013.[36] The stops occurred in higher-crime neighborhoods, and most of those affected—by both the crime and the police actions—were blacks and Hispanics. More than half of the people who were stopped were also frisked,[37] and yet, overall, 88 percent resulted in no further action. In only 1.5 percent of the stops did police find an illegal weapon (including about 4,400 guns that were then taken off the streets).[38]

For Bloomberg, the policy made sense. It was not about race, he argued; it was about behavior. It was about identifying offenders in high-crime areas. Reduce the number of illegal guns on the streets and a reduction in the number of shootings and murders would follow. At one point, Bloomberg argued that anybody in America "has a right to walk down the street without being targeted by the police because of his or her race or ethnicity. At the same time, every American has a right to walk down the street without getting mugged or killed. Both are civil liberties," he wrote in 2013.[39] Despite such arguments, the mayor failed to recognize the power of the complaints or realize that the phrase "stop-and-frisk" would become shorthand for the biggest hole in an otherwise imposing record at city hall.

The tactic had moved over the Bloomberg years from "a necessary tool," as Kelly once described the standard, Supreme Court–approved practice, to a disturbing overreach in the name of crime prevention. And the numbers of these frisks only dropped after criticism became intense and a detailed federal lawsuit began gaining power through the courts.

In June 2012, Bloomberg made an important visit to the First Baptist Church of Brownsville, in one of the higher-crime areas of Brooklyn, to list the ways his administration had worked, and often succeeded, in trying to lower crime in black and Hispanic neighborhoods. Bloomberg said that many of those young men who felt abused by police were right to be angry. "I would be angry as well," he told parishioners.[40]

Bloomberg acknowledged that morning that many in the black and Hispanic communities wanted him to end stop-and-frisk (one of the few lines that day that drew applause from his mostly African American audience), but he borrowed a well-worn phrase from President Clinton and promised to *mend* stop-and-frisk, not *end* it in high-crime areas. He outlined ways police would be retrained and how details of the frisks would be shared more widely at the police department and city hall. "As long as I'm mayor, we will not choose between safety and civility," he promised.[41]

Bloomberg publicly defended Kelly time and again, but "after much internal discussion," as one aide described a few meetings between the mayor and the commissioner without elaboration, Bloomberg told Kelly his people needed to do a better job on the city's roughest streets. Indeed, the stops went down slightly to 532,000 for the year 2012.

Still, Bloomberg continued to support Kelly publicly; that kind of loyalty was a key tenet in the Bloomberg code. One particularly unapologetic version of Bloomberg's defense of stop-and-frisk came when he had been out of office more than a year. Bloomberg was speaking at a forum in Aspen, Colorado. The Aspen Institute refused to release the transcript or video of the speech, insisting that Bloomberg's people wanted it kept private. A young journalist, Karl Herchenroeder, then of the *Aspen Times*, had taped the event, and here is how the former mayor described his record on stop-and-frisk that evening:

He began by explaining why he felt stop-and-frisk was necessary.

"It's controversial," he said, "but the first thing is all of your—95 percent of your murders and murderers and murder victims—fit one MO. You can just take the description, Xerox it, and pass it out to all of the cops."

The perpetrators and victims are mostly male—blacks and Hispanics, aged fifteen to thirty-five, he said. And that profile was true in "virtually every American city." The idea, he explained, was that to keep this group alive, you needed to take away their guns.

"The psychologists say that they think they are going to get killed anyway because all their friends are getting killed. So they just don't have any long-term focus. It's a joke to have a gun. It's a joke to pull the trigger," he told the Colorado audience.

While he was being criticized for stopping and frisking these young people, he emphasized that they were also trying to keep them out of jail.

"We brought down the incarceration rate by a third," he said. "You send a young kid to jail. We don't correct them, although we call it a correction department. We teach them how to be a worse person. And [after] about two or three times, he really does have a gun and starts killing people."

Instead of jail, he said, he put more cops in those neighborhoods where the crime is, "and the first thing you can do for people is stop them getting killed.

"And the way you get the guns off the street is you throw them up against the wall and you frisk them. And these kids don't wanna get caught so they don't bring the gun," he concluded. "They may still have a gun but they leave it at home."[42]

Kelly would make much the same case, although far less dramatically. Their argument, bared to its essence, was this: Stop-and-frisk was not about racial profiling. It was about looking at the data and going to the places where the crimes were being committed—in black and Hispanic neighborhoods—and trying to stop crimes before they happened. It was about public health, saving lives.

U.S. District Court Judge Shira Scheindlin would see it altogether differently. In 2008,[43] a group of black and Hispanic residents charged Bloomberg and Kelly with unreasonable searches and seizures and the right to due process. The case—*Floyd, et al. v. City of New York, et al.*—was amended and challenged and updated over the years. Eventually Judge Scheindlin issued a searing, 198-page ruling in mid-August 2013.[44] She wrote that the Bloomberg administration's version of stop-and-frisk violated the constitutional rights of minorities because police targeted black and Hispanic youths. She made the point that between 2004 and mid-2012, city police stopped 4.4 million people—about 83 percent of them black or Hispanic. About half of those who were stopped were also frisked, but weapons were found on only 1.5 percent, she noted. Supporters of Bloomberg responded that even using her numbers, that meant the city police had found 33,000 weapons.

The court record included details that Bloomberg and Kelly should have dealt with years earlier. In 2009, for example, one NYPD officer was so disturbed by the increase in harassment of these mostly young males that he wrote a letter to his commanding officer. The letter said, in part, that the police were "handcuffing kids for no reason. They [superiors] would just tell us handcuff them. And boss, why are we handcuffing them? Just handcuff them. We'll make up a charge later. Some of those kids weren't doing anything. Some of those kids were just walking home (from school)."[45] Judge Scheindlin's opinion was full of such painful stories—some from innocent people standing outside or really doing nothing extraordinary. Yet they were stopped, frisked, and demeaned, she wrote. The judge made it clear that "universal suspicion," especially about blacks and Hispanics, was destructive of the society and the individual. As she put it, borrowing a phrase from columnist Charles Blow, "It's like burning down a house to rid it of mice."[46]

When the Scheindlin decision came out, a furious Mike Bloomberg responded—nowhere did she mention the number of lives saved, he said indignantly. The decision was based on the flimsiest of evidence, he argued, and it was "pretty clear from the start" that she was going to deny the city a fair trial.[47]

Judge Scheindlin's ruling helped limit a policy that had gone haywire. Even Kelly recognized that it was a tool, "not a panacea."[48] But the Bloomberg lawyers were ready to appeal, and a few months later Scheindlin was removed from the case by a federal appeals panel for a lack of impartiality—mainly for her encouragement to lawyers to file the lawsuit and to the media.[49] But when the court failed to throw out her actual ruling, the Bloomberg attorneys continued their appeal. That was in the last months of Bloomberg's last term, and when his Democratic successor, Bill de Blasio, arrived, he quickly abandoned efforts to overturn the Scheindlin ruling on stop-and-frisk and promised to end Kelly's version during his time in city hall.

Kelly's response was curt: "People will lose their lives as a result."[50]

In short, maybe they were humiliated, but they were still breathing. Their argument would lose much of its force as data provided by Kelly's successors listed far fewer Terry Stops, and the crime rate still kept going down in New York City anyway.

There were other excesses by Kelly's police force. When Bloomberg held the Republican convention in 2004, Kelly's troops rounded up more than 1,800 protestors. Many were demonstrating against the Iraq War, but some of those arrested were just watching or failing to move out of the way. The city faced more than six hundred claims of abuse by those arrested and eventually paid out about $18 million to settle those cases as Bloomberg left office.[51]

Far more serious were what some civil rights advocates called the "manufactured misdemeanors" mostly of black and Hispanic youths. The law allowed possession of a small amount of marijuana as long as it was not out in public. Some officers would stop youths and order them to empty their pockets. If marijuana came out, many were then arrested for having their weed "in public." Many of these charges were dismissed by the courts, but they could also bring a $500 fine and three months in jail. For too many people caught in this unfair practice, it meant loss of job prospects, going to the military, even for a cab license.[52] More than fifty thousand people were arrested in 2010 alone for possession of small amounts of marijuana before Commissioner Kelly issued an explicit order not to use such tricks. Displaying the drug must be an "activity undertaken of the subject's own volition," he decreed. The mandate almost halved the number of arrests overnight.[53]

Overall, Kelly fulfilled Bloomberg's mandate: the city was indeed safer after Kelly's twelve years as his commissioner. Crime kept going down, eventually by a record 32 percent from 2001 to 2013, according to the city's official crime statistics. And Bloomberg noted that the crime drop did not come because more people were imprisoned; the incarceration rate also dropped by 36 percent.

Bloomberg would continue to face criticism for allowing policies like

Kelly's version of stop-and-frisk to continue for so long, but even years later he would defend those efforts as a way to save lives, especially black and Hispanic lives. During his time, the murder rates did go down. There were 587 homicides the year he took over in 2002, and 332 as he left in 2013. It was still too many, but the drop in crime allowed Bloomberg to brag that, under his watch, New York was "the safest big city in the nation."[54]

THE FORGOTTEN
ISLAND

"You send a young kid to jail, you don't 'correct' them.
You teach them how to be a worse person."
—*Michael Bloomberg, 2015*

As Manhattan shimmered in the distance, the tiny island once over-run with horse manure and garbage from New York City festered in the East River. Just a few hundred yards offshore between the Bronx and Queens, Rikers Island housed one of the most notorious jails in America. With room for fifteen thousand prisoners, the inmates on Rikers spent their days trying to survive the guards, the gangs, and a blatantly unfair judicial system that kept many behind bars because they did not have enough money to post bail while they waited for a judge to hear their case.

The very name Rikers provoked nightmares for many New Yorkers who knew anything about the place. If there are some spots that retain the ghastly fetor after years of grief and iniquity, Rikers is one of them. The island itself was named for the Rycken, or Riker, family. Richard Riker, a prominent nineteenth-century lawyer, state attorney general, and city politician, became known as a supporter of the "Kidnapping Club." The club was a group of brigands who encouraged the capturing of free blacks on the streets of New York City, including children taken from their schoolrooms, to be sold in the South as slaves.[1]

After the Rikers sold the island to the city for $180,000 in 1884 (around $4.6 million in 2019 dollars),[2] it became the dumping ground for city refuse that was eventually used as a landfill. As a result, the island expanded over the years from just under 90 acres to 415 by the 1930s, when it eventually became a jail, then a series of jails.[3] It became the place to put away the unwanted, the criminal, and too often the mentally ill. The dreaded complex housed those who were lost for months and sometimes years waiting to go to trial. And those torturous hours on Rikers convinced too many inmates to confess to almost anything in order to get out or to serve a longer term at a prison upstate or go home with a new criminal record.

As mayor, Bloomberg talked about how the jails did not "correct" anyone, even though his department was labeled Correction. "You send a young kid to jail, you don't 'correct' them," he said after he left office. "You teach them how to be a worse person."[4]

He could boast that the city's incarceration rate during his time had hit an all-time low—declining by 36 percent between 2001 and 2012, or by almost 20,000 people, while the national rate grew by 3 percent.[5] Bloomberg favored programs that reduced the prison population, replacing Rikers with sentences to community service, day custody for misdemeanors, and treatment for non-felony drug abusers. The emphasis was on crime prevention, not incarceration, and on giving judges greater latitude to grant pretrial release.

But for those sent to Rikers, it was another story.[6]

When Bloomberg took over as mayor, the city's sixteen jails, including Rikers, seemed under control. His first commissioner of correction, William J. Fraser, a rare holdover from the Giuliani years, was considered a reasonable choice, but within a year Fraser was out after reports of corruption within his administration.[7]

Bloomberg then passed the job to his parole commissioner, Martin Horn, who had been chief operating officer for New York State's parole division and later served as Pennsylvania's secretary of corrections. Horn would add the jail network to his other job overseeing parolees in early 2003. And by tradition, Bloomberg announced the news to the media and then whispered to Horn, "Don't fuck it up." Horn managed the jails from up close. He stayed around. As he once put it, "Managing a prison or jail is like tending a garden. If you don't weed it every day, the weeds take over.[8]

"The mayor never told me to back down. He never interfered," Horn said years later. That could have been Bloomberg's well-advertised management system—you hire good people, then you let them do their jobs. But in this case, Bloomberg was also focused elsewhere—banning tobacco, righting the economy, and instituting such reforms as 311. "I never got the sense that this was really an area he wanted to delve into. It was not on his list of priorities," Horn said.[9] Rikers was, once again, the forgotten island.

Fortunately, Mayor Giuliani had appointed his criminologist and budget expert, Michael Jacobson, as the city's correction commissioner in 1995 when Rikers was known as "a hoodlum counter-city within the city."[10] To identify inmates and guards causing trouble, Jacobson used data much like the CompStat system used by police. He also ramped up activities in the jails to keep inmates occupied. When he began, there were more than one thousand slashings or stabbings a year—a crucial number because inmates can usually hide a fight or even a rape, but it's a lot harder to keep an open wound from the authorities. By the time Giuliani's team left,[11] "the jailhouses were as under control as the nature of the beast allowed," as city historian Chris McNickle wrote in 2017, and the number of slashings and stabbings stayed down for Bloomberg's first term.

Horn felt Rikers had been "stabilized"[12] in those early years, but soon the number of attacks began growing again.[13] While the drop in the number of prisoners at Rikers and other city jails was good news, across the river in city hall, officials felt they could reduce the budget and staff on the island. For overworked correction officers facing gang members or the mentally ill, it was an almost perfect recipe for trouble at the massive complex.[14]

Bloomberg left Horn to deal with the problems at Rikers during his six years as correction commissioner. Horn appeared at press conferences, but he said that Bloomberg only called him personally about Rikers on two occasions. The first time was not about problems at the jails. It was about Canadian geese.

Rikers is in the flight patterns of LaGuardia Airport, and the geese grazing on the island were always viewed as a potential hazard. (A skein of geese would later bring down a US Airways flight on a cold January day in 2009. Captain Chesley "Sully" Sullenberger would become a national hero for landing on the Hudson and managing to save all of his passengers.)[15]

On the phone to Horn one day early in his new job at correction, Bloomberg explained that he was going to an event where the animal rights groups had planned to protest the killing of Canadian geese. Are we killing the geese on Rikers Island, he asked? Horn said his staff was trapping the geese for the U.S. Fish and Wildlife Service. "When we turn them over to the feds, they're alive." Horn remembered telling the mayor that "You can say we're not killing any geese. Whether the feds kill 'em, I can't say."[16]

The second call from the mayor was in 2009 when a sudden outbreak of the flu appeared to be so dangerous that Norman Seabrook, then the arrogant, bullying leader of the correction workers' union, wanted to close the jails to avoid spreading the flu to his workers. Seabrook,[17] who had endorsed Bloomberg in his first two elections in 2001 and 2005, had already made a name for himself by repeatedly threatening to disrupt the jails and the court system if he did not get his way.[18] He boasted to commissioners about his access to the mayor—that he, not they, could get Bloomberg on his personal cell phone.

Seabrook saw another opportunity to throw his weight around over the flu, and Horn was furious. No way are you closing the jails, Horn stressed as he called the city health commissioner and asked him to talk

Seabrook down. When that didn't work, Horn called his top city deputy to warn her that Seabrook was "on a rip."

That night, he got that second call from Bloomberg. According to Horn, the mayor simply said, "Marty, Norman Seabrook is the easiest guy in the world to manage. You just gotta kiss his ass."[19] Horn managed to keep the jails open during the flu, but he would resign a short time later. It was not just the call, he said, it was that he was tired and the mayor was running for a third term. Horn had also lost too many budget battles with city hall, and some of the guards had organized inmate gangs to help maintain order. "The Program," the guards called it.[20] When an eighteen-year-old inmate named Christopher Robinson refused to cooperate, the gangs run by the guards beat him to death.[21] (Two guards would eventually go to prison, and the city would pay $2 million to the Robinson family.)[22, 23] Horn quit to join the criminal justice faculty at John Jay College in New York City. "I was spent," he said later.

Horn's replacement, Dora Schriro, an experienced correction officer, had run the correction facilities in Missouri and Arizona and spent a year as an administrator at the Department of Homeland Security. During her four years as commissioner—in Bloomberg's last term—Rikers, once again, began to seethe with violence. The numbers of stabbings and slashings in city jails went up even as the inmate population went down. In 2009, there were twenty-five such incidents; forty-eight in 2010; thirty-five in 2011; seventy-three in 2012; seventy-three in 2013 (and ninety the year after Bloomberg left, in 2014).[24]

It took a U.S. prosecutor to catalog some of the ugliest ways that Rikers guards were treating prisoners—especially the younger ones. As Bloomberg left office, Preet Bharara, then the powerful U.S. attorney found that there was such a "culture of violence" against teenage inmates that Rikers had become like something out of *Lord of the Flies*.[25]

The details of Bharara's report on the years 2011 to 2013 are horrifying. One young man fell asleep in a class and was then dragged into the hallway and beaten so viciously he was crying for his mother. For these younger inmates, aged sixteen to eighteen, guards were rarely punished for pulling them into some corner, out of range of the prison's video cameras. The guards would often yell "Stop resisting," even if the inmate was subdued or had never resisted at all. That way the guard could argue self-protection as part of a flimsy reporting process that seldom resulted in any discipline or loss of status. In one year (FY 2012), guards used violence 517 times to subdue youthful inmates in two facilities that housed a total of 791 adolescents. There were 1,059 injuries reported during that period.[26]

The most famous case involved a sixteen-year-old African American named Kalief Browder, who was charged with being one of a group that stole a backpack. Browder denied he was involved, but because he had a previous record for taking a truck on a joyride, the judge set his bail at $3,000. That was far too much for his family to pay which meant the youth was automatically sent to Rikers to await trial. Browder stayed in pretrial detention at Rikers for three agonizing years. He repeatedly protested his innocence and refused to plead guilty to get out of Rikers. He was savagely beaten by guards and other inmates and spent much of his time in solitary confinement—a teenager alone in a cell twenty-three hours a day. Eventually, charges were dropped, but Browder was thoroughly broken.[27] He had tried several times in Rikers to commit suicide. In 2015, at home, he succeeded.[28] His story in the *New Yorker* magazine finally prodded the city to do away with solitary confinement for the youngest inmates. And it helped expand some efforts to deal with the widespread mental problems that plagued as many as half of those caught in the hell of Rikers Island. As for the arbitrary and often unfair system of requiring cash bail that punishes the poor, that was like a lot of reforms for New Yorkers—it would be stuck in the state legislature in Albany for another four years.[29]

Norman Seabrook continued to protect guards, even when they brutally abused prisoners. One particular incident toward the end of the mayor's third term finally ignited the full Bloomberg outrage. An inmate had charged guards with assaulting him and a rare court date was finally set. On the day when the inmate was scheduled to appear in court, Seabrook's guards suddenly declared all prison buses unsafe, and they refused to transport more than seven hundred prisoners anywhere,[30] even for medical care. When Bloomberg heard about it, he was furious and called for legal action against the guards. When an aide worried about what Seabrook would think, Bloomberg reportedly pounded the table and shouted, "I don't give a shit. Take him to court. File charges. Do it."[31] The outcome was less than helpful. The guards accused of attacking the prisoner were found not guilty. And the city's effort to punish the union went almost nowhere. After guards were docked two days' pay, the union paid them back.[32] (Years after Bloomberg left office, Seabrook would be found guilty of accepting a $100,000 kickback for investing $20 million of the union's pension money in a hedge fund in 2014 that went bust.[33] In 2019, he was sentenced to fifty-eight months in prison.)

Bloomberg and his commissioners found no long-term solutions to the Rikers problem, but he would try at least one innovative way to deal with young people who kept returning again and again to the courts and the dreaded Rikers system. Bloomberg offered private investors a sort of wager, in what was believed to be New York's first "social impact bond" that would allow the wealthy to gamble on a city reform. In this case, Goldman Sachs would put up $7.2 million to pay for several programs designed to keep 10 percent of the troubled teenagers from returning to Rikers. Bloomberg added $6 million through his philanthropies, in part as a guarantee to Goldman in case the program failed. The city taxpayers would only pay the full bill if the program succeeded.[34]

Bloomberg's experiment failed to work, at least in the way he tried it in New York. Three years into the project, the Vera Institute of Justice ruled that the program "did not reduce recidivism (by 10 percent as required) and therefore did not meet the pre-defined threshold of success."[35] Bloomberg Philanthropies paid the $6 million guarantee to Goldman. Goldman lost $1.2 million on the deal—barely a blip for both enterprises. More important, it was free for the city's taxpayers, and advocates still saw possibilities for future social impact bonds.

For the unfortunates at Rikers, the social impact bond was simply another experiment gone wrong. And even with the number of prisoners steadily decreasing, the place continued to be dangerous and unforgiving. Linda Gibbs, who was Bloomberg's deputy mayor for health and human services, which included Rikers, once simply shook her head when she was asked what should have been done about the island. "It should be closed," she said long after Bloomberg had left city hall.[36] Bloomberg's successor soon promised to close Rikers in ten years (after he left office),[37] thus, once again, handing off this inmate purgatory to some future New York City mayor.

THE CITY GROWS
UP AND UP

"Government's role is not to command, but to
catalyze, not to dictate development but to create
the conditions that will allow it to take place."
—*Bloomberg to British conservatives, 2007*[1]

The Conservative Party of Great Britain welcomed Michael Bloomberg like a superstar when he spoke at their annual conference in the seaside resort town of Blackpool. They laughed at his jokes, like the one about how an American can't speak in Britain without quoting Churchill, in his case, twice that day. He also made a prescient comment then in late 2007, about how the global economy was sliding into bad times because of our "borrowing bacchanalia." A year later, the Great Recession hit and, as he predicted, the world suffered a massive economic meltdown.

There was more tucked into that speech than old jokes and savvy forecasts, however. Bloomberg also gave a very telling explanation of how he saw his role as mayor, how he believed in government unlike many in his financial stratum. He did not think government should be dismantled like some of his Republican friends. He thought government should actually work.[2]

A few of his goals were standard for city leaders. A mayor's first duty is to provide a decent quality of life—that includes protection from crime and terrorism, clean streets and decent schools, and regular garbage pickup. Second, the public's money must be kept safe, and the budget must be balanced with a good bit tucked away for the inevitable bad turn in the economy.

Still, the real meat for that conservative audience was in the third and fourth items on his list. His third task, he said, was to "unleash and incentivize the private sector." And finally, he wanted to lay the groundwork, sometimes literally, for houses and offices for the masses of people who were steadily moving into the cities, especially his own.

From the first day of his tenure, Bloomberg had touted New York like a cheerleader, projecting that one million more people would live and work in the city by 2030. The question, of course, was where? Building to prepare for a bulging city was fuel for the economy, and Bloomberg would help create the beginnings of a building boom that would continue long after he left office. "Government's role is not to command but to catalyze," he stressed that day in England, "not to dictate development but to create the conditions that will allow it to take place."[3]

The business community in New York, much like the British conservatives in Blackpool, applauded such talk. Developers wanted the mayor to build public amenities like his new subway line to the underdeveloped West Side of Manhattan and to hand out fat tax benefits or low-interest bonds, to get rid of complicated and restrictive zoning and then, basically, move out of the way. For the builders and the architects and the construction workers of New York, Michael Bloomberg was their kind of guy.

While Bloomberg saw his job as something of a layup shot for the developers in his city, he would also demand environmental protections. His elaborate PlaNYC in 2007 was an outline for such progress. He also wanted the city to return to its waterfront, by converting the wharfs and old ports into parks and clusters of housing and businesses with access to the shore.

Plus, Bloomberg was a strong believer in the power of capitalism and the wisdom of the markets. He enjoyed their rewards personally, and he argued that business—from start-up entrepreneurs to giant corporations like Google—made a city thrive. They helped with entry-level jobs to bring people out of poverty. Better businesses gave the middle class jobs for the necessary stability and even provided the wealthy with the means—ideally—to pay city taxes or, at the very least, to spend money on local luxuries.

For decades New York City seemed off-limits for big, grandiose projects after "master builder" Robert Moses had bulldozed too many areas after the Depression and World War II, all in the name of progress. Moses lost power by 1968 and died in 1981,[4] but the city was slow in regaining its building muscle. Mayor Koch managed an important affordable housing program and other commercial developments to lure businesses around the city, and David Dinkins helped re-create a bustling Times Square, but every move to develop a part of the city was excruciatingly slow and difficult.

Bloomberg and his development team worked hard to defy what many saw as the Moses curse.[5] By the time he left office, developers had either built or started or proposed massive projects in every borough. There were alluring new parks around the Brooklyn Bridge and the High Line, Manhattan's elevated park, Hunters Point in Queens, and the High Bridge linking Harlem to the Bronx, and even Governors Island off the tip of Manhattan. There were proposals for new schools and libraries—all to help lure development.

There was a new way to pay for a $2.4 billion subway extension from midtown Manhattan to the West Side of the island. Under Bloomberg's plan, the subway line conceived in the 1920s and stalled in the 1970s could be built if the city essentially paid up front. The city issued bonds with the expectation that the burst in new construction would eventually provide tax revenue to pay back these loans. The "value capture" plan or "tax incremental financing" took longer than expected, since the economy slowed in 2008.[6] But the extension would have taken decades for the old state-controlled Metropolitan Transportation Authority to do on its own. Instead, work started on the Bloomberg extension in early 2008, and the new station at Thirty-fourth Street opened in 2015, giving new life to a dreary patch of Manhattan's West Side.

A favorite project of the engineer/mayor was the massive $4.7 billion Water Tunnel No. 3 to guarantee fresh water from upstate reservoirs. It was "one of the largest infrastructure projects in the city's history," Bloomberg said after the completion of the Manhattan leg of the project.[7] He insisted on visiting the site deep underneath the city to talk to the Sandhogs, the way the engineers in Local 147 liked to be called. At one point, the mayor asked the chief engineer when the tunnel would be completed. His troops "all had mortgages," the union boss explained, and the full tunnel would "not be finished in your lifetime."

The $4.7 billion addition to the tunnel also offered some insight into the way Bloomberg dealt with pressure from outsiders, even powerful friends. In the summer of 2005, John Whitehead, a prominent New Yorker who knew Bloomberg socially, wrote the mayor to complain that work on a planned section of the water tunnel had disturbed neighbors in his posh Sutton Place enclave on Manhattan's East Side. Whitehead wrote in his letter, "We would like you to know that our community is aroused" by the blasting and vibrations caused by the Sandhogs' work. A few weeks later, Peter Madonia, Bloomberg's chief of staff, wrote back to Whitehead explaining that while the mayor recognized the problem, Whitehead's area was the best of several being considered for "one of the City's most important infrastructure projects."[8] Translated, the mayor gave the tunnel a priority over his rich friends in Manhattan.

At first, Bloomberg's developments were dictated by the needs of a battered city and its crushing deficit. He canceled former mayor Giuliani's grand plans to spend $800 million on lavish new sports palaces for the Yankees in the Bronx and the Mets in Queens.[9] Bloomberg also surprised his friends on Wall Street by backing out of a deal to build a new

New York Stock Exchange. The city would have to buy nearly half a billion dollars' worth of property for a new building—a costly venture with
Bloomberg facing a $4.7 billion budget deficit.[10] By the time he left city
hall, however, the economy and the city's budget had made it possible to
add elaborate new stadiums for the Mets and the Yankees—with the city
contributing nearly $500 million to each for extras like parking lots or
site repairs (plus an estimated $480 million in city, state, and federal tax
breaks).[11]

In Brooklyn, Bloomberg and his team supported the building of the
Barclays Center, an arena that would eventually be attached to a business
and residential complex. It was a classic development above and near a
transit hub, but it drew plenty of opposition from old-line Brooklyn residents. They argued that the traffic on game days—it would be the home
for the Brooklyn Nets—could suffocate the entire area. And there was
widespread concern about one proposed design that looked like the upended half of a huge barrel before a new round of architects from SHoP
created a giant bird's nest, as much sculpture as architecture.[12] The Barclays Center also had plenty of government help (estimates ran to more
than $2 billion in city and state benefits by 2008,[13] four-plus years before
it opened). Bloomberg was so pleased with the project and its prospects
for giving the city another financial boost that he held his last State of the
City speech at the arena.[14]

Finally, perhaps Bloomberg's most important venture for his own
personal legacy was a new graduate school on Roosevelt Island that began
to take shape after he left office, some of it with a generous helping from
Bloomberg's considerable stash of funds.

How did all this happen? Development is as complicated as the economy
and the humans who live in it, of course, but it is worth focusing on two
important events in the Bloomberg years. One was Dan Doctoroff's push
to win the Olympics in 2012. The other was the drive by Amanda Burden, Bloomberg's planning commissioner, to rezone the city.

Doctoroff, who would be deputy mayor for economic development for nearly seven years, was widely viewed inside city hall as the son Bloomberg didn't have. A New Jersey native and graduate of Harvard and the University of Chicago Law School, Doctoroff was a tall, striking figure whose years at Lehman Brothers and a private equity firm called Oak Hill Capital Partners provided his cushion while he worked for $1 a year, like the mayor. Doctoroff did not hide his views or his intelligence, and he could suddenly begin to shout when he disagreed with someone (including journalists). People either loved working for him or they took early retirement. (When he left city government, the talented but mercurial Doctoroff skillfully managed Bloomberg's prize asset, the mayor's multibillion-dollar data and media business, Bloomberg LP, until the owner returned from city hall.)

Burden—that is, Amanda Jay Mortimer Burden—was then the fifty-seven-year-old daughter of the elegant Babe Paley and a frequent nominee for best dressed in the fashion courts of New York. She also had a degree in urban planning from Columbia, and she had helped develop the landfill in Lower Manhattan into a well-run, resort-like community called Battery Park. Burden knew Bloomberg slightly from the same social circles. She gladly escorted the candidate to places ripe for development like East Harlem, the under-loved sections of Brooklyn's industrial waterfront, and Manhattan's Lower East Side.[15]

Bloomberg quickly appreciated that beneath all that expensive couture and the dismissive title of socialite, Burden was a smart urban planner, knowledgeable about the most arcane and convoluted city zoning issues. He admired her enthusiasm and, most important, her skills with people. Doubters could be reminded that at Columbia University, Burden's master's degree thesis on waste management was widely viewed in the department that year as a must-read.[16]

Burden and Doctoroff were not exactly a team, but they both worked to reinvent the city.

Doctoroff had been trying to lure the Olympic summer games to New York since 1994, and when the Olympic judges said no for that round, Doctoroff and his supporters immediately began aiming for 2012.[17] When Bloomberg hired him to be deputy mayor, he knew Doctoroff would be focused on his elaborate plan to turn the city's five boroughs into a massive Olympian campus. But he also expected Doctoroff to serve another mission—this Olympics plan had to be good for New York City even after the athletes and their fans had moved on. Doctoroff and his lead planner, Alex Garvin, essentially did just that. They reengineered many old ideas about where the city should develop. The New York City bid was a cohesive plan to change old industrial areas into vibrant new spaces for work, play, or places to live in the city.[18]

The centerpiece of Doctoroff's bid turned out to be a major problem, however. It was an elaborate stadium on the West Side of Manhattan that would stretch over a field of rail yards and, like a giant version of the Transformer gadgets beloved by wonky kids, it would convert from an Olympic arena for 86,000 to a football stadium for the New York Jets. Its ceiling would open, and underground it would have room for trucks and a subway. The stadium quickly became unpopular with two tough neighbors: the Dolan family, who owned Madison Square Garden, and, more important, then assembly speaker Sheldon Silver, who represented Lower Manhattan. The Dolans saw the stadium as competition, and they played rough, as they often did. Their ads before Bloomberg's 2005 campaign showed sewage pouring into the Hudson River from the stadium and a bobbleheaded Bloomberg nodding to the Jets' owner, Robert Wood "Woody" Johnson.

But Albany had the final say. It came with the secretive state body known as the Public Authorities Control Board, which met somewhat erratically in the state capital, its agenda often made public only a few minutes before a session. The three important board members (or usually their representatives) were the governor, the senate leader, and the assembly speaker—often referred to in Albany as the three men in a room who essentially controlled the state. Their vote had to be unanimous, and the top two legislative leaders refused to vote in favor of the project, arguing that the development would undermine the slow revival of Silver's district downtown. That killed the stadium, and Bloomberg was livid.[19] Publicly he said simply that "rejection of the stadium will seriously damage our chances at winning the 2012 Games." It would also slow development on the West Side by years, he warned.[20] Bloomberg would be correct about the Olympics. Despite a last-minute alternative plan for a stadium in Queens, in July 2005 the Olympic committee chose London instead of New York.

Even years after the city's Olympics bid was rejected, Doctoroff would talk and write about it with an open nostalgia. Bloomberg, who had spent millions of dollars and too many hours supporting Doctoroff's dream Olympics, was not big on nostalgia. After the news came out that the Olympics would go to London, the mayor responded with one of his favorite comments: "So, what's plan B?" Plan B would take longer, but it mostly turned out to be an important branch of the Bloomberg legacy—proposals for more than 100 million square feet of new office or residential space, three more stadiums, a key subway extension, 2,400 acres of parks, affordable housing for 500,000 people, and a new graduate center for technocrats.[21] In fact, plan B looked a lot like plan A, without the swimming pools or the racetracks or Doctoroff's $2.2 billion stadium.

Some urban experts believed that by losing the Olympics, the city actually won. A team working with Mitchell Moss, director of the Rudin Center for Transportation Policy and Management at New York University, reported that within a few years after the Olympics went to London, "the New York City Olympic Plan has largely been implemented..." Doctoroff's plan focused on seven areas of the city that had been studied for years but were still underdeveloped (the far west side of Manhattan, Brooklyn's East River waterfront, Long Island City in Queens, the Flushing area, Harlem, the South Bronx, and Downtown Brooklyn).[22] Those areas began coming to life under Bloomberg's watch.

• • •

The second bonus for developers was that Burden made certain that nearly 40 percent of the city was rezoned during Bloomberg's reign. Before he arrived, zoning was generally viewed as a negotiation with city officials, and there were so many adjustments to the rules that sometimes it was hard to see how they even existed in some areas. Amanda Burden would earn the name "Demanda" for her forceful control over design and open space as Bloomberg's planning commissioner. But she also doggedly pursued the first citywide rezoning in forty years. It was a crucial gift to those who wanted more stability from the city before they began to invest. That need for new zoning was especially true in areas that had been industrial sites like in Brooklyn or distant parcels like the Far Rockaways, a seaside section of Queens. As a result, during and soon after Bloomberg's time as mayor, there seemed to be cranes and bulldozers and workers in hard hats everywhere.

Not everyone rejoiced in all this building business. There was intense criticism of the tall buildings that seemed to sprout overnight with little or no vetting from the community. The Bloomberg era would be remembered by many as a time when the city built up, when skyscrapers aimed higher and higher, many of them so thin they looked like the narrow "chopstick" buildings of Hong Kong.

The very rich wanted apartments in these tall thin buildings, buildings with wraparound windows. Rich people from other nations, especially Russia and China, parked their money in apartments that could run $10,000 a square foot. Some real estate insiders referred to these palaces as the world's largest safety-deposit boxes, each a high-end security with a fabulous view.[23]

Critics complained that the new owners who spent only a few weeks a year in their plush Manhattan apartments left too much of the city vacant—too dark and lifeless. Many didn't stay around long enough in a year to pay New York City and state taxes.[24] Instead of lamenting the loss of revenue, Bloomberg saw these rich buyers as investors bringing money for restaurants and shopping, limos and furs, and spas and silverware, plus a small troop of workers required for each moneyed guest. "Wouldn't it be great if we could get all the Russian billionaires to move here?" he mused.[25] (This was, of course, long before Russia began meddling in America's elections.)

Bloomberg's development team members insisted that they did not change the rules or the zoning to allow this sudden rise in high-rises. They pointed out that since the 1960s builders collected the rights to build taller by buying development or "air" rights from smaller buildings nearby.[26] A three-story-high church, for example, could sit on a lot that allowed a ten-story building. Instead of ten stories that the church didn't want, it could sell that "air" above its three stories to a developer nearby. Some of these builders had been quietly collecting air rights until the market made it possible to use them, the Bloomberg officials noted. Developers were also allowed to offer amenities like a school or a plaza in the downstairs areas to help them negotiate ways to build up.[27]

It would be hard to argue too vigorously against taller buildings in a city where there is a limited amount of land. But the question often asked was whether there was a pattern for these towers or whether they simply sprouted without warning like weeds. The city's Municipal Art Society raged about these structures in an interactive report called "The Accidental Skyline." The report, which noted that too many of these towers were built without public input, lamented that New York could become a city that is "darker, drearier, and more austere than its people deserve . . . A place where ordinary New Yorkers can't find an affordable apartment while faceless corporations stockpile vacant investment properties."[28] Their solution, repeated more urgently every year since the end of the Bloomberg era, was to change zoning laws that allow this swapping of air rights and other ways to build sky-high, to give the public a better chance to comment on a new tower, and to make certain developers live up to their promises to have plazas or parks open to the public or to build schools or affordable housing.

Bloomberg encouraged this high-end development, primarily as a sign of vitality in his city. Billionaires' Row, as the stretch just south of Central Park became known, brought good construction jobs. Those well-paid workers crafted $10/$50/$100 million Manhattan penthouses with views that said, "I'm really, really rich. Just look. I can see the Tappan Zee Bridge from midtown."

Bloomberg repeatedly welcomed the moneyed class to New York City. He did not want to discourage them with taxes or off-putting talk of the one percent. "If we can find a bunch of billionaires around the world to move here, that would be a godsend," he said, "because that's where the revenue comes [from] to take care of everybody else."[29]

As Bloomberg left office, the independent real estate publication *Curbed NY* catalogued the surge of architectural tower-envy in New York. There were more than twenty skyscrapers in various stages of development, some so tall they needed approval from the Federal Aviation Administration.[30] Nine of them in Manhattan were taller than the Empire State Building's historic 1,250 feet.

One of the first to be completed rose to 1,396 feet at 432 Park Avenue (near Fifty-seventh Street). It is a tall thin box that could be seen around much of the city, which was obviously part of the point. Architect Rafael Viñoly said that the facade was inspired by a trash can—albeit a fancy Josef Hoffmann trash can that cost $225.[31] Then came Central Park Tower, which soared to 1,550 feet and where apartments started in the eight-digit range. The SHoP Architects tower at 111 West Fifty-seventh Street rises to 1,428 feet and looks needle-thin. In midtown, One Vanderbilt climbs to 1,401 feet.[32] At one point, Paul Goldberger, the architecture critic, wrote that the row of towers would create striped shadows on Central Park.[33] But the upward trend was true across the city with new high-rises under construction in midtown Manhattan, Chelsea, Chinatown, and Brooklyn, with more being considered every month.

• • •

For all of Bloomberg's efforts to "incentivize" the corporate world, the most important building site and the tallest office towers in his city were not under his control. The sixteen acres that were once the World Trade Center were still smoldering after the September 11 attacks when Bloomberg took office a few blocks away, but plans for its memorial and the tallest building in the city (at 1,776 feet) would be controlled by the state.

Former mayor Rudy Giuliani and then governor George Pataki, both Republicans, had believed the polls in 2001 that suggested the next mayor would be Democratic candidate Mark Green, a fast-talking consumer advocate who might try to block their every whim. So they created a new group that would essentially allow the governor to oversee the rebuilding of the site. Called the Lower Manhattan Development Corporation, the new structure allowed Pataki to control the site and much of the federal money that Congress had given the city to rebuild.

Early on, Bloomberg and Pataki were supposed to review the two finalists in a global contest to design the master plan for the site. But somehow Bloomberg was not told about the key meeting. The event did not even show up on the mayor's calendar, and it[34] was hard to believe it was a mistake, knowing the firecrackers on Bloomberg's staff. So Pataki alone decided the master planner would be Daniel Libeskind. Libeskind's proposal allowed five skyscrapers, the tallest one being a symbolic 1,776 feet. The losing plan by Rafael Viñoly featured latticework towers, and Pataki decided they looked like two giant skeletons. Bloomberg later agreed. He said they reminded him of "two beer cans," supersized receptacles at the center of the now-hallowed site.[35]

In some ways it should have been a relief to Bloomberg that others were in charge. At the time, he had his own troubles trying to keep the city from sliding back into the desperate 1970s. And the site was intensely complicated—a wall to keep out the river, trains that ran underneath, all kinds of pipes and wires and substructures, plus the need to please and pacify victims' families and mourning New Yorkers, and even the security experts at the city police department. There were 19 public agencies, two private corporations, 101 contractors, and 33 designers eventually involved.[36] And the developer Larry Silverstein, who had leased the towers six weeks before the attack, argued that he had the right to build the towers just the way they were.

After a few years and endless conflicts, the site became as quiet as the tomb some wanted it to be. Only the wind stirred as politicians and Silverstein and the architects and the Port Authority of New York and New Jersey wrestled for control.

Meanwhile, the mayor did not keep quiet about how the Trade Center should fit into his city's landscape. He told his team in city hall that the future of finance would not be confined to Wall Street—there was also midtown, where his own offices were built, and there was already excitement about the possibilities of a new business district on Manhattan's West Side. To Bloomberg, the idea of immediately building back the ten million square feet of office space destroyed in the attack seemed daft.[37]

Bloomberg was one of the few people who dared to be blunt about what it meant to lose the two now-iconic towers. "If we are honest with ourselves," he told the Association for a Better New York in late 2002, "we will recognize that the impact [of the Trade Center] on our city was not all positive." The World Trade Center megaliths and their gale-swept plazas had added to the sterility of the neighborhood, especially after trading hours when the financiers of Wall Street rushed to the suburbs. And he reminded the crowd of business leaders that the unrented space at the Twin Towers had for years "weakened the entire downtown real estate market."[38]

He and his staff did come up with a plan to revitalize the rest of Lower Manhattan—to make it, as they said repeatedly, a working part of the twenty-four-hour city. That would require public amenities to attract private development, the Bloomberg people decided. Their plan, which took many of its ideas from such urban experts as Alexander Garvin of Yale,[39] included extensions to the waterfront parks, ten thousand new apartments, libraries, schools, a new transit hub, ferry service, and a one-seat ride to New York or New Jersey airports. Much of that eventually got done in Bloomberg's twelve years—although the ferries were on and off and the uncomplicated, one-seat rides to the airports never happened.[40]

Bloomberg's downtown did begin to thrive, however. Population in the area more than doubled from 22,700 in 2000 to 49,000 in 2014, and there was suddenly more available housing with Frank Gehry's dramatically torqued skyscraper and other apartment complexes. At least a third of the residents made $200,000 a year and two-thirds of them were under forty-five years old. It was a retailer's dream, a demographic group that could easily drive the economy at full speed.[41]

Finally, in 2005, Bloomberg got his chance to intervene at the Trade Center site. Silverstein, the developer, needed money to build his towers, and he asked for some of the city's $3.35 billion in tax-free Liberty Bonds that were part of the federal effort to help New York after the attack.[42] Bloomberg and Doctoroff quietly commissioned Lehman Brothers to run the numbers on what it would cost for Silverstein to rebuild the World Trade Center site. What they learned was alarming. The analysis found that Silverstein would not have the money even with help from the city and the federal bonds to construct the elaborate arc of tall buildings as proposed by star architect Libeskind. Bloomberg and Doctoroff saw that the hole in the center of Bloomberg's city could remain a wound for years to come, especially if Silverstein went bankrupt and walked away.[43]

It took a while, but in 2006 all parties signed onto a "watershed" agreement to get back to work.[44] Even more important for Mayor Bloomberg, he would take command of the foundation that was supposed to raise money to build the central memorial—two massive voids and waterfalls where the towers had been. Big donors knew about the chaos, and it sounded like an uninviting way to burn money.

Mike Bloomberg, the philanthropist, knew just who to grab by the shoulders to get the necessary millions, and he would, of course, reach into his own bank account for $15 million in seed money.[45] Bloomberg, the engineer, was also anxious to oversee the complex mechanisms needed to build and maintain giant waterfalls almost three stories high that were at the center of the memorial. And the manager-mayor knew how to get things done. Not in twenty years. Tomorrow.

That impatience was on display one day when Bloomberg met with families of the victims. This was a group of people who felt they had a lot of say about what happened on this site, and officials went out of their way to be solicitous. In this case, the family members were arguing about how to arrange the names of the victims around the edges of the great voids. Should the dead be listed alphabetically, clustered by floor? Randomly? Bloomberg talked to—and listened to— the families. He had learned about how names were listed on other memorials like Maya Lin's poignant monument to those lost in Vietnam. Then, listening to the back and forth and then back again that day, Bloomberg suddenly erupted. Red-faced and clearly annoyed, he lectured the mourners about how it was time to move on. He had moved on when his father died while he was in college, he told them. Now it was their turn.

The people running the meeting for the Port Authority were stunned after Bloomberg marched out, leaving behind a roomful of family members as angry as hornets. The Port Authority experts would spend a good hour trying to calm the crowd, but they knew he was right. It was time to move on, and as one official said, "Maybe that's what it's like to be a billionaire and you can say anything. Whatever you think, you say it."[46] It was certainly classic Bloomberg. Whining and malingering and even extended mourning were not part of the Bloomberg way.

Bloomberg, who believed in the power of deadlines, also wanted the memorial to be finished on the tenth anniversary of the attack—September 11, 2011. Soon, however, he began hearing about delay after delay at the site. The design called *Reflecting Absence* by Michael Arad, a young Israeli-American architect then working for the city's Housing Authority,[47] was as complex as it was dramatic. The Port Authority had started working on Arad's massive waterfalls dropping into the footprints of the old Trade Center, but there were also so many other pieces of the site being built at the same time. Each piece seemed to depend on another part like a huge interactive puzzle. The museum would not be ready, that was a given—but, the waterfalls? The names of the victims? The rows of nearly four hundred swamp white oak trees designed to give life to Arad's severe but stunning memorial?

Early in the fall of 2008, Christopher Ward, the executive director of the Port Authority, was summoned to city hall. It was not a friendly request. When Ward arrived and the mayor escorted him to the balcony overlooking his famous bull pen, Bloomberg was primed for battle.

"'I can't believe what I'm hearing,'" Ward remembered the mayor saying. "'I just want you to know that my patience has run out.'" The memorial now had to be the number one priority for the site, Bloomberg demanded. Everything else could slide, but not the memorial. It had to be ready for the ten-year anniversary. Period. No excuses.

That was exactly the kind of direction Ward needed. "That meant I could get back to [the developer, the governor, the families] everybody and when they asked for something else, and I could say, get the fuck in line."[48] The Port workers scrambled for the next three years, and shortly before the opening, the engineers and observers stood around the voids for a test of the giant waterfalls. After a momentary rumble, like a geyser gaining force deep within the earth, the water suddenly crashed down around the massive stone squares. The memorial had worked. Somebody yelled, "Yippee." It felt like a miracle, a marvel of engineering and art after years of delay and disorganization. The powerful cascade also sent a spray of mist as cover for tough construction guys and a few outsiders who were trying unsuccessfully to maintain a tearless, professional reserve.

On September 11, 2011, the memorial opened for the families and for the annual service remembering those lost at that site a decade earlier. On that first day, visitors sobbed as they touched the names of their loved ones engraved around the pools. They left American flags and roses, and some brought paper and charcoal to get a rubbing of a special name.

Presidents Barack Obama and George W. Bush and their wives came to pay their respects along with virtually every politician in the area. Soon as many as six million people would come every year to see the waterfalls and the names and, later, the museum. Bloomberg's fierce deadline deserved much of the credit for that opening day.

As Michael Arad said of his memorial and the city's driven mayor, "It wouldn't have happened without him."[49]

19

TAKING THE HIGH LINE

"It's a no brainer."
—*Bloomberg, in 2001*

In one of his last actions before leaving the mayor's office in 2001, Mayor Rudy Giuliani signed an order to demolish a decrepit elevated railway that darkened the streets of Manhattan's West Side Meatpacking District.[1]

The merchants in the area were relieved. They saw only a seventy-year-old hulk, its rusting bits, crumbling concrete, and pigeon droppings landing on their sidewalks and discouraging their dreams of development. But a small group of enthusiasts, led by two young activists Robert Hammond, an entrepreneur, and Joshua David, a magazine writer, saw a different future for the structure. They were determined to turn the 1.45-mile elevated railway into a park stretching from Fourteenth Street to the Javits Center on Thirty-fourth. Pie-in-the-sky, local critics called it when they were being charitable.

Giuliani's jackhammers failed to arrive before Michael Bloomberg was sworn in as mayor. And the city's new leader believed in parks, as he said repeatedly. They were the city's lungs, as Frederick Law Olmsted once rhapsodized about his Central Park creation. And they were the "catalysts" that Bloomberg so often talked about to help revive his battered city. Parks were attractions that lured people and developers and money.

Early in Bloomberg's first term, Amanda Burden, his planning guru and zoning expert, joined a few early supporters of the High Line, imagining a park that would be unique in all of America. The old railway that Giuliani wanted to tear down could be the city's version of the Coulée verte René-Dumont in Paris, a tree-lined elevated viaduct that had opened nearly a decade earlier. After much very-French disdain, the Coulée soon became one of the city's treasured landmarks. In much the same way, New York City's High Line park could help a fairly seedy area of Manhattan become a vital place with restaurants and shops and offices and apartments, Burden and the advocates argued. But, as she and the friends of the High Line knew, it would not be easy.

In fact, in those first days of the Bloomberg era when the mayor was busy trying to balance a lopsided city budget and working to keep the city intact, the High Line looked like a goner.

Deputy Mayor Dan Doctoroff, who was in charge of development, said at the time that he was skeptical. (He later suggested that was something of a negotiating position.)[2] Doctoroff was at the center of the campaign—one side pushing to get rid of the "blighting influence" of the old railway, the other desperate to save it as a city treasure.

The advocates even used what was usually the clincher in their attempt to convert a skeptic. They invited Doctoroff to see the High Line firsthand. Early in 2002, on an extremely cold, gray day, Doctoroff remembered that "you had to crawl through the chain link fence—it was authorized by CSX [the company that owned the rail bed]—and your first impression was it's cold up here. It's miserable. What's the big deal?"[3]

Doctoroff also worried privately that the High Line might somehow affect his plans for a stadium on the West Side and his obsession with bringing the Olympics to New York City in 2012.[4]

In those early Bloomberg days, the opponents of the High Line—the merchants and landowners—felt confident they could get Doctoroff on their side. In 2002, a group of angry owners of the parking lots and other buildings in the area met with Doctoroff to argue that he must demolish the railway as Giuliani had promised. These Chelsea property owners were escorted by their lawyer, Randy Mastro, once Giuliani's fast-talking deputy, who by then was working for one of the city's biggest law firms.

Mastro arrived dragging a little red wagon, like something borrowed from the children's park nearby. On it was a large piece of concrete, a dangerous chunk that Mastro said had recently fallen from the High Line, the overhead railway.[5]

The property owners also worked the streets, passing out flyers with disturbing photos of rusty holes in the beams and heavy debris that looked ready to drop on members of the fashionable set just beginning to discover the area. One flyer said, "Five engineering firms have said the High Line is dangerous. Take it down before someone gets hurt."[6]

Mastro sent a follow-up letter to Doctoroff warning that property owners were "adamantly opposed to attempting to preserve the High-line [sic] as a trail park, and they view such a trail proposal as a 'pipe dream' and an impediment to economic development in the area . . . Indeed, it is difficult to imagine how such a proposal could possibly become a reality in the face of adjoining property owners' unanimous and unwavering opposition."[7]

The Mastro people seemed to be winning in the courts and even inside the Bloomberg administration. A state court issued an order that might have given the city more authority to tear down the structure, and a representative of the city's Economic Development Corporation, a group in Doctoroff's bailiwick, expressed some relief. "It's about eliminating a public safety hazard," Janel Patterson of the EDC told reporters. "But it's also about enabling the city to move forward and better develop the area."[8]

Once again, destruction loomed. But advocates for the High Line had a surprise waiting for the naysayers. In late 2002, they put out a report titled "Reclaiming the High Line." It made all the arguments about how great the elevated park would be, but the big news for most people was at the front of the book. The foreword was written by Michael R. Bloomberg, the new mayor of New York City.[9]

"Today, on the West Side of Manhattan, we have an opportunity to create a great, new public promenade on top of an out-of-use elevated rail viaduct called the High Line." The mayor had spoken.[10]

For High Liners it was a reminder that Bloomberg had made them a promise about the railway park when he was running for office in 2001. One of the original advocates, Joshua David, had paid $20 to go to a breakfast session and ask the candidate about the possibility. He was so nervous, he wrote his question down and read it over and over before his chance to ask it. David described the High Line, called it a unique opportunity, and asked the candidate if he supported turning it into a park.

Bloomberg did not hesitate that day. "Yes," he said. "It's a no brainer." Bloomberg followed up by signing a letter to the railroad that read, in part, "I'm running for mayor, and I support the High Line so please don't take any action to threaten it."[11]

With memories suddenly restored about how the mayor viewed this venture, the odds shifted again at city hall. Planning Commissioner Amanda Burden and Vishaan Chakrabarti, then city planner for Manhattan, began to work on the details. City Council Speaker Gifford Miller, whose mother, Lynden Miller, was one of the city's premier urban gardeners, gave his support as well. Their problem? The railway owner, CSX, wanted what seemed impossible. Battling a lawsuit by the property owners near the line, rail executives made it clear that they would only release the High Line to the city if every single property owner agreed to drop the suit. It was a classic tangle that most city officials would have resolved with a quick call to the demolition crew.

Not Bloomberg. He had given his word and he expected his development team to "figure it out."[12]

Burden and Chakrabarti spent months trying to get approval of the property owners and, in the end, they essentially bought them off by creating a new zoning district. The Special West Chelsea District became a complicated mix of air rights from the railway park and new rules that would allow builders to build far higher than the previous industrial limits. Burden proposed allowing the developers to add even more height if they contributed to the High Line or created plazas or loggias—open walkways—through their buildings.[13] The rigid industrial zoning would disappear, making way for housing or offices near an entirely new park. It did not take long before the landowners realized they had suddenly won the zoning lottery. Property near the park became prime real estate. Their parking lots or storage vaults were suddenly worth a fortune.

On a sweltering June day in 2009, a beaming Mike Bloomberg cut the ribbon on the High Line park he had endorsed eight years earlier. He was surrounded by dignitaries including Diane von Furstenberg and Barry Diller who had contributed $20 million to the new venture.[14] The state had put up $400,000 and the federal government pitched in $20 million. But the Bloomberg administration had put in the most, adding about $112 million including the money Doctoroff and Bloomberg had spent in the city's financially shaky early years to shore up the literally shaky structure.[15]

When it opened, though, Bloomberg knew it had all been worth it. "Ten years ago, detractors thought the High Line was an eyesore," he said, adding that the visionaries who "recycled" the railway had presented an "extraordinary gift to our city's future." With oversized scissors in hand, he declared that "today we're about to unwrap that gift." [16]

It was indeed a gift to the city. When Bloomberg left office, you could wander along the High Line and see its plantings of 350 species of perennials. There were views of the Hudson River and a nice panorama of what was once the rough terrain of refrigerator plants and cobbled streets for Manhattan's butchers and meat handlers. One high-rise hotel with windows facing the High Line became a particular attraction for a while when guests seemed to enjoy appearing in nude to shock park visitors.[17]

The park was free and often crowded, and by 2018, the railway was drawing as many as seven million people a year from around the world. Even Bloomberg's successor finally visited the park in 2017. Bill de Blasio, who had made a point of staying away from what was clearly a Bloomberg success, eventually toured the city attraction with a herd of schoolchildren whose main job seemed to be helping him avoid the media. Begrudgingly, it seemed, de Blasio managed to christen at least one section of the prized park "very cool." [18]

By then, the High Line had more than paid for itself. City officials at first estimated that the building boom in the area would bring in about $30 million a year. Instead, real estate taxes from the High Line neighborhood reached $100 million in 2010 and were expected to bring the city an additional $900 million over twenty years.[19] There were new buildings on almost every corner, and new apartments were anything but cheap. [20]

One of the most strident opponents of the High Line and a leader in the group working hard to destroy it was Jerry Gottesman, a New Jersey real estate baron who owned parking lots around the New York City area. Gottesman owned land around the High Line including a large parking area beside the old railway. He had purchased the underused land in the early 1980s for $2.4 million. When he finally dropped his opposition, the city began to create the park. And in 2014, Gottesman sold his property for $870 million.[21]

While the area improved considerably with the High Line, there were housing projects nearby that did not get their share of attention. Some advocates for the park lamented that it brought an economic boost to everybody but those on limited incomes who could not afford groceries in the swanky new shops in their area. These advocates suggested that some of those rich tax revenues should go to help the people who can't afford the luxuries around them.

For city lovers, there is another worry that the railroad will become a canyon, a thin green line surrounded by tall, opaque buildings. The desire for an apartment or hotel or office building near the beautifully landscaped railway could become so intense that developers would block the views of the park and the river for all but their own fortunate residents.

The High Line's creators insist they have made it impossible for developers to create a dismal pathway through the area. But the city is a living beast, and if Bloomberg and Burden could change the zoning to create the High Line, a new crowd of city officials could adjust it again to wall off the park.

That said, the High Line was a clear Bloomberg success and an example of how he saw one big part of his job as mayor. As he told the British conservatives, government's role is "to create conditions that will allow development to take place."[22] The High Line fit that requirement almost perfectly.

20

FROM LOW POINT
TO LANDSLIDE—2005

*"You always want to press, and you want to tackle issues
that are unpopular, that nobody else will go after."*
—*Bloomberg, on low polls as mayor*[1]

It was clear to anybody who watched the mayor buzz from event to
event, making policy pronouncements, cutting ribbons, even snarling
at the press, that Michael Bloomberg loved being mayor of New York
City. It was not so clear that New Yorkers felt the same way about him.

To begin with, Bloomberg was competent but not lovable. The property tax increase was so jarring that at one point he earned a 24 percent
approval rating, the lowest for any mayor since the *New York Times* had
been polling such questions. To a city full of Democrats, he brought in the
Republicans—*the Republicans, mind you*—to renominate George Bush for
president at the Republican convention in 2004. Hundreds of protesters
were arrested that week, and some were so roughed up by Ray Kelly's police that the city eventually paid nearly $18 million in settlements.[2]

With the city souring on their billionaire mayor, Bloomberg had a
ready supply of quotes to explain his sudden unpopularity. Besides the
staple about the short attention span for the media—i.e., "Eventually

even Monica got off the cover"—he could be more serious. His version was always: If everybody loves you, you're doing something wrong—or doing nothing at all. Or, if you don't fall, you're skiing on the baby slopes. Great, his political advisers grumbled, but if nobody loves you by election season 2005, you go back to private life. Instead, the savvy political team scrambled to find ways to make their candidate palatable.

One afternoon in early 2004, two of Michael Bloomberg's most seasoned aides slipped out of a city event and reconvened at an Irish bar in uptown Manhattan. Marc Shaw, now the first deputy mayor for operations, and Bill Cunningham, the mayor's communications director, were dressed in their business attire that day—suits, ties, good shoes, the works—and the regulars suddenly grew silent and eyed them warily. "They thought we were the Feds," Cunningham recalled with a chuckle. Instead, the two were trying to figure out a way to help the mayor politically without hurting the city's finances, and after a few rounds of Dewar's for the budget man and Jamesons for the media expert, they hatched a solution. They would not cut the property tax, now a stable source of funds for the city. But since there was extra money coming in, they would give some of it back to the voters as a kind of annual bonus.

Their plan was a classic political solution—a rebate, a check with the mayor's name on it to offer taxpayers a little relief. It was a modern version of the roasted turkey or fifth of bourbon handed out by the politicians of old. When they brought the idea to Bloomberg, he saw the deal as a cheap political ruse. Cunningham remembered the mayor's first reaction. He said, "Cunningham, you're crazy." So Cunningham, Shaw, the budget director Mark Page, and a city lawyer began working on the mayor, showing him exactly how it could be done. The average homeowner's property taxes increased by about $400, so why not send a $400 check to every homeowner who paid that much more in taxes. That would include owners of houses, co-ops, and condo apartments—many of them Bloomberg voters. Renters got zilch, and commercial real estate got zip. Even Donald J. Trump got a $400 rebate on his gilded apartment. "That is just wonderful," the future president sniffed after he complained about commercial real estate taxes in the city. "Today that buys one tank of gas." For a limousine, maybe.[3]

With approval from Albany, the city gave out relief checks every year from 2004 to 2008. It cost the city about $250 million a year in rebates, but, more important, Shaw and company preserved 80 percent of the revenue from the property tax increase.[4]

After grumbling privately about the checks as a political gimmick, when the first batch of over 600,000 went out to homeowners in September 2004, Bloomberg looked like the real winner. He stood beside a large cardboard version of the $400 check, like one of the mock-ups for lottery winners. This was not a gift from the mayor's office, he insisted; he was returning people's own money.

When journalists pointed out how big his name was on the mock-up, he grinned. "For some reason, they put my name on it, too. It doesn't hurt."

It also didn't hurt later when another round of checks went out in October 2005, a few weeks before Bloomberg was facing reelection.

Bloomberg's staff never expected an easy slide into a second term. Many Democrats saw him as an outlier, the accidental mayor who only won last time because the city was busy nursing its wounds from 9/11. Fernando Ferrer, the Bronx Democrat, was the early front-runner who vowed to become the city's first Hispanic mayor.[5]

Plus, even after four years, Bloomberg was still awkward on the campaign trail, and his speeches read a lot better when he wasn't the one reading them. He didn't see political opportunities naturally, like an old pro. New York's senior U.S. senator Charles Schumer recalled being at an event with the mayor when they spotted a sweet-sixteen party, a crowded celebration for a young teenager. Schumer said he told Bloomberg, "Come on, let's go. Parents vote." Bloomberg, however, was reluctant. They weren't invited, he said. Wouldn't politicians ruin such a personal event? Schumer practically dragged him through the door, and once inside, the mayor worked the room so expertly that aides were tapping on their watches, trying to get the two back on the road. As they emerged, Schumer remembered that Bloomberg was elated. "They loved me," he said, clearly surprised.[6]

It also helped that Bloomberg quickly bumped his only Republican competitor from the city ballot. A former city council member, Tom Ognibene, submitted what he thought were enough signatures to challenge the mayor in the Republican race, but Bloomberg's operatives quickly moved in and challenged every name, ultimately bouncing Ognibene from the ballot. It was a stunning turnaround from when Bloomberg complained that it was time "to end this 'gotcha' kind of technique when lawyers comb petitions to find some technical violation." He was talking about such attempts to keep his friend Senator John McCain out of the running for president in New York in 2000. When he had changed his mind, Bloomberg told the *Times*, "The law is the law. You either follow the law, or you don't."[7]

There had been harder lessons for the businessman-turned-mayor. Only one union had openly supported Bloomberg in 2001—the correction officers. To be reelected this time, he needed more. One way was to give the workers better, cushier contracts since the city's finances were getting back to normal. In April 2004, Bloomberg had announced a tentative labor agreement with DC 37, the city's union of public employees with more than 120,000 members.[8] That agreement included a $1,000 lump sum cash payment for every employee, a 3 percent retroactive wage increase for the previous year, and 2 percent plus an extra 1 percent if the union agreed to productivity changes. The total one-time cost to the city was $73 million plus an extra $98 million a year.[9] A year later, the union endorsed Bloomberg for reelection. Some union members argued that the endorsement—which came in mid-July—was made before the Democrats had even chosen their candidate. Wayne Barrett, the city's watchdog at the *Village Voice*, was particularly outraged. His article was illustrated by a picture of a goofy-looking Bloomberg holding up a T-shirt that read "Everyday Heroes." Barrett's headline read "Billionaire Buys Union."[10]

That endorsement was like a quiet announcement that the 2005 election was over. The loss of DC 37 for a Democratic candidate for mayor meant that a full legion of campaign workers had defected to the Republican side. Even worse for the Democrats, Bloomberg and Randi Weingarten, head of the United Federation of Teachers union, negotiated a contract that boosted teachers' salaries considerably and gave principals more power over which teachers worked in their schools. It was not perfect, but it was a good deal, and to the chagrin of the Democrats, the UFT did not endorse that year.

The Bloomberg team was not ready to relax, of course. They would fight through Election Day. They would spend $85 million[11] of his then net worth of $5.1 billion to tout his successes ($11 million more than in 2001)—the smoking ban, the mayoral control of schools, an economy that had revived, a city budget that was looking good for the next few years. Crime was down. Garbage was picked up. The city was humming along at a comfortable pace for most people.

In the end, voters agreed that Bloomberg should keep running the city. He won by a stunning 20 percent of the vote, landslide territory. Out of 1.3 million ballots, Bloomberg got 753,089 votes to 503,219. The Democrat Ferrer had tried a campaign warning that New York had become a tale of two cities—the few rich and the growing poor. (It failed Ferrer, but Bloomberg's eventual successor, Bill de Blasio, used the tale of two cities theme to win in 2013.)

Two important events would stand out among those many changes during those next four years as mayor. He began the fight against guns and the National Rifle Association (see chapter 16), increasingly getting other mayors to join him. And in 2007, he launched another mission that would carry him through the next decade and beyond. Welcome Michael Bloomberg, environmentalist.

Bloomberg made his real debut as one of the city's most active environmentalists during a dazzling event on Earth Day in April 2007. Under the ninety-four-foot-long, fiberglass replica of a blue whale [12] at the city's Museum of Natural History, Bloomberg enjoyed praise (on video) from California's then governor Arnold Schwarzenegger. In the room packed with city dignitaries, including most of the environmental advocates in the region, Bloomberg announced 127 separate initiatives to reduce green-house gases and improve the environment as the city was expected to add a million people by 2030. It was called PlaNYC—A Greener, Greater New York, and it was widely viewed as one of the most ambitious city plans to deal with everything from transportation to air and water quality to the changing climate. Bloomberg promised to push for fewer cars during rush hours, to plant one million trees, to paint more roofs white to save electricity, to demand cleaner heating oil, clean up brownfields, add housing.[13] Every year until he left office, Bloomberg would issue a progress report, a reminder of how far the city still needed to go.

The updates from his staff were one of many ways Bloomberg tried to make certain his press releases weren't simply a politician's airy promises. Where are we? he would ask. What's been done about, you name it? And if it wasn't already clear that Bloomberg didn't want anybody to waste a minute of that second term, which was expected to be his last, there was the new countdown clock. Installed within view of everybody who worked in Bloomberg's open office, the clock began ticking on January 1, 2006. That meant the mayor and his people thought they had until December 31, 2009, or 1,460 days, counting weekends and holidays and long, long workdays. It was a chance to refine and reform and complete the 349 promises made four years earlier—unless, of course, he could find a way to add extra time as mayor.

21

A CITY ON THE MOVE

"It takes a special type of cowardice for elected officials
to refuse to stand up and vote their conscience . . ."
—Bloomberg, furious at Albany legislators refusing to vote on congestion pricing

A massive orange ferry named after Andrew Barberi, a respected high school football coach, churned through the Hudson River from downtown Manhattan toward its usual docking site on Staten Island. It was the afternoon of October 15, 2003, and many of the 1,500 passengers were waiting along the ferry ramps, anxious to get home. Instead of slowing down and sliding into its usual berth, the ferry suddenly turned off course and slammed into a maintenance pier. The huge splinters from the wooden and concrete pier sliced through the ferry, killing eleven people and injuring dozens of others. One law enforcement official reported that bodies had been ripped apart as the pier and the ferry collided.[1]

When the Bloomberg transportation commissioner, Iris Weinshall, got to the site, even she, a veteran of almost fifteen years in top city jobs, was shaken by the apocalyptic scene. Police and transit officials began relaying details, including the bizarre news that the pilot of the ferry had run home and tried (unsuccessfully) to kill himself with a pellet gun.

Mayor Bloomberg, who was making a requisite appearance at a Yankees game, quickly commandeered a helicopter and came to the terminal. He saw a pale Weinshall, who told friends she had expected to be called before the cameras and fired instantly. Instead, the mayor said quietly, "Why don't you tell me what's going on?" He listened, somber, and then when she was apologizing and agonizing, he said, "Well, hey, at least I got to leave the Yankee game." It was a classic Bloomberg attempt to relieve her distress with a weak joke, in this case by mentioning a well-known personal quirk—he was never really comfortable sitting and passively watching much of anything, be it opera or an awards ceremony or, as a born-and-bred Boston Red Sox fan, another Yankees game.

At about 2:00 a.m. the next morning, as Weinshall waited at the Staten Island terminal for federal investigators, her cell phone rang. "This is Mike," the mayor said. "Do me a favor. After they come, I want you to go home, have a stiff scotch, go to sleep and tomorrow morning we'll start fresh and deal with whatever we've got to deal with."[2]

There would be plenty to deal with. The law required two pilots in the wheelhouse for docking, but only the cocaptain, Richard Smith, was at the wheel that day, and he was short on sleep and running on painkillers when he blacked out at the fateful moment. Both he and Patrick Ryan, the ferry supervisor, were sentenced to just over a year in jail for manslaughter.[3] And the city would pay out nearly $100 million to victims and their families. One family member testified that her brother "was so mangled and maimed that we could not see his body."[4]

Reports on the tragedy blamed the pilots and ferry operations, as well as the transportation commissioner. But Bloomberg supported Weinshall for four more years when she reorganized the department including new, tougher rules for piloting the Staten Island ferries. And when she resigned in January 2007, he praised her "extraordinary seven year tenure."[5]

Some of her critics thought "extraordinary" was a loaded word; she was, after all, the wife of U.S. Senator Charles Schumer. But Weinshall saw it as support and fierce public loyalty to his staff. The ferry crash was a powerful example of how Bloomberg could be a solid mensch, she figured, good on his promise to let people work and to back them, publicly at least, when they failed. Or, as she knew firsthand, when something went terribly wrong.[6]

Things easily go wrong in a city with 8,000 miles of streets (about a quarter of the landmass of the entire city),[7] 12,750 miles of sidewalks,[8] and more than 250,000 streetlights.[9] The Staten Island Ferry, normally a boon to commuters and once the favorite way for the young Bloomberg to entertain dates on the cheap, carried about 65,000 passengers a day, or 22 million every year, across the Hudson between downtown Manhattan and Staten Island.

On average, the streets and bridges carried nearly two million private cars—fortunately most of the city's commuters take the bus or subway. Trucks brought in 400 million tons of freight each year, so much that advocates for more public transit began referring to congestion caused by these big rigs as the city's constant "clustertruck."[10]

There were 13,300 yellow taxis in Bloomberg's day and nearly 8,000 apple-green cab licenses were allowed for the outer boroughs. Uber soon cut into taxi fares with 25,000 vehicles every week, and eventually 5,000 more provided by Lyft. More than 5,700 city buses bounced along the city streets, and nearly 8,000 bigger, sleeker buses brought in commuters from the suburbs.

Crossing the street was still a risk. There were 187 pedestrian deaths in 2002 and 184 in 2013 before Bloomberg's successor made it an issue and cut the number to 148 in 2016.[11] There were more than 36,000 private bikers and 5,670 of Bloomberg's Citi Bikes for sharing by 2013, plus 1,461 licensed pedicab drivers mostly looking for clueless tourists with fat pockets. From the sky, the whole manic city could look like a panicked ant colony with every critter on some urgent, death-defying mission.[12]

Over twelve years, Bloomberg and his team touched almost every aspect of transit, warning that without some progress this "most critical" network could create "the greatest single barrier" to the region's growth.[13] To make getting around the city easier, they improved pedestrian signals at crosswalks. (The city even painted eyes on busy sidewalks to help tourists know which way to look before crossing the street.) They added bike lanes and green taxis for the outer boroughs and vehicles called by app. They reordered bus routes and extended a subway line, normally a state matter. And mostly they revolutionized the use of the city's streets. They were no longer lanes reserved for motorized vehicles. They became "complete streets" shared by cars, trucks, buses, bikes, and people. "The Bloomberg people simply changed the way the streets in the city were managed and used,"[14] said Mitchell Moss, professor of urban planning and director of the Rudin Center for Transportation at New York University and an occasional consultant to Bloomberg.

For any city, such a catalog of changes would be a big deal. For New Yorkers, it was another seismic development brought on by Bloomberg's innovators. But it would take the mayor quite a while to figure out exactly what he wanted for the streets and waterways in his city.

In his first days in office, Bloomberg was like most public officials who saw easing city traffic as the main transportation problem. For that early Mayor Bloomberg, Weinshall was a good fit. She had been transportation commissioner under Rudy Giuliani, and some of the mayor's advisers told him that it was a mistake for her to stay on because she was married to such a powerful politician. Never hire somebody you can't fire, one Bloomberg aide kept muttering.[15] Weinshall worked hard to make the city traffic run smoothly, and Bloomberg also clearly loved watching the complex transportation patterns in his city. He pestered Weinshall and her experts with questions about how the streets worked, how the stoplights were timed. Finally, Weinshall and her team took him on a tour of the traffic control center in Queens, where traffic engineers manipulated the timing for red lights and flashing pedestrian walk signs—all on a bank of blinking computers. A small group of transit experts watched as their sixty-year-old boss, their mayor, suddenly morphed into a kid transfixed as if by a new Lionel train set. This was his element, computers tracking what was going on much like the Bloomberg Terminals back at his company. He kept asking questions, kept saying he, too, was a trained engineer, until a nervous press aide finally coaxed him to his next scheduled event.

Near the end of his first term, however, the press began criticizing him for failing to think creatively about transportation, not that such criticism mattered, as he would let you know quickly, if asked.

"The mayor doesn't have a large-scale transportation accomplishment to point to, but rather a collection of smaller, but worthwhile initiatives," Jon Orcutt, executive director of the Tri-State Transportation Campaign, a public transit advocacy group, said in 2005.[16] That was an election year and Bloomberg wasn't a man satisfied with "smaller, but worthwhile initiatives."

It was time to bring in big-change agents, especially since his team of environmentalists predicted another million people in the city by 2030. Would they live in one, big dirty traffic snarl? A permanent gridlock?

Bloomberg's most surprising move was to appoint Janette Sadik-Khan, the kind of transportation renegade who would "disrupt," to put it in a businessman's jargon, the way New York commuters moved around their city. Sadik-Khan had solid credentials. She was born in California but spent some of her youth in the city (her mother was a reporter for the old *New York Post*).[17] A graduate of Occidental College, majoring in political science, she earned a law degree at Columbia, worked with Mayor David Dinkins, then moved to the Federal Transit Administration in D.C. under President Clinton. Finally, she was working in the transit section at Parsons Brinckerhoff, an international transportation engineering and design firm, when the city beckoned again.[18]

Few people would forget meeting Janette Sadik-Khan. She was physically striking, a biker herself who was slim, athletic, and often animated. She was also a powerful saleswoman—that last trait being the key to anybody's success, as Bloomberg often said. Streets, buses, boring old infrastructure issues—she could make it all sound sexy.

When she came to make her pitch for the job in early 2007, Bloomberg sat quietly—so quietly Sadik-Khan thought she had talked herself out of a position she wanted badly. She seemed unafraid to shatter the old way of doing things. She did not talk about how to ease traffic jams. That was the old way, she said. She wanted to "calm" traffic in order to make it safer for people on foot and on bicycles as well as those in cars and trucks. ("Calming" traffic seemed to be the preferred term for slowing it down, a concept that was not always popular with drivers.)

She even wanted to limit traffic coming into Manhattan the way London and Stockholm had done so successfully. (Using what was called "congestion pricing," London had charged more to enter the city center, cut traffic by 15 percent and made it easier to get from here to there more quickly.)[19] Make it cost more, she advised. People will take the bus. She also proposed a bike-sharing program being tried in other cities, plus dedicated lanes on city streets for bikes and buses.

These were still difficult ideas for New Yorkers perpetually stalled in traffic or stuck in the subway, but Bloomberg saw his kind of agitator, and he recognized her high-energy marketing skills. Sadik-Khan was also more like his health commissioner, Tom Frieden, or his education chancellor, Joel Klein—high energy, high impact. Bloomberg hired her a short while later at a breakfast of "burned toast and coffee" at Viand, his favorite diner on Manhattan's Upper East Side, as she remembered.[20]

It turned out that Sadik-Kahn's proposals were many of the same ideas that Bloomberg and his staff had been quietly circling for their massive environmental agenda, PlaNYC 2030. That plan, announced a short while later,[21] would call for all kinds of environmental changes, including those aimed at curbing city traffic or promoting ways to cut down on contaminated air by improving mass transit or making bikes more convenient. The plan noted that without such changes, "by 2030, virtually every road, subway and rail line will be pushed beyond its capacity limits."[22]

Sadik-Khan would quickly take on two issues that would define Bloomberg's transportation policy and stir controversies for years to come. One was the addition of pedestrian plazas, first in Times Square—forcing cars to share the streets with tourists and buskers dressed up as characters like Elmo and Dora the Explorer. The other was making room on more streets for more bicycles. During her time, cyclists began with a little over 500 miles of bike routes, which doubled to more than 1,100 by the time she and Bloomberg left office. She made New York into a cycling city with 45,000 New Yorkers biking to work in 2015, compared to about 16,000 when Sadik-Khan took the job. [23]

Bloomberg said he was often skeptical about Sadik-Khan's ideas, at least in the beginning. Closing traffic lanes in Times Square was clearly a radical move. "My first thought was that it was the stupidest idea I'd ever heard," Bloomberg said. "Ten minutes later, she had convinced me." [24]

Sadik-Khan wanted to get around the normal systems for tampering with city streets. If she had to wait for the community to approve her new designs, the traffic pattern would almost certainly stay put for years. She decided to try it as a pilot project with orange traffic cones and cheap patio chairs to make the plazas pedestrian friendly. (They were so friendly that at one point somebody set up an outdoor bedroom with a rug, lamp, and a small cot—some New Yorker's very brief attempt to comment on the city's housing crisis.)

Sadik-Khan would take her pitch to anybody who would listen. When she came to the *Times* to promote more room for people, not cars, in these plazas along Broadway and in Times Square, Andrew Rosenthal, then the editorial page editor, was a car man who tended to be skeptical about sharing more of the streets with pedestrians. Remove pavement for sidewalks and you add problems for cars, he argued. After Sadik-Khan made her pitch that plazas would be better for people *and* cars, he bristled, then softened, then relented and allowed a piece to run in favor of the new public spaces.

Bloomberg's transportation saleswoman was also unafraid of entering the combat zone between people who ride bikes and almost everybody else. In New York City, you could easily start a shouting match about whether bikers were a menace or they deserved a bigger share of the road. Sadik-Khan began adding bike lanes,[25] but it was not always easy.

During an anti-bike lane protest near Prospect Park in Brooklyn in 2010, several dozen residents were on the streets to challenge a bike path that had become, in the words of one local columnist, "the most controversial slab of cement outside the Gaza Strip."[26] If that seemed a bit over the top, Sadik-Khan quickly countered by convincing about two hundred pro–bike lane advocates to show up and support her new cement slab for cyclists. Sadik-Khan claimed that her protestors had created "likely one of the largest public demonstrations regarding a single transportation project since Jane Jacobs held the line against Robert Moses's Lower Manhattan Expressway half a century earlier."[27] Bloomberg had to deal with the outrage (even his former commissioner Weinshall and her powerful husband were reportedly unhappy with the bike lane in their Brooklyn neighborhood). But the mayor did little more than listen, and Sadik-Khan got her way.

A real key to the city's bike revolution was Citi Bike—New York's version of bike sharing that had worked for commuters in Paris, London, and Washington, D.C. At the debut of Citi Bike, Sadik-Khan declared that she and Bloomberg were launching "a new public transportation system for New York City."[28] It was not cheap—Citibank contributed $41 million[29] for the first five years, and in 2013, bikers would each cough up $95 plus tax for a year's worth of unlimited forty-five-minute rides.[30] There had been repeated delays before the first six thousand bikes became available in Bloomberg's last year in office, some stalled because of a faulty system, another time because of flooding with Hurricane Sandy in 2012.[31] But soon the bikes were spotted across Lower Manhattan and midtown, plus a few parts of Brooklyn, and the number of bikes would more than double and spread into other areas with more than 140,000 paying members by 2019.

Mike Bloomberg seemed to relish the controversies stirred by his transportation guru. He clearly admired her energetic style, but more than that, he approved of the goal to open city streets for more than trucks and cars. Did he ever ride a Citi Bike? He sat on one, at least once, according to his staff.[32]

• • •

As for taxis, Bloomberg was an airplane (or helicopter) guy who rode in chauffered SUVs. Sometimes those SUVs took him to the subway, and the billionaire mayor often boasted that he used his senior MetroCard that gave cut-rate fares for anyone over sixty-five.

Bloomberg also knew that the taxi system needed fixing, and he did indeed make dramatic changes. Riders had more choices at the end of his dozen years, but his administration's efforts to make the city money by selling taxi medallions that are needed to operate a cab contributed to the plight of unsuspecting taxi drivers, who were essentially tricked by unscrupulous private lenders into taking out predatory loans. Like other mayors, Bloomberg counted on the profits from selling these medallions, which became like any bubble, with prices soaring to more than $1 million, and then, deflating as the taxi industry changed. City officials argued that federal regulators were supposed to catch these scams, but immigrant drivers who had taken out loans they could not pay back were destroyed financially in the process.[33]

But Bloomberg's focus when it came to taxis was not on the company or the driver. It was on the person hailing the cab or looking for a ride to outer Queens. Other politicians in the city and state had too easily bowed to the demands of the Yellow Cab owners who too often abused the overworked drivers who, in turn, often refused to take fares outside the city's hot zones. If you tried to hail a cab from downtown Manhattan to, say, upper Harlem, good luck. Bloomberg wanted something that hadn't happened in the taxi business for years—competition.

David Yassky, a former member of the City Council who became the chairman of the New York City Taxi and Limousine Commission in 2010, was a Princeton graduate with a law degree from Yale. He promised to add competition and fairness to the hired-car business in the city. Yassky would push for more taxis and other hired cars like Uber and then Lyft (a company he later joined as a consultant).

When the politically powerful taxi fleet owners began to protest and flex their considerable muscle, Bloomberg prepared to go to war, if necessary, to support his commissioner. When Yassky introduced a new taxi—

the Nissan NV200—fleet owners hated it. So did many customers, and finally the fleet owners sued the city. After the taxi crowd won the first round, Bloomberg was so furious that when he encountered Gene Freidman, then the owner of the largest fleet of yellow taxis in the city, the mayor threatened to "destroy your fucking industry" once he left office. He later denied the outburst when it was reported in the *New York Post*, but the encounter came at a New York Knicks game at Madison Square Garden, and there were witnesses.[34]

The mayor and Yassky also wanted people to have access to hired cars—another revolutionary idea that infuriated the Yellow Cab operators. There were 13,300 yellow taxis, designated as such with the valuable "medallions" then owned by just a few companies. Most cruised downtown Manhattan or waited for a nice fare at the airports.

So Bloomberg and Yassky created licenses for the apple-green taxis. These cars were designed to pick up stranded commuters who needed a ride outside of the city center or the airports. But Bloomberg also encouraged Uber to begin its work in the big city to take people where yellow cabs didn't want to go.

By the time Bloomberg left city hall, the green cars, like the yellow taxis, were beginning to lose ground to Uber and Lyft. The bright green cabs[35] were earning $386,965 a day for about 3,500 cabs in 2018, compared to $862,099 a day three years earlier. But Bloomberg could find success in a better array of choices for the customer. Finally, it was easier for somebody outside of the Manhattan airport corridors to hail a ride.

If there was one big setback in Bloomberg's transportation goals during his time as mayor, it was the effort to limit traffic coming into central Manhattan by charging more during rush hours. Congestion pricing, as it was known, would be tough, he knew, when his administration proposed a three-year pilot project. (Some of his advisers wanted to change the name, arguing, not entirely facetiously, that it sounded more like the remedy for a sinus condition than a traffic problem.)

Bloomberg's data showed that the average New Yorker spent forty-nine hours stuck in traffic every year in 2007, up from eighteen hours a year in 1982.[36] And it could only get worse. The problem, he knew, was Albany—New York's state legislature, often referred to as the place where good ideas in New York go to die.

Indeed, Bloomberg's "congestion pricing" plan in 2008 turned out to be too futuristic for the state politicians who could not see beyond the car culture in their own neighborhoods. Some called it a tax on people who lived outside Manhattan. The word "elitist" was used frequently by opponents in Albany. Even with a few changes to relieve costs for lower-income commuters, the proposal drew noisy criticism from noisemakers outside the city's central zone.

With the deadline looming for a federal grant, Bloomberg worked hard to convince state lawmakers to just give his plan a try. Just three years. But Bloomberg also made matters worse for some in the Albany crowd. State Senator Liz Krueger of Manhattan remembered when an exasperated Bloomberg came to argue privately for congestion pricing. The meeting with Democrats quickly grew "unproductive," as senators kept reminding Bloomberg that he gave campaign contributions to their Republican opponents.

Bloomberg grew more perturbed by the minute, Krueger remembered, in part because New York would lose $350 million in federal matching funds if Albany didn't agree to his plan. Finally, he said, "'Okay if we lose that federal money, you guys have to come up with it, $350 million among you,'" she recalled. "Then he says, 'Oh, wait, I'm the only one in the room who has $350 million.'"

The Democrats did not take it well, and after Bloomberg stormed out, Krueger saw him in the hall of the state capitol. "I said something like, 'Mr. Billionaire . . . did you really think that was an effective model? I think this was a wasted trip for you.'"

A few minutes later, he found Krueger and said, "'My staff says I owe you an apology.'" When Krueger agreed, she said they laughed and worked together fairly well for years afterward.[37] "He likes people who are blunt, who tell him exactly what they think," she concluded.[38]

Congestion pricing died formally that year when the Assembly Democrats decided not to bring it to the floor for a vote. Not even a vote. The mayor was understandably furious. "If that wasn't shameful enough," Bloomberg said of the loss in the assembly, "it takes a special type of cowardice for elected officials to refuse to stand up and vote their conscience . . ."[39] And shortly afterward, a federal grant of $364.5 million for traffic "calming" that could have gone to New York City went instead to Chicago and Los Angeles.[40]

In a few years, the Bloomberg congestion plan would be back, and by 2019, state officials looking for ways to fund the century-old subway system agreed to charge fees and tolls for anyone driving into the busiest streets of Manhattan starting in 2021.[41] Bloomberg wasn't wrong to push for congestion pricing, as it turned out. He was just early.

22

SILICON ISLAND

"The world is about to end tomorrow."
—*Bloomberg on the eve of the financial meltdown, 2008*

Michael Bloomberg was scheduled to board his plane for the West Coast for a major event with the then California governor Arnold Schwarzenegger, when he suddenly contacted his top political organizer, Kevin Sheekey. "I think we have to cancel our trip," Bloomberg said. "The world is about to end tomorrow."[1]

Treasury secretary Hank Paulson had called that evening of September 14, 2008, to alert the Mayor of Wall Street that the mighty Lehman Brothers was going down and taking much of the economy with it. A few hours later, the Lehman Brothers investment bank with more than $600 billion in assets filed for bankruptcy. It would be the largest bankruptcy filing in U.S. history, the stunning failure of a firm that had survived nearly 150 years of financial turmoil including the Great Depression.[2]

All day and into the evening of September 15, the sidewalks near Lehman Brothers' headquarters in Times Square were overrun with gawkers, journalists, and dozens of bewildered Lehman workers holding boxes overstuffed with personal files, family photos, and mementos. A Wall Street recruiter handed out cards beneath what was once Lehman's three-story-high electronic television crawl. A street artist nearby had crafted a scowling caricature of Lehman chief executive Dick Fuld. Across the bottom, one ex-worker had scratched a bitter goodbye note: "I hope his villa is safe." [3]

For all the agony in Times Square and Wall Street, the Lehman implosion was not a local problem. It was another powerful signal that the whole world was sliding into the worst financial crisis since the 1930s. And Michael Bloomberg's city, with so much of its wealth tied to the financial industry, was about to fall into another of its slumps that seemed to come and go with alarming regularity. This time, the city would lose roughly 150,000 jobs and suffer from an unemployment rate rising to 10.2 percent. [4]

Bloomberg would be forced to trim his city budget and try to hold on to commercial real estate taxes set to expire. Even more dramatically, the man who had stepped in to save the city after the financial effects of the World Trade Center attacks on 9/11 would use the sudden downturn in 2008 as another reason that he should stay in charge and run the city for a third term a year later (see chapter 24).

But perhaps Bloomberg's most important response to what became known as the Great Recession would not be fully recognized for nearly a decade.

Like other Wall Street veterans, Bloomberg knew only too well how New York City suffered from the bears of the marketplace. Sometimes, looking at the government balance sheets, this city of over eight million people could seem like a one-industry town, with Wall Street and its lavish bonuses funding the gaps in city and state budgets. When those bonuses withered, so did New York.

Bloomberg's answer was to expand the kinds of businesses in the city, to provide more of a buffer against the dreaded Wall Street cycles. He was not the first mayor or public official or concerned New Yorker pushing for diversification of the city's businesses (and its tax base), but Bloomberg pursued it in a particularly intense way. He wanted more culture, more entertainment, more tourists, of course, but even tourists could be fickle, and Bloomberg wanted some of his smartest and most intense young aides to find a solution.

To do that, Bloomberg and his top advisers created a group that would soon call themselves the "game changers." They were led by Seth Pinsky, a graduate of Columbia College in ancient history and then Harvard Law School. Bright, intense, and straightforward, Pinsky had become a real estate lawyer, then joined the city government in 2003 as vice president of the NYC Economic Development Corporation, the city authority that managed or encouraged many of the city's top real estate ventures. By 2008 and still in his midthirties, he was president of the development corporation and just the kind of intense leader Bloomberg wanted for this task.

To help out, the mayor offered Pinsky and the game changers his star-studded address book. Armed with numbers and emails for about 350 of the city's biggest names in business, academia, media, government, politics, and community affairs, the small group of interviewers soon focused on one main question: "If there is one thing about NYC that you could change that would have the greatest impact on the city's economy, what would it be?"[5]

The idea was to get people to think big. This was not about a zoning change or tax break. Nothing from Albany. The game changers wanted something that would establish a new economic foundation to help New York City thrive for the next hundred years. Think grandchildren, they suggested. Great-grandchildren.

The response was dramatic. While the city was indeed a mecca for the high school soprano or the fashion designer or TV journalist or business kid who wanted to make it big, another kind of talent was in short supply. Corporations needed super-savvy engineering graduates including the "quants" or math whizzes who would know about quantitative analysis and applied sciences, people who had the technical expertise, the engineering know-how, to start or save companies stuck in the compli-cated, computerized world of the twenty-first century.

What New York City needed was a new university, some ventured. New York had some excellent universities, they agreed, but the city needed its own MIT. New York was attracting high-tech business, but it lacked the city's own Stanford University, which had helped feed many of the big winners in Silicon Valley.

A new science and technology university was indeed a big thought, so big that it sounded almost whimsical, like another futuristic proposal from a think-tank seminar. But creating the future out of thin air was exactly what Bloomberg wanted the game changers to do.

Pinsky remembered the evening at city hall when he and then deputy mayor Bob Lieber nervously took their findings to the mayor. They laid out the proposal for a brand-new academic center, somewhere in the city. It could be an arm of an established university, they ventured—a New York City branch of Stanford or Cornell.

As Pinsky and Lieber made their pitch for a project that could take years, Bloomberg sat quietly through the presentation. He did not inter-rupt, but he also did not fidget or sigh or send any signal of how he felt, up or down. Finally, when the presentation was finished, Bloomberg said it was a great idea with one glaring flaw. "Your time line is not aggressive enough," he said. "And if we're going to do this, we're really going to have to be aggressive." As he left for his next evening appointment, it was hard for some in that room to resist doing cartwheels.[6]

Then the project stalled. Pinsky and his colleagues had reached out to a few universities and quietly asked whether they might be interested in some kind of deal—land from the city in exchange for building a tech graduate center.[7] The response was encouraging, much better than inside city hall. The budget office worried about how you could give away city land. Others simply thought it was too far-fetched, even for a mayor who promised to pursue big ideas.

Then in June 2010, the mayor hired Robert Steel to replace Lieber as deputy mayor. Like Bloomberg, Steel knew the inner workings of modern business. He had been at Goldman Sachs for almost thirty years, served as undersecretary of the Treasury for President George W. Bush and orchestrated the sale of Wachovia Bank to Wells Fargo in 2008. Perhaps more important for Pinsky and the game changers, Steel was a dynamo whose abrupt and sometimes-abrasive manner could offend almost as easily as he could inspire. He was not enchanted with the city's social scene or its prying media. He once told a New York *Daily News* reporter that he lived mostly in Connecticut because he had dogs, and "where would you rather live if you were a dog?"[8] But Steel moved at Bloomberg's preferred high speed, and the mayor clearly admired him.

When Pinsky took the plan to Steel, the new deputy rushed over to Bloomberg's desk to confirm that the mayor really wanted this new university. Steel had been chairman of the board of trustees for Duke University, and this was the perfect task for him. A competition to create an entirely new university? Once the mayor told Steel he had already approved it and it was a great idea, "that was basically the moment when the whole thing was unleashed," Pinsky said.

Four very short months later, a whisker in government time, Bloomberg announced that the city was "seeking responses from a university, applied science organization facility or related institution" to create a new branch in New York City. He wanted the new facility to focus on the science and research that "particularly . . . lend themselves to commercialization."

The city was willing to do its part, the mayor announced.[9] There would be land available, he said, overruling some in his budget department. And he suggested four sites—the Brooklyn Navy Yard, Roosevelt Island, Governors Island, and the Farm Colony, a former poorhouse on Staten Island.

A few weeks later, Bloomberg explained in a letter to dozens of select "members of the higher education community" that the city was offering "full-throated support" in order to be "not just a leader but the leader" in the academic fields of "science, technology, engineering and mathematics," often known by simple shorthand as STEM. The letter was co-signed by twenty-three New York leaders including U.S. Senator Charles Schumer, former mayor Ed Koch, former CEO of AOL Tim Armstrong, several real estate and other business executives, British editor Sir Harold Evans, and fashion designer Diane von Furstenberg.

Bloomberg was now in top gear on the project. He met with presidents of universities. He took university representatives to breakfast at Gracie Mansion and arranged for tours of the New York Stock Exchange. This was a "once-in-a-generation" opportunity he told them. This was free land. Free land!! In New York City!! And grants, even some it would turn out, from his own vast supply of funds. The salesman Bloomberg was on full-throttle. How could they resist?

Within two months, Bloomberg announced that the city had received eighteen expressions of interest from top universities. They came from Finland, Korea, India, and in America, included Carnegie Mellon, NYU, Columbia, Cornell, Cooper Union, Purdue, Stanford, and the University of Chicago.[10]

There was grousing, of course. This was New York, and Bloomberg had already irritated many in the city's large academic community by suggesting that New York City lacked a top-flight engineering school. City Councilman Ydanis Rodriguez was miffed that incentives were being offered to outsiders when the city budget still had gaps from the economic crisis. Money should go to city schools, he argued. "We have great programs here."[11]

In the next few months, the contestants narrowed to two—Stanford and Cornell. And they were competing for one spot—Roosevelt Island, the stretch of twelve acres in the city's East River. The island once housed a decrepit New York City Lunatic Asylum that was exposed as a "human rat-trap" by the intrepid journalist Nellie Bly in 1887 and was later used as a facility for smallpox victims.[12] By 2011, however, there were rows of apartment buildings, some of them offering high-end places with stunning views of Manhattan. And for commuters, there was also a cable car over the river and a subway for those nervous about heights.

The word among city leaders in those days was that nobody could beat Stanford. Perhaps most important, Stanford's representatives in New York City seemed to believe that nobody could beat Stanford. As Steel said at one point of Stanford's competitors, "They're a bit like lining up against the Yankees."[13] Cornell, the early underdog, dismissed such talk and simply fought harder. The officials in Ithaca, New York, where Cornell has its main campus, saw this contest the same way Bloomberg was selling it. This was indeed the opportunity of a lifetime. Despite having a medical school and other facilities in New York City, Cornell's academic center was about 250 miles away from Manhatttan, a distant, Ivy League gem often underrated by New York's Harvard-Yale-Princeton crowd.

Cornell was so hungry for this spot that an army of Cornell alumni in the city were organized to rally for their team. Every day Cornell made another pitch to somebody—the business community, the cultural mavens, the media. When Cornell's president, Dr. David Skorton, presented his university's proposal to a few journalists in 2011, he said, "Our campus is absolutely electrified by this proposal."

Some in the Stanford crowd back in California were not so thrilled about a new campus on the other side of the country, and shortly before the winner was announced, Stanford suddenly pulled out.[14] City hall insiders said that Stanford had come up with an impressive proposal, but the school's representatives worried about how hard it was to build anything in New York City. They wanted more assurances that the city would protect them from all kinds of New York City construction problems.

"From their perspective, it was kind of an experiment, and if it worked, they would be all in, and if it didn't, they could pack up and go back home," one insider said.[15]

Cornell, in contrast, promised they would be there to stay. Also, Cornell had a secret weapon. Very quietly—first in Beijing and then at the Cornell Club in Manhattan—top officials of Cornell met with leaders at the Technion-Israel Institute of Technology, Israel's MIT. They began working out a deal to win the Roosevelt Island contest together. They would be joint tenants, an unbeatable combination.

On December 19, 2011, almost exactly a year after announcing the contest, Michael Bloomberg revealed that Cornell University and Technion-Israel Institute of Technology would build a $2 billion, eleven-acre tech campus designed "to make New York City home to the world's most talented work force." The city would provide the land with a ninety-nine-year lease and an option to buy the land at the end of that term for $1. Bloomberg's city would also provide $100 million to cover capital costs to prepare the site.[16] The billionaire club had helped considerably. A Cornell alumnus, Charles Feeney, who made billions of dollars with his Duty Free Shoppers Group, pitched in $350 million.[17,18] And Bloomberg himself soon produced $100 million for a building that was named for his two daughters. The entire project would be built to serve 2,500 students and 280 faculty members by 2043.[19]

When Bloomberg left office at the end of 2013, his genius university was still a muddy field on Roosevelt Island. Technion-Cornell had promised that the first phase would open four years later.

On a warm September day in 2017, with engineers still putting the finishing touches on two elaborate buildings and gardeners hastily tamping down bits of sod to make a green space, Cornell Tech invited the former mayor to the formal opening of the Roosevelt Island campus.

Under a large tent set up for the occasion, political all-stars from the city, the state, and Washington had arrived to celebrate. Congresswoman Carolyn Maloney of New York City declared that this was finally "New York City's MIT." Governor Andrew Cuomo called the campus "an extraordinary, extraordinary, singular achievement," comparing Bloomberg to Franklin Roosevelt, who "recognized the possibility of government—to make a difference in people's lives," Cuomo said. "He was not about theoretical change, or change in the abstract. He was about change in practical terms. FDR knew that holding office was not the real goal of an elected official, that pontification and mere advocacy are not the goals of an elected official.[20]

"Mike Bloomberg had the formula—vision plus confidence plus

achievement equals progress," Cuomo added, then pulling the ultimate Cuomo compliment, he compared Bloomberg to his own father, Mario Cuomo. He is "a progressive who gets things done."

The room was tense and silent. Mayor Bill de Blasio, who had offered a little faint praise for his predecessor, was uncommonly still, perhaps trying not to register the pointed comparisons. Bloomberg, however, now had his Silicon Island. And Technion-Cornell would cement his efforts to create the talent needed to turn New York into a haven for the tech world. Google would soon expand its presence in the city—purchasing the massive old Port Authority building in Chelsea and start adding more jobs, more real estate.[21] Twitter had a natty office for about four hundred people in Manhattan that included a bar for lattes with your initials or your favorite rose. Microsoft had added people and office space. Another bonanza seemed on the way when Jeff Bezos announced plans to create a massive new facility for Amazon in Queens, adding 25,000 New York City workers to his gigantic company. That fizzled when local Queens politicians said no way. But even Amazon couldn't deflate the city's new technology sector. By 2018, the city boasted 320,000 tech workers with more to come. Another pillar of the city's economy was slotting into place, and this one had Bloomberg's name on it.

23

AS FOR THE
OTHER HALF

"We've pioneered new ideas—some of them
controversial, but all of them worth trying."
—*Bloomberg, 2013*[1]

Like other New Yorkers, Bloomberg had seen them. The shivering
woman with a dog wrapped inside her coat. The scraggy man with
his hand-lettered sign about trying to get back to Omaha. The paper or
plastic cups that added their sad rattle to the city's richest streets. But as
New York's billionaire mayor, a man who would soon own fourteen es-
tates from New York to Bermuda to London to Florida, Bloomberg's life
was far removed from the desperate plight of the poor and what it meant
to drag your children to a homeless shelter, night after dangerous night.

On a Sunday morning seven months after he took office, Bloomberg's homeless commissioner, Linda Gibbs, wanted to show the mayor
what poverty in his city really looked like. A seasoned expert in the city's
social services, Gibbs took him to the Emergency Assistance Unit in the
Bronx, the dreaded EAU, as it was called. A grim building even by government standards, the EAU was the "front door" to the city's homeless
shelters, and it was the city's version of a Victorian poorhouse. Homeless

families came here by the dozens every day to ask for help. And because so many people were still in line when the EAU closed for the weekend, the building often became a makeshift dormitory where the homeless would stay until the offices opened again on Monday.

That August morning, the hallways were crowded with people sleeping on the floor, on benches designed to lack comfort. In a desperate search for relief, they were draped over their belongings and one another. And, by any Sunday, the place reeked—of garbage pails stuffed with used diapers and spoiled food.

The mayor was silent as he stepped over children and tried not to wake the exhausted people around them. A stoic by nature, his face still betrayed his dismay about the wretchedness he witnessed. As the tour ended, Bloomberg turned to Gibbs and said, "Okay, do what I understand you need to do."[2]

When Michael Bloomberg took over city hall as the richest man in New York in 2002, advocates for the city's 1.5 million poor and the 31,000 homeless worried that the new Republican mayor would have little time or understanding for those who were not rich or, at least, comfortable. Instead, he tried to calm the doubters, promising to find safer shelters, especially in dangerously hot or cold weather. Within two years, he even vowed to end chronic homelessness altogether in a decade.[3] And by 2006, he predicted a "major reduction" in the number of poor people in his city within the next four years.[4]

His efforts to provide enough relief for the poor would eventually fall short as the gap between his wealthy class and the desperately needy only widened in New York and elsewhere. And Bloomberg's most innovative attempts to fix the growing homeless problem for families failed as the family shelter population nearly doubled from about 31,000 to more than 50,000[5] while he was in office. At the same time, the city's public housing stock for about 600,000 people continued its steady deterioration— "sinking into the loam like a Mayan ruin," as one critic put it.[6]

The businessman-engineer-mayor would push his staff to experiment with new methods for relieving poverty and homelessness, and his team would try a wide array of new programs—some sensible, some not. He committed nearly $8 billion to more affordable housing, and focused on ways to help the poor get and keep jobs ("If you want to work, we want to help you," one official explained).[7] At the end of his three terms, Bloomberg's administration announced they had added jobs for more than 400,000 people.[8]

He would help the poor save on taxes. He would create a program to help young black and Hispanic males that was so promising President Obama adopted it as a national model. He would demolish the old EAU and build a new intake center, and the street homeless would benefit as the city turned to programs that provided housing first, then added support later.[9]

Bloomberg kept many of the hard rules about giving out public assistance from his miserly predecessor, Rudy Giuliani, although he made it somewhat easier to apply. As he said early in his time as mayor, "We will not allow our city to recede to a culture of dependency."[10]

The data mayor also adjusted the number of people on poverty upward to reflect the high cost of trying to survive in his city. As a result, instead of a poverty rate of 19.3 percent, according to the federal government, Bloomberg's data showed that 21.3 percent of the city's population were below the poverty line. He would make it easier to get food stamps, but require fingerprinting by applicants, an offensive prerequisite that was eventually stopped by the governor. And to try some of the most untested programs, he would use his own funds and the help of his rich friends to experiment.[11] For all the effort, he did not end chronic homelessness in five years as he promised in 2004,[12] and under his watch, there would not be the "major reduction" in poverty he had envisioned in his early years as mayor. Family homelessness would double, and the city's poverty rate would remain at nearly 21 percent after he left office.[13]

Bloomberg's scripted comments about the poor were thoughtful: "Our motive is the simple belief that every human being deserves better than to sleep on the streets,"[14] he said, announcing one new effort in 2006.

His unscripted comments did not help shed his image as a cold and distant tycoon. When the city council wanted to demand a "living wage" for employees of any company doing business with the city, Bloomberg railed that the higher costs for companies would mean fewer jobs and that "the last time we had a big managed economy was the USSR and that didn't work out so well."[15]

And he fumed about the court rulings that required the city to provide shelter to any homeless New Yorker. "You can arrive in your private jet at Kennedy Airport, take a private limousine and go straight to the shelter system, and walk in the door and we've got to give you shelter," he said as he prepared to leave office.[16] An exaggeration, certainly, an outburst of frustration, undoubtedly, but it was another statement that added to the widespread view he had a lack of empathy for those who couldn't get rich like him.

Overall, Bloomberg's approach to fixing the problems of the poor and the homeless leaned toward his Republican side, and the anti-poverty community soon had its own way to describe Bloomberg's method as a hand up more than a hand out. Critics accused Bloomberg of creating too many "small bore" solutions to poverty that failed to help the growing numbers of people without homes or enough money to live on. And, like his friends in the Republican Party, Bloomberg backed programs during his years as mayor that provided basics but not too much comfort for anyone using public benefits. Open-door policies would only provide a "perverse incentive" for more of these needy people to sign on for help, the most conservative critics of welfare and relief argued, mostly in private.

Others found that he should not be faulted for trying "some of the most innovative ideas" even if they failed, especially in dealing with homelessness. Philip Mangano, who served as the "homeless czar" for Presidents George W. Bush and briefly for Barack Obama, saw Bloomberg's policies coming straight out of his business experience—the search for different solutions, the assessments of costs per person, per family, the search for hard data, not heartrending, individual stories. Bloomberg wanted to fix the problem, not manage it, and failure at one program meant you dropped that idea and tried something different.[17]

Some of the innovations for dealing with the homeless were the result of an urgent, daily scramble to find places for people to stay. An empty jail in the Bronx provided one early solution. It lasted three weeks. A special master panel quickly ruled that the walls contained lead, plus it was inhumane to store homeless people in a prison, even if it had a fresh coat of paint.[18]

Then there was a plan to use old cruise ships—"Operation House Boat" it was called. Bloomberg allowed Gibbs and her aides to take his private plane to the Bahamas to inspect three ships once used for tourists. The price was modest by city standards—about $40 million for a capacity of four hundred cabins, an estimated cost of $43 to $51 per person.[19]

But the cruise ship idea foundered as well. For one thing, the city was having trouble finding a bit of shoreline to secure these large, cumbersome vessels. The waterfront was becoming more valuable every year as the Bloomberg team emphasized a return to the shore for housing and parks. Gibbs located a spot in Brooklyn, but it was in a part of the borough that, at the time, was still desolate and thus possibly dangerous for families.

In the end, the fire department rejected homeless cruises. Imagine a fire, these officials argued. Think about an emergency, with families and children scrambling and panicked, trying to figure out how to get out of the lower decks and up—*up*, not down, and out—to safety. The cruise ships had disaster written all over them, the FDNY said, and Bloomberg finally agreed.[20]

At one point, the city would pay some of the homeless to leave town, to return to relatives elsewhere. The mayor and his staff provided a total of $500,000 for one-way tickets by bus, train, and airplane. Favorite destinations appeared to be Puerto Rico, Georgia, the Carolinas, and Florida. One family got the city to send them to Paris, at a cost of more than $6,300, about the same as keeping them in some homeless shelters for less than a few months.[21]

Bloomberg later explained that his one-way travel program saved the taxpayers of New York City an enormous amount of money. "The average cost is trivial," he insisted, adding that most leave town by bus. According to city data at the time, 48 percent of the travel by families was actually by air. Even so, a one-way tourist seat was cheaper than a bed for a few days at one of the city's homeless hotels.[22]

Bloomberg was mocked for trying to ship poor people out of his town, but it was not such an unusual idea. Other cities had tried it, possibly shipping their homeless back to New York. And eventually even Bloomberg's antagonist and successor, Mayor Bill de Blasio, made the same old offer under a new name. Project Reconnect[23] was designed to send the homeless back to their original home.

It is worth remembering that Mayor Bloomberg inherited a modern homeless crisis that really began in the mid-1970s. The city was then a frightening place. People were fleeing—to the suburbs, to other cities, to the South. Good jobs were scarce, real estate and tourism were not doing well, and city leaders were scrambling to ward off bankruptcy. At the same time, the numbers of people on the streets had expanded into a large, ragged army. Many came to the city after the state began closing hospitals for the mentally ill. At the same time, single-room-occupancy hotels were beginning to shut down, and the homeless could sleep on the streets legally after the Supreme Court decriminalized vagrancy.[24]

Soon "vagrants and panhandlers," as the *Times* called them, were camping out in Central Park, under the Brooklyn Bridge, in Times Square and Herald Square, and in the rough streets and alleyways of the Bowery. The city shelters were notoriously dirty and dangerous, and in the late 1970s a young lawyer named Robert Hayes was so outraged about the "abominable" conditions for the homeless that he sued, arguing that the New York State Constitution, Article 17,[25] required the city to provide shelter.

Mr. Hayes, who was twenty-six at the time, had never tried a case.[26] He took the city to court on behalf of three homeless men (*Callahan v. Carey*), and to the surprise of most old court hands, he won. (Hayes found the lead plaintiff, Robert Callahan, on the streets of the Bowery. Despite his crucial role in the city's history, Callahan, a chronic alcoholic, failed to find much relief from the courts, the city, or even Hayes. He died on those same hard streets in 1980.)[27]

The Callahan case, however, was the beginning of a series of court rulings that essentially assured the right to shelter in New York City. In 1982, Hayes also coestablished the Coalition for the Homeless, which had doggedly pursued that right to shelter in court and in the media for more than two decades by the time Bloomberg became mayor.

In his early years as mayor, Bloomberg's hope was that the relentless court monitoring would stop. In what Bloomberg labeled a "tremendous victory" in the dealing with homeless issues, the court ceded its powers for two years in 2005 to a special master panel headed by the respected attorney John Feerick.[28] It was a brief respite, and Bloomberg's administration and advocates for the homeless were soon back in court, with the mayor complaining that the "litigants" would sue every time his people tried something new.

At the beginning of his second term, Bloomberg began a more intense effort to deal with the city's poor. First, he brought in the experts. Two of New York's most prominent African Americans—Geoffrey Canada, the charismatic charter school leader from Harlem, and Richard Parsons, then chief executive of Time Warner—ran a commission trying to find better ways to meet the needs of the city's poor. They quickly determined that any new programs should concentrate on three areas affecting more than 700,000 people: the working poor, young adults sixteen to twenty-four, and families with children.

Michael Bloomberg's personal mission was to use his vast wealth and considerable energies to improve the health of the earth and its people. That meant fighting not only
guns, obesity, traffic deaths, and smoking—among the worst plagues of his time—but
also combatting the ignorance about climate change. Here, a grim Mayor Bloomberg
walks through a once lovely section of Queens ravaged by the "perfect storm," Hurricane Sandy in 2012, that killed forty-three New Yorkers and caused $70 billion in
damages. Climate change had already begun to make its mark, even on New York City.

Born in Boston, Mike Bloomberg grew up in the modest, comfortable suburb of Medford. After some trouble buying a house in an area that once forbade Jews, this strong family found a comfortable and accepting place in this community. Even on a tricycle, young Mike was a handful by most accounts, but this very lucky kid grew up with a doting father and a strong mother. He liked to collect snakes from a nearby wood.

The Bloomberg family portrait—his mother, "Lottie," who lived to be one hundred and two, stayed at home, cooked kosher, and kept the family running smoothly. Mike's father, William, was an accountant who made about $6,000 a year and gave an annual contribution to the NAACP, a family tradition mentioned later when his son gave out billions. Mike looms at the left, his sister Marjorie at the right.

Once Bloomberg decided he wanted to be a Boy Scout, he wanted to be the top Boy Scout. At age twelve, he became one of the youngest Eagle Scouts in the country—even managing to get the badge required from his school for being a good citizen (and not Mr. Mischief). The Jewish youth sold Christmas wreaths to earn enough to go to camp, where he loved food that would never touch his mother's table.

BLOOMBERG CONTROLS BALLOTING WITH CUSTOMARY APLOMB

Described as "argumentative" by his high school classmates, Bloomberg emerged as a leader at Johns Hopkins where he received an engineering degree and organized his fraternity house and much of his senior class. Here he is helping with balloting for a student council race "with customary aplomb," as yearbook writers would add.

Michael Bloomberg, second from right (in white socks), became president of his senior class. His leadership qualities (and good grades after his father suddenly died in 1963) helped him go on to Harvard Business School to get a masters in business administration. It was the Vietnam era, but he was not a marcher, and he did not go into the military—rejected for having flat feet. Instead, he went to Wall Street.

Bloomberg, the Harvard MBA, would start his Wall Street career counting stock and bond certificates in a sweaty bank vault at Salomon Brothers & Hutzler. He moved up slowly, and here he is a year later—still a minion, but already offering advice to his elders in a way that would eventually get him into trouble.

Bloomberg steadily moved up. He became a partner in the firm in 1972, and here he is in 1975, a star on Wall Street. He came in early and worked late so that he could often get a ride home with John Gutfreund, right, the chairman of Salomon Brothers. Bloomberg was known in this era for telling Gutfreund and others they needed to update their computer systems.

Mike Bloomberg, fired from Salomon and given a $10 million payout, convinced these three colleagues to help start a new computer system for Wall Street. Bloomberg, at left, is drinking his ever-present cup of coffee. With him as they launch the company in 1982 are Charles Zegar, Thomas Secunda, and Duncan MacMillan. All four would become members of the three comma club—i.e. billionaires.

Nearly a decade after starting his company, Bloomberg and former *Wall Street Journal* reporter Matthew Winkler start Bloomberg News. Winkler, his famous temper barely-camouflaged with a bow tie, would create a massive, worldwide news operation, widely respected for covering finance. He was replaced in 2015 by smooth and erudite British editor John Micklethwait.

After nearly two decades in business, Bloomberg, the billionaire, wanted a new adventure. The newly-declared Republican candidate for mayor of New York City took to the streets while he spent millions on political ads. Bloomberg's uphill race would shift in his favor after the attacks of September 11, 2001.

Former mayor Ed Koch endorsed Bloomberg and helped introduce him to the city beyond Wall Street. Even with help, however, the candidate (still in his tie) needed a fork to spread extras on his hot dog.

Mayor Rudy Giuliani finally endorsed Bloomberg shortly before the election in 2001. At the time, Giuliani had infuriated minorities and unions, but he had also reduced crime and rallied the city after September 11. Bloomberg looks a little embarrassed here, as if he knows Giuliani will later become a front man for President Trump.

14

With Bloomberg's mother at his side and his daughter Georgina watching, the chief judge of New York's Court of Appeals, Judith Kaye, swears the new mayor into an office he will eventually hold for twelve years. He won reelection in 2005, but invited controversy for engineering a third term after the Great Recession of 2008.

15

Patti Harris, Bloomberg's top adviser, will become first deputy mayor for all twelve years. Hired as his assistant at his company years before he became mayor, she would help guide his political campaigns, his city, and his philanthropy. She became his prime confidante and "run it by Patti" was often the first order of business in the Bloomberg universe.

Early in Bloomberg's administration, this looked like a love match—Randi Weingarten, head of the NYC teachers union, gives a congratulatory hug to the new mayor. They would cross swords many times as Bloomberg tried to revolutionize public schools, but ultimately this duo would work together to promote increases in teacher pay.

Bloomberg tried to erase the raw feelings between the African American community and Giuliani's City Hall. Here he meets with Al Sharpton at a Martin Luther King Jr. celebration in 2004. Gifford Miller, city council speaker, is at the mayor's left side, and a future political opponent, then comptroller, William Thompson watches warily.

After a few years and too many polls showing he was extremely unpopular—a tax increase didn't help—the mayor's team wanted him to show voters he was an ordinary guy. Opening fifty-three city pools on a hot June day would help, and, to the surprise of some, Bloomberg took an enthusiastic leap.

Big name golfers line up for Joe Torre's Safe At Home Foundation golf tournament in 2008 to help kids from violent homes. From left: former mayor Rudy Giuliani, club owner and budding politician Donald Trump, Mayor Bloomberg, President Bill Clinton, former Yankees manager Joe Torre, and comedian Billy Crystal.

Bloomberg and Susan Meyer wed in 1976, had two daughters—Emma, on the far left, and Georgina, on the right. They divorced in 1993 but remained on good terms. The former Mrs. Bloomberg even worked on his campaigns. Here he helps her celebrate in 2003 as the American Cancer Society's "Mother of the Year."

In his most important speech as mayor, Bloomberg defended the right of Muslims in 2010 to build a community center a few blocks away from the World Trade Center site. With the Statue of Liberty pointedly over his shoulder, he rebuffed conservatives and even many in the Jewish community by saying that on September 11, as police and fire officials rushed into the burning buildings to save people, "not one of them asked, 'What God do you pray to? What beliefs do you hold?' "

Mayor Bloomberg began making a name for himself as a fierce enemy of the National Rifle Association, and he was part of an intense effort to cut back the illegal weaponry coming into the city. Here he and police commissioner Ray Kelly (right) and Manhattan District Attorney Cyrus Vance (left) announce the indictment of sixteen gun traffickers. Soon, however, the city's overuse of stop-and-frisk was ruled unconstitutional, even as Bloomberg and Kelly insisted they were not targeting blacks and Hispanics, they were going to high-crime neighborhoods to find illegal guns.

In what was clearly an uncomfortable meeting above the outgoing mayor's famous bullpen, Bloomberg tries to share his advice with incoming mayor Bill de Blasio. De Blasio campaigned as the anti-Bloomberg candidate, and he would continue for years to blame many of the city's problems on his predecessor.

With only one day to go on his countdown clock, Bloomberg and staff meet with incoming mayor Bill de Blasio. Patti Harris keeps her grim composure; Howard Wolfson, next to Bloomberg, leans in to listen. It would not be a smooth transition.

Outgoing Mayor Bloomberg and longtime companion Diana Taylor endure the frosty inauguration of his successor, Bill de Blasio. Governor Andrew Cuomo's partner, Sandra Lee, is on his right. Bloomberg would later receive a new title from the United Nations, a Genesis prize from Israel, and an honorary knighthood from the Queen of England. But there was little praise on this day, and one speaker set the tone by accusing him of running the city like a "plantation." Michael Bloomberg's face says it all.

When President Trump pulled the country out of the Paris Agreement in 2017, Bloomberg vowed to meet America's goals for cleaner air—city by city, state by state, and business by business. Exactly twenty-two hours after Trump's announcement, Bloomberg was in Paris to seal his promise. In a telling green tie, he confers with French President Emmanuel Macron and Paris Mayor Anne Hidalgo.

After Hurricane Irma destroyed much of the U.S. Virgin Islands in 2017, Bloomberg quickly commandeered his airplanes and his colleagues to help out. Here, he and Bloomberg LP cofounder Tom Secunda unload supplies for a local health center.

Michael Bloomberg prepares to make a speech, one of thousands he will give over the years—as a politician, a philanthropist, a businessman, and an adviser—especially at graduation ceremonies across the country. He wants his voice to be heard, and he has the money to amplify that need. A restless man who chafes at an empty hour on his overloaded schedule, Bloomberg has few quiet, contemplative moments like this one.

In 2006, the group created the Center for Economic Opportunity—or CEO, appropriately enough for a mogul mayor. It was designed to be an "innovation lab," and over nearly seven years, Bloomberg's CEO created more than sixty different programs to relieve poverty. Some worked, but Bloomberg also canceled seventeen programs that failed.[29]

Bloomberg would claim among his successes the programs to "promote financial literacy" and help families get more than $100 million in tax relief.[30] The city would help with tax preparation and guide taxpayers in ways to get child care tax credits or earned income tax credits. Another successful program helped support accelerated study programs for low-income students at City University of New York. Still another provided what the city called a "non-stigmatized" environment in schools for sex education and help for mental health problems.

The failures included a parks department effort to get young people to help plant trees—employment opportunities in this area had "dwindled." And the most famous experiment that failed was Bloomberg's own effort to try Mexico's successful anti-poverty program called Oportunidades.[31] The program in Mexico provided nearly 25 million poor people with cash rewards when they made certain their children went to school (about $61 a month) or checked in with the local health clinic.[32] After a visit to Mexico City in April 2007, where Bloomberg could enjoy speaking his distinctive Spanish, the results looked promising enough to try in New York.

Bloomberg and his wealthy friends put up $40 million for a new program called Opportunity NYC—Family Rewards. The rewards included $100 for taking the child to a dentist, a little more every month for holding down a full-time job. If your child passed the difficult Regents Exams in high school, the family earned a hefty $600. A few families did well, like one single mother in Brooklyn who collected more than $7,610 in two years.[33] But only $14 million had been paid out to 2,400 families before the program was canceled in 2010.

Unlike in Mexico, New Yorkers had access to other social services—

food stamps, shelter, other assistance. Plus, the rewards program was simply too complex for most people whose lives were already overloaded with complexities. Gibbs, by then the deputy mayor for health and human services, acknowledged that there were "too many things, too many details, more to manage in the lives of burdened, busy households," she said. "Big lesson for the future? Got to make it a lot more simple."[34]

Perhaps more important for Bloomberg personally, he publicly acknowledged that paying the poor to improve their own lives in New York City had not been enough of a success to start using the public's money. That did not mean the project failed altogether.

"In order to find what works in solving difficult problems, you must have the freedom to try new things with the understanding that some things might fail while others succeed," Bloomberg explained at one point.[35] He would continue to talk about how the rich—instead of the taxpayers—could provide a financial cushion for governments (and timid politicians) by paying for untested programs.

In other ways, Bloomberg made good use of his contacts with the city's wealthy, many of whom agreed to contribute to his riskier projects. One of Bloomberg's most important anti-poverty programs began over lunch with George Soros. To the billionaire Soros, Bloomberg provided disturbing data: the poverty rate among black and Hispanic youths aged sixteen to twenty-four was 50 percent higher than Asians or whites from the same age group. Their unemployment rate was 60 percent higher, and they were the ones most likely to die from gun violence on the streets of the city.[36]

As two of the world's richest men talked about the city's poor, Bloomberg tried to convince Soros to put in $30 million to help start the Young Men's Initiative. The initiative would help black and Hispanic youths in the city to stay in school and get jobs, the mayor argued. Soros agreed that it was a worthy idea, with one caveat. He would put in $30 million if Bloomberg matched it. Expensive lunch, Bloomberg would joke later.[37] Begun in 2011 with those two gigantic checks and at least $70 million from the city, the initiative focused on 315,000 New Yorkers who were "disproportionately undereducated, incarcerated and unemployed," as the *Times* put it.[38]

The ambitious plan included nine hundred paid mentors and new satellite offices for probation officers to make it easier for some of these youths to check in, as required. It was designed to help the participants get driver's licenses or other identification. It would help with internships and even jobs. President Barack Obama so admired the Bloomberg system that in February 2014, he used many of its ideas for a five-year $200 million federal program called My Brother's Keeper.

If Bloomberg wanted to find new solutions, he also wanted data, which, as it turned out, could be extremely controversial. A program called HomeBase, designed to keep people in their homes as long as possible, started in 2004 in six of the hardest-hit communities of New York. It seemed to be working, so in 2008 Bloomberg's homeless experts hired a consultant to run the numbers. The company tracked one group that got the city's full support from HomeBase services, and a control group of about 150 who were on their own. To almost no one's surprise, those with services did far better than those without.

But what about the control group—about 150 people stumbling along without the extra help? The *Daily News* and a slew of city politicians suddenly were outraged that two hundred families (it became more, it seemed, every day) were being denied aid. They were like "rats in a lab experiment," as one homeless advocate put it. Scott Stringer, then the Manhattan Borough president, called it a "bone-headed experiment." Melissa Mark-Viverito, a member of the city council at the time, said, "Just when you think you've heard it all. It's inhumane. How cold-hearted and callous."[39]

Bloomberg did not blink. "In the end," he said, "we are only going to spend money on things that work, so we have to find out what works."[40]

As he had already made clear when he announced a new program in 2006, "The status quo, the familiar pattern, the shopworn methods of the past: these must be abandoned if we are to finally end homelessness in America. We must recognize that the 'tried and true' has actually far too often been the tried and failed."[41]

Bloomberg's real hope of ending chronic homelessness began to slip away in his first term when his administration stopped allowing homeless people to jump to the head of a long line of those trying to get federal housing.[42] One reason given for this new policy was that some city officials suspected that people were gaming the system. Some families were claiming to be homeless in a tragic attempt to get public housing, they argued. Linda Gibbs, who would eventually become Bloomberg's deputy mayor in charge of a multitude of issues involving the poor, said at one point, "We don't want people to think that the best way to get housing is to bundle their children up and take them to the [homeless intake center]."[43]

Bloomberg later observed that "you never know what motivates people. One theory is that some people have been coming into the homeless system, the shelter system, in order to qualify for a program that helps you move out of the homeless system"[44] and into more permanent housing. Homeless advocates were outraged that the city would make it harder for such desperate people to find places to live.

Bloomberg and Gibbs tried other ways to deal with the growing homeless problem, and eventually the city adopted a program called Advantage.[45] Advantage participants got a rental subsidy for one or two years. It was not a perfect fix. There were reports of confusion about details among city workers, and some participants had to pay the landlord on the side to keep their apartments.[46] But Advantage was better than nothing, as long as it lasted.

In 2011, Governor Andrew Cuomo made a disastrous decision to cancel the state's share of the money for the city's Advantage program. That cancellation caused a loss in matching federal dollars as well. While the city was pleading with Cuomo to stay with the program, city staff had seen encouraging numbers from Advantage. On a budget of $148 million a year, the city had helped 10,000 clients and only 12 percent of them had returned to the streets.[47]

Bloomberg's city budget had been contributing $48 million a year, but, in February 2012, he ended the Advantage program. Without state or federal help, the city's full cost would rise to $148 million. Bloomberg decided the city could not afford it, especially after his budget advisers argued that they should not take on another burden that belonged in Albany or Washington.

The loss of the Advantage program only added to the city's homeless problems. By the time Bloomberg left office, the number of homeless people on the streets had declined, but the total number including families had risen to 53,173, compared to 31,000 when he arrived in 2002.[48] If Bloomberg and his housing team tried and failed, it should be noted that the numbers kept going up when the progressive mayor Bill de Blasio took over. By 2019, six years after Bloomberg had left office, there were nearly 64,000 homeless people[49] in the city, the highest levels since the Great Depression.

The gap between rich and poor grew during the Bloomberg years, but the alarming inequality was not confined to New York City. The increasing wealth of the few and the struggle to survive for everyone else were part of a national, even global, crisis. Economists and political theorists gave their reasons—corporate greed, a shift to the tech world, diminished unions, outsourcing of secure old manufacturing jobs, the rising cost of rent and health care, just to name a few.

Bloomberg never moved away from his central theme that the best defense against poverty was a good education and a good job, and as mayor, he emphasized programs—including in schools—to help New Yorkers find work and employers to find workers. For all his efforts to improve schools and training and find thousands of people jobs, the poverty rate in the city barely changed. In 2006, 20 percent of New Yorkers were struggling below the poverty line, according to the city's tougher poverty analyses. When he left office and after the city was still fighting the remains of the Great Recession of 2008, the rate was 20.7 percent.[50]

As he often did, Bloomberg found a nugget of good news in the data: New York was doing better than other big cities. In November 2013, six weeks before he left office, Bloomberg released his version of his record. Of the twenty largest cities in the country, all saw poverty rates increase since the 2000 census except New York City, where the poverty rate was essentially flat.[51] Using that same measure, Philadelphia's poverty rate increased 17 percent, Chicago and Houston 22 percent, Memphis 37 percent, and Indianapolis 88 percent.[52] As he gave out those numbers, Bloomberg's staff released the speech he was preparing to give as he received an award for his anti-poverty efforts from the Children's Aid Society. It would be his final statement on poverty as mayor, and he would tout his record on education, health care, crime control, housing, tax assistance, and social services. And he would sum up his administration's fight on poverty this way: "We've pioneered new ideas—some of them controversial, but all of them worth trying."[53]

24

OVERTIME

"The overturning of term limits—when this happens
in another country, we call this a coup."
—*Fran Lebowitz*[1]

"Term limits unfairly limit voters' choices."
—New York Times *editorial*[2]

Bloomberg had said repeatedly that eight years as mayor were enough. New York's voters had twice voted to limit city politicians to two four-year terms in office. It was also a personal rule for Bloomberg that you could overstay your welcome, outlive your usefulness. He said he was outraged in 2005 when city council members considered extending their own to terms from two to three—from eight years to twelve. They had been there too long, he decided. "There's no organization that I know that would put somebody in charge for a long period of time. You always want turnover and change. Eight years is great. You learn for four years. You can do for four years."[3]

It turned out that there was one exception to his diktat—Bloomberg himself. As the red digital clock at the city hall bull pen began to click down in his second term, the mayor became restless. He clearly loved running the city, or, as his friend Michael Steinhardt said of that time, "I think he likes hearing himself talk publicly."[4] Returning to his private world would be a retreat. He was not ready to leave public life, mothball the tux, or cede the microphone that he had learned to master enough for people to resist mocking his delivery.

One option seemed particularly tantalizing. He could run for the only public job more important than mayor of New York. After eight years of President George W. Bush, the nation would pick his successor in 2008. Bloomberg's name was on the media's lists of potential candidates, and for months, his staff did their best to keep him there. But where would he land in the political landscape? He was a former Democrat who became a Republican because the Democratic field for mayor was crowded in 2001. But he was a Republican who approved of gay marriage and a woman's right to choose an abortion, and he was a very unorthodox Jew who often said religion should be a private matter. That pretty well ruled out the Republican roster and had already earned him their tag as a RINO, or Republican in Name Only. His proud capitalist credentials and his attachment to the hard rules of the marketplace would make him suspect as a Democrat.

There was a third option. He would now shift to the lonely center in American politics. In June 2007, he filed papers to change his party affiliation. He would be an independent. "I believe this brings my affiliation into alignment with how I have led and will continue to lead our city," he said.[5]

Bloomberg, the self-described nonpolitician, had long advocated an end to New York City partisanship. He wanted the mayor to be nonpartisan. Even though he contributed lavishly to the political parties over the years (mainly to state Republicans and the Independence Party in New York during this period), he campaigned for a charter amendment in 2003 to convert the city to nonpartisan elections, and New Yorkers soundly rejected a nonpartisan mayor by a vote of more than two to one.[6]

The announcement of his switch to the independent center quickly ignited speculation that he was really planning a third-party run for the presidency in 2008, but after enjoying the attention, he looked at the data for third-party candidates. In an op-ed for the *Times* on February 28,

2008, the mayor argued the case for an outsider who could be independent of both increasingly strident parties. But he made it clear it wouldn't be him: "I listened carefully to those who encouraged me to run, but I am not—and will not be—a candidate for President."[7]

Bloomberg had his own plan B, as always. In this case, he wanted to shake up politics on a more local level. He had asked a few people about running to replace him as mayor in 2009—Richard Parsons, a moderate Republican then chairman of Time Warner, was a favorite.[8] But when his choices said no, he knew a candidate who really wanted the job—himself. When he told his top political advisers, including Patti Harris, Kevin Sheekey, and Ed Skyler, they were stunned and solidly against it. For one thing, it was an abrupt reversal of his own very-public record in favor of term limits. Moreover, he had established himself as a man of his word, and falling from such a lofty perch would tarnish his credibility, or worse.

Clyde Haberman, the city columnist at the *New York Times*, was one of the journalists who dug out the details of Bloomberg's protests when the city council had tried earlier to add four more years. "This is an outrage," Bloomberg had said, promising at the time to veto any effort to change the law. "The people themselves have twice explicitly voted for term limits," he added. "We cannot ignore their will. They want the openness new faces bring. And they will get it. We will not go back."[9] Plus, he had benefited from those limits when the state legislature refused to grant Rudolph Giuliani more time in office after September 11.

More worrying for his advisers, a third term was historically jinxed. Top staff members are exhausted and many simply leave. Mistakes creep in, and good reputations wither all too easily. Corruption got so bad in the third term of Mayor Koch[10] that he confessed (in his videotaped obituary for the *Times*) that he had considered suicide. People are also tired of your face; some even grew weary of the later sanctified Fiorello La Guardia, who served three terms from 1933 to 1945.

The decision to consider a third term was classic Bloomberg, who admired stubbornness, especially his own. And when he wanted something, he usually reached for it and took the necessary risks to get it. For his aides to warn him that this was a mistake was in itself a mistake, as it turned out. It simply hardened his resolve. Plus, why couldn't he change his mind about something? Even term limits.

It would not be simple, overturning the city's law on term limits. Some city experts suggested giving the voters another chance to vote on the issue after New Yorkers had already voted in 1993 and 1996 that term limits were a good thing for the city government. But polls showed that another referendum probably would not turn out his way.[11] Plus there was an easier option. Instead of a referendum, the city council could simply pass a bill to add a third term for him and—this was crucial—for themselves. And he would, of course, sign it into law.

As the mayor began to pitch his plan for four extra years, the business community was desperate to have him there. After some vigorous internal debate, the city's most powerful business group, the Partnership for New York City, welcomed a third term for a fellow financier. Even Donald Trump, then a mere real estate mogul, offered his support. Two terms for mayor was "a terrible idea, an artificial barrier,"[12] he huffed as encouragement.

Rupert Murdoch quickly offered the support of his local tabloid, the *New York Post*. Mort Zuckerman, who owned the *Daily News*, agreed as well. Both tabloids even ran the same headline, "Run, Mike, Run."

The *New York Times*? That would be more difficult. Bloomberg complained that Arthur Sulzberger, then publisher of the *Times*, had agreed that the paper would support his third-term bid, "then they killed me every single day."[13] What Bloomberg didn't get at that point was that Sulzberger would promise support only from the editorial team, which he controlled and which did, after a little skepticism, support a third term. Sulzberger would not tell the news reporters how or what to write.

For the *Times* editorial board, the voice of the paper's management, the third term for Mike Bloomberg would become a subject of intense internal debate. Over the years, *Times* editorials had stressed that term limits limited voters' choices. But the Bloomberg case was a little different. Some editorial writers were adamant that Bloomberg should not get a third term unless the question went back to voters. The first editorial about the mayor's bid for term three in June 2008 hinted at the paper's opposition. It concluded, "We are wary of changing the rules just to suit the ambition of a particular politician."[14] The *Times* brass was not so wary, as it turned out. The publisher and managers wanted another Bloomberg term, especially as the economic downturn had started to look worse. The final editorial restated the paper's established policy against term limits and enthusiastically endorsed Bloomberg in 2009 as a "first-rate steady hand during unsteady times."[15]

Behind the scenes, Bloomberg and his aides unabashedly solicited the support of charities and civic organizations that he had funded over the years. One administrator of a social service group that had received Bloomberg money and a city contract received a phone call from Linda Gibbs, deputy mayor for health and human services. Gibbs asked the administrator to lobby city council members still unconvinced about Bloomberg's third term. Other recipients of Bloomberg's generosity—the Doe Fund, the Public Art Fund, the Alliance of Resident Theatres, the St. Nicholas Neighborhood Preservation Corporation, and Jazz at Lincoln Center—helped pitch the idea of four extra years to their friends in the city council.[16]

Still, there was one powerful and very strident proponent of term limits in Bloomberg's path—Ronald Lauder. Lauder, the son of cosmetics tycoon Estée Lauder, had already bankrolled the two city referendums when New Yorkers had approved term limits. When Lauder realized that Bloomberg was trying to overturn his work, he put out a TV commercial that compared politicians (like the mayor) to dirty diapers "They need to be changed regularly."[17]

Bloomberg's high-powered friends began trying to talk Lauder over to their side, making the pitch that the city needed a manager, a businessman at this economically fragile moment. Financier Henry Kravis, Richard Parsons, developer Jerry Speyer, public relations executive Howard J. Rubenstein, and Ronald's own brother, Leonard Lauder, former chairman of the Estée Lauder firm, were among those trying to convince Lauder not to fight a one-time exception for Bloomberg.[18]

Bloomberg invited Lauder to Gracie Mansion, where, over coffee and cookies, the two moguls eventually agreed on a one-term extension just for Bloomberg. For his part, Bloomberg promised to help engineer another vote on city term limits in 2010. (Term limits would pass for a third time. When that did indeed happen by a vote of 73.9 percent for limits and 26.1 percent against,[19] the *Times* headline in 2010 was all you needed to know: "Bloomberg's Latest on Terms: 3 for Him, but only 2 for Everyone Else.")[20]

With Lauder out of the way, Bloomberg had to convince the city council to allow this one-time extension. He needed a majority, or twenty-six of fifty-one votes. One by one, he and his advisers found ways to get them to go along. For many, the idea of another term was too enticing to turn down. The council speaker, Christine Quinn, who planned to run for mayor herself when Bloomberg quit and who wanted his support, signed on. A delay of four years could also bring her some distance from a scandal in her office when staff members were indicted as part of a scheme to hold money in fake accounts during budget negotiations.[21] Some council members were reluctant to help themselves to another four years, but Bloomberg assured them that "people do forget about things like this."[22]

What really helped Bloomberg make his case for more time on the job was the economy. Lehman Brothers collapsed in early September 2008, Washington was talking about bailouts, and New York once again seemed to be in trouble. He felt that it strengthened the argument that he needed to be the one guiding the city because he had already done it once after September 11.

On October 2, a year before the 2009 election, Michael Bloomberg announced his plan to run for another four years as mayor. He used the economy as his main reason, and when a reporter noted that he was courting yet another heated controversy about term limits, Bloomberg shot back, "Everything we do is controversial. That's what democracy is all about."

Opponents quickly pounced. The comptroller, Bill Thompson, who would run against Bloomberg in the 2009 race, said this was "an attempt to suspend democracy." Gene Russianoff, the reform prophet at the New York Public Interest Research Group, lamented, "Sadly, the move is worthy of 'democracy' in a banana republic."[23] Fran Lebowitz, one of the city's toughest wits, told the *Times*: "The overturning of term limits—when this happens in another country, we call this a coup."

Later that month, the city council began to hold hearings on the mayor's and their third terms. The sessions were like something straight out of a wrestling arena—democracy at its noisiest. The mayor's people had already packed the chamber with about fifty supporters to applaud speeches by the likes of former governor Mario Cuomo and former mayor Ed Koch, who both backed Bloomberg.[24] But opponents lined up for a chance to bellow at the council during these open hearings—a total of twenty hours of testimony before the council dared to vote. People were furious, and they expressed their fury again and again, in the two-minute intervals permitted to mere citizens. One fourteen-year-old captured the tone for the adults when he pleaded with the council to choose "honesty over bribery"—a line that drew raucous applause from the gallery.

The council eventually voted 29–22 as the crowd booed and someone yelled "Shame on you" from the audience. City councilman from Brooklyn, Bill de Blasio, sounding like a prophet of doom, warned that "the people of this city will long remember what we've done here today, and the people will rightfully be unforgiving. We are stealing like a thief in the night their right to decide the shape of democracy." (Four years later, de Blasio was still hammering that outrage into the political weapon he would use against Michael Bloomberg's favored candidate to replace him as mayor, Christine Quinn. Quinn, who had voted for a third term, lost badly in the Democratic primary for mayor in 2013.)

On November 4, 2008, what was usually a pro forma bill-signing ceremony became another angry public forum. By tradition, the public is allowed to make a last-minute appeal to the mayor at these events, and normally a protester or two would show up and then quickly disappear.

This time 137 people came to speak. The mayor sat, his face tight with obvious irritation and resolve, as 68 New Yorkers displayed their outrage in a variety of accents, idioms, and decibels.

"To hell with your agenda," yelled one participant. "Please don't make me and countless other parents explain to our children that good men craving power pushed aside the people's voice," pleaded another. Others were far less polite.

George Arzt, former press secretary to Ed Koch and a seasoned expert on New York City politics, said he had seen nothing like it, "not even close." As the marathon ended, a somber Bloomberg then said he had, over a period of time, changed his view about how long somebody could be in office. "Nobody is irreplaceable," he said, "but I do think that if you take a look at the real world, at how long it takes to do things, I do think that three terms makes more sense than two." Then, with his left hand, he picked up a pen and, "with a flick of his wrist, rewrote New York City's term limits law," as the *Times* reported that day.[25]

For some pundits, New York's 2009 election would be another ho-hum, lopsided race with Bloomberg's money wiping out the competition. As a result, most of them would miss the real story—how Bloomberg almost lost the election, even with all his money and all his success curbing smoking and creating 311 and controlling schools and managing the difficult city.

It was not for lack of funds. Bloomberg spent about $74 million for his race in 2001 and $85 million for his second term in 2005 and, as it would turn out, a stunning $102 million on the 2009 race, or $174 per vote.[26]

The money went to pollsters, advisers, consultants, helpers of all kinds. Even Goodfella's Brick Oven Pizza, which provided numerous meals for the campaign staff, was $8,892 richer by the end of the campaign. At one point, Brooklyn Borough President Marty Markowitz said, "Now that term limits have been extended, so many in the city are looking forward to the mayor's massive job creation program. By the way, it's also known as the Bloomberg re-election campaign."[27]

Bloomberg not only hired the best political operators he could find; he also hired some of the most effective members of the Democratic opposition. Howard Wolfson, who had been Hillary Clinton's tough guy during her 2008 presidential campaign, was the Democratic operative famous for the quick, biting jab, even at Mike Bloomberg. Wolfson had criticized Bloomberg's effort to make city government nonpartisan as a "cynical power grab." He scorned Bloomberg's stadium plans for the West Side and the Bloomberg money replenishing various party slush funds. In the art world, Wolfson became famous as the one who criticized the bright orange panels that the artist Christo installed in February 2005 along the pathways in Central Park. Wolfson called them "schmattas on sticks."[28] The Bloomberg team hired him in time for the 2009 reelection, and he eventually became deputy mayor for governmental affairs from 2010 to 2013, then moved to run Bloomberg's political fund-raising arm once he left city hall.

Poaching the other side's talent is always good business. Bloomberg had already hired the man who had done all the opposition research on him in his first race in 2001. Stu Loeser, who was Mark Green's oppoman that year, had become Bloomberg's press secretary four years later. Loeser was too good, too dangerous, to stay with the Democrats, the Bloomberg people figured. Although many in the press grumbled about Loeser's bruising tactics, he was one of the few people who could berate Bloomberg in private.[29]

Another hire, Bradley Tusk, had worked in city hall with Bloomberg before moving to Chicago to help Rod Blagojevich, the pretty boy governor of Illinois who was later impeached and imprisoned for taking bribes. Tusk was not tainted by the actions of his "sociopath"[30] boss, as he eventually labeled Blagojevich. And when Tusk returned to New York, Bloomberg welcomed him with a "gift"[31]—making him campaign manager for the 2009 race. Tusk said he saw early on that his prize came with a heavy burden—the Bloomberg team knew their man was vulnerable. After two terms, almost everybody is mad at city hall about something, water bills, property taxes, rising costs of parking tickets, the construction noise next door.

But this was different. Early focus groups revealed a raw and stubborn anger about what people saw as Bloomberg's brazen power grab to get that third term. Some of Bloomberg's regular supporters threatened to sit out the vote.[32]

Tusk was particularly worried about who would oppose his man, and the team figured then Congressman Anthony Weiner would be the most dangerous challenger. This was long before Weiner became an international figure for texting photos of his private parts to women who then shared those unsavory disclosures with the world. And it was almost ten years before Weiner went to prison for texting pornography to a minor.[33]

Back in 2008, however, Weiner was a "wisecracking policy wonk," as one writer cooed approvingly,[34] a five-term congressman who had his eye on the top city job. The Bloomberg campaign figured they had to convince Weiner it was a lost cause. Or, as the relentless Tusk put it less artfully, they had to "strangle the baby in the crib."[35] (Tusk insisted that Bloomberg was not told of this strategy until later. In that way, Bloomberg's campaign team used a favorite adage from the mayor himself—it's easier to ask for forgiveness than for permission.)

The goal was to make Bloomberg look invincible. They had social media targeted to Weiner's zip code, and campaign aides knocked on doors to promote the mayor in Weiner's neighborhood (and his parents' neighborhood) long before the normal political armies came through. They leaked stories to the *New York Post*, where editors salivated at any headline denigrating Democrats. A favorite was Weiner's congressional record. He had passed only one bill in his decade in the house—to help foreign models get visas.[36] Another item revealed how Weiner missed votes in Washington every Tuesday for his local ice hockey game in the city. The *Post* headline: "Weiner's a Pucking Goof-Off."[37] The Bloomberg team ran pro-Bloomberg ads early and got Weiner's supporters including his one-time mentor, Senator Chuck Schumer, to call and try to talk him out of running. In late May 2009, Weiner finally took the hint and announced that he'd prefer to stay in Congress.[38]

Outgoing city comptroller William Thompson became the Democratic nominee and he ran a gentlemanly race but could not resist riding the anger over Bloomberg's term-limits vote. "Does the richest man in New York City get to live by one set of rules while the rest of us live by another?"[39] he asked in one campaign speech.

A Marist Poll three days after the only debate gave Bloomberg a 15-point lead with the election a week away. But Bloomberg's approval rate was falling and Thompson's support was ticking up. The trend lines did not look great.[40] In the end, Bloomberg's winning margin of nearly 20 points in 2005 had narrowed to a scant 4.4 points in 2009—from a healthy landslide to an embarrassing trickle. (Of the 1.178 million votes, 585,466 went to Bloomberg and 534,869 to William Thompson.) Some voters clearly believed polls that showed Bloomberg ahead and simply decided to skip the vote. Many others were still angry that a rich and powerful man could bend the rules in his favor.

At a very modest swearing-in ceremony, Bloomberg promised to work on immigration reform and promote innovation. "Conventional wisdom holds that by a third term, mayors run out of energy and ideas," Bloomberg told the crowd of about four thousand. "But we have proved conventional wisdom wrong time and again, and I promise you, we will do it once more."[41]

Bloomberg's four-year extension as mayor would not be conventional, he promised. He did not coast. He overscheduled himself and those around him, shortening deadlines and lengthening workdays for almost everybody. This was a last chance to build on his legacy as mayor and to make good on the hundreds of promises he had made eight years earlier. There would be mistakes that would haunt him, especially as he considered a future as a public figure. And when the countdown clock stopped at midnight on December 31, 2013, his supporters and opponents busily charted his many wins and notable failures.

The success side of the ledger was heavier. For starters, he had steadied New York City after 9/11 and helped New Yorkers weather the Great Recession from late 2007 to June 2009. He inherited a deficit and left his successor a balanced budget with a surplus of $2.4 billion.[42]

The crime rate kept going down, and Police Commissioner Ray Kelly's army foiled sixteen terrorist attempts on the city.[43] At the same time, incarceration rates were down by more than about a third.[44] He organized other mayors to fight gun violence and illegal guns, and he challenged the powerful National Rifle Association at a time when the very idea of being anti-NRA terrified most politicians into silence.

Bloomberg created the city's 311 telephone service, New Yorkers' much-needed way to call and complain to a real human being. Then his team took on a more politically hazardous task—consolidating the way the city responded to emergency 911 calls. Before he left, police, fire, and emergency management services were all working in the same place and mostly starting to use the same systems.

He focused on improving the public's health—a ban on smoking indoors (and later in parks), no more trans fats in restaurants, and the elimination of the dirtiest heating oils fouling the city's air. His health officials gave restaurants letter grades beginning in 2010, and cases of salmonella went down 14 percent.[45] He required comprehensive sex education in schools, gave out free condoms, and tried to warn Orthodox parents about a dangerous and ancient circumcision ritual. Overall, he took a great deal of heat as "nanny mayor" and "Grandma Mike," but he also claimed credit for increasing the life expectancy of New Yorkers by three extra years.

Mayoral control of city schools allowed Bloomberg to abolish layers of turgid bureaucracy, closing 164 failing schools and opening more than 650 new smaller schools including new pubic charter schools.[46, 47] He increased teachers' base salaries by more than 40 percent and almost doubled the amount of city funding for schools during his years in office.[48] His team gave principals more control of schools. He increased graduation rates and cut dropout rates.

He opened streets for bikes, pedestrians, and even weary tourists who could often find a seat on the twenty acres[49] of new open plazas like the ones along the busiest sections of Broadway. Under his watch, his team created more than four hundred miles of bike lanes, and Citi Bike began offering short-term rentals. He made it possible for the city to add an extension on the number 7 subway line and create a new station, in a public-private deal that became the road map for big projects in other cities. He opened the way for more taxis and the apps like Uber and Lyft.

His administration added more than eight hundred acres of parkland, almost half of it along the waterfront. He gained control of a neglected Governors Island from the federal and state governments. Then he hired Leslie Koch to repair and transform the 172-acre island into an urban oasis and the dramatic 40-acre park off Manhattan's southern tip. Brooklyn Bridge Park, long a dream caught in government inertia and community squabbles, finally morphed from a seedy row of wharfs and warehouses into an elaborate park and play space. The High Line railroad, set for destruction in 2002, was turned into a gracious walkway through Manhattan that lured more development and tourists every year after Bloomberg left office.[50] And the High Bridge, the oldest in the city, was restored as a walkway across the Harlem River between the Bronx and Upper Manhattan.

His team rezoned nearly twelve thousand blocks, or almost 40 percent of the city, including many waterfront or industrial areas[51] that were underused and often dangerous or dilapidated. With new zoning and other encouragements like parks, schools, and tax breaks, a building boom followed in every borough. The *Times* tracked forty thousand new buildings of all sizes including clusters of skyscrapers in Manhattan,[52] Brooklyn, and Queens. "Bloom Town," some of the mayor's fans call his city.

In 2002, Bloomberg had canceled Rudy Giuliani's contract to build

Yankee Stadium. Later, with Bloomberg's encouragement, plus millions of dollars in tax breaks and public money, the Yankees built a new stadium in the Bronx, the Mets got a new field in Queens, and Barclays Center opened in the Atlantic Yards in Brooklyn.[53]

He organized the funding of the 9/11 memorial—the massive voids and waterfalls at the former World Trade Center site—and made certain it was ready in time for the tenth anniversary of the attack.[54]

He pushed for same-sex marriage—"Near equality is no equality," he said, and presided as mayor over the city's first official same-sex marriage a month after the law passed in Albany in 2011.[55]

He defended the right of Muslims to have a mosque in Lower Manhattan a few blocks from the World Trade Center site. In a powerful speech on Governors Island, Bloomberg said of the four hundred responders who died in the World Trade Center attack, "Not one of them asked, 'What God do you pray to?'"[56]

His "game changers," a group created to figure out how to diversify the city economy, devised a competition for a new graduate school that became the Cornell Tech graduate school on Roosevelt Island. New York became a center for tech-based companies—Silicon Alley, one area was called—and the number of tech workers began to increase steadily after 2010 to make the city highly competitive for Google, Twitter, and others.[57]

After cutting back recycling in 2002, he soon became an avid environmentalist and created a detailed road map for improving the environment by 2030 with PlaNYC in 2007. He joined city tree lovers like Bette Midler to plant nearly 700,000 trees on the way to a million. New Yorkers painted nearly six million square feet of rooftops white—thereby cooling city buildings and reducing CO_2 pollution. As he left office, air quality in the city was the cleanest it had been in fifty years.[58]

Two days before Halloween in 2012, Hurricane Sandy slammed into New York City with a fourteen-foot wall of water at high tide made worse by a full moon. Bloomberg and other officials had scrambled to warn those in low-lying areas to evacuate, but Sandy killed forty-three people and destroyed or damaged thousands of structures across the city. In his last months as mayor, Bloomberg only started the work to help people rebuild and repair, but he wanted those buildings to be able to withstand the next Hurricane Sandy or worse. His experts created a highly detailed proposal that they called "A Stronger, More Resilient New York."[59] It listed ways to prepare for storms and ways to buffer the city's 520 miles of shoreline—tasks that would fall to future mayors. Sandy also added to his urgent concerns about climate change, and while still mayor, Bloomberg began organizing other cities around the world in the fight against a warming planet.[60]

The Young Men's Initiative to help black and Hispanic youths began in 2011 and was so successful that President Obama adapted the initiative for a federal program called My Brother's Keeper.

He maintained a poverty rate that was essentially flat after twelve years while it rose in other cities—an increase of 17 percent in Philadelphia, for example, and 22 percent in Chicago.[61]

He opened one important section of Water Tunnel No. 3, one of the most important infrastructure projects in city history, in 2013. After six decades of dithering, Bloomberg promised a whopping $4.7 billion in capital funds to create the tunnel to assure that future New Yorkers had enough fresh drinking water. "It's not sexy. Nobody says thank you," he said.[62] But the city would shrivel and die without enough clean water.

If the positive side was a longer list, his critics had their tally as well. Most glaringly, Bloomberg failed until late in his time at city hall to monitor and correct the excesses of his police department in their vigorous search for illegal guns. The number of so-called "Terry stops" rose from 100,100 to nearly 700,000 in 2011 when mostly black or Hispanic youths were stopped and frisked in ways soon judged "unconstitutional." Bloomberg and Police Commissioner Ray Kelly cut down stops to about 200,000 by 2013,[63] and Bloomberg continued to defend Kelly's street stops long after he left office.

The number of homeless people rose to the highest levels since the

Great Depression with more than 53,000 people in shelters, nearly 23,000 of them children.[64] Bloomberg, who had wanted to "end" chronic homelessness, helped find more places for the street people to move indoors, but even with his housing program—175,000 affordable units built or preserved—too many families were pushed into temporary shelters. He streamlined the system for helping those without housing and built a new intake center, but the number of homeless families continued to rise, even long after a new mayor took over.

Bloomberg's administration tried new systems for encouraging reform among those in jail. But an investigation by U.S. prosecutor Preet Bharara found gruesome stories about life on Rikers Island, especially for the young prisoners. Bharara said Rikers was run like the brutal culture described in William Golding's *Lord of the Flies*.

The New York City Housing Authority, the largest public housing authority in the country, was designed to provide the basics for about 400,000 people. Without enough federal or state funds, the authority was burdened with a $168 million operating deficit[65] and a structural deficit of between $50 million and $100 million a year.[66] In 2013, Bloomberg, promising not to desert the NYCHA residents, dedicated $40 million for "essential" repairs before he left office. That barely touched the problem, and his successor faced the possibility of a federal monitor imposed on the city's housing team in 2018 because of lead paint and other problems.[67]

He imposed fingerprinting on nearly two million food stamp applicants (until Governor Cuomo ended the practice in 2012).[68]

The increasing use of outside contractors instead of city workers led to a major scandal during the Bloomberg years. Started by Mayor Giuliani, the budget for the CityTime system for employees rose from $63 million to nearly $700 million before investigators found a nest of corrupt individuals who "treated the city like it was their own giant A.T.M. machine," as one prosecutor said. Bloomberg was not involved directly, but his administration failed to monitor the culprits stealing from the city. Prosecutors got much of the money back,[69] and Bloomberg promised more surveillance over contractors.

Bloomberg's record on public education drew more criticism with each reorganization of the system. Chaos, some called it. After the mayor and school officials celebrated a drastic improvement in test scores, state officials decided the tests were too easy and predictable, and scores dropped dramatically. Although graduation rates improved, an unnecessarily high percentage of those students had to take remedial courses in college.

Bloomberg hired an array of superstars, dozens of high-powered people who took the time to work and work for the city's 108th mayor. But he made a few unfortunate choices. One was Stephen Goldsmith, a former mayor of Indianapolis. Bloomberg picked Goldsmith in 2010 to be deputy mayor for operations, one of the most important jobs in city government. Goldsmith began trying to reorganize the city workforce including the sanitation department that was still in turmoil a few months before a disastrous snowstorm in December 2010.[70] Both Bloomberg and Goldsmith were out of town when the storm hit, and the city's traditional snow-clearing protocols broke down. After the storm, "Blizzageddon" it was called, Bloomberg inappropriately suggested that people should take in a Broadway show before later admitting the city had not done its job and also Broadway was dark on Mondays. Goldsmith left the job eight months later.[71] An even more public mistake was his hiring of Cathie Black, a social friend and former president of Hearst publications. Bloomberg surprised and horrified New York's education establishment in 2011 when he picked her to be chancellor of city schools. She lasted ninety-five days.[72]

In a dozen years as mayor, or 4,380 days, counting weekends and holidays, there would, of course, be missteps and mistakes. But Bloomberg had tried to use his heavily scheduled time as mayor mostly for the benefit of eight and a half million New Yorkers. He encouraged inventive solutions to old problems and did not worry excessively, or sometimes at all, about making hard decisions. He was the city's executive, the manager, the boss-mayor who oversaw substantial improvements in the health, economy, and stability of his charges. He would pass along to his successor a far stronger New York City than he inherited.

On the afternoon of his last day in office, December 31, 2013,[73] Michael Bloomberg stood on his desk in his famous bull pen—he'd always wanted to do that, he said—and thanked his cheering crowd of current and former staffers for all their work. Then at 5:05 p.m, he walked out into the cold and shook hands with a crowd of admirers as he headed to his subway stop outside city hall. The seventy-one-year-old mayor then took his retiree's MetroCard out of a well-ordered wallet, and he and a few companions rode the subway uptown for a private staff party. His audience the next morning would not be so adoring.

25

BACK TO BUSINESS

"You have to understand that when God comes
back, things are going to be different."
—*Dan Doctoroff, head of Bloomberg LP, on Bloomberg's return*

January 1, 2014, was a cold, bitter day, the sun offering little relief as Michael Bloomberg ceded New York City to his successor, Democrat Bill de Blasio. Bloomberg's time as mayor had earned him praise from people on the street and leaders around the globe. He was "dean of our profession," offered London's then mayor Boris Johnson. He was "the mayor's mayor," a label bestowed by Philadelphia's mayor, Michael Nutter,[1] and even "a proper rock star,"[2] as Bono once said of the outgoing Bloomberg. The *Times* declared that, despite any flaws, "New York is in better shape than when he became mayor."[3] Citizens Union gave him their public service award in 2013 for making the city "safer, stronger and greener."[4] But for all the congratulations coming his way as he walked out of city hall on his last day, the inauguration of de Blasio less than twenty-four hours later would not be a graceful transfer of power. Instead, there was an undisguised bitterness to this routine event, an attempt at public shaming.

De Blasio had campaigned as the anti-Bloomberg candidate, accusing the outgoing mayor of cleaving New York into "two cities" divided between the few satisfied rich and everybody else. One of the new mayor's chosen speakers railed against the "plantation" created by his predecessor, and when it was his turn to speak, de Blasio promised to create a "fairer, more just, more progressive place." Bloomberg's face was tight; the veins in his neck pulsed with anger, and even when former President Clinton, de Blasio's highest-profile speaker, tried to soften the tone—to make it more of a celebration for the new mayor and less of a public mudslinging at the old one—Bloomberg crossed his arms against the cold and the criticism.

An ordinary person might have carried that wave of indignation into some suitable hiding place. Bloomberg, now a civilian, had many fortresses to choose from including those in Bermuda or Vail or Florida or London. Instead, he and his companion, Diana Taylor, took off for a high-profile, luxury tour, mainly to play golf in Hawaii and New Zealand. He went to try out the plush golf courses run by his friend Julian Robertson, one of America's earliest hedge fund managers. Bloomberg's aides said it was the ex-mayor's first normal, two-week vacation in more than a dozen years. But, two weeks off would be a trial for someone so restless most of the time that he could barely make it through a long weekend, and when rain overwhelmed New Zealand's perpetually green golf courses,[5] Bloomberg rushed back to New York City, arriving at his sleek Bloomberg LP offices as the sun was rising the next workday morning.

Some colleagues saw a Mike Bloomberg who seemed to wander through his enterprises looking for a fitting role, even in the gleaming office tower in midtown Manhattan that flashed his name at every turn. He would go to his philanthropy headquarters on East Seventy-eighth Street, where former city officials were preparing a new venture to offer free help for cities that wanted to try Bloomberg's methods for dealing with urban problems.

But it was still clear his calendar had too many empty hours.

Meanwhile, at city hall, de Blasio was busy focusing on Bloomberg's policy failures—the poor, the homeless, and the overreach by police in the name of gun control. De Blasio would dismiss Bloomberg's efforts to deal with these issues, offering only images of the frosty billionaire who could be blamed for any criticism coming the new mayor's way.

The rising partisan clamor from de Blasio's camp was obviously infuriating to the Bloomberg loyalists. But the former mayor sent out word that no one—absolutely no one—should fight back. When the media asks for a response, don't bite, he decreed. Instead, his old city staff seethed in silence until de Blasio's former campaign treasurer accused Bloomberg's efforts to reform the 911 emergency system as a shocking case of mismanagement. Only then did Bloomberg allow former deputy mayor Cas Holloway to respond with a point-by-point rebuttal.

Bloomberg had already moved on, and he was shelving the criticism and harvesting praise elsewhere. On January 31, 2014, four weeks after he left office, the United Nations made him a special envoy for cities and climate change. That meant the ex-mayor was now a diplomat, helping the UN secretary general mobilize cities as a way to fight global warming.[6] A little more than three months later, Israel gave him their first Genesis Prize, soon dubbed the Jewish Nobel. The prize was created to promote the best of Jewish values. He seemed thrilled, obviously, but he carefully made the award more inclusive. He said that, yes, his parents had instilled in him the best Jewish traditions, but "the values I learned from my parents are probably the same values that I hope Christians and Muslims and Hindus and Buddhists learned from their parents. They're all centered around God put us on earth and said we should take care of each other. We have an obligation not to just talk about it, but to actually do it."[7] Bloomberg took the $1 million prize and decided to "pay it forward," as he said at the time.[8] He set up a contest to find young entrepreneurs whose work would help follow a Jewish code of *tikkun olam*, a way to repair the world and make it a better place. As one example, Bloomberg's Genesis winners included a group called BIP, which stood for Building with Israelis and Palestinians. They took their $100,000 to help Jewish and Palestinian youths work together on the basics, creating water and sewage facilities in the Palestinian territories.

A few months later, Queen Elizabeth named Bloomberg an Honorary Knight Commander of the Most Excellent Order of the British Empire in recognition of his multibillion-pound business headquartered in London and his philanthropy to promote the arts and education in Britain.[9, 10] He was on the board of both the Serpentine gallery and the Old Vic theater, and he had become such a presence in London that one of the noisier tabloids started predicting he might run to replace Johnson as mayor.[11] The *New York Post* immediately featured a front page with Bloomberg in the high black fur hat and red coat of the Queen's royal guards.

At the home office, Bloomberg found that his own backyard had become far more challenging. The computerized financial markets had morphed into a hyper-complex world—super-fast and convoluted, the primary domain of "quants" or quantitative analysts with algorithms and all the new, ever-changing double back flips of finance. While he was mayor, Bloomberg had asked his former deputy mayor Dan Doctoroff to take charge of his company. Doctoroff, Peter Grauer, Tom Secunda, and Lex Fenwick had increased revenues from $5.4 billion in 2008 to just under $9 billion in 2014.[12] Doctoroff and his colleagues had created both a workable incentive plan for employees and new profit centers and acquired such business stalwarts as *BusinessWeek* and BNA, an important source of detailed tax, legal, and regulatory information. (The additions became *Bloomberg Businessweek* and Bloomberg BNA.)

The core was still Mike Bloomberg's idea—serve the customer, give the broker the data and news he or she needs and wants—and Bloomberg LP now provided a daily avalanche of information, elaborate analyses, customer support, and news of all kinds from all kinds of places around the world. The financial news division, Bloomberg News, was now quoted regularly by mainstream news organizations, and the company had hired a slew of expensive media types to talk about politics on air or redo and modernize some of the publications.

Bloomberg began turning up at more company meetings, gatherings where employees inevitably turned to him, not Doctoroff, for approval. Doctoroff's friend and then colleague Norman Pearlstine tried to warn him that he was sitting in a very temporary seat. Pearlstine, a former news executive at the *Wall Street Journal* who went on to edit the *Los Angeles Times*, knew the lure of the top job. "I was one person who told Dan he [Bloomberg] was coming back," Pearlstine remembered, "and Dan said, 'Absolutely not. He never goes back. He always goes forward,' and I said, 'He's gonna come back. The company's three times the size it was when he left, and he's going to want to run it.'"[13]

Doctoroff finally realized Pearlstine was right. It had always been Bloomberg LP, not Doctoroff, Inc.

As he announced his departure nine months after Bloomberg's return, Doctoroff made his choice sound biblical. "Mike is kind of like God at the company," he said. "He created the universe. He issued the Ten Commandments, and then he disappeared, and then he came back. You have to understand that when God comes back, things are going to be different. When God reappeared, people defer."[14]

If that sounded a bit excessive, Bloomberg apparently liked joking about his status as deity, at least in his world of finance, politics, and philanthropy. Once, when I bumped into him at his philanthropy offices, he smiled mischievously and suggested an alternate title for this book. "What about *God*?" he said as aides nearby laughed nervously.[15]

Back at the company, Bloomberg had already begun emphasizing a few of his old office rules. Emails registered the time you came into the office—8:00? How could you? A stickler for all kinds of details, he grumbled about the way the paper towel racks were hidden artfully behind the mirrors in the men's room. (He had arrows added to help direct others wandering around the rooms with dripping hands.)[16]

As a passionate believer in the value of open work areas, where people can collaborate or at least know what's happening nearby, he saw that in his twelve-year absence some executives had carved out a little private space.

"A number of the senior people in the company had conference rooms next to their desks, and in the conference rooms there were family pictures," he said a few years after he returned. "Literally, the next Monday when they came in, the walls were no longer on those 'offices.' I had the glass taken out of all of them."[17] He soon learned that some people also managed to get bigger desks, so "when they came in on Monday, every desk was the same."[18]

Shortly after he regained full control of his company, Bloomberg sent out this memo:

To all Bloomberg people

Hi. It's great to be back and start to meet all 16,000 (full time) hard-working Bloomberg employees.

  One thing that helps are the badges we all wear around our necks. Unfortunately when one puts our B-unit [used to sign onto the machine] on the same lanyard as the badge, 50 percent of the time we block our names and photos. It makes the memory process for someone my age more difficult (and creates an issue for hard-working security guards). To help everyone, it makes sense to do what I do. Badge on the lanyard, B-unit in your pocket.

Tks, Mike.[19]

That sounded like a factory whistle to everybody in the company, a reminder that Bloomberg was back. For his now-massive operation of nearly twenty thousand employees (including part-time workers), that memo would be little more than window dressing. Bloomberg soon began to dig deeper, to analyze the newest details of his company. It was as if the corporation had a new executive, one colleague said. "And they always look under the carpets. They look in the cupboards. They look on the shelves."[20] Bloomberg was clearly startled by some of what he found.

One day shortly after his return, he sat at his famous terminal with the head of engineering and product development at his elbow. As an executive listened from afar, he could just hear Bloomberg and his tutor talking about "screen shot functionality." The reconstituted boss was trying to catch up, going through the functions on the terminal, getting updated on the convoluted markets of the day. It was no easy task, even for an expert. The animal kingdom of finance had grown far beyond bulls and bears. There were unicorns and zebras and black swans and dead cats and cockroaches. There were Bitcoins and dark pools and exchanges, swaps and new, complicated packages of all sorts. With it came the ultra-fast, high-frequency trading and all the intricacies that accompanied such speed in the marketplace.

As the executive approached, Bloomberg suddenly challenged him. "You've looked at the top 500 functions on the terminal?" he asked before quickly returning to the head engineer and his own lessons on the latest tools available to Bloomberg clients. Most Bloomberg executives knew the stunning breadth of data and analytics and research available on their machine, but the newest refinements could be a mystery, especially as the questions from traders or others using the terminals became more detailed by the hour.

Bloomberg wanted to understand why this item was here on the computer system, the logic of that function there. It had to be easily understood—no computer speak or even Wall Street jargon. As he said, repeatedly, his job was often to ask the questions that others were embarrassed to ask because they might sound dumb. It was a key part of his management system: whenever somebody came to him with a problem or an opportunity, "they've got to describe it to me in language I can understand. Again and again, if that's what it takes. Describing 'how and when' forces them to face all those things they initially glossed over when they thought about the 'what' . . . They have to satisfy me, a novice."[21]

He confessed later to being surprised by how stunningly complex the financial world had become in his absence. The 320,000 Bloombergs around the globe processed 80 billion market transactions a day with terminal users sending one another 20 million instant messages.[22] Later, asked how he saw his return to the company, the former mayor shook his head and said, "It has become so complicated."[23]

As the returning leader, Bloomberg had a few disruptions in store. He began reorganizing management structures that, in his view, had become too independent from the group, straying from Bloomberg LP's basic mission to work together to feed the terminal. He soon focused on the division with the highest profile—Bloomberg News.

Matthew Winkler, the incendiary hired from the *Wall Street Journal*, had created Bloomberg's massive financial news operation over a quarter of a century, expanding from a few dozen people in 1990 to more than 2,500 by the time Bloomberg returned.

As the news operation spread into every medium from radio to broadcast to magazines to web fare, Winkler made Bloomberg News into a big-time player in the media field—a robust rival for the *Wall Street Journal* or *Financial Times* or network news. He would eventually win prizes for broadcast and print and digital media including the Pulitzer, the establishment's ultimate acceptance of Bloomberg News as a force in the media world.[24]

Winkler had worked hard to weather the mayor's political years, attempting to provide a little distance when covering the government of New York City. Bloomberg News had a full-time reporter at city hall, Henry Goldman, who covered his boss, the mayor, very carefully. It was a "difficult assignment," he admitted, but he managed by sticking to "documents, what he says, what he does and what others say. There were no real investigations of Mayor Bloomberg by Bloomberg News, and Goldman did not get exclusive access. At a holiday party during his first term, Bloomberg gave Goldman a piece of stone and explained that it was his

'Rock and a Hard Place Award.'"[25] By standards of most of his colleagues, Goldman hewed a straight line in his coverage of the mayor.

The effort by Bloomberg News to cover the financial and political world without mentioning Bloomberg, the company or the man, was more tortured. When *Forbes* listed Michael Bloomberg in 2017 as the tenth richest man "on the planet" with $47.5 billion,[26] Bloomberg's own Bloomberg Billionaires Index failed to mention the owner in the list that was "updated at the close of every trading day in New York." On April 4, 2017, for example, the index jumped from David Koch at $47.7 billion down to Larry Ellison at $47 billion, skipping Mike Bloomberg's $47.5 billion altogether.

There were other similar quirks. Bloomberg liked to boast about how he promoted and encouraged women. He insisted he wanted "gender equality" so that the company could eventually be 50 percent male and 50 percent female "at every level, in every function, in every one of our offices."[27] Three years after he left city hall, the company created the Financial Services Gender-Equality Index[28] to give investors an idea of the percentage of women in a company's workforce. The reports were voluntary, but with more than a hundred companies by 2018, one is missing from the list—Bloomberg LP. Asked about the gap, a Bloomberg aide explained that the index was to help investors decide whether to invest in *public* companies. Bloomberg was private.[29] One Bloomberg insider suggested defensively that perhaps the number of engineers—about five thousand and mostly male—might skew the numbers as more male than female.

From its birth in 1990, Bloomberg News was designed to spew unadorned facts on the terminal, and Winkler had spent nearly twenty years trying to wring opinion out of his news report. Yet in 2010, while he was still mayor, Bloomberg decided to create Bloomberg View, an opinion and editorial package for the news side. It would become a kind of combination think tank and op-ed section. George Soros had his Open Society. There were Cato and Heritage and Brookings, all places where ideas were the main commodity. Bloomberg wanted a whole section of superstars giving their opinions. The mayor, Winkler, and Doctoroff gathered a host of big names, most of them somewhere in the middle of the road politically. They would include Washington writers Al Hunt and Margaret Carlson; Peter Orszag, who had been director of the Office of Management and Budget for President Obama; Michael Lewis, author of *Liar's Poker* and *The Big Short*; Michael Kinsley and Jonathan Alter, both famous authors and columnists; to name only a few.

The mayor had also hired some of the best opinion editors at the *Times*, including the *Times* op-ed editor, David Shipley. Shipley started out with a coeditor, James Rubin, who had worked as an assistant secretary of state under President Clinton. Each was paid about $500,000 a year, then a stunning salary for a journalist, and the idea was that neither would be the boss. They would share the opinion side with Shipley focusing on national opinion and Rubin covering the foreign side. With two strong personalities, it was a matchup made for divorce. Ten months later, Rubin was out and Shipley was in charge.

Andrew Rosenthal, then editor of the *Times* editorial page, recalled the day when then mayor Bloomberg called to talk about running his new opinion section, in particular how the page editor and the publisher run an editorial board. Rosenthal explained that occasionally your editorial staff is going to disagree with you and you are just going to have to back off and let the writers have their way. Arthur Sulzberger, then the *Times* publisher, had occasionally disagreed with his editorial writers but watched contrary views appear in print, Rosenthal told the mayor.

There was a brief silence, Rosenthal recalled. Then the owner of all things Bloomberg said, "Really? Hmmm."

Rosenthal, who figured that Bloomberg had just rejected the whole concept of an editorial writer disagreeing with the boss, never heard from Bloomberg again.[30] Started in 2011, Bloomberg's View was very much Bloomberg's view. He would use the platform occasionally over the years to write about climate change or trade policy or immigration or whether he planned to run for president. But, even with a talented staff and Bloomberg's deep pockets, the View struggled to get noticed in the early years. By the Trump era, however, View was making its mark, even as the name changed to Bloomberg Opinion in 2018. Long accustomed to serving a financially sophisticated audience, including those working at the company terminals, Bloomberg's editorial writers and columnists were well positioned to comment for a wider audience about why Trump's policies were as shaky and disreputable as his finances.[31]

Even while Bloomberg was concentrating his energies on city hall, the Bloomberg news operation had shifted and grown and matured far from the old bulletins for the Bloomberg Terminal to more in-depth reporting around the world. And the conflict between the news side and the business side selling terminals was beginning to show. Journalists, being journalists, wanted to report the big story, the big investigation, the inside scoop. The Bloomberg sales staff wanted companies to continue renting their machines—even if flaws in those companies were being revealed by the Bloomberg news teams. It is a conflict as old as journalism when newspapers tiptoed around their advertisers or failed to do so as a matter of principle (losing ads but perhaps gaining subscribers). That conflict was even more noticeable at Bloomberg LP. As far as the top officials were concerned, the news operation was there to serve the data information business. News was unofficially designed to be another function on the machine.

When Bloomberg returned from city hall, Winkler was still dealing with the aftermath of two major problems at his news operation. First came word that reporters were snooping on consumers using the Bloomberg Terminals—a breach of confidence that drew widespread concern among the Bloomberg users around the globe. Second, an incident in China exposed a bitter conflict between Winkler's journalists and the sales force peddling the Bloomberg Terminal in Asia.

One workday in early 2013, an official at Goldman Sachs got a strange call from a Bloomberg reporter who asked whether a Goldman employee was still with the firm, because she noticed that he had been "off his terminal for weeks."

Off his terminal? Alarm bells rang at Goldman where there were hundreds of these terminals. How was a Bloomberg news reporter able to monitor when a Goldman employee turned on the Bloomberg machine? How did the news side of Bloomberg know anything about what the business user was doing? Goldman executives "took a hard look then at the Bloomberg contract" and worried that those on the other side of the screens at Bloomberg could probably scrape data from inside their firm.[32]

As the word spread to other banks and financial institutions, the *New York Post* and then the *Times* reported that Bloomberg reporters had been trained to spy on Bloomberg clients to get news. Financial news analysts (not at Bloomberg) began calling it "the Bloomberg Breach," and there were reports on CNBC, for example, of widespread concern about how far the snooping had gone.[33] A spokesman for the Bank of England called the intrusion "reprehensible."[34] For users of those expensive terminals, it was a reminder that the central Bloomberg brain—that colony of expert researchers and analysts—had to know what clients were asking in order to provide the answers. Did they pass those questions and answers on to the news side?

One Bloomberg contract, revealed by the digital business news website Quartz, stipulated that Bloomberg could monitor customer usage "solely for operational reasons." That had the sound of engineers or customer support workers. But somewhere in the same network were the people who reported for Bloomberg News. That wall between news and business apparently had a few holes in it. There had been hints two years earlier when a Bloomberg TV anchor reported that the news operation had used "one of the unique tools that we have at our disposal, to find out a little bit about" a trader who lost millions of dollars for UBS.[35] But the Goldman incident shook the belief for many clients that the business they were conducting on the Bloomberg system was safe and private.

Winkler moved quickly to apologize and announce that reporters no longer had access to even basic activity by clients, including log-on information. "Our reporters should not have access to any data considered proprietary. I am sorry they did. The error is inexcusable," he said in an editorial in Bloomberg View.[36] Winkler also insisted that reporters could only see log-on information and how many times a client used "aggregated" functions akin to seeing how many times a client used Excel or Word. "At no time did reporters have access to trading, portfolio, monitor, blotter" or other parts of the Bloomberg system, he wrote. And he added that they could not see messages and stories or securities that clients were examining on the terminal. Finally, Winkler also promised that no Bloomberg reporter would be allowed to poke around in a client's terminal ever again.

CEO Dan Doctoroff apologized personally to dozens of clients. He labeled it a "mistake," and when users signed onto their terminals, an apology and statement about privacy for clients was the first thing they saw. Doctoroff, who had taken over the company in 2008, tried to organize Bloomberg's freewheeling management system, often described as throwing cats in a bag to see who claws a way out. He had argued for a few new concepts to help various divisions like news make more money. He had been known to remind editors that the terminal paid their mortgages. He often called the machine "the sun" or sometimes "the giver of life," and on his desk, he had a model of the known planets circling a sun with the image of the terminal attached to it.[37] A loss of confidence by Bloomberg's customers was the last thing he needed.

The Chinese episode, which came to a head a few months later, jeopardized both Winkler's hard-fought reputation in journalism and the Bloomberg company's access to a growing market. Across the globe, China's economy was booming, a lucrative market for Western businesses including Bloomberg LP. By late 2013, there were more than two thousand Bloomberg Terminals in China[38] with plenty of room to grow. The Bloomberg operations in Beijing and Hong Kong were also busy feeding Chinese data and news into the more than 320,000 terminals around the world. It was good for business, but Bloomberg company officials always worried about whether Bloomberg News coverage of China would offend Chinese officials. To keep the Chinese data coming, some of Bloomberg's managers found a way in 2011 to block items that might cause the Chinese to hamper the Bloomberg business. It was called Code 204. When Code 204 was attached to a story, it automatically stopped at the borders of Mainland China.[39]

At the same time, Winkler was creating a strong investigative unit, and the Hong Kong news bureau included editor-at-large Ben Richardson and Michael Forsythe, the chief investigative reporter, plus three other investigators. Amanda Bennett, who won a Pulitzer for work at the *Wall Street Journal* and had been the first woman editor of the *Philadelphia Inquirer*, ran the investigative team, which made international news in 2012 for a series called China's Red Nobility. The stunning report gave details about the family finances of Xi Jinping, who would soon become president of China. The family, with its holdings in minerals, real estate, and mobile phone equipment, had assets of $376 million. It was a gutsy report, so widely admired in the journalism community that it won a Polk Award[40] and came close to winning the Pulitzer, which went instead to the *Times* for its piece on the Chinese "princelings" making money because of their connections to outgoing premier Wen Jiabao.[41]

The *Times* Pulitzer disappointed and infuriated Winkler. Even worse for the company, China's officials blocked or slowed access to press events for Bloomberg reporters. The Bloomberg News website was also blocked in China,[42] and Chinese officials suddenly appeared at Bloomberg offices for unannounced inspections for "safety" or "security."[43] The company had become another news organization (like the *Times* and the *Journal*) that was having great difficulty getting residency visas for its journalists.[44] The sales of Bloomberg Terminals stalled, and it became harder to get the kind of financial data out of China that Bloomberg's terminal users needed around the world.

Bloomberg officials were not happy with a drop in terminal sales, but they could cope. The real problem was that the Bloomberg system could not thrive without the best and fastest possible financial data out of China, and the top officials in China knew it. "If you're half a second slower than Reuters, there's trouble," said one former Bloomberg insider. "That was huge leverage over Bloomberg for the Chinese."[45]

After the Polk Award and praise from Winkler, Richardson and Forsythe and the team in Hong Kong prepared another investigative package they believed was ready to go. It had footnotes, the okay from lawyers, and even praise from Bloomberg editors back home.[46]

Then, as they waited for final approval in late October 2013, the bureau got a call from Winkler. On speakerphone,[47] he explained that their latest investigative effort would not be published as written because, frankly, it could offend China's prickly leadership. Winkler as much as acknowledged that it was an act of self-censorship, and Bloomberg sources told the *Times* for a front-page story that Winkler had compared it to the way foreign bureaus curbed their outrage in order to cover Nazi-era Germany.[48]

Winkler publicly denied for a while that the China stories were actually killed. He said that what the Hong Kong bureau had produced was a proposal, not a story, and he thought the *Times* was "unfair" and even "dishonest," first by failing to write glowingly about Bloomberg's original blockbuster series and then accusing him—on the front page, no less—of killing what was an unfinished follow-up series. Winkler also fumed about the reporting of a "private" conversation on speakerphone that was taped by a member of his Hong Kong bureau and passed along to the media. Even years later, he remained furious at Bloomberg's top investigator, Michael Forsythe, the thirteen-year veteran at Bloomberg,[49] who Winkler decided had leaked the tape. Forsythe, who never actually denied passing the conversation along to other reporters, was suspended then fired from the Hong Kong bureau within a few days after the *Times* article. He later joined the *Times* staff in Asia.[50]

The firing of Forsythe began the unraveling of the Bloomberg investigative unit. The editor, Amanda Bennett, moved on shortly after the Winkler phone call. Ben Richardson held on for a few more months, but he said, on leaving, that "I left Bloomberg because of the way the story was mishandled, and because of how the company made mislead-ing statements in the global press and senior executives disparaged the team that worked so hard to execute an incredibly demanding story."[51] One former Bloomberg reporter said that many of them signed on to the Bloomberg Way because Bennett and Winkler had said they wanted Bloomberg News to be the most influential news organization in the world. "And we believed it," the journalist said sadly.

Anyone who missed the message after Winkler's call and Forsythe's firing got the word clearly enough a short time later when Peter Grauer, chairman of Bloomberg LP and a longtime personal friend of Bloom-berg, came to Hong Kong.

"We have to be there," Grauer told a group of business leaders at the Asia Society, meaning that Bloomberg LP had to expand in China. He said that the news operation "should have rethought" publishing some pieces—a comment that appeared to point directly at the Hong Kong investigations. Grauer also reportedly told the Hong Kong reporters that the company's sales team had been forced to do a "heroic job" repairing company relations with the Chinese.[52] And one source at the bureau re-ported that Grauer warned the company would be "back in the shitbox" if "we were to do anything like that again."[53]

Bloomberg himself had withheld any public comment about China or Goldman Sachs while he was finishing his last hectic year as mayor. But soon after he left office, Andrew Ross Sorkin asked Bloomberg on CNBC whether his company had "muzzled" its journalists cover-ing China. Bloomberg avoided a direct answer. The Chinese "have rules about what you can publish," he said. "We follow those rules and if you don't follow the rules, you're not in the country."[54]

At his first meeting with the news staff after he was mayor, he re-peated the point that if a country gives you a license with restrictions, you either comply or you leave. "The thing that hurt me the most is that some people tried to make this something we should be ashamed of, and we have nothing to be ashamed of," he told the staff. "There are things that the press shouldn't be doing and can't," he added. As for the ethics of Bloomberg News while he was away as mayor, "We have zero to be apologetic for."[55]

Even so, Bloomberg recognized that he had a problem with Winkler. Before he announced plans to retake control of the business at the end of 2014, Bloomberg had started asking who should replace him.[56] Soon, he produced his answer. Ever an Anglophile with two homes and what would become a showplace European headquarters being built in London, Bloomberg had sometimes been mentioned as a billionaire reputable enough to buy *The Economist*. Instead, he hired its editor, John Micklethwait, a fifty-two-year-old former banker who had been running the magazine for eight years.

If Mike Bloomberg was looking for Winkler's opposite, he had found it in Micklethwait. The new editor was British born, Oxford educated, and every ounce the classic Anglo-aristocrat who could chart his bloodline back to William the Conqueror.[57] Micklethwait had briefly tried banking and then moved to *The Economist*, one of Bloomberg's favored publications. It was an elite, 171-year-old operation, excellently written (no bylines) with claims to sit in the "radical center"[58] of British politics. Bloomberg, an avowed centrist himself, saw a soul mate, but it would still be a big step for the Brit. Micklethwait went from overseeing a collegial operation with 130 mostly well-behaved employees to Winkler's fast and turbulent media arena with 2,500 employees across the globe.[59]

Micklethwait took over Bloomberg News in February 2015, and two months later, Winkler's team finally won the golden Pulitzer Prize. Zachary Mider, one of the stars remaining on Winkler's investigative team, won for explanatory reporting about how corporations dodge taxes by hiding U.S. profits abroad. The Poynter Institute columnist James Warren spoke for many in old-line, mainstream media when he wrote, "Goliath came out of the shadows Monday."[60] At the company ceremony, when Micklethwait made the announcement, Bloomberg nudged Winkler and said, grinning, "What took you so fucking long?"[61] It was supposed to be a joke.

Winkler had made his mistakes in twenty-five years, but he had achieved what he thought Bloomberg wanted. From a few rewrite serfs churning out public relations updates for terminal users, Winkler had created a massive news organization rivaling Dow Jones and the *New York Times* and Reuters in day-to-day coverage of business and finance. But Bloomberg News had outgrown Winkler's red-faced, nitro school of management.

Bloomberg, the boss redux, also saw parts of the new media world that did not fit with his original mission of business news for business-people. He would soon fire some of the bright, young editors brought in to give buzz to *Bloomberg Businessweek* or to add luster to the television coverage. He reportedly rejected some efforts to increase viewership of Bloomberg Television. (In 2013, the audience was so small it was not rated by Nielsen.) Doctoroff had overseen the hiring of two star political journalists, Mark Halperin and John Heilemann, at a reported $1 million each. Their television show, *With All Due Respect*, which ran on the Bloomberg News cable channel and MSNBC, didn't get much respect from viewers, however, and Bloomberg had to apologize for one of his jokes about the duo. He called them Haldeman and Ehrlichman during a talk with the Washington staff. Their lush contract expired with the 2016 elections.[62]

Micklethwait had already started returning the news operation to basics. Six months after he arrived, he had sent out a long memo about where Bloomberg News was going. It sounded very familiar.

Micklethwait's memo, which he released after he had fired eighty people (including at least one who had written a memo complaining about chaos at Bloomberg News),[63] referred to his downsizing as "refocusing our considerable resources." And he decreed that Bloomberg News would be "the chronicle of capitalism." He vowed to "expose financiers' mistakes and vanities," in short to alert terminal users to the flaws around them. But he wanted Bloomberg News to distinguish itself by also showing "our passion for business, finance and markets."

"So, if you are not intrigued by how people make money, or are inclined to sneer at those who are good at it, or yearn to practice 'gotcha journalism' on investment bankers simply because they've chosen to be bankers, Bloomberg is probably the wrong place for you."[64]

Micklethwait's job was to organize all the various news arms into one structure. He wanted the news side to be less hierarchal. He wanted more collaboration—a Bloomberg mantra since those early days of four guys in a one-room office. Micklethwait gave a brief nod to investigative journalism but noted that he would continue to "cut back on lengthy self-indulgent stories."

Winkler stayed on in an emeritus position after having "stepped down" in late 2014, as he put it later.[65] From the sidelines, he had to watch as Bloomberg moved Micklethwait onto the international stage. Newsroom regulars groused about the distant and inscrutable Brit, but Micklethwait soon became a prime Bloomberg interviewer of global leaders at Bloomberg's increasing number of global meetings in New York and Asia. For example, at Bloomberg's economic meeting in Singapore in 2018, where Bloomberg was launching his Asian version of Davos, Micklethwait talked with outgoing prime minister Lee Hsien Loong, who declared that his outpost was like a "Bonsai Tree Model of What China Is."[66] With that comment, Micklethwait, Prime Minister Lee, and Bloomberg all made the news.

If the news division was a little more than 10 percent of Bloomberg's army of nearly 20,000 people, it was the public face—in every medium and on every new gizmo. Inside, the company also worked to adapt to every shift in the digital stratosphere. Analytics, plain old data, new data, pricing data, regulations data, buy, sell, hold, a complete cafeteria of access and data from every business market—Bloomberg offered it all. Then there was help with managing risk, accounting. You could even estimate how much it would probably cost your two-year-old to go to a private college. While there was a lot of grousing about long hours at the company—and who doesn't like to complain about their job?—the independent employment site Glassdoor analyzed hundreds of comments from Bloomberg workers (some anonymous) and determined in 2018 that Bloomberg got a 90 percent approval rating as CEO.[67]

By that time, the Mike Bloomberg company code was cast in stone. Hire the smartest people you can find who work the hardest. Demand collaboration (especially hard for bigger egos at or near the top). Demand loyalty (but also get them to sign an agreement not to talk about the company or to disparage the bosses and the terminal). Return that loyalty with nice, warm paychecks and top-of-the-line health care and bonuses and, of course, free food—breakfasts or snacks or a complete cafeteria like the one in Princeton, where delis were a car ride away.

His company had open spaces in every office in every major country. "I issue proclamations telling everyone to work together, but it's the lack of walls that make them do it," he insisted.[68] He once admitted that in the early days when there were more people than office space, he had a carpenter come in on a Friday night and cut eighteen inches off of each worker's desk. Apparently workers were so accustomed to being a tightly knit operation, it took a while for them to catch on.[69]

But for all the lack of personal space for his people, Bloomberg also wanted to have splendid offices so that workers would be proud to stay at work. That meant a tall glass tower like the "mother ship" in Manhattan or an elegant three-story office in Hong Kong. Then there was London.

On a cool October day in 2017, a very proud Michael Bloomberg stood with London's mayor, Sadiq Khan, installation artist Cristina Iglesias, and the famous architect who designed the two buildings that served as his stunning backdrop, Lord Norman Foster.

Foster was famous for the "gherkin," the bullet-shaped skyscraper that vied for notice in London's skyline with other high-end works— a needle-thin tower called the Shard (Renzo Piano) and another that looked like a giant, old-fashioned walkie-talkie (Rafael Viñoly). In Hong Kong, Foster had built a bank that was supposed to be like a Lego building that you could change or even dismantle if mainland China became too unfriendly. Perhaps more important for Bloomberg, Foster was one of the first high-end architects to create open-plan office buildings.

Bloomberg, who often called London his second home (although he actually had two homes in the city), did not want a splashy office skyscraper. He wanted a building that inspired his employees, of course, a place that could fit less conspicuously in the historic center of London. As an engineer, he wanted every possible technology to save energy and make the building a showplace for sustainability. And he wanted to show the world that an American businessman cared about public art and archaeology.

He began working on his new European headquarters while he was still mayor. For the then-mayor's rare visits to the Bloomberg offices in Manhattan, he often inspected a model of the Foster building. Foster took notes at their first meeting. They said the exterior had to be "respectful, fitting in, understated, classy." Inside, it was to be "organic and dynamic." By some accounts, with two strong personalities involved, it became a long and difficult birth. Bloomberg kept a close watch on the builder and the building, and he joked at the opening that "some people say that the reason it took us almost a decade to build this is that we had a billionaire who wanted to be an architect working with an architect who wanted to be a billionaire."[70] For Bloomberg and the architectural world, it was worth the struggle.

The design is meant to sweep people up a wide corridor into a central hub (with food and fish tanks and mingling, as is the Bloomberg way). Workers labor at round desks throughout the 3.2-acre site (1.1 million square feet of office space). There is art, big public art like a large bas-relief sculpture by Cristina Iglesias, and there are environmental details that were an obvious source of pride for the billionaire/engineer. The windows, for example, have huge fins that open to real air. "Gills," the architect called them. The ceiling was a field of LED lights, and the whole package was designed to save six hundred metric tons of carbon dioxide emissions every year.[71]

Besides the agonies over which stone and what kind of ventilation, the building also took longer because it was built over a site where ancient

Romans practiced their mysterious worship of the god Mithras. Bloomberg had given archaeologists plenty of time and support to dig up more than fourteen thousand artifacts that ranged from a phallic-inspired pin that might have held together some early Roman's toga to tablets with early messages written in wax that appear to be the first written mention of the town London. Bloomberg reimagined the meeting hall for the mysterious cult that seemed to include the idea of Mithras killing a bull, a somewhat counterintuitive symbol for many of Bloomberg's customers on Wall Street. But what mattered most for London's archaeologists was that the billionaire and his team gave them time to carefully unearth the layers of British history.

There were a few snarky reviews, of course. The *Guardian* complained that it was "chubby and prosaic," that it looked like a "regional department store," and that the Iglesias sculpture brought to mind a "fetid swamp." [72] Another writer praised the new complex, but compared it to Willy Wonka's magic emporium. Most saw a successful effort to make the London headquarters into the ultimate, futuristic office building where workers had an open invitation to come together and work very, very hard, since everybody could see everybody else. When the building won Britain's top architectural prize in 2018, Ben Derbyshire, president of the Royal Institute of British Architects, said that Foster and Bloomberg "had not just raised the bar for office design and city planning, but smashed the ceiling." [73]

Bloomberg was immensely proud of his European headquarters, but as the elaborate complex was being finished, Britain suddenly voted to leave the European Union. The vote for "Brexit" sent some companies scurrying from London to Germany or Brussels to deal with their European operations. Bloomberg had argued against the withdrawal before the vote in June 2016. Two weeks before he opened his London office in 2017, Bloomberg spoke at a technology conference in Boston. Blunt as ever, he said exactly what he was thinking. "We are opening a brand new European headquarters in London—two big, expensive buildings. Would I have done it if I knew they were going to drop out? I've had some thoughts that maybe I wouldn't have." He quickly added, "But we are there [and] we are going to be very happy."[74]

Leaving Britain? Never, he later assured his friends. His ex-wife was a Brit; his two daughters had British passports. He owned two elaborate homes in London. One of them, purchased in 2015 for $25 million, $1 million over the asking price, was the historic mansion where writer George Eliot had spent her final days.[75] Brexit wouldn't send him packing, but he wouldn't be shy about how he viewed the whole, clumsy mess. As he put it, on several occasions, Brexit was "the single stupidest thing that any country has ever done, but then we Trumped it."[76]

26

MOVING TARGETS
NOT SITTING DUCKS

"Growth makes us a moving target,
no growth makes us a sitting duck."
—Bloomberg by Bloomberg, *2019*

A t 8:30 a.m. London time on April 17, 2015, traders at Bloomberg Terminals around the world suddenly saw their normally hyperactive screens offer one alarming message—"CONNECTION LOST." Across the globe, Bloomberg users groused and howled as the markets stalled. In Britain, officials in the government's debt management office were so nervous about the sudden outage that they delayed a treasury bill auction worth more than $4 billion.[1]

It was as if some huge plug in the central Bloomberg socket had suddenly been dislodged, instantly shutting down a global network of 320,000 machines. Some traders took to Twitter—"If markets move, but there is no Bloomberg Machine operational to report it, does it make a sound?" asked one. Another reported, "Millions of traders are looking out the window for the first time in years." And the *Daily Mail* speculated mischievously that the entire blackout was caused by a Coke spilled somewhere on one of the main Bloomberg servers.

Within about two hours, most of the terminals were back running after the Bloomberg company declared an "internal network issue" and began to reexamine the "multiple redundant systems," which had failed one by one.[2] The sudden loss of Bloomberg power had embarrassed the army of computer engineers at the company, but the global outage also sent out another blunt reminder of the Bloomberg hold on financial data, research, analytics, and news. In the years since 1982 when Mike Bloomberg and his team of smart, young techies created the Bloomberg machine, it had grown from a curiosity to a necessity. The *Financial Times* called it "the central nervous system of finance."[3] *Institutional Investor* described "a one-stop, perma-blinking information pleasure dome encompassing data, news, analytics and much much more—the financial product world's answer to the Broadway show."[4]

The reckoning also alerted a small army of hopeful competitors. For them, the Bloomberg Terminal was too big and too complex and far too expensive for the normal needs of finance. The "breach"— how some financiers had called reports about Bloomberg News reporters spying on terminal use in 2013—had already energized a group of bankers to look elsewhere. And any weakness in Bloomberg's fortress would ignite talk of another potential "Bloomberg killer."

Bloomberg liked to scoff at the latest competitor, but he was known for having such a competitive drive that his dismissals often sounded faintly hollow. He had always argued that the best defense against potential rivals was to keep moving. "As long as we continue to be driven by our forward-thinking culture, instead of looking over our shoulders and following what the competition is doing," he said, "we'll be fine."[5]

Bloomberg, the salesman, could quickly list the reasons that his machine had survived and prevailed in the marketplace. Better data, better research, better customer service, better employees, better you name it. Plus, they kept going back to the customers to ask what they needed, what worked and what didn't. But beyond that chest-thumping was a tough competitive heart. He showed it at his company when it became clear they needed to move fast to outpace some rival who had come up with a good idea. Outpace it or adapt it.

Thomson Reuters was causing the most dyspepsia at Bloomberg in 2014 after the established news organization linked up with a group of bankers who had created a financial chat service called Symphony. The group, Symphony Communication Services, which included Goldman Sachs, Bank of America, Bank of New York, BlackRock, Inc. Citigroup, Credit Suisse, JPMorgan Chase, and others, put up $66 million and[6] went straight for one of the most popular parts of the Bloomberg system—the internal email. When a terminal user told a business associate to "Bloomberg me," it was like a secret handshake among the power brokers in finance. If you had a Bloomberg system, the internal email provided contact with the 320,000 others who had enough money and probably clout to have a Bloomberg. This was not standard email, not Gmail with nearly a billion users worldwide. This was Bloomberg's instant messaging for the top tier in global finance—or anybody with a $24,000 terminal.

The CEO of Symphony, David Gurle, later claimed that the firm didn't actually want to kill off Bloomberg and its expensive email. They merely wanted to expand the messaging to thousands of workers beyond the corporate boardroom. Instead, he described it as moving from Bloomberg's private, gated road to a superhighway that allowed more kinds of traffic (including young quants on motorcycles or bots, as robots were now called).[7]

But Bloomberg LP reacted in a surprising way to the Symphony challenge. Normally, to have any Bloomberg service you had to buy the big package, which included messaging. Bloomberg suddenly began selling the message service for $10 a month to other employees in a company that had already purchased the Bloomberg systems (but perhaps didn't have a Bloomberg of their own).[8]

By late 2018, still another threat loomed. Blackstone, the investment behemoth, bought a majority stake in the massive Thomson Reuters data and news business. The move was quickly seen as setting up a mega-battle between Stephen Schwarzman, chairman and CEO of the Blackstone Group, and Michael Bloomberg.[9] Schwarzman, who founded the Blackstone private equity firm in 1985 with former commerce secretary Peter Peterson, later built it into what *Forbes* described as "the world's largest buyout firm" with $500 billion in assets by 2019.[10] But the differences between the Bloomberg and Schwarzman were also political. Bloomberg had become a big giver to Democratic candidates in 2018, Schwarzman contributed to Republicans. The political divide could only add to the tension between the two camps.

Blackstone's new venture with Reuters would be called Refinitiv, and it immediately led the pack of at least six others out there trying to tap into the $30 billion data market[11] dominated by Bloomberg.[12] One of the most inventive was Money.net, created by Morgan Downey, an engaging Irishman who once ran Bloomberg's global commodity division. Downey offered what he hoped would be the people's terminal. Instead of $24,000 a year for a Bloomberg by 2019, Downey said he was charging about $1,500 a year. Like other competitors, Downey disparaged Bloomberg's system as old-fashioned and overly complicated. As he put it, Bloomberg is "your grandfather's trading tool."[13] Of course, a lot of those grandfathers ran corporations and governments around the world.

By the beginning of 2019, however, Bloomberg had still managed to beat the competition and stay on top with his gold standard machine. Douglas B. Taylor, managing director of Burton-Taylor International Consulting, estimated that Bloomberg led the market with nearly 33 percent, with Reuters (or Refinitiv) the closest competition at 22 percent. Others trailed with bits and pieces of the market, in the single digits or less.

"Any news of Bloomberg's demise is greatly exaggerated," Taylor said in early 2019. One of the top analysts of the market data and analysis business including the privately owned Bloomberg, Taylor said that, except for Reuters, Bloomberg's competitors were nibbling around the edges. And Bloomberg LP's revenues were rising to more than $10 billion in 2018. As for potential Bloomberg killers, he added that "generally the people that come after Bloomberg's business end up as roadkill."[14]

In the meantime, Bloomberg had redirected his company's main focus to the terminal users, still his core business, and, as the company grew stronger each year, he turned to one of his favored pastimes, giving out all sorts of advice to young entrepreneurs about how he became such a powerful billionaire. Besides the mantra—get in early, work hard, don't go to the bathroom (a joke, maybe), and leave late—occasionally he looked back more at nearly thirty years of success and mentioned another requirement—luck.

"People that are successful think they're smart, and I think they're lucky, me included," Bloomberg said. "We started [the Bloomberg Terminal] at the right time, but if we'd zigged instead of zagged it wouldn't have turned out that way . . . I think what happened with our luck is we did something that nobody else did; so the competition in the beginning wasn't there."[15]

Later, he added: "We had what Jeff Bezos would tell you was the reason for most of his success—first mover advantage. Because by the time they realized that, 'Oh, what Bloomberg was doing is valuable and people will take the data from him because he has done something else with it,' it was pretty hard, late for them to catch up."[16]

That did not mean he was lucky enough to let things slide. Chairman Bloomberg, who had a maxim for everything, made it clear to his employees that to compete in their hyper-fast world, the company had to grow and adapt constantly. "Growth makes us a moving target. No growth makes us a sitting duck."[17] Or, a corollary: "Any supplier who offers today what it sold yesterday will be out of business tomorrow."

He still claimed he didn't worry about competitors who are always promising to deliver a cheaper, faster, easier machine. As he put it dismissively, "They compare Bloomberg, an operating F18 jet fighter, with their still-being-developed witch on a broomstick."[18]

By 2019, the fighter jet was still working just fine for Michael Bloomberg.

27

GIVING BACK

*"When I get to heaven, I'm not sure I'm going to
stand for an interview. I'm going right in."*
—*Bloomberg to CBS's* 60 Minutes, *2017*[1]

Michael Bloomberg is a generous billionaire. He has been repeatedly ranked as one of the top donors in the country by *The Chronicle of Philanthropy*, coming in second place in 2018 after Jeff and MacKenzie Bezos, who gave away $2 billion to Bloomberg's $767 million.[2]

Bloomberg had already signed the Giving Pledge along with Warren Buffett, Bill and Melinda Gates, and more than one hundred other wealthy people who promised to give away at least half of their fortunes before they died.[3] Bloomberg vowed to do even better. When asked about his philanthropy, Bloomberg would often say that he planned for his check to the undertaker to bounce, a view that echoed Andrew Carnegie's famous line that "the man who dies rich, dies disgraced."[4]

Over the years, Bloomberg has given privately and publicly. His personal generosity was often reflexive and heartfelt—from millions for hospitals and facilities in Israel and Johns Hopkins, his beloved alma mater, to much smaller gifts to friends, employees, even his critics and people he hardly knew. Most of his public giving has been strategically directed to improve the health of the planet and its people—including an emphasis on curbing guns, obesity, tobacco, and climate change. There would still be plenty of money left to support his other pet causes—money for the arts and education and innovations, particularly in cities. And he would carve out millions for his favored candidates who supported climate change and gun control and anybody but President Donald Trump.

Privately, Bloomberg seemed to seek out people in trouble. When he learned that the wife of one top city employee had leukemia, Bloomberg got her into an advanced medical program. A professor once told a Bloomberg employee that he was having heart trouble. "Next thing I knew, *the* helicopter took me to Johns Hopkins" to see Bloomberg's preferred cardiologists. He paid for the funeral of a campaign worker whose family was struggling. And he reached out to people in trouble. "He called my mom every day when she was dying," the son of a Bloomberg friend reported. And if he knew you were fired, Bloomberg was often among the first to offer support and a reminder that being axed did not mean you had been extinguished as a human being. He had been there.

Even some of his political opponents were visited by Bloomberg's better angel. The late Wayne Barrett, a veteran investigative reporter for the *Village Voice*, had repeatedly scorched Bloomberg in print. "I really hammered the guy," he said, "because that's what I do."[5]

To cite only one example of Barrett's Bloomberg work, when the mayor used his money and political clout to run for a third term—breaking his own promise to retire after two terms—Barrett wrote an article with the headline "The Transformation of Mike Bloomberg: How the Benevolent Billionaire with No Political Debts Ended Up Owning Us All."

Yet, when Barrett was ill and in the hospital, the head nurse came running down the hall one day and burst into his room. "It's the mayor on the line," she said breathlessly, holding out her cell phone.

"For ten or more minutes, he was telling me what a good journalist I am and wishing me good luck and all that. It was totally surprising," Barrett recalled. Plus, he noted, his care improved considerably.

And then there were the little surprises, flashy reminders that he had deeper pockets than most. Early in his first term, Bloomberg and a few city officials stopped at a Greek diner for a late-night meal. The owner rushed over and said how honored he was to have the mayor and how the food was on him. The mayor smiled and said thank you. Then, as he left, he pulled out a hundred dollar bill, gave it to the waiter, and said, "Have a good night."[6]

There are plenty of these stories—the sudden handout, the calls to those in pain, the help finding good medical care. Was this, as one skeptic put it, guilt for gilt? Maybe. But a more generous explanation was that Bloomberg had the power to help and enjoyed using it.

Like his peers, Bloomberg gave to museums and major charities, but his public philanthropy was different for one major reason: he had been a mayor for twelve years, and he knew the gritty problems that cities faced every day. He would argue that cities were where changes could be made for the better—not in Washington, where politics too often had hardened into perpetual gridlock. As a result, his public giving began to focus on cities, and he concentrated on finding smaller innovations that could be adopted by urban areas across the world.

Shortly after he left city hall, Bloomberg appeared before a group of philanthropists and their representatives to explain his view. The "public sector traditionally hasn't innovated very well," he said, because there are "powerful disincentives" in case the new idea is a flop. "If there's anything that scares elected officials, not to mention their consultants, it's failure. The press magnifies failure. They harp on it. They sensationalize it, and opponents exploit that so politicians play it safe." A waste of taxpayer money on a faulty experiment simply writes the political ad for an opponent, he said. So, "That's where philanthropy comes in,"[7] he said.

Bloomberg Philanthropies, the umbrella organization created in 2006 to manage his many charitable ventures, operates in an elegant Stanford

White mansion on East Seventy-eighth Street in Manhattan.[8] Bloomberg purchased the historic building in 2006 for a somewhat high, pre-2008 crisis price of $45 million, and, after substantial renovations, he opened his charity headquarters there a short time later.[9] The grand residence was once owned by one of New York's oldest and richest families, whose most famous member in the nineteenth century was Hamilton Fish, governor of New York, U.S. senator, and secretary of state. The house was built for his son, Stuyvesant Fish. Outside there is still a wrought-iron fence with a fish theme, a reminder of the family's golden days.

Behind a somber exterior, the doors now slide open to a burst of light and glass, with transparent stairs and walls and a variety of art, from very ancient to very last week. Bloomberg's own favorite is a seventeenth-century painting called *The Library of Euclid* by Domenico Maroli,[10] which dominates one wall. It shows Euclid of Megara disguising himself as a woman because Megaran males were banned from entering Athens, where Socrates was teaching. Elsewhere, a collection of the latest contemporary art changes more often than the seasons. It is a see-through workplace where people are laboring with a visible intensity, and in some ways, this formidable glass castle feels like an architect's version of the man himself. Staid on the outside, full of energy and unpredictability on the inside.

Bloomberg Philanthropies has been a small operation for the largesse it dispensed over the first dozen years. Some two hundred employees around the world scrambled to find worthy recipients for grants that ranged from a few thousand dollars to tens of millions. Bloomberg planned to dole out more with every birthday with $10 billion of his $50 billion–plus fortune promised by the end of 2019 at age seventy-seven.[11] (He sometimes said he planned to live to 125, which would give him a little extra time to spread his wealth around. But if he pushed the wrong pedal on the helicopter or skied into a tree, of course, like the heirs to the Rockefeller and the Carnegie fortunes, his trusted friends and family could take over.)

Bloomberg put his most-important employee, Patti Harris, in charge of his charity, even though, at the time, she was still his top deputy mayor with plenty on her schedule. She was already the chief guide for Bloomberg's political adventures; she had untangled many of his problems at city hall; and she was generally the one who made certain that his job and his life ran as smoothly as possible. Now she would add control over the organization created to give away billions of dollars in five main areas: public health, arts, government innovation (especially in cities), education, and the environment.

"Patti has been the eyes and ears. She's been the moral standard. She's been the disciplinarian. She's been the one with common sense," Bloomberg explained in an interview in 2018. "She's the one that ties together the family, the foundation and the company.

"It's hard to overestimate the value that Patti has brought to the city and to the worldwide philanthropy and this company. Now she is my confidante. Everybody knows that." Bloomberg was at a glass table in his New York office that day. He nibbled blueberries, passing them around. Suddenly he grinned, unable to resist a little aside. "She already bought a coffin for me and a burial plot. She said, 'You want to go see it?' I said, 'No, I'm not going to see it. I'm going to be six feet underground, for chrisssake.'" [12]

By most accounts, Bloomberg's philanthropy was very "Bloombergerian," the term often used by many in the Bloomberg network. That usually meant that the boss demanded they find or create the data—find numbers for an "unmet need," as his workers said. Then his staff tried to find a way to meet that need, and finally, Bloomberg asked for reports on what had worked and what hadn't.

Following the Johns Hopkins public health creed of saving lives by the millions, Bloomberg gave to combat the deadly issues of the day. Beginning with millions of dollars to fight tobacco use ("even Beijing is now smoke free," he boasted in 2016, after the city banned indoor smoking). [13, 14] He added financial assaults on obesity and guns. He tried to cut traffic deaths around the world by funding such basic changes as pedestrian paths in Ghana or seat belt laws in Shanghai. He fought accidental drowning in Bangladesh and helped provide basic medical care in Africa.

One program for the East African nation of Tanzania trained high school students to do emergency C-sections and appendectomies. It was the kind of gamble most politicians would avoid—the downside being far too disastrous if some teenager accidentally killed a patient. Not Bloomberg, who explained it this way: "These high school graduates, how can they do an operation? It turns out they're relatively simple. Most times it works. And if it doesn't work, you were going to die anyways," he explained to an audience at a synagogue in Atlanta where a few listeners laughed somewhat nervously. "But you've got to be willing to take risks like that. Everybody laughs about it. What would you do, let them die? They'd let them die rather than let a few die. I don't think that way."[15] Only a numbers man would put it quite so bluntly.

Bloomberg would spend hundreds of millions of dollars fighting the thickening air near coal-fired power plants, the dying oceans, and even, above and over it all, climate change. Once, when a fellow business executive tried to convince him that climate change was a hoax, he angrily questioned the guy's intelligence.[16] And as climate change became more important to him personally and politically, he said, "The only thing I know that could literally wipe out every single living thing down to microbes on this planet is global warming," adding, "If you turn this planet into Mars, it never comes back."[17]

Bloomberg's emphasis on education was his view that a good schooling was the main route out of poverty. Data showing that only 6 percent of students at top colleges were poor encouraged him to create a way for "high-achieving, low income" students to apply and go to top universities. Most top universities signed onto his program to make room for bright but poor students—Harvard, Princeton, Yale, Stanford, UCLA, the long list of top universities. Their goal was to graduate 50,000 lower-income students at 270 participating colleges by 2025.[18] For his part, Bloomberg contributed $1.8 billion in 2018 to his alma mater, Johns Hopkins, to help low-income students apply and make it through to graduation.

(Some residents of New York City immediately complained that the money would be better spent at the public City University of New York than the elite private university in Baltimore.)

Bloomberg's philanthropy expanded beyond a few checks here and there in the 1990s, and in New York he became a top name on the begging roster for the city's cultural and educational organizations. His tuxedos in those days got a lot of use as he joined the glamorous society-donor circuit.

A girlfriend of the newly divorced Bloomberg recalled introducing him to Beverly Sills, the famous soprano who quickly made sure he was added to the board of Lincoln Center.[19] At the time, Bloomberg gave freely (and got on the boards) of the city's cultural centers like the Metropolitan Museum of Art and the New York Public Library, to name a few. He was part of the Central Park Conservancy, where he began to promote the Christo orange *Gates* for the park as part of the millennium celebrations in 2000. His friend Harvey Eisen once said that "he wanted to be a player, wanted to be a fancy guy in the city. He's not a phony. He's not a jerk like Trump, but he crossed over [to the elegant side], you know. Do you have any idea of the dirty mouth this guy has? He used to be impossible, but you can't do what we used to do. He adapted."[20]

Ever the Anglophile, Bloomberg courted London in much the same way. Julia Peyton-Jones, director of the adventurous Serpentine Gallery in London from 1991 to 2016, remembered how Bloomberg organized a dinner party in 1996 for people in the arts. At the dinner, when the glamorous Peyton-Jones sat next to Bloomberg and pitched her struggling museum, Bloomberg promised that he planned to spend more time in London (and, of course, more money). "It was like having a very exotic bird in our midst," she remembered.

Peyton-Jones, who believed Bloomberg enjoyed modern, even "provocative" art, convinced her New York billionaire friend to invest heavily in her struggling museum housed in London's Kensington Gardens. She said Bloomberg fearlessly sponsored a major project featuring the works of Piero Manzoni. Manzoni was best known for tantalizing and mocking the commercial art world, using his own fingerprints, a balloon described as his own breath, and small cans called *Merda d'artista*, or the artist's shit. (One can sold for 182,500 pound sterling in 2015).[21, 22]

Patti Harris and later Kate Levin, the city's cultural affairs commissioner, would encourage Bloomberg's tuxedo-driven interest in the arts, especially public art to enliven cities around the country. Bloomberg would later give $75 million to the Shed, the odd but memorable name for a gigantic new cultural center near the High Line railroad park on Manhattan's far West Side. The donation was for the 200,000-square-foot adaptable, moveable, multipurpose structure that could morph from art galleries to a five-hundred-seat theater, with a massive sliding contraption that allowed for cultural events both indoors and out. For his share of the cost of the Shed—$475 million—Bloomberg earned the rights to call it the Bloomberg Building by the opening in 2019.[23, 24, 25]

There would always be questions about whether his philanthropy and his politics were in sync. He gave freely to state politicians as he decided to run for mayor. And as he moved from being the private billionaire to the political candidate in 2001, his gifts to charities looked like something other than simple gifts. David Jones, president of the Community Service Society of New York, was one of those who became increasingly wary of the Bloomberg giveaways. His organization promotes economic progress for the poor but had not taken Bloomberg money. "I do think [the contributions] had a chilling effect on the willingness to take strong positions in opposition to the mayor,"[26] he observed. Such talk infuriated Bloomberg, who insisted he wanted his money to improve the city, not muffle the complaints.

Sometimes Bloomberg even chose to remain anonymous. A few days after he was elected mayor in 2001, Bloomberg was stepping out of a restaurant when he bumped into Vartan Gregorian, president of the Carnegie Corporation of New York.[27] Gregorian, who counted Bloomberg as a friend, quickly explained to the mayor-elect that after 9/11 and a souring economy, many of the smaller arts and nonprofit groups that provide so much vitality to the city were suffering. Could his billionaire friend help set up an emergency fund? Gregorian asked. Bloomberg agreed, as long as the donations were anonymous and Carnegie would administer the fund for free.

Bloomberg sent a donation every December until 2010 when he shifted to his own foundation, and the Bloomberg money allowed Carnegie to give out 3,150 grants across the city. Soon, of course, these anonymous donations were no longer anonymous. Almost everybody in the nonprofit world knew about the Carnegie deal. The *Times*, which referred to Bloomberg as a "modern-day Medici," declared in 2005 that his donations through his family charity and his corporation and Carnegie amounted at least $140 million a year to eight hundred institutions.[28, 29] Moreover, Bloomberg told friends that he loved the idea that any anonymous gift in the city always made people think it was really him, trying to be humble about giving away his billions.

In many important ways, his post-mayoral charity became far more important as an extension of his time in city hall. As mayor he banned smoking in the city and tried (but failed) to limit sugary colas to sixteen ounces. As philanthropist, he announced that he had given nearly $1 billion by 2016 to help fifty-nine countries pass anti-tobacco laws and curb tobacco use even in smoke-filled societies in Turkey, China, India, Indonesia, and Bangladesh.[30] He fared better by promoting soda taxes in Mexico and Philadephia.

As mayor, he fought for cleaner air and water. As philanthropist, he pledged half a billion dollars in 2019 to help close coal-fired power plants and move to a clean energy economy by 2030. And he would fight climate change at every level, from the city to the states to the White House.

He began battling against illegal guns as mayor. And even though he was criticized for his stop-and-frisk policies targeting minorities, his support for gun control turned into a nationwide political and moral challenge to the National Rifle Association. As he left city hall, and with gun deaths mounting to more than 33,000 Americans a year,[31] Bloomberg announced a $50 million grant to merge two groups—Mayors Against Illegal Guns and Moms Demand Action for Gun Sense in America. The new group would be called Everytown for Gun Safety, and its main purpose would be to energize voters to support gun control and candidates unafraid of the NRA.[32] By 2018, Bloomberg and a group run by former congresswoman Gabby Giffords, who survived an assassination attempt in 2011, vowed to fight the NRA at the polls. In the congressional midterm elections that year—$37 million went to candidates who promised to control guns, compared to $20 million from the NRA.[33]

The political donations had to be separate by law, but with his Independence USA PAC (political action committee), Bloomberg was becoming a prime king and queen maker among those in his billionaire class.

For all the money that went out under the Bloomberg name, perhaps nothing was as radical in the world of philanthropy as his emphasis on cities as the major engines of change. After twelve years in city hall, meeting mayors from around the world, talking about how to keep these clusters of human beings healthy and prosperous, Bloomberg was a believer in the power of mayors to do more than march in parades and tub-thump into microphones.

Bloomberg called cities the "laboratories for democracy." And, "If we can help them along, we can sleep well at night."[34]

As he would say repeatedly, his mission was to supplement government and pay for experiments that most city politicians wouldn't dare try. Plus, as mayor for twelve years, he had seen problems up front and in agonizing detail, problems he believed cities could fix.

At one private dinner with a group of mayors in 2012, Bloomberg said, "There's one thing mayors can agree on, whether they're Republican, Democrats or Independents—and I'm the one person in the room who can speak with authority on all three—we don't have the luxury of giving speeches and making promises."[35] That was when his fellow mayors, like Philadelphia's then mayor Michael Nutter, began offering constant encouragement. "Mayor Bloomberg is the mayor's mayor,"[36] Nutter said.

"Mayors do things," Bloomberg added shortly before he left his own mayoral hub. "Mayors make things happen."[37]

Out of office, he turned cities into international testing grounds by using a series of contests, offering funds up to $5 million worth of grants and support for a winning idea that could also help other cities. He also created a consulting firm of top city officials to help other cities gratis, courtesy of his philanthropy.

Here were a few of the ways he used his money to get cities to experiment:

- In 2013, he gave $1 million each to Chicago for "predictive analytics" data and to Houston for a new recycling program. Chicago's effort was a clear success, using department data to predict problems. (For example, the city's data experts cross-checked water-main leaks and garbage complaints to predict sudden surges in the rat population in an area.)[38] Houston's proposal for a high-tech, one-bin recycling program was junked by a new mayor who opted instead for a contract with a standard garbage hauler.[39]

- The grand prize of $5 million that year went to Providence, Rhode Island, for a program called Providence Talks.[40] Researchers had found that children from poor households heard about a third as many words as those from wealthier homes, and this limited vocabulary often held them back in school. To help out, children in 170 families wore recording devices that were analyzed by machines tracking the number of words said by adults in the home. When their word count got low, coaches from the city would come to help with books and other teaching aids. Those children who heard the fewest words in the beginning of their survey—about eight thousand adult words a day—soon heard more than twelve thousand words as adults talked more about cooking, the news, the household, et cetera.[41] Brown University researchers found that the program provided a "promising strategy" to "advance early learning,"[42] and the program began to spread to other cities.

- Cary, North Carolina, a town of 130,000, got a Bloomberg grant to test sewage to determine where people were overusing opioids.[43] Their idea was to direct more help to these areas where opioids were plentiful.

- Santa Monica won $1 million in 2013 to measure the well-being of its residents. (That meant details of people's health, fears, access to the community, and opportunity, etc.) The results were hopeful. Data from the city and from interviews of some of the 92,000 citizens showed that people in one poorer area were not eating enough fruits and vegetables. So they increased the value of food stamps in the area, made them easier to use at a nearby farmers market, and started basic cooking classes in the neighborhood.[44]

In 2014, Bloomberg looked for new ideas in European cities, offering a million euros each to try different programs in Athens, Stockholm, Warsaw, and the Kirklees, a district in West Yorkshire, UK. The grand prize of five million euros went to Barcelona for a digital "trust network," an online community of volunteers to help care for the city's growing number of senior citizens.[45]

By 2017, his focus was back on America, and he announced another $200 million for what he called the American Cities Initiative. He had granted $1 million each in 2018 to Denver, Durham, Fort Collins, Georgetown (Texas), Huntington (West Virginia), Los Angeles, New Rochelle (New York), Philadelphia, and South Bend. Then came the $70 million American Cities Climate Challenge that provided expertise and support to another twenty-five cities finding inventive ways to reduce their carbon footprint.

Still, the help for so many cities came in such small numbers that complaints came from another direction. This money was a pittance, that $100,000 wouldn't even buy a "public toilet," some groused. Henry Grabar, an urban affairs writer for Slate, noted that such grants were small potatoes for cities with billion-dollar budgets. Bloomberg often made the same point himself—that he was not trying to make up for cuts to local or federal budgets. He could give millions to private anti-smoking campaigns, but as a mayor banning indoor smoking, he would enhance the lives of 8.5 million people. No mere philanthropist could do that. As a private citizen, he could not replace city governments, he could only encourage innovations at a local level that might work in other cities.

The Bloomberg contests would be only one way to help mayors around the world. Bloomberg also brought some of the biggest names from his city hall into the charitable operations, creating what the *Times* would call his "urban SWAT team."[46] Near the end of his third term as mayor, Bloomberg had asked George Fertitta, who was running the city's tourism campaigns, to create a group of his top aides who could share their expertise with other cities.

Fertitta, another former tycoon in perpetual motion, had been a successful marketing expert who once helped Bloomberg peddle his news operation by giving out radios that had only one channel—Bloomberg Radio. "It was Mike's idea," Fertitta insisted. At city hall, Fertitta had helped lure more than 54 million tourists to the city by 2013 (up 20 million from the lean years after 9/11).[47]

Fertitta was Bloomberg's kind of guy. Even in his seventies, he often got to the office at 6:00 a.m. (an hour earlier than his boss) and made decisions (or took advice from the ex-mayor) on the run. Fertitta's appointment to head the group was typical. After a brief conversation about the idea, Bloomberg told Fertitta, "'Okay, we're gonna do this. You're gonna be the CEO, and I'm gonna pay you this,' and I said, 'Fine.'"[48]

Fertitta's group included Amanda Burden, former planning commissioner; Janette Sadik-Khan, former transportation commissioner; Rose Gill Hearn, who was commissioner for the city's Department of Investigation; Kate Levin, who had been Bloomberg's cultural affairs commissioner; Linda Gibbs, former deputy mayor for health and human services; and others.

Word quickly got around that the "Associates" did not charge for their services. The bumptious London mayor, Boris Johnson who was a Bloomberg friend, got help to improve Internet capability in his city. The mayors of Mexico City and Los Angeles impressed Bloomberg and then also made the cut.

Cities could not hire the Bloomberg consultants. They were not clients; cities would receive advice, not buy it. That arrangement meant the Bloomberg people could be frank, since they were not angling for another contract, and, of course, the cities were free to reject the advice with minimal grief from taxpayers. By 2018, the Associates had encouraged fourteen cities to allocate $1.3 billion for 280 local projects.[49] Along with London, Los Angeles, Mexico City, and Rio, they worked with Athens, Atlanta, Bogotá, Detroit, Houston, Kansas City, Milan, Nashville, Oakland, and Paris.

With the help from Bloomberg's former city hall deputies, Athens officials provided $14 million to fund local health and economic improvements, including a pedestrian plaza and assistance ridding the city of graffiti. In Detroit, the team helped struggling residents get thousands of dollars in tax credits and advised city officials on how to carve out more public space for pedestrians.[50]

As survivors of New York City's bureaucracy, the Bloomberg Associates knew how to get around notoriously difficult city bureaucrats. And their help ranged from city plazas to an exotic way to entice tourists into a town. When Sony wanted to use Mexico City for an opening scene in a new James Bond movie, the company got nowhere with city officials: Enter Fertitta and his film team. They negotiated to keep 007 in Mexico City for the first twelve minutes of *Spectre* when the Bond producers created a dramatic parade of giant skeletons for the Day of the Dead (as in Halloween). "That's a billion dollar commercial" for the city, Fertitta crowed, adding a zero or two for emphasis. Some viewers said it was the best part of the film, and Mexico City began having a Day of the Dead parade to boost the local economy by drawing tourists from around the world.

There were also the disappointments. The Associates turned down Toronto, for example, because the city took away much of any mayor's power after former mayor Rob Ford refused to resign after using crack cocaine.[51] The Bloomberg group also had to pull out of Rome after the mayor was accused of using city money for repeatedly taking his wife to dinner. There were some questions about whether he had merely offended the wrong people, and after a dead crow was left in front of his home one morning, a deposit viewed by some as an invitation to resign, the mayor decided it was time to go.

One side effect of all this charity that often went unnoticed—it clearly made Bloomberg happy. Yes, it was part of his Jewish heritage, his answer to the call to repair his world.[52] But for Bloomberg it seemed to be more than duty. He enjoyed coming to the rescue like his boyhood hero Johnny Tremain. But with far more resources than the fictional spy from America's Revolutionary days, Bloomberg could direct his team to move fast in any direction. They could suddenly grab medical supplies, as they did in 2017, and hop on his planes to help those devastated by Hurricanes Irma and Maria on Saint John's Island in the Caribbean. *Forbes* magazine, noting how the Bloomberg team had organized rebuilding in the U.S. Virgin Islands, called it "All-In Philanthropy."[53]

Bloomberg had set aside plenty of money for his luxurious lifestyle, his planes, helicopters, houses, golf memberships, and exclusive clubs. And there was enough for his family, even an ex-girlfriend or two. But as for his philanthropy, he told a crowd in Atlanta, "I don't know how else I could get satisfaction. I've got, in terms of material things, anything I want. But you don't look in the mirror and say, 'God, isn't it wonderful I have a bigger house than the guy next door.' No, you want to do something that's really unique. And so Bloomberg Philanthropies tries to make people's lives longer and healthier [and] better."[54]

Not one to belittle his own generosity, he told Steve Kroft of CBS's

60 Minutes in 2017, "I like what I see when I look in the mirror . . . We've probably saved millions of lives, and certainly we'll save tens of millions of lives going forward. There aren't many people that have done that.

"So, you know, when I get to heaven, I'm not sure I'm going to stand for an interview. I'm going right in."[55]

GREEN FOR GREEN

"In the long term [climate change] could literally turn the
planet into a barren sphere like Mars and kill everybody."
—*Bloomberg, 2017*

At 3:32 p.m. on June 1, 2017, Donald Trump strutted into the White House Rose Garden and declared that the United States was pulling out of the international Paris accords to combat climate change.[1] That agreement by 195 countries was a voluntary effort to reduce greenhouse gas emissions, and until then, the only nations not participating were Syria and Nicaragua. (These two soon agreed to join,[2] leaving the United States as the only outsider.)

Yet, on that warm, sunny afternoon, a crowd of mostly white men sweltering in dark business suits applauded enthusiastically as the president announced, "We're getting out." The accords were not fair to America, he complained. "We don't want other leaders and other countries laughing at us anymore," adding as his alliterative punch line that he was elected to take care of the citizens of Pittsburgh, not Paris.

Trump's decision was, of course, a bow to the coal, oil, and gas barons, all the corporate types who pretended that the ice caps weren't melting and that the storms and fires and floods weren't growing more dangerous by the season. But the president also presented Bloomberg with a gift, a powerful opportunity to become more outspoken about this global issue and even to use it as a platform to support Trump's opponents in 2018 and 2020.

Trump was, in many ways, the perfect adversary—an increasingly erratic, divisive, pro-pollution president of the United States who once said climate change was a "hoax" and reacted to a damaging and in-depth report on climate by his own administration by saying, "I don't believe it."[3] Trump's decision on Paris had been expected, and his critics were ready. The mayor of Pittsburgh, Bill Peduto, fired off a tweet that his city was standing firmly with Paris. And in New York, Bloomberg's political team released his prepared statement declaring that Americans would "honor and fulfill the Paris Agreement by leading from the bottom up . . . And there isn't anything Washington can do to stop us," Bloomberg said, adding that he would personally pay the $15 million a year that the U.S. had pledged to the accords, making good on another invoice that Donald Trump had no plans to honor.

As Trump made his Rose Garden announcement, Bloomberg was in Europe, on his way to his first emotional visit to the Nazi concentration camp at Auschwitz. Kevin Sheekey had already arrived in Poland to join Bloomberg for the tour. As Bloomberg's car sped from the Kraków airport, Sheekey was on the ground near the camp and on the phone to his boss.

"What do you think about going to Paris?" Sheekey asked. He envisioned a meeting in the very city where the accords were signed, a high-impact press briefing alongside the French president, Emmanuel Macron, and Paris mayor, Anne Hidalgo, both strong supporters of the accords. "Why don't we do it tomorrow?" Sheekey suggested.

Tomorrow? Sheekey should have known better. "Why would we do it tomorrow?" Bloomberg shot back. "Let's just do it today."

Bloomberg, a Jewish former mayor of the American city with 1.1 million Jews, had no plans to shorten what would be a wrenching tour of Auschwitz. As Bloomberg visited Hitler's death camp, Sheekey stayed outside near the horrifying gate that read "Work sets you free" and focused instead on creating an instant press event. Bloomberg aides in London were ordered onto the next train to Paris, political aides in Paris adjusted and readjusted schedules. That evening, after storms had delayed Bloomberg's flight, he finally arrived at Le Bourget, the airport for private planes, and was rushed by police escort into central Paris. President Macron was waiting on the Élysée Palace steps to greet him.

A scant twenty-two hours after Trump's Rose Garden announcement—the president of France, the mayor of Paris, and the former mayor of New York stood side by side to promise that they would fight Trump's shift backwards.

"I want the world to know that the U.S. will meet our Paris commitment," Bloomberg declared. He did not mention Trump by name, but he added, "The fact of the matter is that Americans don't need Washington to meet our Paris commitment, and Americans are not going to let Washington stand in the way of fulfilling it."[4]

America "cannot stick our heads in the sand," he said, especially as the earth's temperature continued to rise. Because the U.S. is the "world's second largest contributor of greenhouse gases" after China, he added, it was in America's interest to limit these pollutants or "pay for it in worse health, lost jobs and a weaker economy."[5]

The Paris setting offered an impressive backdrop as Michael Bloomberg began increasing his attacks on President Trump's policies on climate change. Within five months, he and California governor Jerry Brown would get commitments from more than 100 American cities, 20 states, and more than 1,300 businesses to join the fight—participants representing "more than half of the U.S. economy."[6] And Bloomberg would soon broaden his public criticism of Trump on other issues as well—the lack of gun control, tax breaks for the rich, broken trade agreements, and the president's inhumane immigration policies that separated thousands of children from their parents coming across the country's southern border.

As it turned out, his visit to Auschwitz would also give Bloomberg the chance nearly six weeks later to speak out about American neo-Nazis who would march through the streets of Charlottesville, Virginia, chanting the Nazi war cry, "Blood and soil," and "Jews will not replace us." When Trump said there were "good people" on both sides of the issue, Bloomberg responded: "I recently visited Auschwitz for the first time. It's hard to fathom how such evil could still lurk here in America. But it does, and we must never flinch from rejecting it. Religious tolerance and racial equality are the bedrock of American greatness."[7] Bloomberg was determined to do his part to assure the world that Americans were better than Trump. And, although it was unspoken, he wanted that same world to know that there were better American billionaires than this flawed U.S. president.

As Michael Bloomberg took center stage advocating for a greener world, it is worth recalling how far he had come from his early days in city hall. One of his first acts as mayor was to cancel most recycling as too expensive, alarming the city's ecologists and setting back the city's recycling habits for years. Over time, however, the issue seemed to grow on him, and with a dynamic plan to create a greener New York City—PlaNYC— he set ambitious environmental goals for his city and encouraged others around the world to follow. More fundamentally, to Bloomberg global warming was the ultimate challenge to global health. "Climate change has the potential to do two things," he said in 2017. "One, hurt your and my life, our children's lives and our grandchildren's lives. And two," as he often added, "in the longer term, it could literally turn the planet into a barren sphere like Mars and kill everybody."[8]

Bloomberg's campaign to fight climate change began in 2011 almost by chance. Carl Pope, the longtime head of the Sierra Club, was having lunch one day with the ubiquitous Sheekey to pitch a new clean-air campaign. He was raising money to close aging coal-fired power plants. Pope planned to find donors who could give $50 million, and with an eye on Bloomberg's passion about public health, he mentioned the seven thousand deaths a year and hundreds of thousands of asthma attacks that could be traced to the toxic fumes from these old power plants. Maybe Sheekey's friend, the billionaire, could help a little? Pope was not sure his pitch had touched its mark.

But shortly after the lunch, Bloomberg was meeting with his top philanthropy staff on education. The meeting was not going well, and Bloomberg was beginning to fidget and look impatient, not a good sign. ("I don't do patience," he explained a few years later.)[9] Finally, Sheekey, scrambling for a new idea, brought up Pope's $50 million drive to close coal-fired power plants that were killing people, thousands at a time.

Bloomberg brightened, as he often did, with the prospect of a new public health campaign. "Just give Carl a check for the $50 million," Bloomberg ordered. "And, tell him to stop fundraising and get to work."[10] Of course, no Bloomberg gift that big could be given quietly. To announce the grant, Bloomberg chartered a party boat called *Nina's Dandy* for a floating press conference on the Potomac River. The boat offered a first-class photo backdrop a few hundred yards away—the Potomac River Generating Station, a sixty-two-year-old, coal-fired power plant on the Virginia side of the river. The antiquated smokestacks had served the growing region, even, on occasion, the nation's capital.[11]

Nature helped that day. It was so hot and humid that D.C. officials had issued a "Code Orange" alert, which meant the air was so bad kids shouldn't be outside playing in it.[12] For the event, Bloomberg shed his jacket and rolled up his sleeves, but kept on his pointedly green tie. By the end of the briefing, his hair looked wet and his standard white shirt was visibly damp. A little wilted, but ready for battle.

"Coal is a self-inflicted public health risk," Bloomberg declared, "polluting the air we breathe, adding mercury to our water and the leading cause of climate disruption."[13]

Within a month, the owners of the Potomac River Generating Station announced plans to close—one of many closings during the Sierra Club campaign. And three years later, the *Wall Street Journal* editorial page blamed Bloomberg and his anti-coal army for contributing to a minor blackout in Washington. The *Journal* wrote that Bloomberg's anti-coal efforts had left the nation's capital with "little margin for electric error."[14]

But with Bloomberg's money, the Sierra Club steadily closed some of the dirtiest coal-fired plants around the country. They organized local groups to fight for cleaner air, to bring out testimony by parents with children who had breathing problems. For those unmoved by the pollution, the Sierra Club lawyers soon argued that coal was too expensive compared to natural gas or solar and wind power. By 2016, the campaign called Beyond Coal had helped retire 245 coal plants, almost half of those still operating.[15]

Then Donald Trump was elected president.

The coal industry quickly moved on Washington since Trump's campaign had promised a revival of one of the nation's unhealthiest forms of energy. Trump quickly called for an end to the "war on coal." And he vowed to bring back jobs for coal miners in West Virginia, Kentucky, Wyoming, and Pennsylvania—all states, by the way, that he won in the 2016 election.

Almost immediately, Trump allowed coal companies to dump their toxic residues into local mountain streams.[16] He hired people in Washington who saw coal as money, and his choice to monitor mine safety was David Zatezalo, a former coal executive whose company had been charged with serious safety violations.[17] Scott Pruitt, who had spent earlier years in Oklahoma fighting the environmentalists including the Sierra Club, took over the Environmental Protection Agency (until he had to resign for his lavish spending and ethical lapses).[18] Coal executive Robert Murray, who labeled climate change a mere "theology," said that after Trump was elected he gave the new president a three-and-a-half-page list of ways to help the coal industry. By late 2017, Murray boasted that Trump had already "wiped out page one."[19]

In October that first year in office, Trump's anti-environment team announced plans to repeal the Clean Power Plan created by Obama to regulate pollution from the nation's power plants including those using coal. The next day, an indignant Mike Bloomberg wrote another check to fund Carl Pope's crusade against coal. This one was for $64 million, bringing Bloomberg's total support to $168 million[20] to close America's coal-fired power plants and, of course, to counter Donald Trump.

To promote their campaign, Bloomberg and Pope produced a book, *Climate of Hope: How Cities, Businesses, and Citizens Can Save the Planet.* With help from Bloomberg, who handed out more than a few free copies, it became a *New York Times* best seller. And Bloomberg Philanthropies would later fund a movie titled *Paris to Pittsburgh* that emphasized local city and community details of the coming climate emergency. The film in 2018 came a dozen years after Al Gore's Oscar-winning documentary, *An Inconvenient Truth,* alerting the world to the dangers of global warming. This new film featured Pittsburgh mayor Bill Peduto and emphasized a U.S. government report in 2018 by three hundred scientists on the financial risks of potential natural disasters from climate change."[21] *Paris to Pittsburgh* also emphasized what cities could do. One reviewer from *Forbes* magazine called it "a searing look at the effects of climate change by regular people who are dealing with its effects in their local towns."[22]

Bloomberg did not merely want cities to pledge support for fighting climate change, he was ready to put up $70 million to help. A year after Trump's Rose Garden event, Bloomberg announced a competition to choose twenty mayors who could come up with the best ways to combat the warming climate. The United Nations had just given Bloomberg a title as U.S. Special Envoy for Climate Action, and using that august new perch, Bloomberg eventually provided help to twenty-seven cities, each getting about $2.5 million worth of expertise and assistance as part of his "Climate Challenge."

The cities were in Ohio and Florida—states that might have become important in the 2020 presidential race, if that had become a possibility. Cincinnati earmarked the Bloomberg assistance to provide renewable energy to power the city's water utility. Orlando won for expanding solar energy, adding charging stations for electric cars, and moving to more electric buses and city vehicles. Skeptics, of course, wondered whether there was some pattern here, an attempt perhaps to establish an artful grassroots network, mayor by mayor, to promote a political offensive in 2020.

As Bloomberg helped organize cities, states, and businesses to fight a warming planet, Trump was just as busy unraveling the federal government's efforts to curb greenhouse gases. On August 21, 2018, for example, he moved to let states regulate coal plant emissions and lifted restrictions on building new plants using coal. In February 2019, Trump put together a panel led by William Happer, a Princeton physicist and Trump adviser, whose unwavering belief in the benefits of carbon dioxide once led him to assert that "the demonization of carbon dioxide is just like the demonization of the poor Jews under Hitler."[23] The White House panel was Trump's attempt to turn the science of climate change into a debate instead of a reality.[24]

As the 2020 presidential campaign gathered momentum in early 2019, Bloomberg unveiled plans to extend and expand his green crusade. His money had helped, but it was not enough. He needed to do something about changing the climate in Washington.

29

GOVERNMENT IN EXILE

"To start a four-year job, maybe an eight-year job, at age
seventy-nine, may not be the smartest thing to do."
—*Bloomberg, on his decision not to run in 2020.*[1]

Even after becoming one of the richest people in the world, even after twelve busy years as mayor of New York City, even after making a name for himself internationally as a powerful philanthropist, Michael Bloomberg had always wanted the top American trophy. He wanted to be president of the United States. An unabashed pragmatist when it came to politics, he was prepared to switch parties to better his chances and to use his own money to sway the voters. But he was also a numbers man who knew the odds of winning the White House, and he would often joke about how his chances were slim. "What chance does a five-foot-seven billionaire Jew who's divorced have of becoming president?" he said when his name first began to surface as a candidate.[2] But the odds and his jokes never stopped him from trying. And trying. And trying.

Bloomberg's first real opportunity to run for the White House came in 2008 when he was still mayor of New York. A Democrat in his early years, he became a Republican in 2000 because there were too many

Democrats in the race already. In 2007, he became an Independent, declaring himself to be "unaffiliated with any political party."[3] When word leaked out that he was considering a run that year as an Independent candidate, most pundits scoffed. After a hard look at the numbers, Bloomberg agreed that they were right.

The next chance came in 2012. Although President Obama was the favorite for reelection, Bloomberg was again being mentioned as a possible candidate. (He kept saying, "No way, no how." Publicly, at least.)[4] But, facing the end of his third term as mayor and a return to relative anonymity as another rich city businessman, Bloomberg was being considered for a group called Americans Elect trying to rally support for a third-party or nonparty candidate. But as the numbers hardened against a third party, he endorsed Obama a week[5] before the election.[6]

Then, in 2016, Bloomberg again rallied his aides for another try. Their high-powered political operation included polls in twenty-two states. Mock television ads for his run as an Independent included one titled "All Work and No Party." And the campaign logo (pointedly a mix of Republican red and Democratic blue, in other words, purple) was "Fix it." Bloomberg had even vetted a potential vice president, retired former chairman of the Joint Chiefs of Staff, Michael Mullen, and the campaign staff considered the possibility of announcing an entire cabinet before the election.[7]

Bloomberg's innovative political shop churned out other possibilities. How do you get young people to the polls, for example. Their billionaire candidate could pay for a "voting app" that would call an Uber or Lyft for anyone wanting to vote (for him, they hoped).

And what if the election were so close that it had to be decided by the House of Representatives for the first time since John Quincy Adams was elected in that manner in 1825? The Bloomberg enthusiasts harbored hopes that the then Republican House would not vote a straight party line. "We could be the non-toxic candidate," Bradley Tusk, the seasoned Bloomberg strategist, explained.[8]

Once again, Bloomberg blinked. Once again, he looked at the numbers and saw that an Independent candidate could only sway a presidential election, not win it. He would be taking away votes from Hillary Clinton. He would hand the White House to Donald Trump, and, as he put it, "That is not a risk I can take in good conscience."[9] Later, he would add a more personal reason: "My obit would be I was the guy that gave you Donald Trump. They wouldn't have cared about anything else I had done in my life."[10]

Still, his urge to reach for the top never really went away. In the summer of 2018, rumors of a Bloomberg candidacy surfaced again, and they seemed to be confirmed in the fall when Bloomberg re-registered as a Democrat, his party until he was fifty-eight years old and first ran for mayor as a Republican. Soon he would turn seventy-seven, and in early 2019, he told his most loyal advisers, "I don't want to have any regrets."[11] Let's get ready, he decided. Start the engines.

As his aides began to scramble, the field of other Democrats running for president was growing by the week. The early entrants were mostly progressives, but former vice president Joe Biden, who would later decide to run, was the clear favorite in early polls and a centrist much like Bloomberg. Biden, only a few months younger than Bloomberg, was leading with around 30 percent, while Bloomberg was near the bottom at 2 or 3 percent.[12] That is not to say a Bloomberg candidacy failed to attract any support. Some observers were clearly relieved at the thought of New York's steadier billionaire, after the tumultuous years of Donald Trump. The idea that there could be someone smart, experienced, and sane prompted *New York Times* columnist Frank Bruni to write, "Maybe one superrich old white guy from New York can save us from another superrich old white guy from New York."[13] BuzzFeed News offered an edgier headline that asked, "Can Mike Bloomberg Make America Boring Again?"[14]

Kevin Sheekey, Howard Wolfson, Patti Harris, and the rest of the campaign team soon worked to expand their skeletal political staff into a nationwide political force. They began looking at new rules for key primaries and buying new polls. They planned trips to Florida, Michigan, and other areas where leaders were already receiving Bloomberg's help to fight guns or climate change or receiving his grants to try new programs. Old political associates were being asked for their support—would they join Bloomberg if he ran or, if not, would they still support his alternative political effort?

Bloomberg began to prepare his daughters, his close friends and, most important, himself for the grueling marathon. Colleagues said he was avoiding his glass or so of good wine. He went on his lettuce diet—nothing but greens until his weight got down to something a notch below slim. He purchased new contact lenses and futuristic hearing aids. And he submitted to a full checkup from his doctor in advance.

And what did your doctor say? he was asked.

"He said, 'You're gonna die.'" Bloomberg paused.

"'But not of anything you have now.'"[15]

The candidate was ready. By late February, the team was ready. Bloomberg said he wanted to think, a day, maybe two. He would decide after the first weekend in March.

The morning of March 4, 2019, began as a bright winter day when most of New York City was preparing for a snowstorm that never came. Bloomberg called his team to the glass table near his desk on the fifth floor of his midtown offices. Sheekey and Wolfson once again outlined the possibilities and challenges. Speech writer Frank Barry was there to help craft the statement, in or out.

Bloomberg listened to the unadorned details, the latest numbers that added up to an insurmountable roadblock for a moderate, a lonely spot in the no-man's land of American politics. He could beat Trump one-on-one, the team figured, but the Democratic nomination?

Fired-up progressives—many of them women—were already attacking the rich. Elizabeth Warren had proposed an "ultra millionaires' tax" for the "tippy-top" class, a 2 percent tax on anyone with assets over $50 million that would go up to 3 percent for the nation's five hundred or so billionaires. Bloomberg, in New Hampshire to speak at Saint Anselm

College, had already declared that Warren's plan was "probably unconstitutional," adding, "We shouldn't be embarrassed about our system. You
want to look at a system that's not capitalistic,"he said, adding that in one
of the wealthiest countries in the world, "people are starving to death. It's
called Venezuela."[16] That same day he blasted the progressives that want
"Medicare for all," saying it was "just not practical." And Senator Bernie
Sanders's plans for tuition-free college? Bloomberg said it was "a nice
thing to do but unfortunately professors want to get paid."[17]

The centerpiece of his most recent work to combat climate change
was being challenged by a group of Democrats promoting the Green
New Deal. Advocated most vigorously by New York's left-wing representative Alexandria Ocasio-Cortez of the Bronx and Queens, the Green
New Deal proposed 100 percent renewable energy by 2050. The list included job guarantees and scaling back on farm emissions including "cow
farts" (thus sending opponents into a frenzy of comments about the end
of hamburgers and truckloads of Gas-X needed out in cattle country).[18]
Bloomberg rejected the notion as "pie in the sky"[19] and said that, ironi-
cally, it needed a little meat on its bones, in other words, specific goals.[20]

It became clearer by the day that the new left would target Bloomberg as the Scrooge candidate despite his progressive record on such issues as climate change, same-sex marriage, gun control, and immigration
reform. The path to the Democratic nomination, the only real way to
combat Trump, would disappear in wasted time, energy and, not that it
mattered that much, even money.

If it was now or never, Bloomberg finally decided that morning—it
wasn't then.

Bloomberg's aides tried not to show their disappointment as their
man stated the obvious. Now, after months of speculation and hurried
preparation, there would be events to cancel, excited new staffers to deflate. If Bloomberg himself was disappointed, the stoic kept it to himself.
Aides saw a man who soon seemed at peace with his decision, and instead
of retiring to his Spanish and his golf swing, Bloomberg, who often counseled that the way to heal any wound was to "get over it," seemed relieved

to return to his own demon schedule. He went back to business at dawn the next day, back to London that first week for the Serpentine Gallery, where he was now chairman of the board, back to a routine that, by most accounts, was as exhilarating to him as it was exhausting to almost everybody else around him.

In a more personal way, Mike Bloomberg was released. He no longer had to worry about what he said, not that he watched his words enough for some of those trying to protect him. There was no need to tiptoe around his fellow Democrats and the hundreds of new media outlets that beat the drums across the digital world about any misstep.

Two weeks after Bloomberg said he was out of the running, he both shocked and entertained those at a forum in New York for the Bermuda Business Development Agency. It was a return of the brash old Bloomberg:

"I'd already assembled a team, I was ready to go," he began, talking about his withdrawal from the race. He mentioned his age first. If he won, he would be seventy-nine years old when he arrived at the White House.

"And, well, people say Ronald Reagan was 80 when he left," he continued. "Yea, when he was 80, they carried him out gaga," to titters from the audience, many of whom were undoubtedly Reagan fans.

"I don't mean to exaggerate but that's very close to being true," Bloomberg added quickly. "To start a four-year job and maybe an eight-year job at 79 may not be the smartest thing to do," he continued, adding that if he thought he could win, he would have run anyway. But he just didn't see a path through the Democratic primary, he said, weaving his hands back and forth like a quarterback trying to evade a heavy defense lineup.

"Unless"—he paused for emphasis—"I was willing to change all my views and go on what CNN called an apology tour. Joe Biden went out and apologized for being male, over 50, white." (More titters, and, sitting on one side of him, Brian Duperreault, chief executive of American International Group, broke into an involuntary grin. Bermuda premier David Burt, seated on Bloomberg's other side, did not seem so amused.)

But Bloomberg hadn't finished his screed against apologies.

"And so everybody else, Beto, or whatever his name is, he's apologized for being born." Guffaws this time from the audience. "I don't mean to be unkind, and a lot of people love him and say he's a smart guy and someday if he wins, I would certainly support him."[21]

The untethered billionaire might offend as well as amuse, but if he was relieved, or at least released, so was his family. His daughter Emma had worked hard to stay out of the ever-expanding Bloomberg limelight. This decision could only provide more privacy for her, her husband, Chris Frissora, and their daughter, Zelda Violet Frissberg (their choice for a merged last name).

Georgina Bloomberg, the equestrian and co-author of young fiction books, was more like her father. She immediately went on Instagram with a mock campaign photo. It showed an "I Like Mike" button attached to a placard that said, "BLOOMBERG, Because fuck this shit," which she added was "Officially back to being just our family slogan."[22]

The high-spirited Georgina had already made her views clear in 2016 when she told a reporter that she thought her father would be "great at it,"[23] but she was not looking forward to all the criticism. "When you watch the news, you can't sit there and think, 'Wow, I'd love one of my parents to be involved in that fight.'"

If running for president couldn't work for him, Bloomberg would move on, as always. And if these alternative efforts succeeded, they could make him one of the most important power brokers in American politics.

The first goal was to oust Donald Trump as president.

"I've never made any secret of my belief that Donald Trump is a threat to our country," Bloomberg said in his 2019 withdrawal statement. "It's essential that we nominate a Democrat who will be in the strongest position to defeat Donald Trump and bring our country back together. We cannot allow the primary process to drag our party to an extreme that would diminish our chances in the general election and translate into 'Four More Years.'"

Second, Bloomberg vowed to double down on his efforts to close coal-fired power plants and fight against man-made climate change. He would also put money behind gun control resolutions around the country. He had his heart in these efforts and more and more of his money would follow. And he could back congressional candidates whose platforms included these policies—as he had done in the 2018 midterm elections.

Third, he could shore up the Democrats, perhaps by strengthening party weaknesses in technology and fund-raising. He already had the campaign structure, and many of those who had signed on when he was deciding about a run agreed to stay on for plan B. He was also owner of a major technology empire. He and his people knew plenty about the bots, the memes, the high-energy quarters of the Internet that had become the trolling fields for Republicans and their supporters.

By and large, Democrats proudly argued that they were on top of this advanced tech thing, or that ultimately it should not be a campaign's top priority. Since 2016, when the Democrats were clearly outgunned, the party had taken note of their deficiencies, hired experts, and tried to catch up to the Republicans. But they were still far behind. As the party's chief technocrat, Raffi Krikorian, admitted shortly before the midterm elections, "We are a 30-person technology team that's charged with all the technology strategy for the Democratic Party and that's clearly not enough to get the job done."[24] The party was no real match for Trump's advance team that began working on the 2020 campaign four years ahead of time—fund-raising on day one as Trump was inaugurated. Republicans soon bragged about having a voter data vault, a sophisticated bank of information on almost everybody with a strong political view who ever signed on to Facebook or Instagram or Twitter or the latest new platform.[25] They promised to make designer ads that fit every type, one-on-one campaign ads. The manipulation of voters had gone very high tech.

A digital counterattack from Bloomberg might not win any Democrat the election, the Bloomberg people argued, but it could make a difference if it was as close as it was in 2016, for example, when a few thousand votes made the difference in a few key states.

Bloomberg's visceral dislike of Trump and his deep concern about a Trump presidency had been on full display early in 2016. First, there was his speech at the Democratic National Convention.

The Democrats, realizing they needed independents like Bloomberg and maybe even some Republicans, asked if he would endorse Hillary Clinton and on prime time—for 25 million people. They wouldn't even look at the speech in advance, they promised. The slot was all his.

Some Democrats worried that asking Bloomberg to speak was a gamble, especially for prime time. By the end of his time as mayor, he had become more relaxed in front of the microphone. He could joke and make his points succinctly. But he could not bring the crowds to their feet like Barack Obama or Bill Clinton. He could not turn an audience into a seething mob like Donald Trump. Would Mike Bloomberg send America rushing to *CSI*?

Back at the Bloomberg offices in Manhattan, the political team went to work. Frank Barry drafted the text. Howard Wolfson, who worked on the Hillary Clinton campaign in 2008 before he joined Bloomberg, eyeballed it for political traps. Others took their turn, including Kevin Sheekey and Patti Harris.

Bloomberg then made his marks, always in pencil, a tiny script that aides complained was hard to read. Back and forth it went until the speech was complete. Then Bloomberg did something unusual. He practiced it. Twice.[26]

As he showered to get ready that night, Bloomberg realized he wanted one more line. The speech had already gone out, embargoed, to a few top journalists, his staff explained. But this line was going in. No use even debating.

In the draft as released, Bloomberg's description of Trump already had the hard edges of a Wall Street takedown. There were plenty of good lines, polished into short bursts—a bespoke lineup for a news establishment that was madly sending out quick updates or 140-character messages on Twitter:

"The bottom line is: he is a risky, reckless and radical choice and we can't afford to make that choice.

"Trump says he wants to run the nation like he runs his business. God help us.

"I'm a New Yorker, and New Yorkers know a con when we see one."

Then Bloomberg added his line from the shower. "Let's elect a sane, competent person," he said. The implication was, of course, that Donald Trump was not merely incompetent, he was nuts.

Trump erupted, of course. He had watched the speech and wanted to "hit" one of his critics, he said on Twitter. "I was going to hit one guy in particular, a very little guy. I was going to hit this guy so hard his head would spin. He wouldn't know what the hell happened." He was talking about Bloomberg,[27] who is five eight (or five ten on his driver's license), compared to Trump's bulky six three, counting his blond pompadour. Trump claimed Bloomberg's last term as mayor was a "disaster" and that if he ran again in New York City, he wouldn't get 10 percent of the vote. "They would run him out of town," he fumed.[28]

Bloomberg's army retaliated with videos and other proof that Trump had been full of praise for their man as he left city hall. But the disturbing news was not Trump's personal attack. It was that Michael Bloomberg, the richest member of that exclusive club of rich New Yorkers, business executives, politicians, and philanthropists, had done his best to warn Americans about somebody who claimed he was in their peer group. Bloomberg and his crowd feared that Trump was a fraud who would wreck the country the way he had wrecked so many of his own businesses.

A few weeks after the election, Trump sent word through Bloomberg's associates that he would accept a phone call from his fellow New Yorker. Bloomberg told friends that when he called, he and the president figured they had attacked each other to a draw. Mostly, the president had asked for advice about people he should hire, Bloomberg recalled. He had resisted naming names. But he said he had counseled Trump to hire people smarter than himself, which Bloomberg's supporters decided could not be all that difficult.[29]

Publicly, Bloomberg described the conversation as cordial. He told the new president, "Look, Donald, you don't know anything about this job," adding that Trump "had never run anything." Bloomberg explained, "Trump is not a business guy. He's a real estate salesman." It was a business executive's takedown, and Bloomberg added that during that call he tried to warn the president-elect that he could not change the entire government from the Oval Office. He said he told Trump, "You can't walk away from how our government has developed over 100, 200 years and say it's all bullshit."[30]

If there was a truce, it was soon over. Bloomberg used his own media vehicle to chastise Trump publicly—saying he looked "weak and fearful" when he fired FBI director James Comey for his handling of the Russia probe.[31] The big tax windfall for the wealthy and the corporations? Bloomberg called it "a trillion-dollar blunder" and wrote that "we don't need the money." Corporations were sitting on $2.3 trillion in cash already, and the real worry was that Republicans would take aim at entitlements.[32, 33] And he worried about the loss of global trade, the unraveling of environmental protections, and the separation of children at the border. "This is not who we are as a nation," he wrote.[34] The sniping shifted to a full-frontal assault after Trump backed out of the Paris accords, and Bloomberg began organizing cities, states, and businesses to veto Trump's decision. (See chapter 28.)

But Bloomberg was not done. In an entirely new kind of challenge to Trump's pinched view of how the world worked, in 2017 Bloomberg gathered some of the biggest names in business and government from around the world to talk about global issues. It was Bloomberg's Davos, New York City's own version of the World Economic Forum in Switzerland where powerful people had come together for more than forty-five years, mostly to discuss the ways to guide the world's economy. (He would later add an Asian version in Singapore.)

For the first of what would turn out to be an annual event, scheduled conveniently at the same time as the 2017 United Nations General Assembly, Bloomberg chose the Plaza Hotel in Manhattan for what would be called the Bloomberg Global Business Forum.

The fabled Oak Room, settings for the movies *North by Northwest* and *Arthur*, among others, became a media center. The lavish Palm Court and tearoom changed into a kind of café and schmoozing hall. A ballroom was small enough to give the crowd a little intimacy, and there were assorted other side rooms for cozy meetings and backroom conferences. For most, the irony was not missed—Trump had bought the Plaza in 1988 for $390 million and was forced to sell it seven years later at a loss to cover his debts.[35] The former mayor was taking on the president in the very splendor that Trump had once craved but couldn't manage to keep.

For the first session, the stellar guest list included Jim Yong Kim, head of the World Bank, and Christine Lagarde, managing director of the International Monetary Fund. Emmanuel Macron, president of France; Justin Trudeau, prime minister of Canada; and Recep Tayyip Erdoğan, president of Turkey, all spoke in forums for about several hundred guests (and a small flock of journalists).

The tech stars were there, of course. Tim Cook, CEO of Apple, spoke, as did Jack Ma, head of the massive e-commerce company Alibaba. Fellow billionaire philanthropist Bill Gates roamed the halls. Henry Kissinger spoke to one small group, accompanied by former British prime minister Tony Blair. The rococo rooms of the Plaza were filled with representatives from the United Nation, plus executives from more than 250 companies from around the world.

It was such an elaborate event that BuzzFeed declared Michael Bloomberg president of America's "government-in-exile."[36]

A year later, Bloomberg was ready to spend even more money challenging Trump and his disastrous policies in the midterm elections. He became one of the top donors in 2018, and his mission was to provide a buffer against Trump's worst instincts by getting rid of the president's fawning lackeys in the Republican Party. The Adelsons of Las Vegas were the top Republican contributors in 2018, donating $123 million in political action funds. Bloomberg came in second with nearly $93 million (or $120 million according to his staff), all of it to Democrats this time.[37]

Bloomberg had not always been quite so generous. He gave out about $40 million in 2014 and $60 million in 2016, when two-thirds of his money went to Democrats and the rest to friendly Republicans, according to Howard Wolfson, treasurer of the Bloomberg PAC.[38] But in 2018, Bloomberg's experts did an "enormous amount of polling" and ran ads mostly aimed at suburban districts, Wolfson said. Some voters were interested in how the new tax bill was hurting them, limiting write-offs for home mortgages. Many worried about their health care. Some were angry about the guns—Bloomberg spent $5 million to help Lucy McBath win a congressional seat in Georgia after her son was shot and killed for playing his music too loud at a gas station. They bought the television ads for these races, but they also went digital, "because Mike thought in 2016 the Democrats got really outplayed online," Wolfson added.[39]

On the weekend before the election, Bloomberg appeared in another $5 million ad, which ran on CBS's *60 Minutes* on Sunday night and again on Monday, the day before the election. The two-minute spot featured Bloomberg, still in a telltale nonpartisan purple tie, explaining that he was normally not a party man. But this time, he urged voters to vote Democratic because "we must send a signal to Republicans in Washington that they have failed to lead, failed to find solutions and failed to bring us together."[40] Even though he lost a few, Bloomberg's help winning twenty-one of twenty-five House races meant that he was now more fully engaged in the political battlefield. And he was ready to spend more, many millions more.

Big money would not be new to politics after the Supreme Court decided in 2010 to throw out congressional limits on corporate spending.[41] As expected, their decision that Citizens United could spend freely if ads were independent of any campaign soon unleashed others to spend lavishly, mostly in ways that helped Republicans. With Bloomberg using his own funds to aid Democrats (independently, of course), the playing field was almost level, giving good-government types a new hope that Congress would try to limit this deluge.

Although Bloomberg had plans to give out about $10 billion of his fortune by 2019, he still had plenty to spare. On the same day he announced that he would not run in 2020, *Forbes* came out with its latest billionaires ranking. Bloomberg, who had started out with nothing but a supportive family and a good education, was now the ninth-richest person in the world with a net worth of $55 billion. (Donald Trump, who inherited his start-up wealth starting as a toddler,[42] had moved down 51 spots to 715th place with $3.1 billion.)[43]

Months before the 2020 elections, Bloomberg had already vowed to use another $500 million to fight climate change and bring a "clean energy economy" to America. He promised to phase out every coal-fired power plant in the country by 2030 and to fight in the courts and support local politicians working to convert to 100 percent clean, renewable energy. And finally, he would use his money, and his clout to elect national politicians who agreed with his mission. The message would be simple, he said, "face reality on climate change or face the music on election day."[44]

Bloomberg and his political team would also spend the pre-election months figuring out precisely how to defeat America's polluter in chief, President Donald Trump. At the same time, they were looking at ways to replace local and national politicians under the thumb of the National Rifle Association or those who failed to see the value of immigration in America. It would not be simply television ads. The battleground had moved onto cell phones and into social media, and Bloomberg's team was prepared to help Democrats match the formidable high-tech operation being built by the Trump campaign. As a *New York Observer* headline suggested, if he succeeded, Bloomberg would be the political world's "Obi-Wan Kenobi,"[45] the legendary *Star Wars* guru who knew how to use the forces (or the Force) to guide the universe.

To neutralize damage done by President Trump and his political mob, Bloomberg faced a daunting task. But changing much of Wall Street with

a new computer and becoming a billionaire had been a massive undertaking. Running New York City was a colossal job, managed expertly over
a dozen years. His philanthropy was unusually pointed and inventive as
he became one of the most generous billionaires in the country. Now he
was ready for another extravagant challenge—to counter some of Washington's worst political and policy mistakes, even if he had to do it from
outside the White House.

EPILOGUE

WORTH "EVERY PENNY"

Michael Bloomberg always wanted a Plan B. As his mother advised long ago, if one road is blocked, you go around, take another way. For every action, the engineer Bloomberg argued, there had to be a fallback. And, of course, when things change, you adapt.

Thus, on November 24, 2019, two hundred and sixty-five days after he declared he would not be running for president, Bloomberg announced that he had changed his mind. At age seventy-seven, a few months shy of seventy-eight, he surprised even some close associates when he launched his first real-live, out-front campaign for the White House.

Bloomberg did not step up to the microphone that day and shout his announcement to a live and friendly audience. Instead, he announced in the Bloomberg way—by video. It was a heartwarming version of his life as a businessman who created thousands of jobs, as the mayor who revived a terrorist-torn city, as the philanthropist "who put his money where his heart is." There was no mention of the crowded field of Democrats also running for the top job. Instead, along with a pitch to make the wealthy (like him) pay more taxes, a picture of Trump Tower flashed on the screen. It was the beginning of a blast of Bloomberg commercials supporting Bloomberg and attacking Trump, $37 million worth of ads and other Internet videos for just those first two weeks.

The reaction from the progressive Democrats was swift. Senator Bernie Sanders said he was "disgusted" that any billionaire would try to buy elections. Senator Elizabeth Warren preferred to mock the new entry to the campaign. "I understand that rich people are going to have more shoes than the rest of us. They are going to have more cars than the rest of us. They're going to have more houses. But they don't get a bigger share of democracy, especially in a Democratic primary."[1] Moderates, however, saw a possibility.

Bloomberg recognized that he was late to the presidential race, both in life and in the 2020 primary season. He was months behind other Democrats who had already been debating and spending hours courting the persnickety (and mostly white) voters in Iowa and New Hampshire. But he had something none of the other candidates had—a net worth then estimated at $60 billion and a plan to spend as much of it as needed to campaign for the presidency and, most of all, to defeat Donald Trump.

"If he wins another term in office, we may never recover from the damage," Bloomberg said in a press release as he opened his quixotic adventure.

The Bloomberg presidential campaign of 2020 would be brief, expensive, and humiliating, a 100-day dash to nowhere near the finish line at a staggering cost of $1 billion. But, for a while, it would be inventive and fast and even fun. Workers earned almost twice the going rate, and young activists were being paid handsomely to create Bloomberg memes for such Internet stars as GrapeJuiceBoys or Tank.Sinatra. The memes tapped into a fairly new audience for political operatives, and in some cases they were carefully counterintuitive. One batch had Bloomberg asking the meme creators to make him look cool. The Twitter world enjoyed what seemed like an hourly blast from the Bloomberg team. Most were serious, but one featured a plate of meatballs, one of Bloomberg's favorites. "Spot the meatball that looks like Mike," the tweet said. And there he was, the candidate, faintly emblazoned on a meatball.

In the end, despite his innovative political strategies and the lavish spending, Bloomberg would fade after a disastrous debate performance, while former Vice President Joe Biden would emerge as the moderate choice to beat Trump.

Ultimately, Bloomberg would win only 49 of 3979 pledged delegates in the Democratic primaries.[2] Most notably, especially in the meme world that now seemed to enjoy turning against him, Bloomberg only captured the South Pacific territory of American Samoa. (That is, five islands, 55,000 people and two coral atolls.)

But, if the tally was disappointing, the hangover was worse.

The media mocked Bloomberg as political roadkill. *Rolling Stone* called it "the Most Colossal Flop of a Presidential Campaign in Modern History,"[3] an obvious overreach considering the many other famous flameouts over the years. Staffers would sue for funds they believed they were due after promises from recruiters that they would be paid until the election no matter what. And Trump would keep mocking "Mini Mike" as a loser, at the time the president's favorite insult.

Was it all worth it, the money, the disappointment, the criticism from the media? "I'm happy." Bloomberg insisted months later.[4] "I can look in the mirror and say I did the best that I could, and it didn't work because I didn't do it as well as I could have or hoped to do, but I have no regrets whatsoever." He added, as he often did, "Should've, would've, could've. I don't live my life second guessing or anything."

So, what drew Mike Bloomberg out of his comfortable nest as a political benefactor handing out money at a distance? Word first began to slip out in the early autumn of 2019 that former Vice President Joe Biden, Bloomberg's preferred candidate, was losing to the progressives in the party. Bloomberg's private polls, like a few public ones, were showing that if Senators Bernie Sanders of Vermont or Elizabeth Warren of Massachusetts won the Democratic nomination, they would lose to Trump. Told about the polls one afternoon in early November, Bloomberg advisers urged him to put more money in the Biden campaign. Instead, the next day, he called his political team with different decision: he would step into this race as the Biden alternative.

Bloomberg's ever-ready political crew quickly built back the campaign army they had disbanded nine months earlier. They hired some of the best in the political business. They paid top dollar for polling, advertising, and digital work. But they also knew there would be trouble. An early blast came from New York Times columnist Charles Blow who shouted from the paper's op-ed page: "Let me plant the stake now. No Black person—or Hispanic person, or ally of people of color—should ever ever *consider* voting for Michael Bloomberg."[5]

The column distressed some Bloomberg allies, and a week later the former mayor appeared at the Christian Cultural Center for a very public apology. Before this predominantly Black audience, he acknowledged the pain his stop-and-frisk policies as mayor had caused in Black and Hispanic communities. He said he had always wanted to save lives, but he had also come to realize that "I was wrong, and I am sorry."[6] He looked pained more than relieved, perhaps a recognition that only a few months earlier he had mocked other candidates for going on "apology tours."

Most in the audience for Bloomberg's apology stood to applaud him, the sinner come to repent. But, outside the religious center, many Blacks and Hispanics were not ready to forgive. After he left the crowd, Bloomberg called the Rev. Al Sharpton from his car. Sharpton said that after millions of police stops during his time as mayor, one speech would not erase the pain. For others, the apology was simply too late, little more than a political feint. At the same time, some police officials were said to be furious at his retreat from a tactic they believed could curb crime if done constitutionally.

For the now rapidly expanding Bloomberg army in those early days, even a late apology was enough to clear the way. Within a week, Bloomberg's aides would fly to Alabama to register their man in the state's Democratic primary and to activate one of the shortest and most lavish presidential primary campaigns in American history.

Bloomberg would later tell me that nobody thought he could win, even though he knew, like all candidates, that there was always a chance.

"It looked to me then, and the polls seemed to say it, that Donald Trump was going to get four more years, and I thought that was a disaster for the country and none of the candidates were making any inroads against him at that time, "he said.

"And I thought to myself, you know, everybody said you can't win, everybody said you're much too late to get in, but how would I look at myself afterwards if Trump got another four years, and say, you could've stopped him," he said later.[7] "If I stopped him or somebody else stopped him, he wasn't reelected, so that's good."

Or, as he told another reporter, "Shame on me if I didn't have the courage to stand up and at least try."[8]

Once he announced on November 24, Bloomberg would use his connections as a businessman and philanthropist—in particular, he rallied fellow mayors he'd supported over the years with funds or expert advice or free trips to conferences about city problems. He would gather those who recognized how his energy and money had helped fight for gun control and climate change and better public health. He would have only one donor—himself. He would skip the first four primaries—Iowa, New Hampshire, South Carolina, and Nevada. Then, he would stake his claim on the big ones—especially Super Tuesday, March 3, when Democrats would pick a third of the delegates to their convention.

In live settings—twenty-five states and one hundred and twenty-five cities were his own tally—Bloomberg could charm and make his case cogently. He would give his traditionally wooden speeches, mini-lectures really, to supportive listeners who often seemed relieved at the lack of political hype.

As in his New York City campaigns, he could also fumble. At one event, he could be seen awkwardly patting a baby on the head. At another, he suddenly began shaking a dog's nose instead of its paw. He would misspeak—once trying to say how he planned to help Native Americans like the Shinnecocks living near his estate on Long Island who were a "disaster" because of domestic violence, drugs, and alcoholism. (The Shinnecock community quickly responded that their problems weren't much different from those in the rest of America.)

Even more important, Bloomberg helped create a digital company called Hawkfish to counter Trump's massive campaign machine. The Trump people had been steadily collecting information on how to push or pull voters, one by one, to lure them to Trump or dissuade them from voting for the Democrat. The Democrats were leagues behind. To help with his campaign and later with the Democratic field for 2020, Hawkfish quietly began operation in February 2019 at one of Bloomberg's New York City addresses. (Hawkfish got its name after somebody pointed to a somewhat nondescript creature in one of Bloomberg's office aquariums. The hawkfish is small but it can be aggressive. One per tank is enough.)

But in true Bloomberg fashion, his most important pitch would be on television and other media. The Bloomberg ad blitz had worked during three campaigns for mayor of New York City, and he would use much the same game plan for the nation's top job. In all, he spent nearly $600 million on his campaign ads reminding people that Trump had turned into the presidential "con" man that Bloomberg had predicted in 2016. And if people voted for Mike Bloomberg, these ads promised, he would fix things. He would "get things done," as his campaign slogan rang over and over and over. By the end of 2019, the Bloomberg spots were everywhere. Wall to wall TV, rolling Twitter feeds, and even billboards including one that read "Donald Trump Cheats at Golf: Mike Bloomberg Doesn't."

In a very important way, those ads were different from the usual primary campaign commercials. They did not criticize the other Democrats, at least not directly. His message was aimed at President Trump. And Bloomberg—a successful businessman and former mayor—could beat him in November, the spots argued. Bloomberg's aides would later explain that their candidate was attacking President Donald Trump because the president was enjoying a free ride in those early months. Democratic candidates were still squabbling among themselves, long before they would turn their weaponry on the Republican president.

Bloomberg would also work throughout 2020 to force Trump to

spend his dwindling campaign funds. Bloomberg bought an $11 million ad for gun control to run during the Super Bowl. The ad told the story of a youth killed by gunfire and how Bloomberg was promoting gun control around the country. The buy meant Trump also had to buy a Super Bowl ad—$11 million deducted from his campaign bank accounts.

Bloomberg's wall-to-wall advertising helped him rise in the polls, but it also created a problem. After all the rosy, glorified versions of the man and his record in these commercials, the real, live Mike Bloomberg would come as a shock to many voters.

On February 19, 2020, Bloomberg appeared on national television in Las Vegas for a live debate with five other Democratic candidates running for president. It was Bloomberg's first public debate since a gentlemanly exchange with his opponent, William Thompson, in the New York City mayor's race in 2009. Bloomberg did fine in 2009. He was not ready for the political Olympics.

Aides had warned Bloomberg that he was the fresh, new target. He would be attacked—for trying to buy the election, for comments and treatment of women over the years, and for stop-and-frisk. He had been warned not to sound angry or to go after the women candidates who might lead the attacks. That would only add to his troubles and make him look like another hotshot white male failing to show respect for an intelligent woman.

Instead, as he stood on the stage and faced attacks that evening, Bloomberg seemed to flatten into a cardboard version of himself. He froze under the withering criticism from Massachusetts Senator Elizabeth Warren who came after him for his money and for his treatment of women. She battered Bloomberg for the nondisclosure agreements at his company, and for his comments like the time he allegedly said "kill it" to a pregnant employee. Bloomberg tried to deny and to defend himself and to talk about his record, but too many of his potential supporters were shocked and disappointed. At one point he rolled his eyes after a Warren broadside—a moment that would appear in many of the videos circulating after the debate.

The Bloomberg people tried to argue later that he was the grown-up in the room and that Warren hadn't helped herself by being so vicious and unrelenting. But Bloomberg's friends knew the campaign was over. Van Jones, a CNN commentator, described that evening succinctly: "*Titanic* meets iceberg— Elizabeth Warren."

At the same time, there were other strong currents changing the outcome of the campaign. Three days before the South Carolina primary, representative Jim Clyburn, the highest ranking African American in Congress, enthusiastically endorsed Joe Biden. At that point, Biden began the surge that would eventually win him the presidency.

Michael Bloomberg canceled his campaign on March 4, the day after Super Tuesday. He called Biden to announce his departure and his support. Then Bloomberg gathered his loyalists for a subdued gathering at his posh campaign headquarters in the old New York Times Building in Times Square. Colleagues said he stayed long enough for everybody to get a picture with him, a keepsake in case they wanted one.

"I think I have an obligation to help this country. It's been very good to me and my family, and I'd be disingenuous if I didn't give something back," he would say months later when asked about whether it was worth it to him personally. [9]

About a week after the campaign ended, he made an appearance, as promised, at the League of Cities in Washington to announce a new program with Harvard to help cities fight Covid-19. He looked fit and even joked about how he hoped that Tuesday was better than the Super Tuesday a week earlier. Then, he came back to his estate on Long Island, and as far as the outside world was concerned, he disappeared. One critic gloated that after Bloomberg was so soundly rejected, "It's poof. Vanish. Gone."

Bloomberg's departure from the political scrum coincided with the early surge of the Covid-19 pandemic that would increasingly menace the country. He spent much of his time at Ballyshear, his Long Island mansion on thirty-five acres and a quick ride to one of the nation's best golf courses, Shinnecock Hills. He would take an occasional dip into Manhat-

tan to visit his nearly empty offices and his philanthropy center, his city
home on the Upper East Side, and his new barber after Covid killed his
friend Alberto Rottura who had cut his hair for nearly five decades.

By comparison, losing a mere campaign was not a hardship, of course.
He still had plenty of money and plenty to do. He was still running the
global computer powerhouse at Bloomberg LP, plus a growing financial
news empire and one of the largest and most active philanthropies in the
country. He purchased another estate—this one bought from his fellow
billionaire Henry Kravis. For 4,600 acres, a 19,000 square-foot mansion,
a helipad, and a four-hole golf course, Bloomberg paid $44.79 million.

Still, friends saw an impatient Mike Bloomberg who missed his social life, his beehive of a workplace at Bloomberg LP too often abandoned
in favor of home computers, his easy travel around the world, his head-
liner events like the New Economy Forum that was becoming his version of Davos. But, after years of advocating for public health, Bloomberg
turned his attention and a good deal of his money to fighting Covid. He
began by providing over $331 million to fight the virus in cities around
the world, to help find treatments, and to collect data that was in danger
of being twisted or hidden by Trump's people.

If he was bitter or hurt about the campaign, he told only a few close
friends. One said Bloomberg knew the campaign was a longshot. He was
chagrined about his debate performances, and he generally "blamed himself." Another reported that shortly after his loss, Bloomberg let slip that,
"They didn't want me and to hell with them."

As for the money, by the end of 2020 he had spent a ton of it on politics. According to Ad Impact, a media intelligence company that tracks
campaign spending, Bloomberg forked over $643 million in ads during
the entire presidential campaign season—$582 million of it on his own
campaign. There were big investments, as promised, in the key states of
Michigan ($14.7 million), Wisconsin ($10 million), Pennsylvania ($24
million), Ohio ($17.6 million) and Florida ($47.5 million). He would
go on to pour money into Florida later in the campaign, promising $100
million in all to force Trump to defend the state he eventually won. "If

I spent a lot of money in Florida, Biden didn't have to," Bloomberg explained. "So, he could spend money elsewheres. Is that the thing that made the difference? You can't answer that. Nobody knows."

He would spend $16 million in Arizona, a state that finally deserted Trump in 2020, and the Republicans for the first time since 1996. Bloomberg's digital investment was estimated at over $200 million, and that did not count all the staff, his unsparing campaign offices, travel, phones, pizza, and later the lawyers to defend lawsuits once it was over charging that he had failed to pay his staff until the election in November.

Hawkfish would be an extra expense for any political candidate, but it became Bloomberg's digital army. Eventually, Hawkfish became a big part of "the Cult of Mayor Mike" when he was running, as *Wired*'s Steven Levy wrote.[10] After Bloomberg got out of the race, Hawkfish shifted to become a full division in the fight to help Biden oust Trump. During his campaign, Bloomberg pumped $50 million into software and $50 million into data, according to *Wired*.

Hawkfish soon became part of the Bloomberg strategy to spend money in states Trump could be expected to win—like $110 million promised for Florida, Ohio, and Texas. In the end, Biden lost those states, but Hawkfish and the Bloomberg political team took credit for forcing the Trump people to spend increasingly scarce dollars in these states they would eventually win. They also warned of a "Red Mirage" on election day. Trump and his red-state supporters would vote in person and thus the early count would seem to go to him, they warned. Counting the mail-in ballots would take longer, and they would favor Biden. They hammered this idea so often that when Trump declared victory—as he did right after election—the media would know better.

The final tally would be huge. More than $1 billion, maybe more than $1.5 billion. Was it worth it, Bloomberg was asked?

"Every penny," he answered quickly. "And I tried my best. And I had the resources. What kind of person would I be if I didn't care enough about the country not to spend whatever I thought it took. If I thought we should've spent more money, I would've. But we thought we were spending as much as we could productively employ."[11]

As for the future, even as Bloomberg approached his eighties, his colleagues confirmed that if he could be reduced to one word, it would still be *restless*. If you're a billionaire and one option fails, there are still plenty of possibilities.

A job in the Biden administration always seemed an option, although friends stressed that he preferred to be the boss, not the one who took orders. Younger dreams now seemed distant, like the job he once said he wanted as ambassador to the Court of St. James in Great Britain. He'd have to be talked into that one, one friend suggested. Head of the World Bank? What could he bring to the job that required more travel than even a fifty-year old could manage. A special project on guns or climate change or Covid? Maybe.

After the election, Bloomberg was asked if he saw a role in the new administration. "I have no idea. I have not had a conversation with them. I have plenty of things to do," he said as he listed his company and his philanthropy. "You know, I haven't worked for anybody in a long time."[12]

It was never a very good idea to predict what Michael Bloomberg will do, as I learned when this book originally ended after he said he would not run for president in 2020. But he has never been comfortable sitting on the sidelines, and he is certainly strong enough for another career.

As he began the primary campaign in 2019, his doctor declared him in excellent health—for his age. (He has had a coronary stent since 2000 and his medications included a blood thinner for atrial fibrillation, beta blockers for blood pressure, and a cholesterol medication.) With the best health care a billionaire can afford, he could last long enough to stay engaged for some time in his business, his politics, his philanthropy, or, of course, his next Plan B.

ACKNOWLEDGMENTS

Any biographer acquires many debts, and for this work, mine begin with Howell Raines, who hired me in 1998 as a member of the *New York Times* editorial board. My mission was to opine about city and state matters, and I spent much of the next eighteen years watching and writing about Michael Bloomberg. Gail Collins, columnist and editorial page editor, was a particularly generous colleague and boss, and Andy Rosenthal, who took over the editorial page from Gail, helped me see the mayor from different perspectives.

My other colleagues on the editorial page during the Bloomberg years always raised the standards of any debate. They include editors Robert Semple, Philip Boffey, Philip Taubman, Terry Tang, Ethan Bronner, and Linda Cohn, and board members Vikas Bajaj, Maura Casey, Frank Clines, Adam Cohen, Carolyn Curiel, Lawrence Downes, Lincoln Caplan, David Firestone, Carol Giacomo, Verlyn Klinkenborg, Nick Kulish, Ernesto Londono, Floyd Norris, Eduardo Porter, Tina Rosenberg, Dorothy Samuels, Brent Staples, Ernest Tollerson, Teresa Tritch, David Unger, Jesse Wegman, and Steve Weisman. Mara Gay, who took over my slot on the board, also helped me see other aspects of Bloomberg. Abby Aguirre, Peter Catapano, Rusha Haljuci, Liz Harris, Carol Lee, Phoebe Lett, and Brian Zittel offered expert research, guidance, and support, and especially Eileen Lepping, who generously helped with the manuscript. Copyeditors Juston Jones, Bruce Levine, Alan Mattingly, Steve Pickering, and Bob Rudiger steered me clear of so many errors over the years. The ever-cheerful Maureen Muenster organized almost everything for the *Times* opinion staff, a job she left in 2018 to her expert successor, Elfriede Engl.

Sara Barrett, photo editor for editorial, guided me expertly through the *New York Times* photo galleries, as did Jeff Roth, caretaker of the *Times* morgue, who discovered a trove of photos of the early Mike on Wall Street. Lori Reese helped with *Times* photos as did Frank Barry at Bloomberg.

Although I covered many of the events written about here, I turned often to some of the expert reporters at the *Times* for their valuable writings about Michael Bloomberg. They included Charles V. Bagli, Al Baker, Michael Barbaro, David W. Chen, Michael Cooper, Michael M. Grynbaum, Winnie Hu, Adam Nagourney, William Rashbaum, Jennifer Steinhauer, Kate Taylor, and especially my friends Clyde Haberman and Sam Roberts.

I was especially fortunate to have time with Wayne Barrett, the incomparable investigative journalist who died in 2017. He was generous with his wisdom, his sources, and his files on Bloomberg.

Other authors have tackled Bloomberg's story, including Bloomberg himself. But two deserve extra mention and thanks. To understand how Bloomberg ran the nation's largest city, the best and most encyclopedic work is Chris McNickle's *Bloomberg: A Billionaire's Ambition*, published in 2017. McNickle, an expert historian and trained economist, was also kind enough to read a draft and help me avoid a few real bloopers. (Other mistakes, of course, are my own doing.)

For her invaluable 2009 biography, *Mike Bloomberg: Money, Power, Politics,* Joyce Purnick interviewed many of Bloomberg's friends and family, including those who have died or decided not to give more interviews. A former *New York Times* editor and columnist, Joyce was kind enough to give me very sage advice about this project.

There are legions of people I should thank who spoke to me anonymously. Some simply wanted to be frank and open, but a billionaire like Bloomberg clearly frightens a surprising number of people. Those backgrounders made the people who spoke on the record all the more valuable.

At New York University, where I was a visiting scholar in 2016, my thanks go to Sherry Glied, dean of NYU's Wagner School of Public Service, and especially to Professor Mitchell Moss, director of the Rudin Center for Transportation, who constantly offered the best overview of New York City, its history, and its politics. Thanks also to aides Marilyn Lopez and Kiran Lutfeali.

At the City University of New York, I was fortunate enough to be chosen as a fellow for the Leon Levy Biography Center in 2017 to 2018. That fellowship is such a gift for any biographer—advice, research, and encouragement from those who know how hard it is to pack an entire life into one book. My thanks go to Kai Bird, director and accomplished biographer; Thad Ziolkowski, associate director and poet; and my talented co-fellows, Justin Gifford, Micki Kaufman, Bruce Weber, and Lindsay Whalen. A special thanks to Shelby White, who made the Levy fellowships possible.

Samuel Crawford, a friend and financial wizard, helped me understand the inner machinations of the finance world and its dependence on computers. Others, some of whom worked for Bloomberg, I will have to thank anonymously.

Researchers were vital, including Glenn Speer at CUNY; Donna Davey, Shawn Smith-Cruz and Adriana Palmer, librarians at CUNY's Graduate Center; and Danny Klein at the Jersey City public library. Dr. Jacqueline J. Wisner, a medical doctor with a love of history, provided fascinating information about the early years of Bloomberg's family in New Jersey. Jasper Craven helped with the Massachusetts data, and John Surico provided much-needed assistance, including time spent going through the Barrett documents. Thanks also go to Paul Friedman at the New York Public Library, Mimi Chiahamen and Amy Whyte at Institutional Investor, Joe Halpern and Liz Toner at the *Boston Business Journal*, broadcaster Lisa Napoli, Massachusetts librarians Victoria Schneiderman in Medford and Sarah Gay Jackson in Chelsea, Christina Prochilo from Historic New England and Kelsey Sawyer from the Jewish Heritage Center at the New England Genealogical Society.

The New York City Municipal Archives preserves riches about the city's mayors and issues going back in time. With the help of archivists, I was able to get some understanding of how hard it is to run the nation's largest and most complex city. Pauline Toole, commissioner of the city department of records and information services, provided guidance, as did Sylvia Kollar, director of the NYC Archives. Kenneth Cobb, assistant commissioner, provided his expertise, Nathalie Belkin helped with records, and Rossy Mendez helped with photos. They are keepers of a vast array of city treasures.

Frank Barry, an editor at Bloomberg Opinion and a gifted speechwriter for the former mayor, was especially patient and helpful. He tried very hard to guide me to the best possible versions of Mike Bloomberg and to counter any of the flaws mentioned here. Bloomberg's political ringmaster, Kevin Sheekey, spun his many hours with Bloomberg into intoxicating yarns. Howard Wolfson mapped the political field with expertise. Bill Cunningham helped me gather stories and context, and Ester Fuchs, professor and urban affairs expert at Columbia University, offered thoughtful assessments of the man and his ambitions.

Experts helping at Simon and Schuster include Stephen Bedford, director of marketing, Elizabeth Gay, publicity manager, Ruth Lee-Mui, associate director of interior design, Lisa Erwin, director of production, Jessica Chin, copyediting manager, and copyeditor Robert Sternitzky. Stuart Roberts, now an editor, and associate editor Amar Deol helped untangle editorial, computer, and other complications.

The indomitable Alice Mayhew, my editor and friend, has helped bring this book to life, as she has done with so many biographies of other influential people over the years. David Black provided much-needed enthusiasm and counsel. His patience as a literary agent is phenomenal, and I can only hope it will be rewarded.

Of course, this project would have been impossible without the help of my family. My ebullient and gifted husband, Peter Pringle, took time away from his own projects to read and suggest improvements to this manuscript. Our daughter, Victoria, provided support, joy, and encouragement.

Finally, even with all this help and expertise, I take responsibility for any mistakes, failings, omissions, or misjudgments. That said, I hope this book provided an enjoyable read about this very important man.

NOTES ON SOURCES

As a longtime journalist and editorial board member at the *New York Times* during the Bloomberg years as mayor, I have covered and witnessed many of the events recorded in this book. I have also relied on coverage by the *Times* especially to confirm quotes or details. I conducted more than one hundred interviews of people who knew or know Michael Bloomberg, and Bloomberg himself gave several hours of his time for formal discussions and informal chats to add flavor and context.

For Bloomberg's youth and family, Bloomberg's sister Marjorie Tiven collected much of the family history, as did Dr. Jacqueline Wisner, a physician and amateur historian with a particular interest in New Jersey. Author Joyce Purnick interviewed and wrote about many of those in Medford, Mass. In her 2009 work, "Mike Bloomberg, Money, Power Politics," she was able to talk with many people including Bloomberg's powerful mother before they died. My own visit to Medford gave me a better idea, as well, of the place where Bloomberg thrived as a boy but ached to leave.

Officials at the New York City Municipal Archives kindly provided access to some of the documents from Mayor Bloomberg's time at city hall, including important troves saved by Bloomberg's daughter Emma, Dan Doctoroff, his development deputy, and Peter Madonia, his chief of staff. These papers helped me understand the complexity of the city, and the way the Bloomberg team worked. They also offered valuable guidance in my interviews with Bloomberg's top aides as mayor.

The late investigative reporter Wayne Barrett had saved reams of vital documents, including those that the city's Conflicts of Interest Board had unwisely discarded after Bloomberg left office. His files were also rich in other details about the Bloomberg years. After he died, Barrett's archives were moved to the Dolph Briscoe Center for American History, University of Texas, Austin.

For the business side, I conducted interviews with Bloomberg's colleagues at Salomon Brothers. For the period when he created his business, I had a good number of interviews on background, given Bloomberg's strict rules about talking to outsiders. That said, several top Bloomberg executives were generous with their time and helped explain how the business worked. I have also consulted financial analysts, competitors, business writers, Bloomberg news alumni, and numerous users of the Bloomberg terminals. Bloomberg's autobiography, "Bloomberg by Bloomberg" written with Matthew Winkler in 1997, is also a great primer on the man and the business.

For his philanthropy, I relied on Bloomberg Philanthropies for numbers and details, plus interviews with experts on giving. Some of the experimental work with cities was followed by academic assessments that were helpful, as were federal reports from the Bloomberg family charity. George Fertitta, who runs the consulting group made up of Bloomberg's city officials, vastly expanded my understanding of that new venture. And, Patti Harris, who runs the philanthropies for Bloomberg, helped provide the big picture. By 2019, Bloomberg had given out or promised $10 billion of his more than $50 billion in net worth—virtually all of it sanctioned by Harris.

For Bloomberg's political giving and presidential dreams, Kevin Sheekey and Howard Wolfson repeatedly provided details. Frank Barry, Bloomberg's talented speech writer, patiently worked to provide me with guidance overall, a thankless task.

Any biography of a man as complex and active as this one will only provide a snapshot of the whole person. He is seventy-seven years old at this writing and pledges to keep pushing for a better world until he dies. I have attempted to use important examples to show who he is and how he has operated. But there are many other efforts, especially in his time as mayor, that are barely mentioned here. That doesn't mean they are unimportant. I happily leave those for the next biographer of Michael Rubens Bloomberg.

NOTES

INTRODUCTION

1. Landon Thomas Jr., "Michael Bloomberg's Harder Sell," *New York Times*, August 23, 2014.
2. Author interviews, background.
3. Michael Wolff, "Bloomberg News," *New York*, August 27, 2001.
4. Author interview with Michael Bloomberg, August 16, 2018.
5. Amy Russo, "Michael Bloomberg Says He Won't Go on Joe Biden's White Male Apology Tour," *Huffington Post*, March 22, 2019.
6. Daniel L. Doctoroff, *Greater Than Ever: New York's Big Comeback* (New York: PublicAffairs, 2017), 250.
7. John Sullivan, "2 Arrested in Bloomberg Extortion Case," *New York Times*, August 15, 2000; United States Attorney, Southern District of New York, "U.S. Convicts Kazakhstan Hacker of Breaking into Bloomberg L.P.'s Computers and Attempting Extortion," U.S. Department of Justice, February 26, 2003.
8. Author interview with Bloomberg, August 16, 2018.
9. Author interview with Robert Francis Goldrich, president, Leon Levy Foundation, 2017.
10. Katie Couric, "Michael Bloomberg on Climate Change, the Power of Government, and Why He's Still Hopeful About the Future," *Town & Country*, May 9, 2017.

CHAPTER 1: BORN TO RUN, EVERYTHING

1. Michael Bloomberg with Matthew Winkler, *Bloomberg by Bloomberg* (New York: John Wiley & Sons, 1997), 10.

2. Joyce Purnick, *Mike Bloomberg, Money, Power, Politics* (New York: PublicAffairs, 2009), 11.

3. Michael Bloomberg, *Bloomberg by Bloomberg* (1997; Hoboken, NJ: John Wiley & Sons, updated and digital, 2019), 458.

4. Bloomberg family history, compiled by Bloomberg and his sister, Marjorie Tivens, provided to author by Michael Bloomberg representative Frank Barry, 2018.

5. Ibid.

6. Michael Bloomberg, *Bloomberg by Bloomberg* (reissue, 2019), 518.

7. Ibid, Bloomberg family history.

8. Max Rubens death certificate, Department of Health of the City of New York, Register no. 16454, June 8, 1922.

9. Dr. Jacqueline Wisner, *Hudson Roots* newsletter for the Hudson County (New Jersey) Genealogical Society, June/November 2009.

10. William L. Dickinson High School (Jersey City, New Jersey) yearbook, 1925.

11. Adelaide "Adeline" Gehrig, Museum of American Fencing, http://museum ofamericanfencing.com/wp/gehrig-adeline/.

12. *Commerce Violet*, Accounts and Finance yearbook, New York University School of Commerce, 1929.

13. Elizabeth Harris, "Charlotte R. Bloomberg, Mayor's Mother, Dies at 102," *New York Times*, June 20, 2011.

14. Birth Certificate, Michael Rubens Bloomberg, February 14, 1942, City of Boston.

15. Author interviews with classmates from Medford, 2014 and 2015.

16. Purnick, *Mike Bloomberg*, 39.

17. Bloomberg film for Boston's Museum of Science, https://www.bloomberg.org /press/videos/mike-bloomberg-makes-major-gift-museum-science-boston/.

18. Ibid.

19. Author interview with Michael Bloomberg, May 2015.

20. Randy Kennedy, "John Cameron Swayze, 89, Journalist and TV Pitchman," obituary, *New York Times*, August 17, 1995.

21. Purnick, *Mike Bloomberg*, 21.

22. Javier C. Hernandez, "A Mayor's Recollections of Motherly Advice," *New York Times*, June 20, 2011.

23. Bloomberg, *Bloomberg by Bloomberg* (2019), 40.

24. Purnick, *Mike Bloomberg*, 30.

25. Dean E. Murphy, "Bloomberg Mentions Prayer and His Opponents Pounce," *New York Times*, July 20, 2001.

26. Author interview with Marjorie Stone Glau, 2014.
27. Dean E. Murphy, "Bloomberg a Man of Contradictions, but with a Single Focus," *New York Times*, November 26, 2001.
28. Michael Bloomberg to William Newman, *New York Times* reporter, during Roosevelt Island event, September 13, 2017.
29. Purnick, *Mike Bloomberg*, 8.
30. Jon Meacham, "The Revolutionary," *Newsweek*, November 12, 2007.
31. Purnick, *Mike Bloomberg*, 14.
32. Meacham, "The Revolutionary."
33. Bloomberg with Winkler, *Bloomberg by Bloomberg* (1997), 11.
34. Ibid., 10.
35. Ibid., 9.
36. Author interview with Dorothy Rubin Schepps, Medford High School, Class of 1960, 2014.
37. Author interview with Reverand Richard Black, Medford High School, Class of 1960, 2015.
38. Author interview with Dorothy Rubin Schepps, Medford High School, Class of 1960, April 2015.

CHAPTER 2: THE WAY UP

1. Author interview with Dr. Mary Kay Shartle-Galotto, 2015.
2. Michael Bloomberg, commencement speech, Tufts University, May 20, 2007.
3. Michael Bloomberg with Matthew Winkler, *Bloomberg by Bloomberg* (New York: John Wiley & Sons, 1997), 12.
4. Mame Warren, Michael Bloomberg 1964 interview for Johns Hopkins University, November 17, 1999.
5. Ibid.
6. Ibid.
7. Ibid.
8. "Baltimore '68 Events Timeline," Baltimore 68: Riots and Rebirth, Langsdale Library Special Collections, University of Baltimore.
9. Michael Barbaro, "$1.1 Billion in Thanks from Bloomberg to Johns Hopkins," *New York Times*, January 26, 2013.
10. Michael Bloomberg commencement address, Tufts University, 2007.
11. Author interviews with Dr. John Galotto, July 2015.
12. Ibid.
13. "House Cleaned by Fraternities; Judge Told Sanitary Violations Were Corrected," *Baltimore Sun*, November 8, 1963.

14. Ibid.
15. Barbaro, "$1.1 Billion in Thanks from Bloomberg to Johns Hopkins"; Warren interview.
16. Ibid., Warren interview.
17. Author interviews with Dr. Galotto.
18. Ibid.
19. Barbaro, "$1.1 Billion in Thanks from Bloomberg to Johns Hopkins."
20. Author interview with Dr. Mary Kay Shartle-Galotto.
21. Warren interview.
22. Linell Smith, "He Was Always Working," *Baltimore Sun*, November 10, 2001.
23. Author interview with Michael Bloomberg, August 16, 2018.
24. Michael Bloomberg, speech to Harvard Business School, Fiftieth Reunion, June 2016.
25. Gayle Fee, "Harvard Grades Former NYC Mayor Michael Bloomberg on Curve," *Boston Herald*, March 13, 2014.
26. Jennifer Steinhauer, "Bloomberg Says He Regrets Marijana Remarks," *New York Times*, April 10, 2002.
27. Michael R. Bloomberg, *Bloomberg by Bloomberg*, revised and updated, (Hoboken, NJ: John Wiley & Sons, 2019), digital p. 45.
28. Bloomberg speech to mayors for Harvard Business School, Cities Initiative, July 24, 2017.
29. Ibid., Bloomberg with Winkler, *Bloomberg by Bloomberg* (1997), 13.
30. *Crimson* staff, editorial, "Listen to Bloomberg," *Harvard Crimson*, March 12, 2014.
31. Valerie Strauss, "Bloomberg, at Harvard, Blasts Ivy League 'Liberals' for 'Trying to Repress Conservative Ideas,'" *Washington Post*, May 31, 2014. Video of speech is available on Bloomberg site: https://www.mikebloomberg.com/news/mike-bloomberg-delivers-remarks-at-harvard-universitys-363rd-commencement-ceremony/.
32. "Answers About Michael R. Bloomberg," *City Room* blog, *New York Times*, September 23, 2009, https://cityroom.blogs.nytimes.com/2009/09/23/answers-about-michael-r-bloomberg/.

CHAPTER 3: THE SALOMON BROTHERHOOD

1. Author interview with Michael Bloomberg, 2015.
2. Jonathan Randell, "John Gutfreund, 86, Dies; Ran Wall Street Investment Firm at Its Apex," *New York Times*, March 9, 2016.

3. Michael Bloomberg with Matthew Winkler, *Bloomberg by Bloomberg* (New York: John Wiley & Sons, 1997), 17.

4. Recording of Michael Bloomberg at William Salomon memorial, April 6, 2015, provided by Bloomberg staff.

5. Bloomberg with Winkler, *Bloomberg by Bloomberg* (1997), 23.

6. Michael Bloomberg, *Bloomberg by Bloomberg* (Hoboken, NJ: John Wiley & Sons, updated and digital, 2019), 70.

7. Kurt Eichenwald, "Robert William Haack, 75, Dies; Led Stock Exchange During Crises," *New York Times*, July 16, 1992; FINRA staff, "When Paper Paralyzed Wall Street: Remembering the 1960s Paperwork Crisis," August 19, 2015.

8. Author interview with Salomon colleague on background, 2016.

9. Bloomberg, *Bloomberg by Bloomberg* (2019), 71–72.

10. Author interview with Robert P. Quinn, July 8, 2015.

11. Martin Mayer, *Nightmare on Wall Street: Salomon Brothers and the Corruption of the Marketplace* (New York: Simon & Schuster, 1993), 66.

12. Ibid., 10.

13. Author interviews with former Salomon officials, Robert Quinn, Kenneth Lipper, Donald Feuerstein, and others, on background, 2014, 2015, and 2016.

14. Author interview with Robert Quinn.

15. Author interview with Dr. John Galotto, 2015.

16. Mayer, *Nightmare*, 43.

17. Henry Kaufman, *Of Money and Markets: A Wall Street Memoir* (New York: McGraw-Hill, 1999), 97.

18. Author interview with Gedale Horowitz, Citibank, October 17, 2017.

19. Mayer, *Nightmare*, 62.

20. Bloomberg, *Bloomberg by Bloomberg* (2019), 73.

21. Ibid., 94–95.

22. Ibid., 80.

23. Author interview with Harvey Eisen, 2014.

24. Andrea Bernstein, "The Bloomberg Chronicles," *Observer*, October 22, 2001.

25. Bloomberg, *Bloomberg by Bloomberg* (2019), 99.

26. Chris Welles, "The Fall of Jay Perry," *Institutional Investor* (October 1975): 38.

27. Newton W. Lamson, "Block Trader at Salomon," *New York Times*, November 9, 1975.

28. Ibid., Author interview with Harvey Eisen.

29. Bloomberg, *Bloomberg by Bloomberg* (2019), 86.

30. Joyce Purnick, *Mike Bloomberg: Money, Power, Politics* (New York: PublicAffairs, 2009), 58.

31. Author interview with longtime Bloomberg associate, for background, 2014.

32. Bloomberg, *Bloomberg by Bloomberg* (2019), 86.

33. Author interview with Salomon executive board member, 2017.

34. Bloomberg, *Bloomberg by Bloomberg* (2019), 322.

35. Author interviews with Salomon alumnae, 2014 and 2016.

36. Mayer, *Nightmare*, 101.

37. Ibid., 103.

38. Author interview with Don Feuerstein, October 7, 2014.

39. Wolfgang Saxon, "Richard Rosenthal, Arbitrager," obituary, *New York Times*, April 19, 1987.

40. Michael Bloomberg, interview with John Caddell, "How Michael Bloomberg Got His Start: 'I Brought You a Cup of Coffee,'" "Founder Stories," *TechCrunch*, November 28, 2011, https://techcrunch.com/2011/11/28/founder-stories-how -michael-bloomberg-got-his-start-i-brought-you-a-cup-of-coffee/.

41. Bloomberg with Winkler, *Bloomberg by Bloomberg* (1997), 5.

42. Author interview with Kenneth Lipper, September 10, 2015.

43. Author interview with Harvey Eisen, 2014.

44. Winnie Hu, "Solitaire Costs Man His City Job After Bloomberg Sees Computer," *New York Times*, February 10, 2006.

45. Howard Wolfson, Fordham University, March 26, 2015, author recording. Howard Wolfson in Janet Sassi, "Q-and-A Measures the Metrics of a Mayor's Success," *Fordham News*, March 26, 2015.

46. Elizabeth Kolbert, "The Mogul Mayor," *The New Yorker*, April 22, 2002.

CHAPTER 4: THE MAKING OF A BLOOMBERG

1. Michael Bloomberg with Matthew Winkler, *Bloomberg by Bloomberg* (1997; Hoboken, NJ: John Wiley & Sons, updated and digital, 2019), 34.

2. Ibid., 122.

3. Ibid., 46.

4. Tim Sablik, "Recession of 1981–82," Federal Reserve Bank of Richmond, Federal Reserve History, https://www.federalreservehistory.org/essays/recession_of _1981_82.

5. Charles Grosvenor Jr, "Prices in the Eighties," In the 80s, http://www.inthe80s .com/prices.shtml.

6. "Dow Jones Industrial Average History," FedPrimeRate.com, http://www.fed primerate.com/dow-jones-industrial-average-history-djia.htm.

7. *Wall Street Journal* history of prime rates, http://www.fedprimerate.com/wall _street_journal_prime_rate_history.htm.

8. "*Time,* Machine of the Year: The Computer Moves In," *Time,* January 3, 1983.

9. David Leinweber, *Nerds on Wall Street: Math, Machines and Wired Markets* (Hoboken, NJ: John Wiley & Sons, 2009), 12.

10. Ibid., 18.

11. Ibid., 23.

12. Ibid., 25.

13. Internet Hall of Fame, "Living History Timeline," Internet Society, https:// www.internethalloffame.org/internet-history/timeline.

14. Madeline Berg, "Meet the Newest Billionaire to Mint His Fortune at Bloomberg LP," *Forbes,* March 8, 2018.

15. Author interview with Morgan Downey of Money.net, October 20, 2017.

16. Author interview with Tom Secunda, August 26, 2015.

17. Ibid.

18. Author interview with Dr. Richard Sylla, professor emeritus of economics at New York University, November 3, 2016.

19. Ibid., Internet Hall of Fame, "Living History Timeline."

20. Author interviews with John Holman, 2015 and 2016.

21. Ibid., Bloomberg with Winkler, *Bloomberg by Bloomberg* (1997), 40.

22. Joyce Purnick, *Mike Bloomberg: Money, Power, Politics* (New York: PublicAffairs, 2009), 42.

23. Ibid., Bloomberg with Winkler, *Bloomberg by Bloomberg* (1997), 50.

24. Ibid., Author interview with Tom Secunda.

25. Ibid., Bloomberg with Winkler, *Bloomberg by Bloomberg* (1997), 59.

26. "Intel," WhatIs.com, https://whatis.techtarget.com/definition/Intel.

27. Carol J. Loomis, "Bloomberg's Money Machine," *Fortune,* April 5, 2007.

28. Ibid., Bloomberg with Winkler, *Bloomberg by Bloomberg* (1997), 54.

29. Author interview with Jerome Kenney, president and chief executive officer of Merrill Lynch Capital Markets Group, 1984–1991, remembered watching the machine arrive and, mostly, being surprised that Bloomberg had met his deadline, February 28, 2018.

30. Ibid., Bloomberg with Winkler, *Bloomberg by Bloomberg* (1997), 55.

31. Ibid., Author interview with Jerome Kenney.

32. Bloomberg speech to mayors, July 24, 2018, provided by Bloomberg LP.

33. Michael W. Miller and Matthew Winkler, "Plugging In: A Former Trader Aims to Hook Wall Street on—and to—His Data; Michael Bloomberg Dreams of

Making His Computers Global Bond-Market Hub—Merrill Lynch Plays Key Role," *Wall Street Journal*, September 22, 1988.

34. Ibid.

35. Ibid., Bloomberg with Winkler, *Bloomberg by Bloomberg* (1997), 59.

36. Ibid., 61.

37. Ibid., Miller and Winkler, "Plugging In."

38. Ibid., Bloomberg with Winkler, *Bloomberg by Bloomberg* (1997), 55.

39. Author interview with Michael Bloomberg, August 16, 2018.

40. Michael Lewis, *Liar's Poker* (New York: W. W. Norton, 1969), 44.

41. Julian Hebron, "Paul Volcker's Legacy, 30 Year Anniversary of Floating Rates," The Basis Point, October 6, 2009, http://thebasispoint.com/2009/10/06/paul-volkers-legacy-30-year-anniversary-of-floating-rates/.

42. Ibid., Author interview with Tom Secunda.

43. Ibid.

44. Andrew Marton, "Mastering the Bond Market," *Institutional Investor*, November 1985.

45. Bloomberg, *Bloomberg by Bloomberg* (2019), 283.

46. Andrew Alleman, "Michael Bloomberg's Hilarious .NYC Domain Name Registrations," Domain Name Wire, November 3, 2014.

47. Author interview with John Aubert, May 7, 2018; Bloomberg with Winkler, *Bloomberg by Bloomberg* (1997), 56.

48. Bloomberg with Winkler, *Bloomberg by Bloomberg* (1997), 69.

49. Ibid., 70.

50. Ibid., 69.

51. Ibid., Author interview with Tom Secunda.

52. Ibid.

53. Author interview with Bloomberg executive, background, June 2016.

54. Author interview, Shawn Feeney, chief administrative officer for North America Markets at Citi, October 17, 2016.

55. Ibid., Miller and Winkler, "Plugging In."

CHAPTER 5: BLOOMBERG MAKES THE NEWS

1. Michael Bloomberg with Matthew Winkler, *Bloomberg by Bloomberg* (New York: John Wiley & Sons, 1997), 80.

2. Ibid.

3. Author interview with Matthew Winkler, May 24, 2016.

4. Ethan Bilby, "London's Big Bang at 25, Origin of Today's Financial University," Reuters, October 27, 2011, https://www.reuters.com/article/britain

-big-bang/londons-big-bang-at-25-origin-of-todays-financial-universe-id
USL5E7LO1T720111027.

5. Matthew Winkler, *The Bloomberg Way: A Guide for Reporters and Editors* (Hoboken, NJ: John Wiley & Sons, 2014), xi.

6. Author interview with Matthew Winkler, May 24, 2016.

7. Ibid.

8. This was 1991. Even Netscape was still three years away.

9. Joyce Purnick, *Mike Bloomberg: Money, Power, Politics* (New York: PublicAffairs, 2009), 48.

10. Author interview with Floyd Norris, July 26, 2016.

11. Wharton School management, " 'The Bloomberg Way': An Inside Look at How the News Organization Covers News," Wharton School of the University of Pennsylvania, January 9, 2012, http://knowledge.wharton.upenn.edu/article/the -bloomberg-way-an-inside-look-at-how-the-news-organization-covers-news/.

12. Winkler, *The Bloomberg Way*, xii.

CHAPTER 6: LIFE IN THE BLOOMBERG FISHBOWL

1. Author interview, Thomas Secunda, August 26, 2015.

2. "Bloomberg Chair Steps Down," CNN Money, March 5, 2001, https://money .cnn.com/2001/03/05/news/bloomberg.

3. *Sekiko Sakai Garrison v. Michael Bloomberg, as owner, Bloomberg L.P. Bloomberg Asia, inc and Bloomberg Inc.*, SDHR No. 95-E-MNOS-95-7940474-E, Federal Charge No. 16G-95-9182.

4. Author interview with Bloomberg LP employee, background, 2017.

5. Sheeraz Raza, "Ray Dalio and Michael Bloomberg Talk Leadership," September 22, 2014, ValueWalk, https://www.valuewalk.com/2014/09/ray-dalio -michael-bloomberg-talk-leadership-video/.

6. Michael Bloomberg with Matthew Winkler, *Bloomberg by Bloomberg* (New York: John Wiley & Sons, 1997), 60.

7. Geoffrey Croft, "Bloomberg Throws $9 Million Party in Annual Randall's Island Land Grab," *A Walk in the Park* blog, June 24, 2011, http://awalkinthepark nyc.blogspot.com/2011/06/bloomberg-throws-9-million-party-in.html.

8. Frankie Edozien, "Party-Hearty Bloomberg Wannabe Mayor a Real Ladies' Man," *New York Post*, May 27, 2001.

9. Elizabeth Kolbert, "Big Ticket Item," *The New Yorker*, September 3, 2001.

10. Author interviews with former Bloomberg employees, 2014–2018.

11. Ray Rivera, "Bloomberg @Google, Where Lunch Is Free," *City Room* blog, *New York Times*, January 31, 2008.

12. Ibid., Bloomberg with Winkler, *Bloomberg by Bloomberg* (1997), 61.
13. Ibid., 165.
14. Michael Bloomberg, interview with Andrew Ross Sorkin, *Squawk Box*, CNBC, May 2, 2014.
15. Carol J. Loomis, "Bloomberg's Money Machine," *Fortune*, April 5, 2007; Description in Judge Loretta A. Preska's ruling, October 16, 2011, in *EEOC v. Bloomberg L.P.*, case 1:07-cv-08383-LAP, document 202, p. 6.
16. Sekiko Sakai Garrison interview with Wayne Barrett, Wayne Barrett archives, Austin, Texas; author interview with Wayne Barrett, August 14, 2015.
17. Leah Nathans Spiro, "Is This on Your Bloomberg?," Bloomberg Business News, June 30, 1997.
18. *Sekiko Sakai Garrison v. Michael Bloomberg as owner Bloomberg LP, Bloomberg Asia and Bloomberg Inc.*, SDHR No. 9S-E-MNOS-95-7940474-E, June 19, 1997; Reuters, "Bloomberg Faces Sexual Harassment Suit"; Meryl Gordon, *New York*, April 16, 2001; James Ledbetter, Press Clips, *Village Voice*, August 12, 1997.
19. Bloomberg New York Sales Group evaluation, January 1, 1994, Wayne Barrett archives; author interview with Barrett.
20. Witness affidavit, *Sekiko Sakai Garrison v. Michael Bloomberg*.
21. Robert Polner, "Bloomberg Denies Harassment: Eyeing Mayoral Run, Says He Passed Polygraph Test," *Newsday*, March 29, 2001.
22. Larry Cohler-Esses, "Mike Settled Abuse Case: Bloomberg Paid Woman Over Pregnancy Remark," New York *Daily News*, March 27, 2001.
23. Ibid.
24. Michael Bloomberg interviewed by Samuel Abady, deposition on June 25, 1998, for case of *Mary Ann Olszewski v. Bloomberg LP and Bryan Lewis* (96Civ3393, RPP).
25. Leslie Eaton, "Candidate Hoping New York Is Newest Bloomberg Market," *New York Times*, June 11, 2001.
26. Felicity Barringer and Geraldine Fabrikant, "Coming of Age at Bloomerg LP," *New York Times*, March 21, 1999.
27. Status report from Getman Sweeney & Dunn on overtime pay lawsuit settled in 2018, https://getmansweeney.com/current-cases/bloomberg-analytics-overtime.
28. David W. Chen, "Mayor Shows His Testy Side in Deposition for a Lawsuit," *New York Times*, April 14, 2011.
29. Elissa Gootman, "Bloomberg Discrimination-Suit Ruling Renews Work-Life Debate," *New York Times*, August 18, 2011.

30. *EEOC v. Bloomberg LP*, U.S. District Court, Southern District of New York, No. 07-08383, Case 1:07-cv-08383-LAP-Document 202-Filed 08/16/11, p. 22.

31. Ibid., 32.

32. Ibid., 60; David Chen, "Discrimiation Suit Against Bloomberg L.P. Is Rejected," *New York Times*, August 17, 2011.

33. Goodman, "Bloomberg Discrimination-Suit Ruling Renews Work-Life Debate."

CHAPTER 7: THE BLOOMBERG WOMEN

1. Jonathan Van Meter, "Madam Would-Be Mayor, Hanging Out with the Crude, Playful, Openhearted Front-Runner, Christine Quinn," *New York*, February 2013, p. l.

2. *People of the State of New York v. John F. Haggerty Jr. and Special Operations LLC*, case no. 2589/1, 2011, p. 332.

3. Author interview with Bloomberg official, 2018.

4. Author interviews with city hall aides, Bloomberg aides, 2014.

5. Jennifer Steinhauer, "Bloomberg's New Deputy Has a Velvet Fist," *New York Times*, December 6, 2005.

6. Heidi Evans, "The Quiet Power of Patti Harris: Bloomberg's Confidant 'Can Do Anything,'" New York *Daily News*, November 16, 2009.

7. Email response to author from Patti Harris via Frank Barry, March 14, 2019.

8. Jessica Pressler, "Dating Mayor Bloomberg Is Worth a Woman's While," Intelligencer, *New York*, June 14, 2010, http://nymag.com/daily/intelligencer/2010/06/dating_mayor_bloomberg_is_wort.html.

9. Emma Bloomberg and Christopher Frissora wedding announcement, *New York Times*, June 12, 2005.

10. "Emma B. Bloomberg '01," speakers bio, *She Roars*, Princeton University, https://sheroars.princeton.edu/speaker/emma-b-bloomberg-01/.

11. Michael M. Grynbaum, "Bloomberg's Granddaughter Gets a Hybrid Surname," *New York Times*, July 6, 2015.

12. Emma Bloomberg, born January 20, 1983.

13. Jillian Dunham, "As a Catalog of Pain Shows, She Isn't Riding Just for Show," *New York Times*, August 31, 2012.

14. Office of the Mayor press release, December 20, 2013, http://www1.nyc.gov/office-of-the-mayor/news/426-13/mayor-bloomberg-mta-officials-local-leaders-take-first-ride-7-subway-train-extension/#/0.

15. Alex Williams, "*Mayor* Bloomberg?" *New York*, March 2, 1998.

16. Maureen Dowd, "Liberties; Camelot with Older Babes," *New York Times*, July 8, 2001.

17. Ruth La Ferla, "Her Term Is Up as Well," *New York Times*, December 27, 2013,

18. Author interviews with Bloomberg associates and dinner guests, background, 2014 and 2018.

19. Linette Lopez, "Ray Dalio on How 'Round the Clock Surveillance Makes His Hedge Fund a Place Where Wall Street Is Dying to Work," *Business Insider*, September 22, 2014; Dalio and Bloomberg interview, Bloomberg TV, https://finance.yahoo.com/news/live-ray-dalio-speaking-125005716.html.

CHAPTER 8: RUNNING ON MONEY

1. Michael Bloomberg with Matthew Winkler, *Bloomberg by Bloomberg* (New York: John Wiley & Sons, 1997), 41.

2. Penelope Patsuris, "Forbes Face: Michael Bloomberg," *Forbes*, June 5, 2001.

3. Author interview with Richard Ravitch, July 8, 2015. Ravitch was head of the Metropolitan Transportation Authority from 1979 to 1983 and lieutenant governor of New York from 2009 to 2010.

4. Author interview with Michael Bloomberg, August 16, 2018.

5. Ibid.

6. Ibid.

7. Ibid.

8. John M. Broder, "Bob Squier Is Dead at 65; Master of Political Imagery," *New York Times*, January 25, 2000,

9. Frank Lynn, "Some Major Democratic Incumbents Face Tough Primary Fight," *New York Times*, July 17, 1977.

10. Joyce Purnick, *Michael Bloomberg: Money, Power, Politics* (New York: PublicAffairs, 2009), 89.

11. Dean E. Murphy, "Bloomberg Philanthropy Cuts Two Ways as Campaign Issue," *New York Times*, September 8, 2001.

12. Author interviews with former assemblyman Richard Brodsky, 2014.

13. Andrea Bernstein, "Bloomberg's Golden Army," *New York Observer*, May 28, 2001.

14. David Seifman, "Bloomberg Joins GOP in Party Switch," *New York Post*, October 14, 2000.

15. Bradley Tusk email to author, February 2, 2017.

16. Promises list from Bradley Tusk; author interview with Tusk, September 20, 2016.

17. Dexter Filkins, "Bloomberg Far Outspends Mayoral Rivals," *New York Times*,

August, 11, 2001; Michael Cooper, "At $92.60 a vote, Bloomberg Shatters an Election Record," *New York Times*, December 4, 2001.

18. Cleveland Amory, "The Great Club Revolution," *American Heritage*, 1954.

19. Alexis Jeffries, "A Few Private New York Clubs Still Bar Women," *Village Voice*, April 27, 2010.

20. Julia La Roche, "The 12 Golf Courses Where Wall Street Big Shots Love to Play," *Business Insider*, April 8, 2013.

21. Dean E. Murphy, "Bloomberg Quietly Left Four Mostly White Clubs," *New York Times*, July 25, 2001.

22. Dean E. Murphy and Eric Lipton, "Bloomberg Discloses He's Rich, but He's Frugal with the Details," *New York Times*, July 14, 2007; author interviews with Bill Cunningham and other aides, July 2007 and 2014.

23. Chris McNickle, *Bloomberg: A Billionaire's Ambition* (New York: Skyhorse, 2017), 24.

24. Larry Cohler-Esses, "Mike Settled 'Abuse' Case: Bloomberg Paid Woman Over Pregnancy Remark," New York *Daily News*, March 27, 2001.

25. Maggie Haberman and Susan Edelman, "Bloomberg's Old Suit Fails Dems' Taste Test," *New York Post*, March 28, 2001.

26. Author interview with Bill Cunningham, 2014.

27. Gail Collins, "Public Interest; Bloomberg Beams In," *New York Times*, June 9, 2001.

28. "Unknown Bloomberg Trails Dems in Mayoral Race," Quinnipiac Poll, June 7, 2001, https://poll.qu.edu/search-releases/search-results/release-detail?Release ID=538&What=&strArea=3;0;&strTime=28. (Former city council chair Peter Vallone would lead Bloomberg by 43 points. Public advocate Mark Green would lead by 42 points. City comptroller Alan Hevesi by 37 points. And Bronx Borough president Fernando Ferrer by 30 points.)

29. McNickle, *Bloomberg: A Billionaire's Ambition*, 20.

30. Author interview with former New York governor George Pataki, May 10, 2017.

31. Author interviews with Betsy Gotbaum, 2017–18.

32. *Gotham Gazette*, "Searchlight on Campaign 2001," Campaign Trail Archives, *Newsweek*, April 2, 2001.

33. Author interview with Joe DePlasco, November 3, 2015.

34. 2,763 victims died in attack in New York City, plus nineteen hijackers died in two planes. "September 11 Terrorist Attacks Fast Facts," CNN, updated September 3, 2018, https://www.cnn.com/2013/07/27/us/september-11-anniversary -fast-facts/index.html.

35. Dean E. Murphy, "Bloomberg Expands on Economic Plans," *New York Times*, October 18, 2001.

36. Author interview with Jonathan Capehart, January 27, 2016.

37. Ibid., Murphy, "Economic Plans."

38. Jennifer Steinhauer, "Bloomberg Says He Regrets Marijuana Remarks," *New York Times*, April 10, 2002.

39. Jack Newfield, "Smart $$ Is Against Bloomberg," *New York Post*, May 10, 2001.

40. Michael Wolff, "Chairman Mike," This Media Life, *New York*, September 17, 2001.

41. Author interview with Elisabeth DeMarse, March 9, 2017.

42. Dean E. Murphy, "Campaigning for City Hall: Controversies: Questions Raised over a Gag Gift to Bloomberg from 1990," *New York Times*, September 8, 2001.

43. "The Eye-Opener: Conflicts of Interest Board Approves New Rule to Limit Fundraising from Individuals with City Business," *Gotham Gazette*, May 10, 2019.

44. "Mark Green for Mayor," editorial, *New York Times*, October 26, 2001, https://www.nytimes.com/2001/10/29/opinion/mark-green-for-mayor.html.

45. "Bloomberg White Paper," anti-Bloomberg campaign data compiled for the Green campaign by Stu Loeser in 2001; author interviews with DePlasco, November 3, 2015, and Loeser, November 7, 2016.

46. Michael M.Grynbaum, "With Adviser's Departure, Bloomberg Will Lose a Fierce Protector," *New York Times*, July 30, 2012; NYC press announcement, January 11, 2006.

47. Casey Chamberlain, executive assistant, "My Anthrax Survivor's Story," NBC News, September 19, 2006, http://www.nbcnews.com/id/14785359/#.WPT5tVPyvBI.

48. Ibid., Murphy, "Bloomberg Expands on Economic Plans."

49. Mark Green, *Bright, Infinite Future: A Generational Memoir on the Progressive Rise* (New York: St. Martin's Press, 2016), 199.

50. Adam Nagourney, "Bloomberg and Green Clash over Capability in Debate," *New York Times*, November 2, 2001.

51. Author interview with Bill Cunningham, 2014 and 2015.

52. Ibid., Green, *Bright, Infinite Future,* 189.

53. Dean E. Murphy, "In Homestretch of Campaign, Mayor Endorses Bloomberg," *New York Times*, October 28, 2001.

54. Author interviews with Bill Cunningham, 2014 and 2015, and Kevin Skeekey, 2015.

55. Author interview with Joe De Plasco, November 3, 2015.

56. Ibid., Green, *Bright, Infinite Future*, 193.

57. Author interview with Bill Cunningham, 2017.

58. Ibid., Green, *Bright, Infinite Future*, 194.

59. McNickle, *Bloomberg: A Billionaire's Ambition*, 44; author interview with Bill Cunningham, 2017.

60. Author interview with Kevin Sheekey, September 8, 2015.

61. NYC Board of Elections, official tally of 2001 mayoral race; Michael Cooper and Dean E. Murphy, "Green Calm as Victory Slips away at the End," *New York Times*, November 7, 2001.

62. Ibid., Green, *Bright, Infinite Future*, 195.

63. Meryl Gordon, "Citizen Mike," *New York*, April 16, 2001.

64. Michael Bloomberg campaign expenditures, disbursements by date paid, New York City Campaign Finance Board, campaign finance information system, p. 46.

65. Michael Cooper, "At $92.60 a Vote, Bloomberg Shatters an Election Record," *New York Times*, December 4, 2001.

66. Gail Collins, Bloomberg Beams In, Column: Public Interests, *New York Times*, June 5, 2001.

67. Penelope Patsures, *Forbes* Face: Michael Bloomberg, *Forbes*, June 5, 2001.

CHAPTER 9: FIRST HUNDRED DAYS

1. Multiple interviews with hires, although, in a few cases, he said, "Don't screw it up"—if the new employee seemed too proper for his Wall Street vocabulary.

2. Maggie Haberman, "Mike's Off to a Running Start—Has Meetings with Ferrer and Rudy," *New York Post*, November 8, 2011, https://nypost.com/2001/11/08/mikes-off-to-a-running-start-has-meetings-with-ferrer-and-rudy/; author interviews with Kevin Sheekey, 2015 and 2018.

3. Chris McNickle, *Bloomberg: A Billionaire's Ambition* (New York: Skyhorse, 2017), 47.

4. "Bloomberg sworn in by Giuliani," CNN, January 1, 2002, http://www.cnn.com/2001/US/12/31/newyork.mayor/index.html; author interviews with advisers, 20014 and 2015.

5. Author interview with Chief Judge of New York Appeals Court Judith Kaye, June 2013.

6. "New York City Mayor Inauguration," C-SPAN video, January 1, 2002, https://www.c-span.org/video/?168034-1/york-city-mayor-inauguration Michael Bloomberg inauguration 2002.

7. Joe Carter, "5 Facts About the 9/11 Aftermath," *Acton Institute Powerblog*, Action Institute, September 11, 2018, http://www.history.com/topics/ground-zero.

8. Anemona Hartocollis, "Landfill Has 9/11 Remains, Medical Examiner Wrote," *New York Times*, March 24, 2007.

9. "Working Together to Accelerate New York's Recovery," New York City Partnership report, November 2001; Michael Cooper, "Economic Anguish of 9/11 Is Detailed by Comptroller," *New York Times*, September 5, 2002.

10. Daniel L. Doctoroff, *Greater Than Ever: New York's Big Comeback* (New York: PublicAffairs, 2017), xii, xiii.

11. Eric Nadelstern, a teacher, principal, and administrator in the New York school system for forty years, boiled the Bloomberg management style as mayor to its essence:

   - Recruit the best people you can find
   - Support them
   - Provide incentives for good work
   - Protect them from outside interference
   - Hold them accountable for the highest standard of performance

12. Author interview with Joel Klein, former school chancellor, November 25, 2014.

13. Michael Bloomberg interview with Judy Woodruff, *PBS Newshour*, PBS, December 18, 2017.

14. Jennifer Steinhauer, "Initial Steps by Bloomberg Show Contrast with Giuliani," *New York Times*, November 10, 2001.

15. Author interview with Nathan Leventhal, November 20, 2017.

16. Adam Nagourney, "Bloomberg Fills Nine Posts with Government Veterans," *New York Times*, December 20, 2001.

17. Ibid.; Steinhauer, "Initial Steps by Bloomberg Show Contrast with Giuliani."

18. Christopher Drew, "Sad Search by Kerik to Find His Mother; Family Secret Is Revealed in Autobiography," *New York Times*, November 9, 2001.

19. "Bernard Kerik Fast Facts," CNN March, 11, 2013, https://www.cnn.com /2013/03/11/us/bernard-kerik-fast-facts/index.html.

20. Ray Kelly, *Vigilance: My Life Serving America and Protecting Its Empire City* (New York: Hachette, 2015), 164; author interview with Ray Kelly, September 8, 2015.

21. Author interview with Marc Shaw, October 13, 2017.

22. Author interview with Tom Frieden, October 22, 2014.

23. Author interview with Peter Madonia, December 12, 2017.

24. Author interview with Adrian Benepe, September 24, 2014, October 28, 2015; biography as director of City Park Development for Trust for Public Land, https://www.tpl.org/about/adrian-benepe.

25. Robin Finn, "Public Lives: Away from the Ovens to a Hot Spot at City Hall," *New York Times*, April 16, 2002.

26. Author interview with Peter Madonia; New York City Archives, Bloomberg city files, Peter Madonia, Box 22677, box 4 of 6; Box 22677, box 3 of 3, 2003–2006.

27. Jim Dwyer, "In High Costs of City Litigation, a Litany of Missed Opportunitites," About New York, *New York Times*, August 2, 2013.

28. "Statement by Mayor Michael R. Bloomberg on Resignation of EDC President Andrew M. Alper," press release, NYC.gov, May 8, 2006, http://www1 .nyc.gov/office-of-the-mayor/news/143-06/statement-mayor-michael -bloomberg-resignation-edc-president-andrew-alper.

CHAPTER 10: A BILLIONAIRE'S CITY HALL

1. Julia La Roche, "Mike Bloomberg: 'Happiness Can Never Buy Money,'" *Business Insider*, September 22, 2014. Article about a Bloomberg news interview with Stephanie Ruhle, September, 2014.

2. Jennifer Steinhauer, "Can't Find the Mayor? Well, What's It to You?," *New York Times*, February 20, 2002.

3. Michael Barbaro, "New York's Mayor, but Bermuda Shares Custody," *New York Times*, April 25, 2010.

4. Dean E. Murphy and Eric Lipton, "Bloomberg Discloses He's Rich, but He's Frugal with the Details," *New York Times*, July 14, 2001.

5. Ibid.

6. Ibid.

7. Ibid.

8. Allen Salkin, "Homes Sweet Homes," *New York*, April 15, 2002.

9. New York City Conflicts of Interest Board, Advisory Opinion, no. 2002-1, August 20, 2002.

10. Ibid.

11. Michael J. de la Merced and Louise Story, "Bloomberg Expected to Buy Merrill's Stake in His Firm," *New York Times*, July 17, 2008.

12. New York City Conflicts of Interest Board, Advisory Opinion, no. 2002-1, August 20, 2002.

13. Serge F. Kovaleski and Ray Rivera, "The Roles Blur for the Mayor and the Mogul," *New York Times*, December 8, 2007.

14. Author interview with Peter Grauer, June 14, 2016.

15. Wayne Barrett, "Bloomberg Keeps His Billions Separate from His Mayoral Obligations? Yeah, Right!" *Village Voice*, September 1, 2009, https://www.vil lagevoice.com/2009/09/01/bloomberg-keeps-his-billions-separate-from-his -mayoral-obligations-yeah-right/.

16. Email to author from Michael Henton, editorial assistant, finance and accounting, John Wiley & Sons, April 18, 2017.

17. Ibid.

18. Letter from Jane W. Parver, acting chair of Conflict of Interest Board, COIB case no. 2002-107, February 22, 2002, Wayne Barrett archives.

19. Letter from Jane Parver, acting chair of Conflict of Interest Board, COIB case no. 2002-014, January 30, 2002, Wayne Barrett archives.

20. Letter from Steven Rosenfeld, chairman of Conflict of Interest Board, COIB case no. 2012-123, March 1, 2012.

21. Barrett, "Bloomberg Keeps His Billions Separate from His Mayoral Obligations?"

22. Adam Lisberg, "Mayor Bloomberg: We Love the Rich People," New York *Daily News*, March 6, 2009.

23. Diane Cardwell, "Mayor Says New York Is Worth the Cost," *New York Times*, January 8, 2003.

24. Chris McNickle, *Bloomberg: A Billionaire's Ambition* (New York: Skyhorse, 2017), 137.

25. Author interview with Peter Grauer, June 14, 2016.

26. "Gates Still World's Richest," CNN Money, June 22, 2001, https://money.cnn .com/2001/06/22/news/wealthiest/.

27. Edwin Durgy, "The World's Richest Billionares: Full List of the Top 500," *Forbes*, March 4, 2013.

CHAPTER 11: A LABORATORY FOR URBAN REFORM

1. Sam Roberts, "Listening to (and Saving) the World's Languages," *New York Times*, April 29, 2010.

2. New York State Department of Labor, Current Employment Statistics, OSC analysis, Report 10-18.

3. Robin Nagle, *Picking Up: On the Streets and Behind the Trucks with the Sanitation Workers of New York City* (New York: Farrar, Straus and Giroux, 2013), 13.

4. Restaurant Inspection Information, New York City Department of Health and Mental Hygiene, 2019, http://a816-restaurantinspection.nyc.gov/Restaurant Inspection/SearchBrowse.do.

5. Nancy Hass, "The House That Bloomberg Built," Fast Company, October 31, 1995.

6. Author interview with Ester Fuchs, May 3, 2017.

7. Author interview with Robert Steel, August 28, 2017; Michael Barbaro, "Bloomberg's Bullpen: Candidates Debate Its Future," New York Times, March 22, 2013.

8. Author interviews with numerous city hall officials from Bloomberg years. 2004, 2014, and 2015.

9. Author interview with Peter Madonia, December 12, 2017.

10. Author interview with Marc Shaw, October 13, 2017.

11. Author interviews with numerous city hall aides, 2014, 2015, and 2018.

12. Author interview with Bill Cunningham, 2018.

13. Author interview with Joel Klein, November 25, 2014.

14. "In His Final Major Address, Mayor Bloomberg Delivers Remarks on the Rise of Cities, Their Future and the Labor-Electoral Process That Could Undermine Progress," NYC.gov, December 18, 2013, https://www1.nyc.gov/office-of-the -mayor/news/417-13/in-his-final-major-address-mayor-bloomberg-delivers -remarks-the-rise-cities-their-future/#/0.

15. Author interviews with Kathryn Wylde, January 16, 2014, and March 6, 2018.

16. Michael Cooper, "New York City Budget: The Deal," New York Times, June 20, 2002.

17. Ibid.

18. Michael Cooper, "Officials Brace for a Budget That Spreads the Pain Around," New York Times, February 13, 2002.

19. Jennifer Steinhauer, "The Mouse as Sacred Cow: Mayor's Cuts Spare Technology," New York Times, May 28, 2002.

20. "Mayor Michael R. Bloomberg Delivers Speech on Economic Development and Job Creation," NYC.gov, October 21, 2003, https://www1.nyc.gov/office -of-the-mayor/news/293-03/mayor-michael-bloomberg-delivers-speech-eco nomic-development-job-creation.

21. Cooper, "New York City Budget."

22. Michael Cooper, "Cigarettes up to $7 a Pack with New Tax," New York Times, July 1, 2002.

23. Tali Elfassy, Stella S. Yi, and Susan M. Kansagra, "Trends in Cigarette, Cigar, and Smokeless Tobacco Use Among New York City Public High School Youth Smokers, 2001–2013," ResearchGate, posted online June 11, 2015, https://

www.researchgate.net/publication/278666691_Trends_in_cigarette_cigar
_and_smokeless_tobacco_use_among_New_York_City_public_high_school
_youth_smokers_2001-2013.

24. Michael Cooper, "Mayor Signs Property Tax Increase into Law," *New York Times*, December 3, 2002.

25. "Ferrer Or Miller Beat Mayor Bloomberg, Quinnipiac University Poll Finds," Quinnipiac Poll, November 25, 2003, https://poll.qu.edu/search-releases /search-results/release-detail?ReleaseID=365&What=&strArea=3;0;&str Time=28.

26. Jennifer Steinhauer and Marjorie Connelly, "New Yorkers Have Growing Pessimism About the City," *New York Times*, June 12, 2003.

CHAPTER 12: THE "NANNY" MAYOR

1. Dana Rubinstein, "Bloomberg: 'Just Before You Die, Remember You Got Three Extra Years,'" Capital New York, June 1, 2012.

2. Author interview with Dr. Al Sommer, July 22, 2014.

3. Ibid.

4. Ibid.

5. Johns Hopkins Bloomberg School of Public Health, history, https://www .jhsph.edu/about/history/index.html.

6. James Bennet, "The Bloomberg Way," *The Atlantic*, November 2012.

7. Tom Nugent, "Life on the Cutting Edge," *Oberlin Alumni Magazine*, Fall 2006, http://www2.oberlin.edu/alummag/fall2006/life-on-the-cutting-edge.html.

8. Dr. Tom Frieden official bio, Vital Strategies, http://www.vitalstrategies.org /executive-team/dr-tom-frieden/.

9. Author interview with Dr. Tom Frieden, February 24, 2015.

10. Dr. Tom Farley, *Saving Gotham: A Billionaire Mayor, Activist Doctors, and the Fight for Eight Million Lives* (New York: W. W. Norton, 2015), 29.

11. New York City Municipal Archives, Bloomberg administration, Deputy Mayor for Economic Development, Daniel L. Doctoroff, Box 22665, Projects, 2002, Box 1 of 1; Health file.

12. Ibid.

13. Author interview with Michael Bloomberg, May 27, 2015.

14. Ibid., Author interview with Dr. Tom Frieden.

15. New York State Clean Indoor Air Act "Smoking Regulations in New York," Public Health Law, Article 13-E, July 24, 2003, https://smoking.uslegal.com /smoking-regulations-in-new-york/.

16. Matt Coneybeare, "Vintage Photograph from 1943 Shows Famous 'Smoking'

Camel Billboard in Times Square," Viewing NYC, September 6, 2017, https://viewing.nyc/vintage-photograph-from-1943-shows-famous-smoking-camel-billboard-in-times-square/.

17. Bill Keller, "The Smoke Nazis," *New York Times*, October 19, 2002.

18. Author interview with Ed Skyler, March 14, 2014.

19. Jennifer Steinhauer, "Bloomberg, Heckled, Presses Smoking Curbs," *New York Times*, October 11, 2002.

20. Author interviews with Gerard Maegher, June 2017, 2018.

21. Tina Moore, "Mayor Bloomberg Visits Old Town Bar to Celebrate 10th Annivesary of Smoke-Free Air Act," New York *Daily News*, March 27, 2013.

22. "Dietary Reference Intakes for Energy, Carbohydrate, Fiber, Fat, Fatty Acids, Cholesterol, Protein, and Amino Acids (2005)," National Academies of Sciences, Engineering, Medicine, https://www.nap.edu/read/10490/chapter/1.

23. Sewell Chan, "A New Condom in Town, This One Named 'NYC,'" *New York Times*, February 15, 2007.

24. "NYC Condoms," New York City Health Department release, NYC.gov, https://www1.nyc.gov/site/doh/health/health-topics/condom.page.

25. Ibid., Chan, "A New Condom in Town."

26. Ibid., Farley, *Saving Gotham*, 120.

27. Melinda Wenner Moyer, "It's Time to End the War on Salt," *Scientific American*, July 8, 2011.

28. Farley, *Saving Gotham*, 120.

29. Ibid.

30. Christine J. Curtis, Jenifer Clapp, Sarah A. Niederman, Shu Wen Ng, and Sonya Y. Angell, "US Food Industry Progress During the National Salt Reduction Initiative: 2009–2014," *American Journal of Public Health* (106[10]): 1815–19, National Center for Biotechnology Information, published online October 2016, https://www.ncbi.nlm.nih.gov/pmc/articles/PMC5024394/.

31. Author interview with Dr. Tom Frieden; Farley, *Saving Gotham*, 61; author interview with Dr. Thomas Farley, March 13, 2015.

32. Ibid., Farley, *Saving Gotham*, 209.

33. Ibid., 210.

34. CBS News, "Palin Mocks Bloomberg, Drinks Big Gulp," video, YouTube, posted on March 16, 2013, https://www.youtube.com/watch?v=ebRyYrqMrXU.

35. Holly Yan, "No Soda Ban Here: Mississippi Passes 'Anti-Bloomberg' Bill," CNN, March 21, 2013, https://www.cnn.com/2013/03/21/us/mississippi-anti-bloomberg-bill/index.html.

36. Holly West, "NC Gets 'Anti-Bloomberg' Law," posted by Rose Hoban, North

Carolina Health News, July 19, 2013, https://www.northcarolinahealthnews
.org/2013/07/19/nc-gets-anti-bloomberg-law.

37. Tina Susman, "N.Y. Mayor 'Shocked' by Soda Law Ruling, Takes Shot at Mis-
    sissippi Law," *Los Angeles Times*, March 15, 2013.

38. Dave Mosher, "The Sweetest Drinks in the US: These Bestselling Beverages
    Have the Most Sugar Per Ounce," *Business Insider*, July 25, 2017, http://www
    .sugarstacks.com/beverages.htm.

39. Ibid., Farley, *Saving Gotham*, 213.

40. Ibid., 216.

41. Justia Opinion Summary, *New York Statewide Coalition of Hispanic Cham-
    bers of Commerce v. New York City Dep't of Health & Mental Hygiene,* Justia
    US Law, 2012, https://law.justia.com/cases/new-york/court-of-appeals/2014
    /134-0.html.

42. Michael M. Grynbaum, "New York's Ban on Big Sodas is Rejected by Final
    Court," *New York Times*, June 26, 2014, https://www.nytimes.com/2014/06/27
    /nyregion/city-loses-final-appeal-on-limiting-sales-of-large-sodas.html.

43. John Kell, "Bottled Water Contiues to Take the Fizz out of Diet Soda," *Fortune*,
    April 19, 2017, http://fortune.com/2017/04/19/coca-cola-pepsi-dr-pepper
    -soda-water/.

44. Justin McCarthy, "Americans More Likely to Avoid Drinking Soda Than Be-
    fore," Gallup.com, July 28, 2014, https://news.gallup.com/poll/174137/ameri
    cans-likely-avoid-drinking-soda.aspx.

45. Rebecca Rifkin, "Majority of Americans Say They Try to Avoid Drinking
    Soda," Gallup.com, August 3, 2015, https://news.gallup.com/poll/184436/ma
    jority-americans-say-try-avoid-drinking-soda.aspx.

46. Ryan Jaslow, "New York Raises Smoking Age to 21," CBS News, Novem-
    ber 19, 2013, https://www.cbsnews.com/news/nyc-raises-smoking-age-to-21
    -sets-cigarette-pack-minimum-price-at-1050/.

47. David Walpuck, "The ABC's of New York City's Restaurant Grades," *Food
    Safety News*, June 4, 2013.

48 Jennifer Glickel, "Health Department Launches Graphic Campaign Against
    Holiday Binge Drinking," DNAinfo, November 30, 2010; Lucas I. Alpert,
    "City Department of Health's New Ads Aim to Rein In Holiday Binge Drink-
    ing," New York *Daily News*, December 1, 2010.

49. James Bennet, "The Bloomberg Way," *The Atlantic*, November 2012, https://
    www.theatlantic.com/magazine/archive/2012/11/the-bloomberg-way/309136/.

50. Colin Campbell, "Jewish Pols Demand Bloomberg Apologize for 10,000 Guys
    in Black Hats Remark," *New York Observer*, October 26, 2012, http://observer

.com/2012/10/jewish-pols-demand-bloomberg-apologize-over-10000-guys-in-black-hats-remark/.

51. "Trends in Cigarette Use Among Adults in New York City, 2002–2010," Epi Data Brief, New York City Department of Mental Health and Hygiene, November 2011, https://www1.nyc.gov/assets/doh/downloads/pdf/epi/databrief 12.pdf.

52. Mireya Navarro, "City Issues Rule to Ban Dirtiest Oils at Buildings, *New York Times*, April 21, 2011.

53. Matt Flegenheimer, "After Decades, a Water Tunnel Can Now Serve All of Manhattan," *New York Times*, October 16, 2013.

54. Michael Dhar, "Did Mayor Mike Bloomberg Make New Yorkers Healthier?" *Scientific American*, December 10, 2013.

55. "Mayor Bloomberg: New Yorkers Living Longer than Ever," CBS NewYork, December 27, 2011, http://newyork.cbslocal.com/2011/12/27/mayor-bloomberg-new-yorkers-living-longer-than-ever/.

CHAPTER 13: THE GEEK SQUAD

1. Steven Johnson, "What a Hundred Million Calls to 311 Reveal About New York," *Wired*, November 10, 2010.

2. "Mayor Bloomberg Reveals Sources of Mysterious but Harmless Maple Syrup Odors," NYC.gov, February 5, 2009, https://www1.nyc.gov/office-of-the-mayor/news/059-09/mayor-bloomberg-reveals-sources-mysterious-harmless-maple-syrup-odors.

3. Miriam Kreinin Souccar, "Next Mayor Faces Big Technical Gap; on DoITT List, New Commissioner," Crains, Monday, June 11, 2001.

4, Jennifer Steinhauer, "The Mouse as Sacred Cow: Mayor's Cuts Spare Technology," *New York Times*, May 28, 2002; author interview with Ester Fuchs, May 3, 2017.

5. Taewoo Nam and Theresa A. Pardo, "Identifying Success Factors and Challenges of 311-Driven Service Integration: A Comparative Study of NYC311 and Philly311," Hawaii International Conference on System Sciences, 2013.

6. Author interview with Gino Menchini, October 19, 2018.

7. "Michael R. Bloomberg, Mayor, State of the City Address," NYC.gov, January 30, 2002, http://www.nyc.gov/html/om/html/2002a/state_city.html.

8. Author interview with Ester Fuchs, May 3, 2017.

9. New York City Municipal Archives, Emma Bloomberg, 22683, 4 of 4, Project/issues 2002, NYC 3-1-1 Workng Committee Project Status report, 12-3-02.

10. Ibid.

11. Emma Bloomberg, New York City Municipal Archives, 22683 4 of 4, Project Issues, 9-25-01.

12. Author interviews with aides, Bill Cunningham, and others, 2014 and 2016.

13. Chaleampon Ritthichai, "On Noise," *Gotham Gazette*, July 12, 2004.

14. Winnie Hu, "That Jingle of Mr. Softee's? It's the Sound of Compromise," *New York Times*, December 14, 2005, https://www.nytimes.com/2005/12/14/nyre gion/that-jingle-of-mr-softees-its-the-sound-of-compromise.html.

15. Author interview with Bill Cunningham, July 11, 2015, and July 15, 2017.

16. Alex Howard, "Predictive Data Analytics Is Saving Lives and Taxpayer Dollars in New York City: Explains Why Applying Data Science to Regulatory Data Is Necessary to Use City Resources Better," *The O'Reilly Factor*, FoxNews, June 26, 2012.

17. Debashis Basu, "Data Science for Smart Cities," *Business Standard*, April 17, 2016.

18. Kia Gregory, "New York Tries to Rid Its Sewers of FOG (Fat, Oil and Grease)," *New York Times*, February 14, 2014; https://www.nytimes.com/2014/02/15/ny region/new-york-tries-to-clear-its-sewers-of-fog-fat-oil-and-grease.html.

19. "About the Business Integrity Commission," Business Integrity Commission, NYC.gov, https://www1.nyc.gov/site/bic/about/about-bic.page.

20. Alan Feuer, "The Mayor's Geek Squad," *New York Times*, March 23, 2013.

21. Basu, "Data Science for Smart Cities"; Viktor Mayer-Schönberger and Kenneth Cukier, "Big Data in the Big Apple," *Slate*, March 6, 2013.

22. Mayer-Schönberger and Cukier, "Big Data in the Big Apple."

23. Email to author from Edward Skyler, July 11, 2017.

24. Author interviews with aides and former city officials, background, 2013 and 2014.

25. "Report from Former New York City Deputy Mayor for Operations Cas Holloway in Response to Mayor Bill de Blasio's Critique of the Emergency Communications Transformation Program," January 16, 2015, p. 4.

26. Author's timing of event.

27. Michael Cooper, "The Blackout of 2003: The Mayor; Bloomberg Cast as a Figure of Calm Authority," *New York Times*, August 15, 2003.

28. Ibid.

29. New York City Municipal Archives, Emma Bloomberg, 22683, box 1 of 2, project issue files, 83 NYC Archives. First report on August 14, 2003, blackout.

30. Michael Barbaro, "Blizzard Mystery Solved? Air Bloomberg Was Seen in Bermuda," *New York Times*, January 11, 2011.

31. Alison Gendar, Lisa L. Colangelo, Kathleen Lucadamo, and Helen Ken-

nedy, "Mayor Bloomberg Apologizes for Snow Screw-ups During Blizzard of 2010, Defends Sanitation Department," New York *Daily News*, December 29, 2010.

32. Elizabeth Weinstein and Skip Funk, "Preliminary Review of the City's Response to the December 2010 Blizzard: Report and Recommendations to Mayor Michael R. Bloomberg; Elizabeth Weinstein, Director, Mayor's Office of Operations; Skip Funk, Director of the Mayor's Office of Citywide Emergency Communications," NYC.gov, January 10, 2011.

33. "Mayor Bloomberg Announces Completion of Major Milestones in 911 System Overhaul Sought by City for Decades," press release, NYC.gov, January 5, 2012, https://www1.nyc.gov/office-of-the-mayor/news/004-12/mayor-bloomberg-completion-major-milestones-911-system-overhaul-sought-the-city#/4.

34. Report by New York City Comptroller Scott Stringer on Emergency Communications Transformation Project upgrade, August 5, 2014, SR15-063S.

35. Author interview with Mark Peters, commissioner of the New York City Department of Investigation, 13, 2015.

36. Author interview with Cas Holloway, July 2014.

37. Report from former Deputy Caswell Holloway responding to criticism of 911, January 16, 2015; author interview with Holloway, 2015.

38. "SAIC Deferred Prosecution Agreement, Prepared Remarks of U.S. Attorney Preet Bharara," United States Attorney's Office, Southern District of New York, U.S. Department of Justice, March 14, 2012, https://www.justice.gov/usao-sdny/saic-deferred-prosecution-agreement-prepared-remarks-us-attorney-preet-bharara.

39. Sewell Chan, "New Scanners for Tracking City Workers," New York Times, January 23, 2007.

40. Ibid., "SAIC Deferred Prosecution Agreement, Prepared Remarks of U.S. Attorney Preet Bharara."

41. Benjamin Weiser, "Three Contractors Sentenced to 20 Years in CityTime Corruption Case," New York Times, April 28, 2014.

42. Greg B. Smith, "Mayoral Candidate Bill Thompson Failed Repeatedly as Controller to Intervene as Payroll System CityTime Ballooned in Costs," New York Daily News, July 1, 2013.

43. David Chen, "Years Before Fraud Indictment, City Official Warned About Payroll Project," New York Times, December 20, 2010.

44. Colin Campbell, "Mayor Bloomberg on CityTime: 'We Were Lucky Because of the Fraud,'" New York Observer, July 26, 2013, http://observer.com/2013/07/mayor-bloomberg-on-citytime-we-were-lucky-because-of-the-fraud/.

45. David Seifman, "Bloomberg Claims City Did 'Pretty Good Job' with Scandal-Plagued CityTime," *New York Post*, May 27, 2011.

46. Author interview with former Bloomberg company employee, background, 2017.

47. "Bloomberg Chair Steps Down," CNN Money, March 5, 2001, http://money.cnn.com/2001/03/05/news/bloomberg/.

48. Celeste Katz, "Three Guilty in NY CityTime Corruption Scandal," New York *Daily News*, November 22, 2013.

49. Author interview with city administrator, background, 2017.

50. "A Plan to Make New York the Nation's Leading Digital City," NYC press release, digital announcement, NYC.gov, May 16, 2011, http://www1.nyc.gov/office-of-the-mayor/news/158-11/mayor-bloomberg-chief-digital-officer-rachel-sterne-em-road-map-the-digital#/2.

51. "New York City's Growing High-Tech Industry," Report from Office of State Comptroller, Report 2-2015, April, 2014.

52. Robert Dominguez, "Tech Zone," New York *Daily News*, October 11, 2013.

CHAPTER 14: THAT PUBLIC SCHOOL BUSINESS

1. David M. Herszenhorn, "Mayor Accepts Blame for Lag in Suspensions," *New York Times*, December 13, 2003.

2. "Mayor Bloomberg Discusses Remarkable Progress in New York City Schools and the Challenges of the Knowledge Economy at Education Nation Summit," NYC Public Library, October 8, 2013, https://www1.nyc.gov/office-of-the-mayor/news/323-13/mayor-bloomberg-remarkable-progress-new-york-city-schools-the-challenges-the/#/0.

3. "Mayor Bloomberg Announces Tentative Agreement with the United Federation of Teachers Nearly One Year Before Expiration of Current Contract," NYC.gov, November 8, 2006, https://www1.nyc.gov/office-of-the-mayor/news/388-06/mayor-bloomberg-tentative-agreement-the-united-federation-teachers-nearly-one#/0.

4. Catherine Gewertz, "N.Y.C. Mayor Gains Control over Schools," *Education Week*, July 19, 2002, https://www.edweek.org/ew/articles/2002/06/19/41nyc.h21.html; James C. McKinley Jr., "State Senate Passes Bill Giving Mayor Control of Schools," *New York Times*, June 12, 2002.

5. Chris McNickle, *Bloomberg: A Billionaire's Ambition* (New York: Skyhorse, 2017), 100.

6. Author interview with Merryl Tisch, November 13, 2015.

7. "Silence was Golden for Michael Bloomberg," Opinion, *New York Post*, June 23, 2013.

8. McNickle, *Bloomberg: A Billionaire's Ambition*, 100.

9. Ibid., Author interview with Merryl Tisch.

10. David M. Herszenhorn, "Bloomberg Wins on School Tests After Firing Foes," *New York Times*, March 16, 2004.

11. Ibid.

12. Eric Nadelstern, *10 Lessons from New York City Schools: What Really Works to Improve Education* (New York: Teachers College Press, 2013), 57.

13. Michael Cooper, "So Long School Bureaucrats: 110 Livingston Is Being Sold," *New York Times*, July 9, 2003.

14. Jennifer Steinhauer, "Mayor Wants Tweed Building for School Use," *New York Times*, March 19, 2002.

15. Ibid.

16. Nadelstern, *10 Lessons*, 15–16.

17. "A Slimmed-Down Education Department," editorial, *New York Times*, December 4, 2002.

18. McNickle, *Bloomberg: A Billionaire's Ambition*, 97.

19. New York City Municipal Archives, Letter from Ester Fuchs with names of chancellors being proposed, July 8, 2002, Madonia, 22677, box 3 of 8, project issues, 2000–2003.

20. Joel Klein, *Lessons of Hope: How to Fix Our Schools* (New York: HarperCollins, 2014), 20–21.

21. Michael Tomasky, "No Experience Required," *New York*, August 12, 2002.

22. McNickle, *Bloomberg: A Billionaire's Ambition*, 103.

23. Author interview with David Yassky, June 1, 2016.

24. Jennifer Medina, "On New York School Tests, Warnings Signs Ignored," *New York Times*, October 10, 2010; Jennifer Medina, "State Long Ignored Red Flags on Test Scores," *New York Times*, October 11, 2001.

25. Joel Klein, *Lessons of Hope*, 35.

26. Ibid., 36.

27. Jelani Cobb, "Class Notes," *The New Yorker*, August 31, 2015.

28. Nyc.gov/schoolportals for Jamaica Gateway to the Sciences; Queens Collegiate; Hillside Arts and Letters Academy; the High School for Community Leadership, in 2016.

29. Eliza Shapiro, "$773 Million Later, de Blasio Ends Signature Initiative to Improve Failing Schools," *New York Times*, February 26, 2019.

30. James J. Kemple, "High School Closures in New York City; Impacts on Student Academic Outcomes, Attendance and Mobility," NYU/Steinhardt, November 2015, p. 49, https://steinhardt.nyu.edu/scmsAdmin/media/users/sg158/PDFs

/hs_closures/HighSchoolClosuresinNewYorkCity_ResearchAllianceforNYC
SChools_pdf.pdf.

31. Author interview with Sean Patrick Corcoran, November 11, 2016.

32. Sean P. Corcoran, Jennifer L. Jennings, Sarah Cohodes, and Carolyn Sattin-Bajaj, "Leveling the Playing Field for High School Choice: Results from a Field Experiment of Informational Interventions," Executive Summary, NYC High School Admissions Study, 2015–16 school year, https://static1.square space.com/static/57b20ecbe6f2e157a74c4a3a/t/5ac2371f70a6ad85f4e9bbda /1522677535909/Leveling+the+Playing+Field+for+High+School+Choice+Ex ecutive+Summary+%2803_29_18%29.pdf.

33. Lori Nathanson, Sean Corcoran (IESP), and Christine Baker-Smith, "A Report on the Placements of Low-Achieving Students," Research Alliance for New York City Schools, NYU Steinhardt, 2013.

34. Ibid.

35. "How Do Charter School Lotteries Work?," New York City Charter School Center, 2013–14, https://www.nyccharterschools.org/sites/default/files/re sources/LOTTERIES082713.pdf.

36. Raymond Domanico, director of research, New York City Independent Budget Office, "School Indicators for New York City Charter Schools, 2013-14 School Year," July 2015, pp. 4, 15, http://www.ibo.nyc.ny.us/iboreports/school -indicators-for-new-york-city-charter-schools-2013-2014-school-year-july -2015.pdf.

37. "Study Finds New York City Charter Schools Remain Positive, but with Pockets of Concern," Center for Research on Education Outcomes, Stanford University, February 20, 2013.

38. Sharon Otterman, "Charter Schools Among 12 Chosen to Close," *New York Times*, December 7, 2010.

39. Elizabeth A. Harris, "Report Faults Charter School Rules on Discipline of Students," *New York Times*, February 12, 2015; Paula Davis et al., "Civil Rights Suspended: An Analysis of New York City Charter School Discipline Policies," Advocates for Children of New York, February 2015, https://www.advocates forchildren.org/sites/default/files/library/civil_rights_suspended.pdf?pt=1.

40. "Mike Bloomberg Details NYC's Bold Education Reform Efforts at U.S. Conference of Mayors Winter Meeting," Washington, D.C. NYC.gov, January 20, 2012, https://www1.nyc.gov/office-of-the-mayor/news/028-12/mayor-bloom berg-details-new-york-city-s-bold-education-reform-efforts-u-s-conference -mayors.

41. Author interview with David Weiner, October 13, 2014.

42. Azi Paybarah, "Bloomberg on Randi Weingarten and the New York Education Model," *New York Observer*, November 17, 2008.

43. "Mayor Bloomberg Announces Tentative Agreement with the United Federation of Teachers Nearly One Year Before Expiration of Current Contract," NYC.gov, November 8, 2006, https://www1.nyc.gov/office-of-the-mayor /news/388-06/mayor-bloomberg-tentative-agreement-the-united-federation -teachers-nearly-one#/1.

44. Jennifer A. O'Day, Catherine S. Bitter, and Louis M. Gomez, "Improving Instruction in New York City," in *Education Reform in New York City, Ambitious Change in the Nation's Most Complex School System* (Cambridge, MA: Harvard Education Press, 2011), 121.

45. Stacey Childress and Tonika Cheek Clayton, "Focusing on Results at New York City Department of Education," Public Education Leadership Project at Harvard University June 17, 2008, p. 3, http://pelp.fas.harvard.edu/files/hbs-test /files/pel054p2.pdf.

46. O'Day, Bitter, and Gomez, "Improving Instruction in New York City," 90–91; Stacey Childress, Monica Higgins, Ann Ishimaru, and Sola Takahashi, "Managing for Results at the New York City Department of Education," Digital Access to Scholarship at Harvard, 2011.

47. Childress and Clayton, "Focusing on Results at New York City Department of Education."

48. McNickle, *Bloomberg: A Billionaire's Ambition*, 131.

49. Ibid., Klein, *Lessons of Hope*, p. 47.

50. Ibid.

51. Ibid.

52. Jennifer Medina, "On New York School Tests, Warning Signs Ignored," *New York Times*, October 10, 2010.

53. "Mayor Bloomberg Introduces American Federation of Teachers President Randi Weingarten at National Press Club Breakfast," NYC.gov, November 17, 2008, https://www1.nyc.gov/office-of-the-mayor/news/457-08/mayor-bloom berg-introduces-american-federation-teachers-president-randi-weingarten -national.

54. O'Day, Bitter, and Gomez, Part 1, Chapter 3, Leanna Stiefel and Amy Ellen Schwartz, *Education Reform in New York City*, 55.

55. Author interview with Randi Weingarten, October 10, 2016.

56. "Mayor Bloomberg, Chancellor Klein and UFT President Weingarten An-

nounce Schoolwide Bonus Plan to Reward Teachers at Schools That Raise Student Achievement," press release, NYC.gov, October 17, 2007.

57. Jennifer Li, "What New York City's Experiment with Schoolwide Performance Bonuses Tells Us About Pay for Performance," research brief, Rand Corporation, 2011.

58. Author interview, Michael Bloomberg, August 16, 2018.

59. Sharon Otterman, "New York City Abandons Teacher Bonus Program," *New York Times*, July 17, 2011, fhttp://www.nytimes.com/2011/07/18/education/18rand.html.

60. Mary Ann Giordano and Anna Phillips, "Mayor Hits Nerve in Remarks on Class Sizes and Teachers," *New York Times*, December 2, 2011.

61. Sharon Otterman, "Judge Voids City School Closings," *New York Times*, March 26, 2010.

62. Email to author from Howard Wolfson, December 14, 2018.

63. Ben Chapman, Ben Lesser, and James Fanelli, "More Than a Dozen Teachers Earned Lowest Scores on Controversial Rankings," New York *Daily News*, March 12, 2012, https://www.nydailynews.com/new-york/education/dozen-teachers-earned-lowest-scores-controversial-rankings-article-1.1028113.

64. O'Day, Bitter, and Gomez, "Improving Instruction in New York City," 129.

65. Joseph Viteritti, "Stumbling Through: How Joel Klein Reinvented the New York City Schools," *Journal of School Choice* (v6:n3, 2012): 411–22; author interview with Joseph Viteritti, August 11, 2016.

66. Author interview with Eric Nadelstern, February 10, 2015.

67. Author interview with Joel Klein, November 25, 2014.

68. A.G. Sulzberger, "Democrats Lash Out at Mayor over Control of Public Schools," *New York Times*, July 19, 2009; author interviews with Bloomberg staff, 2017 and 2018, and with Albany politicians, 2009 and 2018.

69. Jennifer Medina, "The Brief Life and Impending Death of a Board of Education," *New York Times*, August 8, 2009; author interviews with Micah Lasher, Bloomberg aide, in Albany, 2014 and 2017.

70. Sharon Otterman and Jennifer Medina, "Klein Resigning as Chancellor of City Schools," *New York Times*, November 10, 2010.

71. Sergio Hernandez, *Village Voice* intern, sued for Cathie Black emails, https://www.villagevoice.com/2011/05/26/michael-bloomberg-sued-by-reporter-over-cathie-black-freedom-of-information-requests/; emails released, seventy-eight pages made widely available by the New York *Daily News*, the *Gotham Gazette*, the *Daily Beast*, https://archive.org/stream/695715-cathie-black-emails/695715-cathie-black-emails_djvu.txt.

72. Author interview with Michael Bloomberg, Klein book party, 2014.

73. Mike Bloomberg's own record on education progress, https://www.mikebloom berg.com/global-impact/education/.

74. Leanne Stiefel, Amy Ellen Schwartz, and Matthew Wiswall, "Does Small High School Reform Lift Urban Districts? Evidence from New York City," SAGE *Journals*, June 25, 2016, https://journals.sagepub.com/doi/abs /10.3102/0013189x15579187.

75. "Small Schools Work in New York," editorial, *New York Times*, October 18, 2014.

76. Al Baker, "With Legacy on His Mind, Mayor Adds More Schools," *New York Times*, April 2, 2013.

77. O'Day, Bitter, and Gomez, *Education Reform in New York City*, 1.

78. McNickle, *Bloomberg: A Billionaire's Ambition*, 132.

79. Sam Roberts, "David Rogers, 88; Took On New York's School Board," obituary, *New York Times*, March 8, 2019.

80. Diane Ravitch, "Breaking News: Mayor-Elect Chooses an Educator to Lead NYC Schools," *Diane Ravitch's Blog*, December 30, 2013.

81. "Michael Bloomberg on Education, Inside the Tweed Courthouse," YouTube, published on October 25, 2007, https://www.youtube.com/watch?v=NSCc QROsOAc.

82. Ibid.

CHAPTER 15: OFF HOURS

1. Michael Bloomberg, *Bloomberg by Bloomberg*, revised and updated, digital (Hoboken, NJ: John Wiley & Sons, 2019), 484–486.

2. Sara Kugler, "NYC Mayor Has His Own Air Crash Experience," Associated Press, October 14, 2006.

3. Bloomberg, *Bloomberg by Bloomberg* (2019), 487–493.

4. Author interview with Michael Bloomberg, August 16, 2018.

5. Allen Salkin, "Homes Sweet Homes," *New York*, April 15, 2002, http://nymag .com/nymetro/news/politics/newyork/features/5890/#print.

6. Author talk with Bloomberg at book party, April 16, 2017.

7. Ibid.

8. Percy Boomer, *On Learning Golf* (1946; New York: Knopf, 2008, digital), 319.

9. "Bloomberg: Illegal Immigrants Help Golfers," UPI, April 1, 2006, https:// www.upi.com/Bloomberg-Illegal-immigrants-help-golfers/85421143938311/.

10. Author interview with John Gambling, radio host, April 18, 2014.

11. Michael Barbaro and David Chen, "For Bloomberg, Golf's a Foe with No Term Limits," *New York Times*, June 17, 2009.

12. Ibid., Author interview with Michael Bloomberg, August 16, 2018.

13. Author interviews on background with Bloomberg golfing partners, 2014 and 2017.

14. Ben Terris, "Does Donald Trump Cheat at Golf?," *Washington Post*, September 4, 2015.

15. Author interviews with golfing partners, background, 2017.

16. Vincent Barone, "LaTourette Park and Golf Course Traffic Light Installed on Richmond Hill Road," SILive, July 1, 2014.

17. Alyssa Melillo, "Club Lobbies for Road Removal," *Southampton Press*, June 16, 2016; author interview with Melillo.

18. Grace Cassidy, "Michael Bloomberg Still wants a Reroute of Tuckahoe Road," *Curbed Hamptons*, May 5, 2017; Grace Cassidy, "Tuckahoe Road Closes for U.S. Open," *Curbed Hamptons*, June 7, 2018, https://hamptons.curbed.com /2018/6/7/17437278/us-open-golf-tuckahoe-road-closure.

CHAPTER 16: BLOOMBERG'S BULLDOG

1. Joseph Goldstein, "Judge Rejects New York's Stop-and-Frisk Policy," *New York Times*, August 12, 2013; *Floyd, et al. v. City of New York, et al.*, Case 1:08-cv-01034-SAS-HBP-Document 373, Filed 8/12/13; Scheindlin ruling, p. 196.

2. Ray Kelly, *Vigilance: My Life Servicing America and Protecting Its Empire City* (New York: Hachette, 2015), 26.

3. Ibid., 175.

4. Chris McNickle, *Bloomberg: A Billionaire's Ambition* (New York: Skyhorse, 2017), 73.

5. Author interviews with Bloomberg aides and advisers, background, 2014.

6. Joseph Goldstein, "Weekly Police Briefing Offers Snapshot of Department and Its Leader," *New York Times*, February 11, 2013.

7. Christopher Dickey, "Al Qaeda Terror Threat to New York City and U.S. Trains Remains High," *Daily Beast*, May 6, 2011, https://www.thedailybeast.com/al -qaeda-terror-threat-to-new-york-city-and-us-trains-remains-high.

8. Author interview with Ray Kelly, April 26, 2016.

9. Kelly, *Vigilance*, 177.

10. McNickle, *Bloomberg: A Billionaire's Ambition*, 78.

11. Al Baker and William K. Rashbaum, "Police Find Car Bomb in Times Square," *New York Times*, May 1, 2010.

12. Kelly, *Vigilance*, 13.

13. Eric Lichtblau, "Trucker Sentenced to 20 Years in Plot Against Brooklyn Bridge," *New York Times*, October 29, 2003.

14. Author interview with Ray Kelly, April 26, 2016.

15. Al Baker and Kate Taylor, "Bloomberg Defends Police's Monitoring of Muslim Students on Web," *New York Times*, February 22, 2012.

16. Jason Horowitz, "Mosque Debate: New Yorkers Take a Dim View of Rabble-Rousing Outsiders," *Washington Post*, August 19, 2010.

17. Bill Hutchinson, "Tea Party Leader Mark Williams Says Muslims Worship a Terrorist 'Monkey God,' Blasts Ground Zero Mosque," New York *Daily News*, May 19, 2010.

18. Michael Barbaro, "Mayor's Stand on Muslim Center has Deep Roots," *New York Times*, August 12, 2010.

19. "Mayor Bloomberg Discusses the Landmarks Preservation Commission Vote on 45-47 Park Place," YouTube, video, published on August 3, 2010, https://www.youtube.com/watch?v=kXm_fUDfJZQ; http://www1.nyc.gov/office-of-the-mayor/news/337-10/mayor-bloomberg-the-landmarks-preservation-commission-vote-45-47-park-place#/0.

20. Barbaro, "Mayors Stance on Muslim Center Has Deep Roots."

21. Author interviews with Jonathan Lemire, Associated Press, March 3, 2016, and 2017; U.S. Constitution, 2nd Amendment.

22. Michael Cooper, "Mayor's Response Breaks with the Past," *New York Times*, April 1, 2002.

23. "NYC Mayor Bloomberg Sworn in for 2nd Term," CrownHeights.info, January 2, 2006, http://crownheights.info/general/1282/nyc-mayor-bloomberg-sworn-in-for-2nd-term/.

24. "Mayor Bloomberg, Boston Mayor Menino and Mayors from Around the United States Stand Up Together in the Fight Against Illegal Guns," NYC.gov, April 25, 2006, https://www1.nyc.gov/office-of-the-mayor/news/129-06/mayor-bloomberg-boston-mayor-menino-mayors-around-united-states-stand-up-together-in#/2.

25. "Mayor Bloomberg Announces the Filing of Federal Lawsuit Against Rogue Gun Dealers," official press release, NYC.gov, May 15, 2006, https://www1.nyc.gov/office-of-the-mayor/news/156-06/mayor-bloomberg-the-filing-federal-lawsuit-against-rogue-gun-dealers.

26. Ibid.

27. Rhonda Cook, "Smyrna Gun Shop Owner Loses Another Round in Legal Fight with New York," *Atlanta Journal-Constitution*, May 5, 2011.

28. Bridget G. Brennan, Special Narcotics Prosecutor, "Over 250 Illegal Guns Sold in Undercover NYPD Investigation: 19 indicted," Office of the Special Narcotics Prosecutor for the City of New York, NYC.gov, August 19, 2013, http://www.nyc.gov/html/snp/downloads/pdf/GUNS.pdf.

29. Barry Paddock, "NYPD Announces 250 Illegal Firearms Seized" New York *Daily News*, August 20, 2013; court citation, http://www.nyc.gov/html/snp/downloads/pdf/WALKER-CAMPBELL-Ind.pdf.

30. Tim Craig, "NYC Defends Running Stings of Va. Gun Sales," *Washington Post*, May 11, 2007.

31. Letter from Michael A. Battle, director of the executive office for United States Attorneys, to John Feinblatt, February 6, 2007. Text made available by NYC Mayor press office. Online at https://www.americanthinker.com/articles/2013/04/michael_bloombergs_gun_stings.html.

32. Kelly, *Vigilance*, 189.

33. Ibid., 190.

34. Jeffrey Toobin, "Rights and Wrongs: A Judge Takes on Stop-and-Frisk," *The New Yorker*, May 27, 2013.

35. Ibid.

36. New York Civil Liberties Union, Annual Stop and Frisk Numbers, https://www.nyclu.org/en/stop-and-frisk-data.

37. McNickle, *Bloomberg: A Billionaire's Ambition*, 88.

38. Ibid.

39. Michael Bloomberg, "Michael Bloomberg: 'Stop and Frisk' Keeps New York Safe," opinion, *Washington Post*, August 18, 2013.

40. Kate Taylor, "Stop and Frisk Policy 'Saves Lives,' Mayor Tells Black Congregation," *New York Times*, June 10, 2012; "Mayor Bloomberg Speaks at First Baptist Church of Brownsville," YouTube video, published on June 22, 2012, https://www.youtube.com/watch?v=Epj_h8rK7NM.

41. "Mayor Bloomberg Speaks at First Baptist Church of Brownsville" video.

42. Karl Herchenroeder tape. It eventually made its way to YouTube: "Bloomberg's Remarks at the Aspen Institute About Minorities and Guns," published on February 16, 2015, https://www.youtube.com/watch?v=5L0Zq0MusGA.

43. *Floyd, et al. v. City of New York, et al.*, Center for Constitutional Rights, https://ccrjustice.org/home/what-we-do/our-cases/floyd-et-al-v-city-new-york-et-al.

44. Ibid., Goldstein, "Judge Rejects New York's Stop-and-Frisk Policy."

45. Ibid., Goldstein, *New York Times* report on ruling (August 12, 2013): p. 113 (116 in Scheindlin ruling).

46. Scheindlin ruling, 196.

47. Goldstein, "Judge Rejects New York's Stop-and-Frisk Policy."

48. Author interview with Ray Kelly.

49. Joseph Goldstein, "Court Blocks Stop and Frisk Changes for New York Police," *New York Times*, October 31, 2013.

50. Kelly, *Vigilance*, 294.

51. Colin Moynihan, "New York Is Said to Settle Suits over Arrests at 2004 Convention," *New York Times*, December 23, 2013.

52. McNickle, *Bloomberg: A Billionaire's Ambition*, 90.

53. "Trouble with Marijuana Arrests," editorial, *New York Times*, September 27, 2011.

54. Michael Bloomberg: "'Stop and Frisk' Keeps New York Safe," *Washington Post*, August 18, 2013.

CHAPTER 17: THE FORGOTTEN ISLAND

1. Mariya Moseley, "Rikers Island was Named After a Judge Who was Eager to Uphold Slavery," *Essence*, April 6, 2017.

2. CPI, Inflation Calculator, amount = $180,000, http://www.in2013dollars.com/1884-dollars-in-2019.

3. Matilda Jaxon, "The History of Rikers Island," ClassNewYorkHistory.com, April 10, 2017.

4. Michael Bloomberg, Aspen Institute talk, Karl Herchenroeder tap, February 5, 2015. It eventually made its way to YouTube: "Bloomberg's Remarks at the Aspen Institute About Minorities and Guns," published on February 16, 2015, https://www.youtube.com/watch?v=5L0Zq0MusGA.

5. "Mayor Bloomberg Announces New York City's Incarceration Rate Hits New All-Time Low," press release, NYC.gov, December 26, 2013, https://www1.nyc.gov/office-of-the-mayor/news/434-13/mayor-bloomberg-new-york-city-s-incarceration-rate-hits-new-all-time-low/#/0.

6. Chris McNickle, *Bloomberg: A Billionaire's Ambition* (New York: Skyhorse, 2017), 278.

7. Diane Cardwell, "Commissioner of Probation Will Run Jails," *New York Times*, December 27, 2002.

8. Jake Pearson, "Widespread Problems on Rikers Island Tough to Fix," AP, December 28, 2014, https://www.apnews.com/1d49c8ea13ac4a57bdb1a75e1ba3e827.

9. Author interview with Martin Horn, February 14, 2017.

10. Frank Straub and Paul E. O'Connell, "Why the Jails Didn't Explode," *City Journal*, Spring 1999, https://www.city-journal.org/html/why-jails-didn%E2%80%99t-explode-11794.html.

11. Ibid., McNickle, *Bloomberg*.

12. Ibid., Author interview with Martin Horn.

13. Michael Schwirtz and Michael Winerip, "Violence by Rikers Guards Grew Under Bloomberg," *New York Times*, August 13, 2014.

14. Ibid.

15. Sarah Zielinski, "Migratory Canada Geese Brought Down Flight 1549," Smithsonian.com, June 8, 2009, http://www.smithsonianmag.com/science-na ture/migratory-canada-geese-brought-down-flight-1549-12575190/.

16. Ibid., Author interview with Martin Horn.

17. Azi Paybarah, "Norman Seabrook Backs Thompson, Regrets the Errors," *New York Observer*, October 13, 2009.

18. Ibid., McNickle, *Bloomberg: A Billionaire's Ambition*, 280.

19. Ibid., Author interview with Martin Horn.

20. Ibid., McNickle, *Bloomberg: A Billionaire's Ambition*, 281.

21. Ibid.

22. Associated Press, "City Pays $2 Million in Case of Inmate Killed at Rikers," *New York Times*, June 8, 2012.

23. Ibid., Schwirtz and Winerip, "Violence by Rikers Guards Grew Under Bloomberg."

24. Chai Park, The City of New York Board of Correction, "Violence in New York City Jails: Slashing and Stabbing Incidents," 2011–2014, NYC.gov, http://www1.nyc.gov/assets/boc/downloads/pdf/Violence%20in%20New%20 York%20City%20Jails_Slashing%20and%20Stabbing%20Incidents.pdf.

25. "Manhattan U.S. Attorney Finds Pattern and Practice of Excessive Force and Violence at NYC Jails on Rikers Island That Violates the Constitutional Rights of Adolescent Male Inmates," U.S. Attorney's Office, Southern District of New York, Department of Justice, August 4, 2014; https://www.justice.gov/usao-sd ny/pr/manhattan-us-attorney-finds-pattern-and-practice-excessive-force-and -violence-nyc-jails.

26. Ibid.

27. Jennifer Gonnerman, "Before the Law," *The New Yorker*, October 6, 2014, https://www.newyorker.com/magazine/2014/10/06/before-the-law.

28. Ibid.

29. Vivian Wang, "7 Takeaways from New York's $175 Billion Budget," *New York Times*, March 31, 2019.

30. Russ Buettner, "Bus Stoppage Said to Target Rikers Inmate," *New York Times*, November 20, 2013.

31. McNickle, *Bloomberg: A Billionaire's Ambition*, 283.

32. Ibid.

33. Zoe Greenberg, "Norman Seabrook Guilty in Bribery Trial That Cast Shadow over de Blasio," *New York Times*, August 15, 2009; Benjamin Weiser and Zoe Greenberg, "Norman Seabrook Was Once a Union Power Broker in New York. Now He Is Going to Prison," *New York Times*, February 8, 2019.

34. Edward Porter, "Wall St. Money Meets Social Policy at Rikers Island," *New York Times*, July 28, 2015.

35. "Impact Evaluation of the Adolescent Behavioral Learning Experience (ABLE) Program," Vera Institute of Justice, September 2016.

36. Linda Gibbs, former deputy mayor for health and human services for Mayor Bloomberg, speaking at Fordham University for series, "The Bloomberg Years."

37. Jeff Coltin, "De Blasio Sets 10-Year Timeline to Close Rikers Island," *City & State New York*, March 31, 2017.

CHAPTER 18: THE CITY GROWS UP AND UP

1. NYC Government Office of the Mayor release, September 30, 2007. "Mayor Bloomberg Delivers Remarks at 2007 Conservative Party Conference in Great Britain."

2. Author interviews with Ester Fuchs, others on background, May 2017.

3. British Conservative Party Conference in Blackpool, England, September 30, 2007, https://www.c-span.org/video/?201279-1/british-conservative-party-conference.

4. Sydney Sarachan, "The Legacy of Robert Moses," PBS, January 17, 2013, http://www.pbs.org/wnet/need-to-know/environment/the-legacy-of-robert-moses/16018/.

5. Daniel Doctoroff, "Making Omelets Without Breaking Eggs: Getting Things Done in the Post-Moses Age," speech, Museum of the City of New York, February 1, 2007.

6. Eric Jaffe, "7 Fun Facts About the New York Subway's New 7 Train Extension," CityLab, September 11, 2015, https://www.citylab.com/transportation/2015/09/7-fun-facts-about-the-new-york-subways-new-7-train-extension/404800/.

7. "Mayor Bloomberg Announces Completion and Activation of Manhattan Portion of City's Third Water Tunnel," press release, NYC.gov, October 16, 2013, http://www1.nyc.gov/office-of-the-mayor/news/334-13/mayor-bloomberg-completion-activation-manhattan-portion-city-s-third-water/#/0l;

"Mayor Bloomberg Turns on Water in Manhattan Portion of Water Tunnel No. 3," YouTube video, October 16, 2013, https://www.youtube.com/watch?v=QyYdXQxB34w.

8. New York City Municipal Archives, Peter Madonia, 22677, box 2 of 2, DEP, Shaft of 33B City Water Tunnel, letter to John Whitehead.

9. Charles V. Bagli, "As Stadiums Rise, So Do Costs to Taxpayers," *New York Times*, November 4, 2008, http://www.nytimes.com/2008/11/05/nyregion/05stadiums.html.

10. Edward Wyatt, "Stock Exchange Abandons Plans for a New Headquarters Building Across the Street," *New York Times*, August 2, 2002.

11. Bagli, "As Stadiums Rise, So Do Costs to Taxpayers."

12. Michael Kimmelman, "An Arena as Tough as Brooklyn, but Street Smart?" *New York Times*, October 31, 2012.

13. Rich Calder, "Your 'Net' Loss," *New York Post*, April 14, 2008.

14. "Mayor Bloomberg Delivers 2013 State Of The City Address," press release, NYC.gov, February 14, 2013, https://www1.nyc.gov/office-of-the-mayor/news/063-13/mayor-bloomberg-delivers-2013-state-the-city-address.

15. Chris McNickle, *Bloomberg: A Billionaire's Ambition* (New York: Skyhorse, 2017), 151–152.

16. Julie Satow, "Amanda Burden Wants to Remake New York; She has 19 Months Left," *New York Times*, May 18, 2012.

17. Mitchell Moss, "How NYC Won the Olympics," Rudin Center, Robert Wagner Graduate School of Public Service, NYU, November 2011.

18. Ibid.

19. Author interviews with Bloomberg staff, 2005 and 2014.

20. Charles V. Bagli and Michael Cooper, "Olympic Bid Hurt as New York Fails in West Side Stadium Quest," *New York Times*, June 7, 2005.

21. Sam Roberts, "Is New York 'Greater than Ever'? Yes, a Former Official Argues," book review, *New York Times*, May 10, 2017.

22. Moss, "How NYC Won the Olympics."

23. Joel Rose, "New York Skyline Sees Boom in Super Tall Skyscrapers," NPR, December 12, 2016.

24. James B. Stewart, "Plan to Tax the Rich Could Aim Higher," *New York Times*, October 26, 2013.

25. Chris Smith, "In Conversation: Michael Bloomberg," *New York*, September 7, 2013.

26. "What Are Air Rights?," description by the Curtis Group, Air Rights New York, 2018, http://www.airrightsny.com/.

27. Jason M. Barr, *Building the Skyline: The Birth and Growth of Manhattan's Skyscrapers* (New York: Oxford University Press, 2016), 683.
28. "Accidental Skyline: A Blueprint for a More Intentioanl City, 2013–Present," Municipal Art Society of New York, https://www.mas.org/initiatives/accidental-skyline/.
29. Michael Kimmelman, "Seeing a Need for Oversight of New York's Lordly Towers," *New York Times*, December 23, 2013, https://www.nytimes.com/2013/12/23/arts/design/seeing-a-need-for-oversight-of-new-yorks-lordly-towers.html.
30. Julie Creswell, "Stratospheric Views and Prices," *New York Times*, November 4, 2013, https://www.nytimes.com/2013/11/04/business/stratospheric-views-and-prices.html.
31. Zoe Rosenberg, "A $225 Trash Can Inspired NYC's Tallest Residential Tower," Curbed, June 1, 2015.
32. "NYC's Supertall Skyscraper Boom, Mapped," Curbed, updated January 28, 2019, https://ny.curbed.com/maps/new-york-skyscraper-construction-supertalls.
33. Paul Goldberger, "Too Rich, Too Thin, Too Tall," *Vanity Fair*, May 2014, https://www.vanityfair.com/culture/2014/05/condo-towers-architecture-new-york-city.
34. Daniel L. Doctoroff, *Greater Than Ever: New York's Big Comeback* (New York: PublicAffairs, 2017), 107. (At first, Pataki gave John Whitehead, a well-known businessman and friend of Bloomberg, what appeared to be the top job. Then, when it counted, he made sure that his own people were actually in charge. That turned out to be a big mistake.)
35. Ibid.
36. WTC Integrates Innovative Technologies, Event at Center for Architecture, November 17, 2010, Charles V. Bagli, moderator, https://www.centerforarchitecture.org/news/wtc-integrates-innovative-technologies/.
37. Author interviews with Bloomberg officials on background, December 2002.
38. Andrea Bernstein, "Bloomberg's Plan for Lower Manhattan," WNYC, December 13, 2002, https://www.wnyc.org/story/85495-bloombergs-plan-for-lower-manhattan/.
39. Paul Goldberger, *Up From Zero: Politics, Architecture, and the Rebuilding of New York* (New York: Random House, 2004), 134–135.
40. Jennifer Steinhauer, "Mayor's Proposal Envisions Lower Manhattan as an Urban Hamlet," *New York Times*, December 13, 2002.
41. J. Jennings Moss, "15 Ways Lower Manhattan Has Changed Since 9/11," *New York Business Journal*, September 7, 2016.

42. Doctoroff, *Greater Than Ever*, 292.

43. Ibid., 293–295.

44. Lynne Sagalyn, *Power at Ground Zero: Politics, Money and the Remaking of Lower Manhattan* (New York: Oxford University Press, 2016), ix.

45. Charles V. Bagli, "Bloomberg Gives September 11 Museum a $15 Million Loan," *New York Times*, May 2, 2013, https://cityroom.blogs.nytimes .com/2013/05/02/bloomberg-gives-sept-11-museum-a-15-million-loan/.

46. Author interview with official at the Port Authority of New York and New Jersey on background, 2014.

47. Michael Arad bio, Handel Architects, https://handelarchitects.com/firm/leader ship/michael-arad.

48. Author interview with Chris Ward, 2018.

49. McNickle, *Bloomberg: A Billionaire's Ambition*, 296.

CHAPTER 19: TAKING THE HIGH LINE

1. Tom Hynes, "Looking Back at the History of the High Line in NYC, New Video from Blueprint," Architecture New York, Untapped Cities, April 1, 2015, https://untappedcities.com/2015/04/01/looking-back-at-the-history-of-the -high-line-in-nyc-blueprint/.

2. Author interview with Dan Doctoroff, 2015.

3. Ibid.

4. New York City Municipal Archives, 22665, box 6 of 11, Deputy Mayor Doctoroff, Economic Development & Rebuilding. Memo from Doctoroff to John Cahill.

5. Author interview with Dan Doctoroff.

6. Flyers from merchants around High Line, 2002.

7. New York City Municipal Archives, 22665, box 1 of 2, 2002, Deputy Mayor Dan Doctoroff. Letter from Randy M. Mastro hand-delivered to Doctoroff, February 15, 2002.

8. Kelly Crow, "Neighborhood Report: Chelsea, Fight Heats Up Again over Grassy Bed of Rails," *New York Times*, January 27, 2002.

9. Joshua David and Karen Hock, "Reclaiming the High Line," Design-Trust for Public Space, February 2002, http://designtrust.org/publications /reclaiming-high-line/.

10. "Reclaiming the High Line," Design Trust for Public Space, with Friends of the High Line, 2002, http://www.solaripedia.com/files/1048.pdf.

11. Joshua David and Robert Hammond, *High Line: The Inside Story of New York City's Park in the Sky* (New York: Farrar Straus & Giroux, 2011), 38.

12. Author interviews with Amanda Burden, 2013 and 2015, Vishaan Chakharbarti, 2015 and 2018, and city officials on background, 2015.

13. New York City Municipal Archives, City Planning File on High Line 22665, box 1 of 1, Dan Doctoroff. Burden memo to Doctoroff on zoning change for High Line area, November 12, 2002.

14. Lisa Foderaro, "$20 Million Gift to High Line Park," *New York Times*, October 27, 2011.

15. "First Section of High Line Park Opens to the Public," Daily Plant, NYC Parks, June 11, 2009, https://www.nycgovparks.org/parks/the-high-line/daily plant/21962.

16. Robin Pogrebin, "Renovated High Line Now Open for Strolling," *New York Times*, June 8, 2009.

17. Lachlan Cartwright, "Highline Hotel Encourages Nude Clientele," *New York Post*, August 26, 2009.

18. J. David Goodman, "Mayor Visits the High Line and Becomes One in Seven Million, Finally," *New York Times*, September 26, 2017.

19. Mariela Quintana, "Changing Grid: Exploring the Impact of the High Line," StreetEasy, August 8, 2016, https://streeteasy.com/blog/changing-grid-high -line/.

20. Kate Ascher and Sabina Uffer, "The High Line Effect," Council on Tall Buildings and Urban Habitat, research document and conference report, 2015, http:// global.ctbuh.org/resources/papers/download/2463-the-high-line-effect.pdf.

21. Daniel Geiger, "Gottesman's Death Leaves Edison Properties Without a Clear Successor," *Crain's New York Business*, September 11, 2017; Edison Properties, the Real Deal, New York, https://therealdeal.com/new-research/topics /company/edison-properties/.

22. British Conservative Party Conference in Blackpool, September 30, 2007, https://www.c-span.org/video/?201279-1/british-conservative-party-confer ence[c-span.org].

CHAPTER 20: FROM LOW POINT TO LANDSLIDE—2005

1. James Bennet, "New York's Mayor on Everything from Campaign Money to Circumcision," *The Atlantic*, October 24, 2012.

2. Haley Drazin, "New York to Pay $17.9 million to 2004 Republican Convention Protestors," CNN, January 16, 2014.

3. Josh Barbanel, "Big Tax Increases, Small Tax Rebates," *New York Times*, September 18, 2005.

4. Author interview with Bill Cunningham, 2015 and 2018.

5. Patrick D. Healy, "If He Has to Lose, Ferrer Wants to Lose with Dignity," *New York Times*, November 7, 2005.

6. Author interview with Senator Charles Schumer, October 20, 2016.

7. Jim Rutenberg, "G.O.P. Rival in Mayor's Race Says Petition Is in Jeopardy," *New York Times*, July 26, 2005. (Ognibene eventually moved onto another line—as the Conservative Party candidate—where he got 14,630 votes.)

8. "Mayor Michael R. Bloomberg and District Council 37 Announce Tentative Labor Agreement," press release, NYC.org, April 20, 2004, https://www1.nyc .gov/office-of-the-mayor/news/090-04/mayor-michael-bloomberg-district -council-37-tentative-labor-agreement.

9. Ibid.

10. Wayne Barrett, "Billionaire Buys Union," *Village Voice*, August 9, 2005.

11. Michael Barbaro, "Bloomberg Spent $102 Million to Win His Third Term," *New York Times*, November 27, 2009; "Bloomberg's Increasing Annual Wealth: 1996 to 2013, Plus Updates on His Annual 'Charitable' Giving," Noticing New York, March 6, 2013, http://noticingnewyork.blogspot.com/2013/03/bloom bergs-increasing-annual-wealth.html.

12. "Blue Whale Model," American Museum of Natural History, https://www .amnh.org/exhibitions/permanent-exhibitions/irma-and-paul-milstein-family -hall-of-ocean-life/blue-whale-model.

13. Mayor Bloomberg Presents: PlaNYC: A Greener, Greater, New York, NYC documents, April 22, 2007.

CHAPTER 21: A CITY ON THE MOVE

1. Janny Scott and William K. Rashbaum, "The Ferry Crash Overview," *New York Times*, October 16, 2003; Michele McPhee and Corky Siemaszko, "Staten Island Ferry Crashes into a Concrete Pier at the St. George Ferry Terminal, Killing 10 in 2003," New York *Daily News*, October 14, 2015.

2. Author interview with Iris Weinshall, June 3, 2015.

3. William K. Rashbaum and Sewell Chan, "Pilot and Supervisor Sentenced in '03 Staten Island Ferry Crash," *New York Times*, January 10, 2006.

4. Ibid.

5. "Statement by Mayor Michael R. Bloomberg on the Resignation of Dot Commissioner Iris Weinshall," NYC.gov, January 29, 2007, https://www1.nyc.gov /office-of-the-mayor/news/030-07/statement-mayor-michael-bloomberg-the -resignation-dot-commissioner-iris-weinshall.

6. Author interviews with Iris Weinshall, 2015 and 2018.

7. Jed Lipinski, "Leaving Footprints on the City," *New York Times*, March 23, 2012.

8. "Infrastructure: Sidewalk Maintenance and Repair," New York City Department of Transportation, NYC.gov, https://www1.nyc.gov/html/dot/html/infrastructure/sidewalkintro.shtml.

9. "Infrastructure: Street Lights," New York City Department of Transportation, NYC.gov, https://www1.nyc.gov/html/dot/html/infrastructure/streetlights.shtml.

10. Raven Rakia, "There are too Many Trucks Coming into New York City," Grist, October 12, 2015.

11. NYC Pedestrian Fatalities, NYC records, NYCDOT-NYPD, https://www1.nyc.gov/html/dot/html/pedestrians/pedsafetyreport.shtml.

12. Janette Sadik-Khan and Seth Solomonow, *Street Fight: Handbook for an Urban Revolution* (New York: Viking, 2014), xiv; "The Mobility Factbook," NYU Rudin Center for Transportation, http://nycmobility.org/.

13. PlaNYC—A Greener, Greater New York, the City of New York, Mayor Michael R. Bloomberg, April 2007, p. 7, https://www1.nyc.gov/office-of-the-mayor/news/119-07/mayor-bloomberg-presents-planyc-a-greener-greater-new-york#/3.

14. Author interview with Mitchell Moss, Rudin Center, 2016.

15. Author interviews with Bloomberg advisers on background, 2002 and 2014.

16. Joshua Robin, "Rating Bloomberg on Transit Work," *Newsday*, March 6, 2005.

17. Sadik-Khan and Solomonow, *Street Fight*.

18. Ibid., xii, xiii.

19. "London Congestion Charge: Why It's Time to Reconsider One of the City's Great Successes," Transport for London Data, The Conversation, March 2, 2018.

20. Sadik-Khan and Solomonow, *Street Fight*, xiii.

21. Bloomberg administration report, "PlaNYC—A Greener, Greater New York," April 22, 2007, 72–97.

22. Ibid., 6.

23. Winnie Hu, "More New Yorkers Opting for Life in the Bike Lane," *New York Times*, July 30, 2017.

24. Sadik-Khan and Solomonow, *Streetfight*, 93.

25. Joe Lindsey, "This Woman Built 400 Miles of Bike Lanes in New York City," Bicycling.com, December 31, 2015.

26. Natalie O'Neill, "The Prospect Park Bike Lane Had Our Presses Rolling All Year Long," *Brooklyn Paper*, December 30, 2011; Sadik-Khan and Solomonow, *Streetfight*, 8.

27. Sadik-Khan and Solomonow, *Streetfight*, 8.

28. Ibid., 180.
29. Matt Flegenheimer, "Citibank Pays to Put Its Name on Shared Bikes," *New York Times*, May 8, 2012.
30. Matt Flegenheimer, "Questions and Answers on Citi Bike," *New York Times*, May 26, 2013.
31. "About Citi Bike," CityBikeNYC.com, https://www.citibikenyc.com/about.
32. Author interview with Bloomberg adviser, 2016.
33. Brian M. Rosenthal, "Taxi Drivers Fell Prey While Top Officials Counted the Money, *New York Times*, May 20, 2019.
34. Emily Smith, "Mike Unleashes a 'Hail' Storm," *New York Post*, May 22, 2013.
35. James Barron, "Where Yellow Cabs Didn't Go, Green Cabs Were Supposed to Thrive. Then Came Uber," *New York Times*, September 3, 2018.
36. Sewell Chan, "U.S. Offers New York $354 Million for Congestion Pricing," *City Room* blog, *New York Times*, August 14, 2007, https://cityroom.blogs.nytimes.com/2007/08/14/us-will-give-new-york-354-million-for-congestion-pricing/.
37. Author interview with New York State Senator Liz Krueger, July 27, 2016.
38. Author interview with State Senator Liz Krueger, 2018.
39. Nicholas Confessore, "Congestion Pricing Plan Dies in Albany," *New York Times*, April 7, 2008.
40. Chan, "U.S. Offers New York $354 Million for Congestion Pricing"; "New York City's Congestion Pricing Experience and Implications for Road Pricing Acceptance in the United States," NYC.gov, published in *Transport Policy*, August 2010, http://www.nyc.gov/html/dot/downloads/pdf/schaller_paper_2010trb.pdf.
41. Winnie Hu, "Confused About Congestion Pricing? Here's What We Know," *New York Times*, April 24, 2019.

CHAPTER 22: SILICON ISLAND

1. Email to author from Kevin Sheekey, October 11, 2017.
2. Nick K. Lioudis, "The Collapse of Lehman Brothers: A Case Study," Investopedia, updated December 11, 2017, https://www.investopedia.com/articles/economics/09/lehman-brothers-collapse.asp.
3. Ben White and Michael Grynbaum, "Life After Lehman Brothers," *New York Times*, September 15, 2008.
4. "New York City Employment Trends," Office of the New York State Comptroller, https://osc.state.ny.us/osdc/rpt10-2018.pdf.
5. Author interview with Seth Pinsky, September 26, 2017.
6. Author interviews with staff and Pinsky, 2014 and 2017.

7. Ibid.

8. Shira Ovide, "Ex-Wachovia Boss Bob Steel Still Drawing Fire," *Wall Street Journal*, September 21, 2011,

9. NYC official mayoral announcement, proposal for new university, December 16, 2010. https://www.nycedc.com/press-release/mayor-bloomberg-announces-initiative-develop-new-engineering-and-applied-sciences; letter sent, January 2011, http://www.nyc.gov/html/om/pdf/appliedscience_letter.pdf.

10. "Mayor Bloomberg Announces City Received 18 Submissions from 27 Academic Institutions for New Applied Sciences Campus," NYC. gov, March 17, 2011, http://www1.nyc.gov/office-of-the-mayor/news/088-11/mayor-bloomberg-city-received-18-submissions-27-academic-institutions-new.

11. Javier C. Hernandez, "Bloomberg's Big Push for an Applied Sciences School," *New York Times*, April 26, 2011.

12. Nicholas Parco, "Roosevelt Island's Rich Frightening History," New York *Daily News*, October 30, 2015, https://www.nydailynews.com/new-york/roosevelt-island-rich-frightening-history-article-1.2418027.

13. Tim Carmody, "How Cornell Beat Stanford (And Everybody Else) for NYC Tech Campus," *Wired*, December 28, 2011, https://www.wired.com/2011/12/how-cornell-beat-everybody-nyc/.

14. Richard Perez-Pena, "Stanford Ends Effort to Build New York Arm," *New York Times*, December 16, 2011.

15. Author interview with Bloomberg adviser on background, 2017.

16. "Mayor Bloomberg, Cornell President Skorton and Technion President Lavie Officially Transfer 12 Acres of Roosevelt Island to Cornell Tech," NYC.gov, December 9, 2013, https://www1.nyc.gov/office-of-the-mayor/news/420-13/mayor-bloomberg-cornell-president-skorton-technion-president-lavie-officially-transfer-12/#/0.

17. Richard Perez-Pena, "Cornell Alumnus Is Behind $350 Million Gift to Build Science School in City," *New York Times*, December 19, 2011, https://www.nytimes.com/2011/12/20/nyregion/cornell-and-technion-israel-chosen-to-build-science-school-in-new-york-city.html.

18. Ibid.

19. NYC press release, December 19, 2011; "Mayor Bloomberg, Cornell President Skorton and Technion President Lavie announce Historic Parnership to Build a New Applied Sciences Campus on Roosevelt Island," https://www1.nyc.gov/office-of-the-mayor/news/420-13/mayor-bloomberg-cornell-president-skorton-technion-president-lavie-officially-transfer-12/#/0; "The Inside Story of Cornell-Tech Campus Win," Crain's, December 18, 2011, https://

www.crainsnewyork.com/article/20111219/EDUCATION/111219897/the
-inside-story-of-cornell-s-tech-campus-win.

20. Author covered September 2017 event; Cuomo administration provided tran-
     script of his remarks.

21. Hamza Shaban, "Google Announced $1 Billion Expansion in New York City,"
     Washington Post, November 17, 2018.

CHAPTER 23: AS FOR THE OTHER HALF

1. "Mayor Bloomberg Receives Award for Anti-Poverty Efforts from Children's
    Aid Society, Releases New Data Showing Every Major US City Saw Increase
    in Poverty Rate—Except for New York City—since 2000, NYC press release,
    NYC.gov, November 14, 2013, https://www1.nyc.gov/office-of-the-mayor
    /news/367-13/mayor-bloomberg-receives-award-anti-poverty-efforts-chil
    dren-s-aid-society-releases-new/#/0.

2. Author interviews with former Bloomberg city official on background, 2017.

3. Leslie Kaufman, "Mayor Seeks 10 Year Plan to Address Homelessness," *New
    York Times*, November 22, 2003.

4. "Mayor Michael R. Bloomberg Delivers 2006 State of the City Address 'a
    Blueprint for New York City's Future,'" NYC.gov, January 26, 2006, http://
    www1.nyc.gov/office-of-the-mayor/news/030-06/mayor-michael-bloomberg
    -delivers-2006-state-the-city-address-a-blueprint-new-york-city-s.

5. "Amidst Unprecedented Homelessness—a New Focus on Housing Can Turn
    the Tide," Coalition for the Homeless, March 12, 2014, http://www.coalition
    forthehomeless.org/state-of-the-homeless-2014/.

6. Jessica Dailey, "10 Surprising Facts About NYCHA, New York's 'Shadow
    City,'" Curbed New York, September 10, 2012, https://ny.curbed.com/2012
    /9/10/10330984/10-surprising-facts-about-nycha-new-yorks-shadow-city.

7. Chris McNickle, *Bloomberg: A Billionaire's Ambition* (New York: Skyhorse,
    2017), 208.

8. "Mayor Bloomberg Announces New York City on Pace to Reach 4 Million Total
    Jobs by End of Year—the First Time in the City's History, Doublecheck NYC
    press release, NYC.gov, December 19, 2013, https://www1.nyc.gov/office-of-the
    -mayor/news/422-13/mayor-bloomberg-new-york-city-pace-reach-4-million
    -total-jobs-end-the-year—/#/0. Bloomberg website on poverty and jobs.

9. Thomas J. Main, *Homelessness in New York City: Policymaking from Koch to de
    Blasio* (New York: NYU Press, 2016), 160–166; hiring of Homeless Commis-
    sioner Robert Hess, April 14, 2006, https://www1.nyc.gov/office-of-the-mayor

/news/111-06/mayor-bloomberg-appoints-robert-hess-commissioner-the
-department-homeless-services-and#/0.

10. Kay S. Hymowitz, "Saving Welfare Reform," *City Journal* special issue, 2013.

11. Kate Taylor, "Bloomberg Lured Donors for New York Programs," *New York Times*, November 20, 2013.

12. "Mayor Michael R. Bloomberg Announces Citywide Campaign to End Chronic Homelessness," NYC.gov, June 23, 2004, https://www1.nyc.gov /office-of-the-mayor/news/157-04/mayor-michael-bloomberg-citywide-cam paign-end-chronic-homelessness#/0.

13. "CEO Poverty Measure, 2005–2014," annual report, Mayor's Office of Operations, the City of New York, NYC. gov, April 2016, https://www1.nyc.gov/as sets/opportunity/pdf/16_poverty_measure_report.pdf.

14. Maria Newman, "Bloomberg Unveils Plan to Reduce Homelessness, *New York Times*, July 17, 2006.

15. Dana Rubenstein, "Living Wage Reminds Bloomberg of Soviet Union," Politico, May 13, 2012.

16. Sam Roberts, "City's Sheltering of Out of Town Homeless, and Mayor's Remark, Stir Debate," *New York Times*, March 18, 2013.

17. Author interview with Philip Mangano, March 16, 2017.

18. Jennifer Steinhauer, "Mayor's Style Is Tested in Sending Homeless to Old Jail," *New York Times*, August 16, 2002.

19. New York City Municipal Archives, Emma Bloomberg, 22683, box 1 of 2, confirmed in interviews with former Bloomberg officials, 2017.

20. Ibid.

21. Diane Jeantet, "As Homeless Numbers Rose, Clashes Over Policies," City Limits, March 11, 2013.

22. Julie Bosman and Michael Barbaro, "Mayor Defends One-Way Tickets for Homeless," *New York Times*, July 29, 2009; Julie Bosman, "City Aids Homeless with One-Way Tickets Home," *New York Times*, July 28, 2009.

23. Project Reconnect Homeless Assistance, NYC.gov, https://www1.nyc.gov/nyc -resources/service/3601/project-reconnect-homeless-assistance.

24. Ian Frazier, "Hidden City," *The New Yorker*, October 28, 2013, http://www .newyorker.com/magazine/2013/10/28.

25. Article 17 of the NYS constitution reads, "The aid, care and support of the needy are public concerns and shall be provided by the state and such of its subdivision (i.e., the city), and in such manner and by such means, as the legislature may from time to time determine."

26. Suzanne Daley, "Robert Hayes: Anatomy of a Crusader," *New York Times*, October 2, 1987.

27. Robin Herman, "Pact Requires City to Shelter Homeless Men," *New York Times*, August 27, 1981, http://www.nytimes.com/1981/08/27/nyregion/pact-requires-city-to-shelter-homeless-men.html.

28. "Mayor Michael R. Bloomberg Applauds Independent Panel's Recommendation to End Court Oversight of Family Shelter System," NYC.gov, February 15, 2005, https://www1.nyc.gov/office-of-the-mayor/news/063-05/mayor-michael-bloomberg-applauds-independent-panel-s-recommendation-end-court-oversight-of.

29. NYC Center for Economic Opportunity, Annual Report, 2012–2013, p. 18, https://www1.nyc.gov/assets/opportunity/pdf/ceo_annual_report_2012-2013_web.pdf.

30. Michael Bloomberg letter, Center for Economic Opportunity Annual Report, 2012–13, p. 4.

31. "Mexico's *Oportunidades* Program, Shanghai Poverty Conference: Case Study Summary, World Bank, http://web.worldbank.org/archive/website00819C/WEB/PDF/CASE_-62.PDF.

32. "Mayor Bloomberg and Delegation Visit Mexico's *Oportunidades* Program," NYC.gov, April 24, 2007, http://www1.nyc.gov/office-of-the-mayor/news/123-07/mayor-bloomberg-delegation-visit-mexico-s-i-oportunidades-i-program#/1.

33. Julie Bosman, "City Will Stop Paying the Poor for Good Behavior," *New York Times*, March 31, 2010.

34. Ibid.

35. Center for Economic Opportunity, Annual Report, 2012–2013.

36. NYC Young Men's Initiative, Annual Report, 2013, p. 4, NYC.gov, https://www1.nyc.gov/assets/opportunity/pdf/ceo_annual_report_2012-2013_web.pdf.

37. "Mayor Bloomberg Receives Award for Anti-Poverty Efforts from Children's Aid Society, Releases New Data Showing Every Major US City Saw Increase in Poverty Rate—Except for New York City—Since 2000," NYC.gov, November 14, 2013, http://www1.nyc.gov/office-of-the-mayor/news/367-13/mayor-bloomberg-receives-award-anti-poverty-efforts-children-s-aid-society-releases-new/#/0.

38. Michael Barbaro and Fernanda Santos, "Bloomberg to Use Own Funds in Plan to Aid Minority Youth," *New York Times*, August 3, 2011.

39. Tina Moore, "200 Families on Brink of Homelessness Treated Like Rats in Lab Experiment," New York *Daily News*, September 10, 2010.

40. "Mayor Bloomberg Defends 'Inhumane' Study on Homeless," *Huffington Post*, September 30, 2010, https://www.huffpost.com/entry/new-york-study -leaves-200_n_745457?guccounter=1&guce_referrer=aHR0cHM6Ly93d3cu YmluZy5jb20v&guce_referrer_sig=AQAAAJpLvg0RAGjea91Fhg7UhjbDC d9KLXLIDBNwgH-uU82Wwb9MSMNxb62CLpMKlZcFFwUHezpQNd DrYUqFrhqGPzpkefh_mOF2nQykEI8hMrHRgzUnzhGvazYxcTAbbmaNb ZmXX5_Py_CdCspk4ycJCZUL4XZEjMrcLm4TzZrGAnte; Main, *Homelessness in New York City*, 172, on HomeBase program.

41. Bloomberg speech, progress report on homelessness in NYC to National Alliance to End Homelessness, July 17, 2018.

42. Main, *Homelessness in New York City*, 155.

43. Leslie Kaufman, "Homeless Families Blocked from Seeking U.S. Housing Aid," *New York Times*, October 20, 2004.

44. Mosi Secret, "Clocks Tick for a Key Homeless Program," *New York Times*, May 31, 2011.

45. Leslie Kaufman, "City Vows to Improve Aid to Homeless Families," *New York Times*, March 19, 2007.

46. Main, *Homelessness in New York City*, 179.

47. Email to author, Bloomberg press office, February 6, 2012.

48. Coalition for the Homeless, "NYC Homeless Shelter Population Report," worksheet, May 2019, pp. 8–12, https://www.coalitionforthehomeless.org/ wp-content/uploads/2019/05/NYCHomelessShelterPopulation-Worksheet _1983-Present_Mar2019.pdf: p.8-12.

49. "Facts About Homelessness," Coalition for the Homeless, January 2019, https://www.coalitionforthehomeless.org/the-catastrophe-of-homelessness /facts-about-homelessness/.

50. New York City Government Poverty Measure 2005–2016, NYC Opportunity, NYC.gov.

51. "Mayor Bloomberg Receives Award for Anti-Poverty Efforts from Children's Aid Society," November 2013.

52. Ibid.

53. Ibid.

CHAPTER 24: OVERTIME

1. Fran Liebowitz, "Voices," *New York Times*, August 18, 2013.

2. Editorial, "For Mayor of New York City," *New York Times*, October 23, 2009.

3. Joyce Purnick, *Mike Bloomberg: Money, Power, Politics* (New York: PublicAffairs, 2009), 179.

4. Ibid., 296.

5. Sewell Chan, "Bloomberg Leaving Republican Party," *City Room* blog, *New York Times*, June 19, 2007, https://cityroom.blogs.nytimes.com/2007/06/19 /bloomberg-leaving-republican-party/.

6. Jonathan P. Hicks, Michael Cooper, "The 2003 Election: City Charter, City Votes Down an Effort to End Party Primaries," *New York Times*, November 5, 2003.

7. Michael R. Bloomberg, "I'm not Running for President, but . . . ," opinion, *New York Times*, February 28, 2008.

8. Author interview with Richard Parsons, February 9, 2018.

9. Clyde Haberman, "Back When the Mayor Loved Term Limits," *New York Times*, October 20, 2008.

10. Garth Johnston, "Remembering Ed Koch's Scandalous Third Term," Gothamist, February 1, 2013, http://gothamist.com/2013/02/01/ed_koch_and _the_curse_of_the_third.php.

11. Michael Barbaro, David Chen, "Bloomberg Expected to Seek Third Term as Mayor," *New York Times*, September 30, 2008.

12. Billy Parker, "More Speculation of a Third Term for Mayor Bloomberg, Gothamist, July 28, 2008, http://gothamist.com/2008/07/28/speculation_of _a_third_term_for_may.php.

13. Author talks with Bloomberg, 2016.

14. "The Seductive Charms of Term Limits," editorial, *New York Times*, June 9, 2008.

15. "For Mayor of New York City," *New York Times* editorial endorsement of Michael Bloomberg, October 24, 2009.

16. Michael Barbaro, David Chen, "Bloomberg Enlists His Charities in Bid to Stay," *New York Times*, October 17, 2008.

17. Sam Roberts and Eric Konigsberg, "Enigmatic Billionaire Is Back in Term Limit Fray," *New York Times*, October 8, 2008.

18. Ibid.

19. "Election 2010: Election Results," *New York Times*, November 3, 2010, https:// www.nytimes.com/elections/2010/results/new-york.html.

20. Michael Barbaro and David Chen, "Bloomberg's Latest on Terms; 3 for him, but only 2 for Everyone Else," *New York Times*, October 25, 2010.

21. Chris McNickle, *Bloomberg: A Billionaire's Ambition* (New York: Skyhorse, 2017), 256.

22. David Chen and Michael Barbaro, "Passions High on Term Limits in City Council," *New York Times*, October 16, 2008.

23. Sewell Chan, "Bloomberg Says He Wants Third Term as Mayor," *New York Times*, October 2, 2008.

24. Chen and Barbaro, "Passions High on Term Limits in City Council."

25. Michael Barbaro and Fernanda Santos, "Bloomberg Gets His Bill and a Public Earful," *New York Times*, November 3, 2008.

26. Michael Barbaro, "Bloomberg Spent $102 Million on Third Term," *New York Times*, November 27, 2009.

27. Courtney Gross, "A Recovery Package from Bloomberg," *Gotham Gazette*, January 16, 2009.

28. Jim Rutenberg and Raymond Hernandez, "In About-Face, Wolfson Now Works for Bloomberg," *New York Times*, July 10, 2009.

29. Michael M. Grynbaum, "With Adviser's Departure, Bloomberg Will Lose a Fierce Protector," *New York Times*, July 29, 2012.

30. Bradley Tusk, *The Fixer: My Adventures Saving Startups from Death by Politics* (New York: Portfolio/Penguin, 2018), 66.

31. Ibid., 67.

32. Ibid., 69.

33. Matthew Choi, "Anthony Weiner to be Released Early from Federal Prison," Politico, October 9, 2018, https://www.politico.com/story/2018/10/09/anthony-weiner-federal-prison-885080.

34. Mark Jacobson, "Anthony and the Giant," *New York*, May 3, 2009.

35. Tusk, *The Fixer*, 71.

36. Ibid., 72.

37. Ibid., 73.

38. "Why I'm not Running for Mayor," op-ed, *New York Times*, May 26, 2009.

39. Clyde Haberman, "Bloomberg Is Betting on Voters with an Elastic Approach to the Law," *New York Times*, October 26, 2009.

40. Adam Lisberg, "Poll: Mike Bloomberg Leads William Thompson by 15 Points . . . for Now," New York *Daily News*, October 30, 2009.

41. David Seifman, "Three-Peat Mike Vows to Beat Jinx," *New York Post*, January 2, 2010.

42. Kate Taylor and David W. Chen, "Bloomberg Says He'll Leave de Blasio No Deficit," *New York Times*, November 21, 2013.

43. Ray Kelly, *Vigilance: My Life Serving America and Protecting Its Empire City* (New York: Hachette, 2015), 2–3.

44. "Mayor Bloomberg Announces New York City's Incarceration Rate Hits New All-Time Low" (down 36 percent from 2001–2012), NYC.gov, December 26, 2013.

45. Eli Epstein, "No Money in a Dirty Kitchen: The Repercussions of NYC's Restaurant Grading System," *The Atlantic*, July 23, 2012, https://www.theatlantic.com/health/archive/2012/07/no-money-in-a-dirty-kitchen-the-repercussions-of-nycs-restaurant-grading-system/260183/.

46. Patrick Wall, "Bloomberg's Early School Closures Benefitted Future Students, New Study Finds," Chalkbeat, November 19, 2015, https://ny.chalkbeat.org/posts/ny/2015/11/19/bloombergs-early-school-closures-benefitted-future-students-new-study-finds/.

47. Laura Bliss, "New York City Closed 29 High Schools. What Happened to the Students?," City Lab, November 19, 2015, https://www.citylab.com/equity/2015/11/new-york-city-closed-29-high-schools-what-happened-to-the-students/416778/.

48. "Mayor Bloomberg Presents Fiscal Year 2014 Executive Budget," NYC.gov, May 2, 2013, https://www1.nyc.gov/office-of-the-mayor/news/153-13/mayor-bloomberg-presents-fiscal-year-2014-executive-budget#/5.

49. Kim Velsey, "Among the last Pedestrian Plazas in the Bloomberg Era, Marcy Avenue Plaza Is Unveiled in Brooklyn," *New York Observer*, September 11, 2013, https://observer.com/2013/09/among-the-last-pedestrian-plazas-of-the-bloomberg-era-marcy-avenue-plaza-is-unveiled-in-brooklyn/.

50. "High Line Fact Sheet," Friends of the High Line, http://files.thehighline.org/pdf/high_line_fact_sheet.pdf.

51. Charles V. Bagli, "Going Out with Building Boom, Mayor Pushes Billions in Projects," *New York Times*, December 16, 2013.

52. "The Physical City, Building Boom," Metropolitan, *New York Times*, August 18, 2013, 6.

53. Charles V. Bagli, "So Many Seats, So Many Tax Breaks," *New York Times*, July 11, 2018; Charles V. Bagli, "As Stadiums Rise, So Do Costs to Taxpayers," *New York Times*, November 4, 2008.

54. Author interviews with officials from Memorial, Bloomberg staff, and Port Authority of New York and New Jersey, 2014, 2015, and 2016.

55. Michael Barbaro, "Bloomberg States Case, Emphatically and Personally, for Same-Sex Marriage," *New York Times*, May 26, 2011.

56. John del Signore, "Bloomberg Chokes Up During 'Ground Zero' Mosque Speech," Gothamist, August 3, 2010, http://gothamist.com/2010/08/03/bloomberg_chokes_up_during_ground_z.php.

57. Ben Casselman, Keith Collins, and Karl Russell, "Even Without Amazon, Tech Could Keep Gaining Ground in New York," *New York Times*, February 15, 2019.

58. Kate Taylor, "New York's Air Is Cleanest in 50 Years, Survey Finds," *New York Times*, September 26, 2013.

59. "Sandy and Its Impacts," NYC.gov, https://www1.nyc.gov/assets/sirr/down loads/pdf/Ch_1_SandyImpacts_FINAL_singles.pdf.

60. "NYC Cool Roofs, Annual Review, 2013," NYC.gov, 2013, http://www.nyc .gov/html/coolroofs/downloads/pdf/annual_report_2013.pdf.

61. "Mayor Bloomberg Receives Award for Anti-Poverty Efforts," NYC.gov, November 14, 2013, https://www1.nyc.gov/office-of-the-mayor/news/367-13 /mayor-bloomberg-receives-award-anti-poverty-efforts-children-s-aid-society -releases-new/#/0.

62. Matt Flegenheimer, "After Decades, a Water Tunnel Can Now Serve All of Manhattan," *Alex Prud'homme*, October 16, 2013, http://www.alexprudhomme .com/the-ripple-blog/bloomberg-unsexy-water-tunnel-3-open-business-40 -years/.

63. Brendan Cheney, "Bloomberg's 'Stop-and-Frisk' Legacy Would Complicate Presidential Bid," Politico, November 22, 2018, https://www.politico.com /states/new-york/albany/story/2018/11/22/bloombergs-stop-and-frisk-legacy -would-complicate-presidential-bid-707075.

64. "State of the Homeless, 2014," Coalition for the Homeless, March 12, 2014, homelessness,http://www.coalitionforthehomeless.org/wp-content/up loads/2014/04/State-of-the-Homeless-2014-FORMATTED-FINAL.pdf.

65. McNickle, *Bloomberg: A Billionare's Ambition*, 220.

66. Ibid., 220.

67. Benjamin Weiser and J. David Goodman, "New York City Housing Authority, Accused of Endangering Residents, Agrees to Oversight," *New York Times*, June 11, 2018.

68. Author interview with Governor Cuomo, 2012.

69. Benjamin Weiser, "3 Found Guilty in CityTime Corruption Trial," *New York Times*, November 23, 2013.

70. Robin Nagle, *Picking Up: On the Streets and Behind the Trucks with the Sanitation Workers of New York City* (New York: Farrar, Straus & Giroux, 2013), 206.

71. Ibid., 181–186, 204–206.

72. Michael Barbaro et al., "After Three Months, Mayor Replaces School Leader," *New York Times*, April 7, 2011.

73. Michael Barbaro, "As the Clock Ticks Down, Mayor Bloomberg Experiences 12 Years of Gratitude," *New York Times*, December 31, 2013.

CHAPTER 25: BACK TO BUSINESS

1. Gabriel Sherman, "The Mayor of Mayors," *New York*, June 1, 2012, http://nymag.com/news/features/michael-bloomberg-2012-6/.

2. "Genesis Prize Inaugural Laureate Mike Bloomberg," YouTube video, published on May 22, 2014, https://www.youtube.com/watch?v=RHQBiD_S4DE.

3. "12 Years of Mayor Bloomberg," editorial, *New York Times*, December 28, 2013.

4. Citizens Union award brochure, bio of Michael Bloomberg, 2013.

5. Christina McDonald, "Bloomberg Dines with CHCh Mayor," *New Zealand Herald*, January 13, 2014.

6. "Secretary-General Appoints Michael Bloomberg of United States Special Envoy for Cities and Climate Change," United Nations, January 31, 2014, https://www.un.org/press/en/2014/sga1453.doc.htm.

7. Jodi Rudoren, "Bloomberg in Israel, Wins a $1 Million Prize, then Gives It Back," *New York Times*, May 22, 2014.

8. Ibid.

9. Matt Flegenheimer, "Bloomberg Named an Honorary Knight," *New York Times*, October 6, 2014.

10. Raf Sanchez, "Michael Bloomberg Is Made an Honorary Knight By the Queen," *Telegraph*, April 8, 2015, https://www.telegraph.co.uk/news/world news/northamerica/usa/11523895/Michael-Bloomberg-is-made-an-honou rary-knight-by-the-Queen.html.

11. Christopher Bucktin, "Michael Bloomberg to be London Mayor? Former New York Mayor Considers Running for Post in 'Second Home,'" *Mirror*, April 5, 2015, https://www.mirror.co.uk/news/uk-news/michael-bloomberg -london-mayor-former-5464806.

12. Andrew Ross Sorkin, "Michael Bloomberg to Return to Lead Bloomberg L.P.," *New York Times*, September 3, 2014.

13. Author interview with Norman Pearlstine, October 18, 2017.

14. Sorkin, "Michael Bloomberg to Return to Lead Bloomberg L.P."

15. Author chat with Bloomberg, March 16, 2016.

16. Ravi Somaiya, "Bloomberg Shakes Up Newsroom Side of His Company," *New York Times*, January 25, 2015.

17. Bloomberg interview with Stuart Eizenstat, Atlanta, July 19, 2016.

18. Eizenstat interview.

19. Keith J. Kelly, "Bloomberg Tells Employees How to Wear ID Tags," *New York Post*, November 7, 2014.

20. Author interview with Bloomberg official, background.

21. Michael Bloomberg with Matthew Winkler, *Bloomberg by Bloomberg* (New York: John Wiley & Sons, 1997), 145.

22. Michael Bloomberg, *Bloomberg by Bloomberg* (1997; Hoboken, NJ: John Wiley & Sons, revised 2019, digital), 54.

23. Bloomberg comment to author, 2014.

24. Bloomberg, *Bloomberg by Bloomberg* (2019), vii.

25. Ashley Parker, "Covering (and Working for) Bloomberg," *New York Times*, April 20, 2011.

26. "Billionaires: The Richest People in the World," *Forbes*, March 5, 2019, https://www.forbes.com/billionaires/list/#version:static.

27. Bloomberg, *Bloomberg by Bloomberg* (2019), 165.

28. "Bloomberg Launches Financial Services Gender-Equality Index," Bloomberg LP press announcement, May 3, 2016, https://www.bloomberg.com/company/announcements/bloomberg-launches-financial-services-gender-equality-index/; the Bloomberg Equality Index at https://www.bloomberg.com/gei.

29. Author talk with Bloomberg aide, 2017.

30. Author interviews with Andrew Rosenthal, 2014.

31. Author interviews, Bloomberg employees, 2018, 2019.

32. Author interview with Goldman Sachs official, 2016.

33. Matt Twomey, "Bloomberg Appoints Former IBM CEO as Privacy Advisor," CNBC, May 17, 2013, https://www.cnbc.com/id/100717504.

34. "Bloomberg Criticized by Bank of England over Data Monitoring," BBC, May 14, 2013, https://www.bbc.com/news/business-22533109.

35. Peter Elkind, "The Trouble at Bloomberg," *Fortune*, December 5, 2015, http://fortune.com/2013/12/05/the-trouble-at-bloomberg/.

36. Matthew Winkler, "Holding Ourselves Accountable," Bloomberg Opinion, May 13, 2013, https://www.bloomberg.com/opinion/articles/2013-05-13/holding-ourselves-accountable.

37. Elkind, "The Trouble at Bloomberg."

38. Edward Wong, "Bloomberg Special Code Keeps Articles from Chinese Eyes," *New York Times*, November 28, 2013, https://sinosphere.blogs.nytimes.com/2013/11/28/bloomberg-code-keeps-articles-from-chinese-eyes/.

39. Ibid.

40. "Bloomberg Wins George Polk Award for International Reporting," Bloomberg LP, February 21, 2012, https://www.bloomberg.com/company/announcements/bloomberg-wins-george-polk-award-for-international-reporting/.

41. David Barboza, "Billions in Hidden Riches for Family of Chinese Leader," *New York Times*, October 25, 2012.

42. Craig S. Smith, "The New York Times vs. the Great 'Firewall' of China," *New York Times*, March 31, 2017.

43. Peter Elkind and Scott Cendrowski "Exclusive: Chinese Authorities Conduct Unannounced 'Inspections' of Bloomberg News Bureaus," CNN Money, December 2, 2013; Dylan Byers, "Report: Chinese Conducted Unannounced 'Inspections' of Bloomberg News Bureau," Politico, December 2, 2013.

44. Author interviews on background, 2013 and 2015; Ben Duronio, "China Blocks Bloomberg.com for Reporting How Much Next President Xi Jinping Is Worth," *Business Leader*, June 29, 2012; Neil Gough and Ravi Somaiya, "Bloomberg Hints at Curb on Articles About China," *New York Times*, March 20, 2014.

45. Author inteviews with former Bloomberg journalist on background, 2015.

46. Howard W. French, "Bloomberg's Folly: The Backstory Is About to Be Told," *Columbia Journalism Review*, May/June 2014.

47. Edward Wong, "Bloomberg News is Said to Curb Articles That Might Anger China," *New York Times*, November 8, 2013; author interviews with Bloomberg employees and ex-employees on background, 2016 and 2017.

48. Wong, "Bloomberg News Is Said to Curb Articles That Might Anger China"; author interviews with former Bloomberg employees on background, 2016.

49. Edward Wong and Christine Haughney, "Bloomberg News Suspends Reporter Whose Article on China Was Not Published," *New York Times*, November 17, 2013.

50. Ibid.

51. Jim Romenesko, "Ben Richardson Quits Bloomberg News Over Handling of Investigative Piece," *Editor & Publisher*, March 24, 2014.

52. Neil Gough, "Bloomberg Should Have Rethought Articles on China, Chairman Says," *New York Times*, March 21, 2014.

53. Howard French, "Bloomberg's Folly," *Columbia Journalism Review*, May/June 2014, https://archives.cjr.org/feature/bloombergs_folly.php.

54. Michael Bloomberg interview with Andrew Ross Sorkin, CNBC, May 2, 2014.

55. Luke O'Brien, "The Mayor vs. the Mogul: Michael Bloomberg's $9 Billion Identity Crisis," *Politico*, July/August 2015, https://www.politico.com/magazine/story/2015/06/mike-bloomberg-mayor-vs-mogul-119111_full.html.

56. Christine Haughney, "Longtime Chief of Bloomberg News to be Succeeded by the Economist's Editor," *New York Times*, December 9, 2014.

57. Ravi Somaiya, "Micklethwait's Balancing Act, After a Year as Bloomberg Editor in Chief," *New York Times*, February 14, 2016.

58. "Is the Economist Left- or Right-Wing?," The Economist Explains Itself, *The Economist*, September 3, 2013, https://www.economist.com/the-economist-explains/2013/09/02/is-the-economist-left-or-right-wing.

59. Joe Pompeo, "At Bloomberg, John Micklethwait Channels an Ancient Ancestor," Politico, July 10, 2015.

60. James Warren, "Bloomberg Gets Its First Pulitzer," Poynter, April 20, 2015, https://www.poynter.org/reporting-editing/2015/bloomberg-gets-its-first-pulitzer/.

61. O'Brien, "The Mayor vs. the Mogul."

62. Dylan Byers, "Can Bloomberg Buy 2016?" Politico, May 5, 2014; Michael Calderone, "Michael Bloomberg Doesn't Expect Mark Halperin and John Heilemann to Remain After the Election," *Huffington Post*, May 6, 2016.

63. Hadas Gold, "Micklethwait Memo Outlines New Focus for Bloomberg," Politico, September 1, 2015.

64. Ibid.

65. Christine Haughney, "Longtime Chief of Bloomberg News to be succeeded by Economist Editor," *New York Times*, December 9, 2014; author interview with Matthew Winkler.

66. Rachel Au-Yong, "Singapore a Bonsai Tree Model of What China Is: PM," *Straits Times*, November 7, 2018, https://www.straitstimes.com/singapore/singapore-a-bonsai-tree-model-of-what-china-is-pm.

67. Glassdoor.com reviews companies, including Bloomberg LP. They rate CEOs and, in 2018, Bloomberg got a 90 percent approval rating from employees, https://www.glassdoor.com.

68. Bloomberg, *Bloomberg by Bloomberg* (2019), 381.

69. Ibid., 379.

70. Laura Clarke, "Is Lord Foster's New Creation the Ultimate Office Building?," BBC Capital, October 31, 2017, http://www.bbc.com/capital/story/20171031-is-lord-fosters-new-creation-the-ultimate-office-building.

71. Bloomberg LP press release book published by company at opening of new London office, Bloomberg European Headquarters, October 2017, Trevor Franfield, services engineer, SWECO, quoted on p. 47.

72. Oliver Wainwright, "Bloomberg Headquarters: A £1 Billion Building That Looks Like a Regional Department Store," *Guardian*, October 25, 2017.

73. Ben Derbyshire, President of the Royal Institute of British Architects, October 10, 2018, https://www.architecture.com/knowledge-and-resources/knowledge-landing-page/bloombergs-european-hq-named-uks-best-new-building.

74. Graham Ruddick, "Michael Bloomberg: Brexit Is the Stupidest Thing Any

Country Has Done Besides Trump," *Guardian*, October 24, 2017; Silvia Amaro, "Michael Bloomberg Says Brexit Is 'Single Stupidest Thing' a Country Has Ever Done ... Besides Trump," CNBC, October 25, 2017.

75. Michael M. Grynbaum, "Former Mayor Bloomberg Buys London Mansion for $25 Million," *New York Times*, July 27, 2015.

76. Barb Darrow, "Michael Bloomberg on Trump, Brexit, and Climate Change," *Fortune*, October 13, 2017.

CHAPTER 26: MOVING TARGETS NOT SITTING DUCKS

1. Julia Kollewe and Graham Wearden, "Bloomberg IT Meltdown Leaves Financial World in the Dark," *Guardian*, April 17, 2015, https://www.theguardian.com/business/2015/apr/17/uk-halts-bond-sale-bloomberg-terminals-crash-worldwide.

2. Nathanial Popper and Neil Gough, "Bloomerg Terminals Suffer Widespread Failure," *New York Times*, April 17, 2015; Associated Press, "Bloomberg Says 'Internal Network Issue' Likely Cause of Big Outage of Its Trading Terminals," April 17, 2015.

3. Philip Stafford, Robert Cookson, and Patrick McGee, "Bloomberg Global Outage Paralyses Investors," *Financial Times*, April 17, 2015.

4. Aaron Timms, "The Race to Topple Bloomberg," *Institutional Investor*, January 30, 2014.

5. Michael Bloomberg, *Bloomberg by Bloomberg*, updated (1997; Hoboken, NJ: John Wiley & Sons, 2019, digital), 286.

6. Justin Baer, "Goldman-Led Group of Firms Buys Perzo to Form Instant-Messaging Company," *Wall Street Journal*, October 1, 2014.

7. Oliver Staley, "To Beat Bloomberg, Symphony Is Letting Banks' Bots Talk with Each Other," *Quartz*, October 19, 2018.

8. Ibid.

9. Matt Scuffham, "Thomson Reuters Closes Deal with Blackstone," Reuters Business News, October 1, 2018, https://www.reuters.com/article/us-thomsonreuters-m-a-blackstone/thomson-reuters-closes-deal-with-blackstone-id USKCN1MB3PY.

10. Stephen Schwarzman: $13.2 billion net worth as of January 20, 2019, *Forbes* List, number 34.

11. Author interview with Douglas B. Taylor, managing director of Burton-Taylor, International Consulting, a division of TP-ICAP, January 28, 2019.

12. Eric Huffman, "Best Alternatives to Bloomberg Terminal," Benzinga, December 11, 2018.

13. Kevin Dugan, "Money.net Now Has More Than 80,000 Subscribers," *New York Post*, November 30, 2017.

14. Ibid., author interview with Douglas B. Taylor.

15. Conversation: Stuart Eizenstat and Michael Bloomberg, Ahavath Achim Synagogue, Atlanta, July 19, 2016. Eizenstat Family Memorial Lecture Series. Transcript provided by Bloomberg Philanthropies.

16. Author interview, Michael Bloomberg, August 16, 2018.

17. Bloomberg, *Bloomberg by Bloomberg* (2019), 162.

18. Ibid., 143.

CHAPTER 27: GIVING BACK

1. Michael Bloomberg interviewed by Steve Kroft, *60 Minutes*, CBS, April 27, 2017.

2. "Special Report: Bezoses and Bloomberg Top Chronicle List of 50 Donors Who Gave the Most to Charity," *Chronicle of Philanthropy*, February 19, 2019.

3. Michael Bloomberg statement on why he has signed on to "The Giving Pledge," https://givingpledge.org/.

4. Alex Eichler, "Buffett and Gates: Billionaires, Give Away Half Your Money! Billionaires—Uh, All Right," *The Atlantic*, June 20, 2010, https://www.theatlantic.com/business/archive/2010/06/buffett-and-gates-billionaires-give-away-half-your-money/345144/.

5. Author interview with Wayne Barrett, January 9, 2015.

6. Author interview with former city official, 2015.

7. Sam Dangremond, "The Inaugural Town & Country Philanthropy Summit," *Town & Country*, May 29, 2014.

8. Diane Cardwell, "Mayor to Put His Charity in Upper East Side Building," *New York Times*, July 2, 2006.

9. Christopher Gray, "An Elegant Design to Complement a Bold Personality," *New York Times*, August 19, 2007.

10. Email to author from Maurizo Canesso, Galleria Camesso Lugano, June 30, 2017.

11. Author interviews with Bloomberg philanthropies officials, 2014, 2017, 2019.

12. Author interview with Michael Bloomberg, August 16, 2018.

13. Conversation: Stuart Eizenstat and Michael Bloomberg, Ahavath Achim Synagogue, Atlanta, July 19, 2016.

14. "New Comprehensive Smoke-Free Law 20 Million People in Beijing, China," World Health Organization, https://www.who.int/tobacco/communications/highlights/beijingsmokefree/en/.

15. Conversation: Stuart Eizenstat and Michael Bloomberg.

16. Author interview, background, August 2017.

17. Conversation: Stuart Eizenstat and Michael Bloomberg.

18. "Enrolling High-Achieving, Low- and Moderate-Income Students into Top Colleges and Universities," College Access and Success, Bloomberg Philanthropies, 2019, https://www.bloomberg.org/program/education/college access/.

19. Joyce Purnick, *Mike Bloomberg: Money, Power, Politics* (New York: PublicAffairs, 2009), 60.

20. Ibid., 61.

21. Author interview with Julia Peyton-Jones, November 18, 2014.

22. Andrew Jack, "Piero Manzoni at the Serpentine Gallery," Culture Kiosque, April 17, 1998, http://www.culturekiosque.com/art/exhibiti/rheserpen.htm.

23. Robin Pogrebin, "Michael Bloomberg Gives $75 million to Shed Arts Center," *New York Times*, May 24, 2017.

24. Jeanhee Kim, "Hudson Yards Arts Center to be Named Bloomberg Building," Crain's New York, January 9, 2019, https://www.crainsnewyork.com/arts/hudson-yards-arts-center-be-named-bloomberg-building.

25. Joshua Barone, "The Shed, a Rare New Arts Center on the Hudson, Is Set to Open," *New York Times*, January 8, 2019.

26. Author interview with David Jones, April 9, 2018.

27. Author interview with Vartan Gregorian, president of the Carnegie Corporation of New York, January 17, 2019.

28. Sam Roberts and Jim Rutenberg, "With More Giving, Bloomberg Forges Ties," *New York Times*, May 23, 2005.

29. Michael Barbaro, "Bloomberg Is Quietly Ending a Charitable Program," *New York Times*, March 18, 2010.

30. "Michael R. Bloomberg Commits $360 Million to Reduce Tobacco Use—Raising Total Giving on Tobacco Control Efforts to Nearly $1 Billion," Press & Media, Bloomberg Philanthropies, https://www.bloomberg.org/press/releases/michael-r-bloomberg-commits-360-million-reduce-tobacco-use-raising-total-giving-tobacco-control-efforts-nearly-1-billion/.

31. National Center for Health Statistics, "Fast Facts, All Firearm Deaths (as of 2016) 38,658," Centers for Disease Control and Prevention, https://www.cdc.gov/nchs/fastats/injury.htm.

32. "Bloomberg to Launch $50 Million Gun Control Initiative," *Philanthropy News Digest*, April 17, 2014, https://philanthropynewsdigest.org/news/bloomberg-to-launch-50-million-gun-control-initiative.

33. Danny Hakim and Rachel Shorey, "Gun Control Groups Eclipse N.R.A. in Election Spending," *New York Times*, November 16, 2018.

34. Matt Stevens, "Santa Monica Gets $1 Million to Measure Residents' Well-Being," *Los Angeles Times*, March 13, 2013.

35. Gabriel Sherman, "The Mayor of Mayors," *New York*, June 3, 2012.

36. Ibid.

37. Ibid.

38. "Chicago Leads a Data-Driven Revolution," Medium.com, June 20, 2017, https://medium.com/@BloombergCities/chicago-leads-a-data-driven-revolu tion-3bf878ca669d.

39. Meagan Flynn, "The Long Rise and Fast Fall of the Ambitious One-Bin Recycling Program," *Houston Press*, July 13, 2017.

40. "Closing the Word Gap Among Young Children," Providence Talks, http://www.r2lp.org/early-childhood-development/providence-talks/.

41. "Pilot Findings & Next Steps," Providence Talks, October 2015, http://www.providencetalks.org/wp-content/uploads/2015/10/Providence-Talks-Pilot-Findings-Next-Steps.pdf.

42. Kenneth Wong, Megan Boben, and Crystal Thomas, "Disrupting the Early Learning Status Quo, Providence Talks . . ." Brown University, February 14, 2018, http://www.providencetalks.org/wp-content/uploads/2018/07/updated-brown-eval.pdf.

43. Rachel Kaufman, "Sewage May Hold the Key to Tracking Opioid Abuse," Smithsonian.com, August 22, 2018.

44. Julie Rusk, "Santa Monica: The First City in the World to Measure Its Residents' Well-Being," Apolitical, January 17, 2018.

45. "Bloomberg Philanthropies Announces Winners of 2014 Mayors Challenge," *Philanthropy News Digest*, September 18, 2014.

46. Michael Barbaro, "Bloomberg Focus on Rest (as in Rest of the World)," *New York Times*, December 14, 2013.

47. "Mayor Bloomberg Announces New York City Will Reach a Record 54.3 Million Visitors in 2013—Increase of Nearly 20 Million Additional Annual Visitors from 2002," NYC.gov, December 10, 2013, https://www1.nyc.gov/of fice-of-the-mayor/news/393-13/mayor-bloomberg-new-york-city-will-reach-record-54-3-million-visitors-2013-/#/0.

48. Author interview with George Fertitta, June 14, 2017.

49. George Fertitta via Frank Barry email, November 16, 2018.

50. Detail for Detroit, Michigan: https://dotorg.content.cirrus.bloomberg.com/annualreport2018/bloomberg-associates/.

51. "Rob Ford's 'Best' Moments," YouTube video, published on November 19, 2013, https://www.youtube.com/watch?v=4QH7vr8XO_s.

52. Genesis Prize, biography video, 2014, https://www.genesisprize.org/laureates/laureate-2014.

53. Alan Fleischmann, "All-In Philanthropy: The Story of Bloomberg LP's Rebuilding Team in the U.S. Virgin Islands," *Forbes*, December 5, 2017, https://www.forbes.com/sites/alanfleischmann/2017/12/05/all-in-philanthropy-the-story-of-bloomberg-lps-rebuilding-team-in-the-u-s-virgin-islands/#2927b1d34cda.

54. Conversation: Stuart Eizenstat and Michael Bloomberg, Ahavath Achim Synagogue, Atlanta, July 19, 2016.

55. Michael Bloomberg interviewed by Steve Kroft, CBS's *60 Minutes*, April 21, 2017.

CHAPTER 28: GREEN FOR GREEN

1. Michael D. Shear, "Trump Will Withdraw US from Paris Agreement," *New York Times*, June 1, 2017, https://www.nytimes.com/2017/06/01/climate/trump-paris-climate-agreement.html.

2. Lisa Friedman, "Syria Joins Paris Climate Accord, Leaving Only US Opposed," *New York Times*, November 7, 2017; https://www.nytimes.com/2017/11/07/climate/syria-joins-paris-agreement.html.

3. "Trump on Climate Change Report: 'I Don't Believe It,'" BBC News, November 26, 2018, https://www.bbc.com/news/world-us-canada-46351940.

4. "Bloomberg Meets Macron, Hildago in Paris," AP Archive, YouTube video, published on June 7, 2017, https://www.youtube.com/watch?v=5N_s_8PJvvU.

5. Ibid.

6. "States, Cities, and Businesses in the United States Are Stepping Up on Climate Action," Phase 1 Report, America's Pledge, 29, https://www.bbhub.io/dotorg/sites/28/2017/11/AmericasPledgePhaseOneReportWeb.pdf.

7. "Mike Bloomberg Statement on Charlottesville," MikeBloomberg.com, August 16, 2017, https://www.mikebloomberg.com/news/mike-bloomberg-statement-charlottesville/.

8. Katie Couric, "Michael Bloomberg on Climate Change, the Power of Government, and Why He's Still Hopeful About the Future," *Town & Country*, May 9, 2017.

9. Author interview with Michael Bloomberg, August 8, 2018.

10. Nolan McCaskill, "The Agenda: War on Coal," Politico, May 29, 2015.

11. Christian Torres and Enid Juliet Eilperin, "N.Y. Mayor Gives $50 Million to Fight Coal-Fired Power Plants," *Washington Post*, July 11, 2011.

12. "Bloomberg Makes a $50M Anti-Coal Bet with Sierra Club," Reuters, July 23, 2011, https://www.reuters.com/article/idIN144034130920110722.

13. "Bloomberg Philanthropies Commits $50 Million to Sierra Club's Beyond Coal Campaign to Move America Toward Cleaner Energy," Press & Media, Bloomberg Philanthropies, https://www.bloomberg.org/press/releases/bloom berg-philanthropies-commits-50-million-to-sierra-clubs-beyond-coal-cam paign-to-move-america-toward-cleaner-energy/.

14. "Washington's 'Beyond Coal' Blackout," editorial, *Wall Street Journal*, April 10, 2015, https://www.wsj.com/articles/washingtons-beyond-coal-blackout-142 8706365.

15. Brian Willis, "Beyond Coal Campaign Hopes to be Catalyst for More Philanthropic Partnerships on Climate Change: The Entire World Depends on It," Sierra Club, December 8, 2016, https://content.sierraclub.org/press-re leases/2016/12/beyond-coal-campaign-hopes-be-catalyst-more-philanthropic -partnerships.

16. Devin Henry, "Trump Signs Bill Undoing Obama Coal Mining Rule," The Hill, February 16, 2017, https://thehill.com/policy/energy-environment/319938 -trump-signs-bill-undoing-obama-coal-mining-rule.

17. Suzy Khimm, "Senate Confirms Trump's Controversial Pick to Lead Mine Safety," NBC News, November 15, 2017, https://www.nbcnews.com/politics/congress /senate-confirms-trump-s-controversial-pick-lead-mine-safety-n821081.

18. Brady Dennis and Juliet Eilperin, "Scott Pruit Steps Down as EPA Head after Ethics, Management Scandals," *Washington Post*, July 5, 2018.

19. Nicole Einbinder, "A Coal Executive's Action Plan for Trump is Made Public," *Frontline*, PBS, January 10, 2018, https://www.pbs.org/wgbh/frontline /article/a-coal-executives-action-plan-for-trump-is-made-public/.

20. Rachel Nagler, email to author from, Bloomberg Philanthropies, February 8, 2019.

21. Caitlyn Oprysco, "'I Don't Believe It,' Trump Dismisses Grim Government Report on Climate Change," Politico, November 26, 2108.

22. Jennifer Kite-Powell, "This New Documentary 'Paris to Pittsburgh' Makes Climate Change Local," *Forbes*, November 27, 2018.

23. Aaron Rupar, "Trump's Pick to Chair New Climate Panel Once Said CO2 Has Been Maligned Like 'Jews Under Hitler,'" Vox, February 20, 2019.

24. Coral Davenport, "White House Climate Panel to Include Climate Denialist," *New York Times*, February 20, 2019.

CHAPTER 29: GOVERNMENT IN EXILE

1. Dylan Stableford, "2020 Vision: Is Biden-Abrams the Ticket for Democrats?" Yahoo News, March 22, 2019, https://sports.yahoo.com/2020-vision-is-biden -abrams-the-ticket-for-democrats-181550555.html.

2. John Heilemann, "His American Dream," *New York*, December 11, 2006, published online, October 24, 2007.

3. Sewell Chan, "Bloomberg Leaving Republican Party," *City Room* blog, *New York Times*, June 19, 2007.

4. David A. Graham, "A Short History of Mike Bloomberg Supposedly Running for President," *The Atlantic*, October 20, 2015.

5. Raymond Hernandez, "Bloomberg Backs Obama, Citing Fallout from Storm," *New York Times*, November 1, 2012.

6. Graham, "A Short History of Mike Bloomberg Supposedly Running for President."

7. Maggie Haberman and Alexander Burns, "Michael Bloomberg Says He Won't Run for President," *New York Times*, March 7, 2016.

8. Author interview with Bradley Tusk, September 20, 2016.

9. Michael R. Bloomberg, "The Risk I Will Not Take," Bloomberg View, March 7, 2016.

10. Tatania Siegel, "Michael Bloomberg on a Near-Presidential Run, a Call to Trump and His 'War on Coal' Movie," *Hollywood Reporter*, November 20, 2017.

11. Author interviews with Bloomberg advisers on background, 2019.

12. Emily Stewart, "Biden and Sanders Lead New Early Polls of Democrats, but It's Still Early," *VOX*, February 12, 2019.

13. Frank Bruni, "Is This Man the Antidote to Donald Trump?," *New York Times*, September 22, 2018.

14. Ben Smith, "Can Mike Bloomberg Make America Boring Again?" BuzzFeed News, October 8, 2018.

15. Author interview with Michael Bloomberg, August 16, 2018.

16. James Pindell, "In N.H., Bloomberg Compares Warren's 'Ultra Millionare Tax' with Chaos in Venezuela, *Boston Globe*, January 29, 2019.

17. Stephanie Murray and Marc Caputo, "Bloomberg Tees Off on Potential 2020 Rivals as He Inches Toward Run," Politico, January 29, 2019.

18. Zachary B. Wolf, "Here's What the Green New Deal Actually Says," CNN, February 14, 2009; https://ocasio-cortez.house.gov/sites/ocasio-cortez.house .gov/files/Resolution%20on%20a%20Green%20New%20Deal.pdf.

19. Allen Smith, "Bloomberg Blasts 'Pie in the Sky' Green New Deal, Rips Warren Wealth Tax as Venezuelan," NBC News, January 29, 2019.

20. Michael Bloomberg Speech to Saint Anselm College, Manchester, New Hampshire, MikeBloomberg.com, January 29, 2019, https://www.mikebloom berg.com/news/mike-bloomberg-delivers-remarks-new-hampshire/.

21. Amy Russo, "Michael Bloomberg Says He Won't Go On Joe Biden's White Male Apology Tour," *Huffington Post*, March 22, 2019; Bermuda Business Development Agency Forum, 2019.

22. Georgina@georginabloomberg, Instagram, March 7, 2019.

23. Ally Betker, "Georgina Bloomberg on Her Father's Aborted Presidential Run," *W*, March 22, 2016.

24. Tim Mak and Alina Selyukh, "Here's What Keeps the Democratic Party's Technology Boss Awake at Night," NPR, August 30, 2018.

25. Leslie Stahl, "Facebook 'Embeds,' Russia and the Trump Campaign's Secret Weapon," CBS News, June 10, 2018.

26. Author interviews with Bloomberg advisers on background, 2016.

27. Theodore Bunker, "Trump: Bloomberg a Very Little Guy," Newsmax.com, July 29, 2016, https://www.newsmax.com/Politics/Trump-Bloomberg-Little -Guy-DNC/2016/07/29/id/741203/.

28. Philip Bump, "Donald Trump Now Hates Michael Bloomberg Because Bloomberg Was Mean to Him," *Washington Post*, July 29, 2016.

29. Author interviews with Bloomberg aides and colleagues on background, 2016.

30. Jack Holmes, "Michael Bloomberg Remembers His First Call to President-Elect Donald Trump," *Esquire*, May 9, 2017.

31. Michael R. Bloomberg, "GOP Must Show Backbone and Stand Up to Trump," Bloomberg View, May 11, 2017.

32. Michael R. Bloomberg, "This Tax Bill Is a Trillion Dollar Blunder," Bloomberg View, December 15, 2017, https://www.bloomberg.com/opinion/articles /2017-12-15/this-tax-bill-is-a-trillion-dollar-blunder.

33. Ibid.

34. Michael R. Bloomberg, "Fix Immigration Without Sacrificing Innocent Children," Bloomberg View, March 8, 2017.

35. Abram Brown, "The Suite Life: Inside the Plaza Hotel's 110 Year History," *Forbes*, December 12, 2017, https://www.forbes.com/sites/abrambrown/2017 /11/21/the-suite-life-inside-the-plaza-hotels-110-year-history/#4c08752 f1010.

36. Ben Smith, "The U.S. Government–in–exile Has a New President," BuzzFeed, September 19, 2017.

37. Open Secrets, www.opensecrets.org.

38. Author interview with Howard Wolfson, November 13, 2018.

39. Ibid.

40. Simon Dumenco, "Bloomberg Spends $5M on Last-Minute 'Vote Democratic' Ad Campaign," Ad Age, November 5, 2018.

41. Adam Liptak, "Justices 5–4, Reject Corporate Spending Limit," *New York Times*, January 21, 2010.

42. David Barstow, Suzanne Craig, and Russ Buettner, "Trump Engaged in Suspect Tax Schemes as He Reaped Riches from His Father," *New York Times*, October 2, 2018.

43. Chase Peterson-Withorn and Dan Alexander, "Trump Jumps 51 Spots on Forbes Billionaire's List," Forbes, March 5, 2019, https://www.forbes.com /billionaires/#564a95a2251c.

44. Michael Bloomberg's Commencement Address (at Massachusetts Institute of Technology), MIT news, June 7, 2019.

45. Arick Wierson, "By Not Running for President, Bloomberg Is Now the Obi-Wan Kenobi of Democrats," *New York Observer*, March 8, 2019.

EPILOGUE: WORTH "EVERY PENNY"

1. William Cummings, "Trump Is 'an Existential Threat': Michael Bloomberg Announces Entry into 2020 Presidential Race," *USA Today*, November 24, 2019.

2. Michael Bloomberg, "Our Highest Office, My Deepest Obligation, I'm not running for president . . ." Bloomberg.com/opinion, March 5, 2019; Cummings, *USA Today*, November 24, 2019; Miles Parks, "Michael Bloomberg Suspends his Presidential Campaign and Endorses Joe Biden," NPR, March 4, 2020.

3. Andy Kroll, "Farewell to Mike Bloomberg 2020, the Most Colossal Flop of a Presidential Campaign," *Rolling Stone*, March 4, 2020.

4. Author interview with Michael Bloomberg, November 16, 2020.

5. Charles Blow, "You Must Never Vote for Bloomberg," op-ed, *New York Times*, November 10, 2019.

6. Shane Goldmacher, "Michael Bloomberg Pushed 'Stop-and-Frisk' Policing. Now He's Apologizing," *New York Times*, November 17, 2019.

7. Author interview, Bloomberg, November 16, 2020.

8. Isaac Stanley-Becker and Michael Scherer, "Mike Bloomberg's Money Buys

Him a Very Different Kind of Campaign. And It's a Big One," *Washington Post*, December 7, 2019.

9. Author interview, Bloomberg, November 16, 2020.
10. Steven Levy, "How Bloomberg's Digital Army Is Still Fighting for Democrats," *Wired* (Backchannel*)*, August 7, 2020.
11. Author interview, Bloomberg, November 16, 2020.
12. Ibid.

BIBLIOGRAPHY

Barr, Jason M. *Building the Skyline: The Birth and Growth of Manhattan's Skyscrapers.* New York: Oxford University Press, 2016.

Bender, Thomas. *The Unfinished City: New York and the Metropolitan Idea.* New York: New Press, 2002.

Bishop, Matthew and Michael Green. *Philanthrocapitalism: How Giving Can Save the World.* New York: Bloomsbury, 2008.

Bloomberg, Michael with Matt Winkler. *Bloomberg by Bloomberg.* New York: John Wiley & Sons, 1997.

Bloomberg, Michael. *Bloomberg by Bloomberg.* Hoboken, NJ: John Wiley & Sons, updated and digital, 2019.

Bloomberg, Michael and Carl Pope. *Climate of Hope: How Cities, Businesses, and Citizens Can Save the Planet.* New York: St. Martin's Press, 2017.

Brash, Julian. *Bloomberg's New York: Class and Governance in the Luxury City.* Athens, GA: University of Georgia Press, 2011.

Brill, Steven. *Class Warfare: Inside the Fight to Fix America's Schools.* New York: Simon & Schuster, 2011.

Brook, Daniel. *A History of Future Cities.* New York: W. W. Norton, 2013.

Callahan, David. *The Givers: Wealth, Power, and Philanthropy in a New Gilded Age.* New York: Knopf, 2017.

Chakrabarti, Vishaan. *A Country of Cities: A Manifesto for an Urban America.* New York: Metropolis, 2013.

David, Greg. *Modern New York: The Life and Economics of a City.* New York: Palgrave Macmillan, 2012.

David, Joshua and Robert Hammond. *High Line: The Inside Story of New York City's Park in the Sky.* New York: Farrar, Straus & Giroux, 2011.

Doctoroff, Daniel L. *Greater Than Ever: New York's Big Comeback.* New York: PublicAffairs, 2017.

Farley, Tom. *Saving Gotham: A Billionaire Mayor, Activist Doctors, and the Fight for Eight Million Lives.* New York: W. W. Norton, 2015.

Fleishman, Joel L. *Putting Wealth to Work: Philanthropy for Today or Investing for Tomorrow?* New York: PublicAffairs, 2017.

Gallagher, Leigh. *The End of the Suburbs: Where the American Dream Is Moving.* New York: Portfolio/Penguin, 2013.

Garson, Barbara. *The Electronic Sweatshop: How Computers are Transforming the Office of the Future into the Factory of the Past.* New York: Penguin, 1988.

Geisst, Charles R. *Wall Street: A History.* 1997; New York: Oxford University Press, updated 2012.

Glaeser, Edward. *Triumph of the City: How Our Greatest Invention Makes Us Richer, Smarter, Greener, Healthier, and Happier.* New York: Penguin, 2011.

Goldberger, Paul. *Up from Zero: Politics, Architecture, and the Rebuilding of New York.* New York: Random House, 2004.

Green, Mark. *Bright, Infinite Future: A Generational Memoir on the Progressive Rise.* New York: St. Martin's Press, 2016.

Jackson, Kenneth T. *The Encyclopedia of New York City.* New Haven, CT: Yale University Press, 1995.

Jacobs, Jane. *The Death and Life of Great American Cities.* 1961; New York: Vintage, updated 1992.

Katz, Bruce and Jennifer Bradley. *The Metropolitan Revolution: How Cities and Metros are Fixing Our Broken Politics and Fragile Economy.* Washington, DC: Brookings Institution, 2013.

Kaufman, Henry. *On Money and Markets: A Wall Street Memoir.* New York: McGraw-Hill, 2000.

Kelly, Ray. *Vigilance: My Life Serving America and Protecting Its Empire City.* New York: Hachette, 2015.

Klein, Joel. *Lessons of Hope: How to Fix Our Schools.* New York: HarperCollins, 2014.

Leinweber, David. *Nerds on Wall Street: Math, Machines and Wired Markets.* Hoboken, NJ: John Wiley & Sons, 2009.

Lewis, Michael. *Liar's Poker: Rising Through the Wreckage on Wall Street.* New York: W. W. Norton, 1989.

Main, Thomas J. *Homelessness in New York City: Policymaking from Koch to De Blasio.* New York: New York University Press, 2016.

Mayer, Martin. *Nightmare on Wall Street: Salomon Brothers and the Corruption of the Marketplace*. New York: Simon & Schuster, 1993.

Mayer-Schönberger, Viktor and Kenneth Cukier. *Big Data: A Revolution That Will Transform How We Live, Work and Think*. New York: Houghton Mifflin Harcourt, 2013.

McNickle, Chris. *Bloomberg: A Billionaire's Ambition*. New York: Skyhorse, 2017.

Mollenkopf, John and Ken Emerson, eds. *Rethinking the Urban Agenda: Reinvigorating the Liberal Tradition in New York City and Urban America*. New York: Century Foundation Press, 2001.

Nadelstern, Eric. *10 Lessons from New York City Schools: What Really Works to Improve Education*. New York: Teachers College Press, 2013.

Nagle, Robin. *Picking Up: On the Streets and Behind the Trucks with the Sanitation Workers of New York City*. New York: Farrar, Straus & Giroux, 2013.

O'Day, Jennifer A., Catherine S. Bitter, and Louis M. Gomez, eds. *Education Reform in New York City: Ambitious Change in the Nation's Most Complex School System*. Cambridge, MA: Harvard Education Press, 2011.

Platt, Rutherford H. *Reclaiming American Cities: The Struggle for People, Place, and Nature Since 1900*. Amherst: University of Massachusetts Press, 2014.

Purnick, Joyce. *Mike Bloomberg: Money, Power, Politics*. New York: PublicAffairs, 2009.

Ravitch, Richard. *So Much to Do: A Full Life of Business, Politics, and Confronting Fiscal Crises*. New York: PublicAffairs, 2014.

Roberts, Sam. *Only in New York: An Exploration of the World's Most Fascinating, Frustrating and Irrepressible City*. New York: St. Martin's Press, 2009; reprinted, New York: Fordham University Press, 2019.

Sadik-Khan, Janette and Seth Solomonow. *Streetfight: Handbook for an Urban Revolution*. New York: Viking, 2016.

Sagalyn, Lynne B. *Power at Ground Zero: Politics, Money, and the Remaking of Lower Manhattan*. New York: Oxford University Press, 2016.

Schroeder, Alice. *The Snowball: Warren Buffett and the Business of Life*. New York: Bantam, 2009.

Smith, Adam. *The Money Game: How It Is Played in Wall Street, What Money Really Is, What We Think It Is and How It Makes Us Behave*. New York: Vintage, 1967.

Sorkin, Andrew Ross. *Too Big to Fail: The Inside Story of How Wall Street and Washington Fought to Save the Financial System—and Themselves*. New York: Viking, 2009.

Stone, Brian, Jr. *The City and the Coming Climate: Climate Change in the Places We Live*. New York: Cambridge University Press, 2012.

Tusk, Bradley. *The Fixer: My Adventures Saving Startups from Death by Politics*. New York: Portfolio/Penguin, 2018.

Viteritti, Joseph P. *The Pragmatist: Bill de Blasio's Quest to Save the Soul of New York*. New York: Oxford University Press, 2017.

White, E. B. *Here is New York*. New York: Little Bookroom, reprint 1999.

Winkler, Matthew with Jennifer Sondag, eds. *The Bloomberg Way: A Guide for Reporters and Editors*. Hoboken, NJ: John Wiley & Sons, 2014.

PHOTO CREDITS

1. New York City Municipal Archives, 2012
2. Bloomberg Family Archives
3. Bloomberg Family Archives
4. Bloomberg Family Archives
5. 1964 Hullabaloo, Sheridan Libraries, Johns Hopkins University
6. 1964 Hullabaloo, Sheridan Libraries, Johns Hopkins University
7. Neal Boenzi, *New York Times*/Redux, 1967
8. Edward Hausner, *New York Times*/Redux, 1975
9. Fred R. Conrad, *New York Times*/Redux, 1982
10. William E. Sauro, *New York Times*/Redux, 1991
11. Dith Pran, *New York Times*/Redux, 2001
12. Dith Pran, *New York Times*/Redux, 2001
13. Suzanne DeChillo, *New York Times*/Redux, 2001
14. New York City Municipal Archives, 2002
15. New York City Municipal Archives, 2002
16. Ruby Washington, *New York Times*/Redux, 2002
17. Shannon Stapleton, *New York Times*/Redux, 2004
18. Marilynn K. Yee, *New York Times*/Redux, 2004
19. New York City Municipal Archives, 2008
20. Thomas Monaster, *NY Daily News*, Getty Images, 2003
21. New York City Municipal Archives, 2010
22. Michael Appleton, *New York Times*/Redux, 2012
23. New York City Municipal Archives, 2013
24. New York City Municipal Archives, 2013
25. Seth Wenig, Associated Press, 2014
26. Michael Nagle, Bloomberg Philanthropies
27. Michael Nagle, Bloomberg Philanthropies
28. Ozier Muhammad, *New York Times*/Redux

INDEX

ABOUT THE AUTHOR

ELEANOR RANDOLPH has covered national politics and the media for the *Washington Post*, the *Los Angeles Times*, and other newspapers. Her articles have appeared in *Vogue*, *Esquire*, the *New Republic*, and other magazines. A member of the *New York Times* editorial board from 1998 to 2016, she focused on city and state politics. She lives in New York City.